Endangered languages

This edited volume provides an overview of the issues surrounding language loss. It brings together work by theoretical linguists, field linguists, and non-linguist members of minority communities to provide an integrated view of how language is lost, from sociological and economic as well as from linguistic perspectives.

The contributions to the volume fall into four categories. The chapters by Dorian, and Grenoble and Whaley provide an overview of language endangerment. Grinevald, England, Jacobs, and Nora and Richard Dauenhauer describe the situation confronting threatened languages from both a linguistic and sociological perspective. The understudied issue of what (beyond a linguistic system) can be lost as a language ceases to be spoken is addressed by Mithun, Hale, Jocks, and Woodbury. In the last section, Kapanga, Myers-Scotton, and Vakhtin consider the linguistic processes which underlie language attrition.

Endangered languages

Language loss and community response

....

edited by

LENORE A. GRENOBLE
Dartmouth College

and

LINDSAY J. WHALEY
Dartmouth College

CAMBRIDGE
UNIVERSITY PRESS

PUBLISHED BY THE PRESS SYNDICATE OF THE UNIVERSITY OF CAMBRIDGE
The Pitt Building, Trumpington Street, Cambridge, United Kingdom

CAMBRIDGE UNIVERSITY PRESS
The Edinburgh Building, Cambridge CB2 2RU, UK   http://www.cup.cam.ac.uk
40 West 20th Street, New York, NY 10011–4211, USA   http://www.cup.org
10 Stamford Road, Oakleigh, Melbourne 3166, Australia
Ruiz de Alarcón 13, 28014 Madrid, Spain

© Cambridge University Press 1998

First published 1998
Reprinted 1999

Printed in the United Kingdom at the University Press, Cambridge

Typeset in 9/13.5pt Concorde BQ Regular, in QuarkXPress™ [GC]

A catalogue record for this book is available from the British Library

Library of Congress Cataloguing in Publication data
Endangered languages: language loss and community response / edited
by Lenore A. Grenoble and Lindsay J. Whaley
    p.   cm.
Includes bibliographical references and indexes.
ISBN 0 521 59102 3 (hardback). – ISBN 0 521 59712 9 (paperback)
1. Language attrition.   2. Language maintenance.   3. Linguistic change
4. Linguistic minorities.   5. Sociolinguistics.
I. Grenoble, Lenore A.   II. Whaley, Lindsay J.
P40.5.L28E63   1998
408´.9–dc21   96–53430 CIP

Contents

Preface

LENORE A. GRENOBLE AND LINDSAY J. WHALEY
Program in Linguistics and Cognitive Science, Dartmouth College

The imminent dawning of the next millennium offers an obvious, if somewhat arbitrary, inducement to evaluate the situation in which the world finds itself. There can be little doubt that a chief characteristic of our current state is extreme dynamism, perhaps most evident in the constant shifting of technology and material culture, but also plainly observable in everything from ecosystems to moral attitudes. In that small niche of the world which falls under the purview of linguists – language and language use – the globe as it now exists is also being transformed at an incredible rate. One particularly striking feature of this transformation is the number of languages which will simply cease to be spoken in the next fifty to a hundred years. The phenomenon of language death, and how various communities have responded and are responding to it, forms the theme of this volume.

It is generally agreed that there are somewhere between 5,000 and 6,000 languages spoken in the world today. These languages are unevenly distributed over the earth and over the world's population: while some countries, like Papua New Guinea, show extremely high language density (approximately 860 languages spoken in a territory of only 461,690 sq. km), other large areas may be characterized by relative scarcity. For example, there are but nine languages found in Saudia Arabia, six of which are varieties of Arabic, even though the country is over four times the size of Papua New Guinea.[1]

Just as the languages of the world are distributed unequally in terms of geography, they vary widely in terms of the numbers of people who use them. Manifold languages are spoken by a thousand people or less, with the extreme cases being those which are no longer in primary use within any community and only remain part of the personal knowledge of a handful of individuals. In contrast, some languages are employed as the first language

[1] Data on the number of languages spoken in Papua New Guinea and Saudi Arabia were taken from Grimes 1992.

of tens of millions of speakers. Mandarin Chinese, with well over 700 million speakers, easily tops the list.

Over the course of the next century, however, the very basic global picture painted here will change drastically. A certain small group of languages (Arabic, Chinese, English, and Spanish, to name a few) will be used by an ever increasing percentage of the world's population, while a great many other languages will completely disappear. Just how many will disappear is a matter open to debate, though according to the more dire predictions of Michael Krauss, over 4,000 of the world's languages will cease to be spoken by the end of the next century (Krauss 1992).

For obvious reasons, then, endangered languages are a topic which has become of particularly great concern to linguists. As a result, work on language endangerment and death has been accelerated over the past decade. Representative scholarship can be found in Brenzinger (1992), Dorian (1989), Fase, Jaspaert, and Kroon (1992), Hinton (1994), and Robins and Uhlenbeck (1991).

As this work on language endangerment has progressed, a number of key points of inquiry have emerged. (In this volume, the chapters by Dorian, and Grenoble and Whaley address subsets of these points in more detail than we do here.) At the most basic level of investigation, we find a need to gain more accurate assessments of current language vitality. While it is widely accepted that a large proportion of the world's languages are nearing extinction, it is difficult to form anything but an educated guess about the breadth of the problem. This stems in no small part from the mundane fact that empirical data on language use is lacking for many parts of the world.

In order to be useful for research on language loss, language assessments need to include not only head counts of speakers and estimates of fluency in native languages, but also evaluations of the likelihood of the continuation, decline or revitalization of the language(s) in any given community. Only with detailed and comprehensive data on language vitality is long-term prediction of the global linguistic picture a real possibility.

Until relatively recently, only the Summer Institute of Linguistics (SIL) collected information of this kind on a large-scale basis.[2] The size of

---

2 The information is available in *Ethnologue: languages of the world* (Grimes, 1992). This resource is constantly being updated and is now accessible on the internet (http://www@sil.org/ethnologue).

SIL, with its force of linguists and missionaries placed into new linguistic communities all the time, leaves it the single most efficient institutional mechanism for gathering demographic information on people groups and their language use. However, there are other large-scale projects currently underway which can supplement SIL's efforts. For example, a UNESCO sponsored program called the International Clearing House for Endangered Languages was initiated in 1995 at the University of Tokyo. Their manifesto is to accumulate information on as many threatened languages as possible and to disseminate the data to interested parties. Of course, there are also many regionally focused institutions around the world which are involved in gathering crucial information on endangered languages within specific locales. (Colette Grinevald identifies several such institutions in South America in her contribution to this volume.)

Inseparably linked to questions about current language vitality is the crucial issue of identifying precisely the kinds of situations which will facilitate or, alternatively, hinder language loss/expansion. Certain factors are well known. For instance, large numbers of speakers or governmental support for a language tend to ensure its spread, while conversely, small numbers of speakers and active repression of a language tend to lead to its loss. However, these factors comprise only two of the most obvious influences on the vitality of a language.

A much subtler, yet move pervasive, predictor of the continued use of a language is the prestige attached to it. The prestige may derive from a number of factors (including the facts just noted – government support and large numbers of speakers); *inter alia*, a language typically grows in prestige if it is associated with a rich literary tradition, is used in local or national media of communication, is utilized in processes of commercial exchange (and thus is associated with economic advancement), or if it is tied to a widely practiced religion. Though any of these variables may prove to be important in imparting prestige to a language, there is no direct causal link. That is to say, a language could be marked by some of the properties listed above, yet still fail to achieve a high enough degree of prestige to ensure its continued use.

A case in point is Irish Gaelic (see Watson 1989 for details). Around AD 1500, Irish Gaelic was in primary use through nearly all of Ireland. Today, however, native speakers are found only in scattered communities in the north and west of the country. According to the 1971 census, only about a quarter of the population claims to speak Gaelic, and the proportion which actually employs Gaelic on any sort of regular basis is but a fraction of this number. Such a decline in Gaelic has occurred despite the fact that it had a large number of speakers and the fact that the language was traditionally utilized in education, commerce, government, religion, etc. The social conditions were just right to establish Gaelic as a high-prestige language, and indeed, it did. Nonetheless, the prestige attached to the language was not enough to maintain the language against the rapid encroachment of English. Why should this be? Why did Irish Gaelic not repel English altogether, or at least contain the spread of English so that both languages came to exist in equilibrium?

Nancy C. Dorian, in her chapter for this volume entitled "Western language ideologies and small-language prospects," argues that such patterns of language loss in Europe and the Americas are understandable only when one recognizes the force of a language "ideology" to undermine the normal maintenance effects of prestige. This ideology, which forms part of the heritage brought to the New World by conquering Europeans crucially carries a bias towards monolingualism. Such a bias highly disfavors situations where a native language exists peacefully with the Indo-European language of colonization. What makes this proposal particularly intriguing is that it underscores the dynamic nature of a social attitude like language prestige. While linguists have made strides toward comprehending what components go into building prestige, they have often ignored the forces which can dismantle, or at least reduce, that prestige. By identifying one such force, Dorian highlights a seriously neglected area of research.

Of course, language prestige is just one among an array of issues which must be addressed in understanding the processes of language maintenance or loss. So complex is the interplay of factors that it may ultimately prove impossible to predict the fate of individual languages over long periods of time. Even so, enough scholarship has been put forth for models which assess the liklihood of language loss with some accuracy to be conceivable. Lenore A. Grenoble and Lindsay J. Whaley outline certain necessary features of such a model in their contribution to the volume, "Toward a typology of language endangerment." Taking as their starting point a proposal laid out in Edwards (1992), they discuss certain vital components of a theoretical model of endangerment situations. For example, they argue that the pressures that combine to enervate or bolster language vitality should be arranged into several parallel levels based upon the source of the pressure, i.e. whether they are internal to the speech community, whether they are external but form part of the immediate context in which the community is found, whether they are a general characteristic of the geographic area where the community is found, etc. A desirable consequence of this architecture is that it accounts for pressures at different levels which run counter to each other.

While the attempt to understand and predict language loss has been a predominant concern of scholarly literature on endangered languages, there are two equally pressing considerations: what happens in a speech community when its traditional language is replaced by another? And what are the possible responses to the threat of language loss? The most fruitful answers to these questions are typically drawn from the experiences of communities which are confronting them first hand. Three of the chapters found in this collection offer insights on the effects of language loss on speakers of Native American languages and the challenges confronting them in the development of language maintenance/restoration programs.

Nora Marks Dauenhauer and Richard Dauenhauer, in "Technical, emotional, and ideological issues in reversing language shift: examples from Southeast Alaska," supply a retrospective view of attempts at language restoration in Alaska. In general, the programs aimed at reversing the precipitous decline in Native-language use have failed in Alaska. Born out of their experience with a number of such programs, the Dauenhauers detail several essential lessons about instigating language-maintenance programs. Chief among them is that a community must properly grasp and address the full range of attitudes it carries about itself and its relationship to other groups before a successful attempt at language restoration is even conceivable. Part and parcel of this is the fact that the community, or a significant part of it, must be committed to the success of a language program before it is initiated. As they aptly point out, "Language reversal can't be done to you or for you by others."

The external situation described by Nora C. England ("Mayan efforts toward language preservation") appears to be quite different than that in Alaska. Mayan languages typically have several hundreds of thousands of speakers, and a majority of Mayas speak a Mayan language as a first language. The driving concern of Mayan communities is not to revitalize their language but to buttress it against the increasingly rapid spread of Spanish. One might say that whereas Dauenhauer and Dauenhauer discuss the efforts of people who find themselves at the end of a process of language shift, England reviews the efforts of those at the beginning.

Despite the difference in language vitality, England also identifies community involvement as the single most important property for determining the likelihood of success of language programs. Though Mayan efforts at language maintenance include lobbying for the official status of Mayan languages in the regions where they are spoken, the lion's share of their work has gone into forming a self-generated, self-directed Academy to control decisions about Mayan language policies and to promote language use among Mayas. Even with the institutionalization of community support for language maintenance, England cites three forbidding obstacles: the lack of resources, the lack of technical expertise to guide decisions about language policies, and internal disagreement about the best course of action in language promotion. The last obstacle in particular serves as a crucial reminder that language use can be a highly political issue.

The theme of active community involvement again plays a key role in the contribution by Annette Jacobs "A chronology of Mohawk language instruction at Kahnawà:ke." The Mohawk immersion school in Kahnawà:ke was not introduced suddenly, but emerged piecemeal over a number of years as resources and opportunities became available. Nevertheless, the school, which represents one of the more successful language-revitalization efforts in North America, could never have developed if it were not for the sustained vision of certain community members.

Linguists also comprise a community which is directly affected by language loss, but in their case the death of a language usually bears professional rather than personal consequences. For this reason, their precise role in language preservation is unclear. Do linguists simply record languages while they are still in use, or should linguists take a more active role to promote language revitalization? Such questions have only recently been addressed in a public way by linguists, and as one might expect, there is no clear consensus. Some argue, along with K. Hale (1992), that a necessary goal of linguists is "safeguarding diversity in the world of people." Alternatively, some (such as Ladefoged 1992), argue for a professional detachment from the issue. Under this view, linguists are acting most responsibly when they leave the preservation of languages to the communities which use them and the political authorities that are charged with overseeing language policies. This, of course, does not preclude linguists acting in the role of professional experts when called upon.

Colette Grinevald, in "Language endangerment in South America: a programmatic approach," offers several insights into this issue from the perspective of a linguist who has been intimately involved with attempts at language preservation in Latin America and South America. She articulates a position which has the linguistic community, in its entirety, actively engaged in the issue of endangered languages while respecting and promoting the authority of speech communities to direct the fate of traditional languages. On the one hand, she asserts that decisions about language maintenance or restoration must be left solely in the hands of speakers of threatened languages. To this end, the linguistic community should also recognize the importance of providing technical training, and not just technical advice, to the speech communities they work with. On the other hand, the linguistic profession must make certain systemic changes to assist in the cause of maintaining linguistic diversity. Among other things, she calls for an increased willingness on the part of top graduate programs to train foreign linguists, an improvement in the training of fieldworkers, and giving due weight to fieldwork on endangered languages which, in tenure and hiring decisions, is oft times assessed as being largely in the realm of "descriptive" and "applied" linguistics.

Because the rapid loss of languages (and concomitant changes occurring in cultures) promises to reweave the social fabric of the world completely in the coming century, one might expect it to be a topic of keen interest for anyone concerned with the nature of social interaction in the not so distant future. On the contrary, attention to the issues surrounding endangered languages has remained mostly restricted to certain segments of academia and to individual communities currently faced with the real possibility of the loss of a traditional language. The general inattention to the issue of language death stems in part from a failure by linguists to adequately explore and to explain questions about what, if anything, is lost when one language becomes obsolescent and is superceded by another.

One popularly held opinion is that very little beyond an arcane linguistic system disappears with the death of a language. While this loss may be regrettable for those who have an emotional attachment to the language, so the wisdom proceeds, it really is of little concern to humanity generally. Indeed, many might argue that the leveling of linguistic diversity is a good thing in that it facilitates communication and, accordingly, intercultural harmony. Besides the fact that recent history (with the interethnic strife between the Serbian-speaking peoples of Bosnia, or the Kinyarwanda-speaking peoples of Rwanda and Burundi) provides too many counterexamples for this misconception to be tenable, there is much reason to assume that language diversity is "good" and should be preserved. A number of chapters in this book provide arguments to this effect.

Marianne Mithun ("The significance of diversity in language endangerment and preservation") points out that language offers one of the most direct glimpses at the creativity of the human mind. As a demonstration of this fact, she contrasts several aspects of the grammar of English and Central Pomo, a language of California now spoken by fewer than ten individuals. The contrast, which is presented in non-technical language, drives home just how different languages can be. Thus, in the death of any language comes the irreplaceable loss of a picture of human creativity.

Using a very different approach, Ken Hale ("On endangered languages and the importance of linguistic diversity") presents further arguments that a decline in language diversity constitutes a huge intellectual loss for humanity. He begins by providing several examples in which data from a single language has confirmed, altered, or vexed theoretically based beliefs about the way language operates. Hale continues by outlining some truly exceptional properties of a now extinct language called Damin, which was created by the Lardil people of Australia. His purpose in doing so is to demonstrate that instances of intellectual genius are often contained in languages. When languages disappear, we are in less of a position to recognize the full breadth of human cognitive capacity, let alone to account for it.

Christopher Jocks ("Living words and cartoon translations: Longhouse 'texts' and the limitations of English") and Anthony C. Woodbury ("Documenting rhetorical, aesthetic, and expressive loss in language shift") both explore the necessary connection between certain types of cultural practices and language. These two case studies are significant in that they offer actual instances of the widely held view that language loss entails cultural loss. Jocks addresses the role of the Mohawk language in understanding Mohawk culture and, in particular, religion. He speaks from a personal perspective, as a native Mohawk who acquired his ethnic tongue only as a second language, and has gone on to specialize in Mohawk religion. He shows that in a culture with a long-standing oral tradition (such as Mohawk), knowledge, memory, language and culture are indivisible. Moreover, language and cultural identity, and language and self-identity, are inexorably linked.

In a similar vein, Woodbury examines a set of suffixes in Cup'ik, a dialect of Central Alaskan Yup'ik Eskimo. These suffixes subtly nuance the nouns to which they are attached such that they are used with great rhetorical effect in Cup'ik speech. Woodbury has found that as Cup'ik is supplanted by English, the affective suffixes are not replaced by any functionally equivalent strategy. Indeed, Woodbury argues they *could not* be replaced. Therefore, the aesthetic and rhetorical value of these suffixes for Cup'ik culture disappears with the language.

A final topic of inquiry which has risen to the forefront of research on endangered languages is the structural changes which occur in a language as it is replaced by another. For the sake of simplicity, discussions on endangered languages are often framed as though speakers suddenly switch from the use of one language to another. The reality, though, is that language shift takes place over the course of a generation or more and can only occur in a context of multilingualism. This being the case, questions arise as to the morphosyntactic modifications to a language which is in declining use. How are they effected? Do they follow any sort of predictable patterns? Are the patterns universal or based on idiosyncracies of individual languages? The answers to such questions not only further general linguistic theory, but also promise to provide insights into the functioning of the human mind.

In this volume, André Kapanga ("Impact of language variation and accommodation theory on language maintenance: an analysis of Shaba Swahili") analyzes three subdialects of Swahili spoken in Shaba, Zaire. He examines several aspects of the phonology, morphology, and lexicon of these subdialects and finds, surprisingly, that the least prestigious subdialect of Shaba Swahili has remained most vital, while the most prestigious has been most affected by French. This leads Kapanga to suggest a set of social factors which might account for this unexpected result.

Whereas Kapanga uses data on language structure to assess language vitality, Carol Myers-Scotton in "A way to dusty death: the Matrix Language turnover hypothesis" uses her Matrix Language Frame model to account for the ways in which language structure is transformed as one language is replaced by another. Her claim is that when two or more languages coexist, one is often the dominant, or Matrix, language. The grammar of this language impinges on the others such that speakers will begin using certain structural components of the Matrix Language (e.g. constituent order and inflectional morphology) even when constructing sentences in a less dominant language. One of the significant points in this chapter is that instances of language shift do not involve one static language system abruptly taking a place of another. Instead, it is a gradual process that includes a transitional state in which the two languages are blended in the speech of individual members of the community.

Nikolai Vakhtin makes the same point but pushes it a step further in "Copper Island Aleut: a case of language 'resurrection'." He argues that language-endangerment situations cannot always be depicted as one language replacing another. There is another possibility – a traditional language can be displaced by new "mixed" or "creolized" tongue. In other words, the gradual shift from one matrix language to another can be arrested before the shift is completed. To make his case, he cites the situation of Copper Island Aleut (or CIA), which takes its lexical base from Aleut and morphology from Russian.

By necessity, we have only hinted here at the full gamut of issues involved in language loss and the responses of communities to such loss. This overview should, however, provide a context for discerning the direction which research into these matters is currently travelling. It should be noted that many of the chapters in this volume were originally presented at a conference on language endangerment held at Dartmouth College in February, 1995 (a summary of the major themes of the conference appears in Grenoble and Whaley 1996). The conference was made possible by contributions from the Steffens Twenty-First Century Fund, the Dickey Center for International Understanding, the Nelson A. Rockefeller Foundation, the New Hampshire Humanities Council, and the Office of the Dean of the Faculty of Dartmouth College. None of these organizations is responsible for the views expressed. We would like to thank them for their generous support. We would also like to thank Brigg Noyes for help in transcription, and especially Kirsten Henschel for work in final editing and proofreading.

Abbreviations and symbols

A	adjective	nom	nominative
ACC/acc	accusative	NP	noun phrase
caus	causative	NSL	Native language as a
CAY	Central Alaskan Yup'ik		second language
	Eskimo	obj	object
CIA	Copper Island Aleut	OBV	obviative
cl	class	part	particle
cont	continuous	PERF/perf	perfect(ive)
cop	copula	pl	plural
CP	projection of	poss	possessive
	Complementizer	PRES/pres	present
CS	codeswitching	prog	progressive
DET/det	determiner	PROX	proximative
EAS	East African Swahili	rel	relative
EL	Embedded Language	RMD	Romani mixed dialects
ERG	ergative	sg	singular
FSU	former Soviet Union	Sh.S.	Shaba Swahili
FUT/fut	future	SIL	Summer Institute of
fv	final vowel		Linguistics
GEN/gen	genitive	semlf	semelfactive
imp	imperative	SV	stem vowel
imperf	imperfect(ive)	SVO etc.	subject–verb–object etc.
indic	indicative	T	tense
INF/inf	infinitive	T/A	tense/aspect
loc	locative	TP	tense phrase
ML	Matrix Language	V	verb
MLF	Matrix Language Frame	=	clitic marker
N	noun	#	morpheme-boundary
n	neuter		marker
neg	negation		

Part I General issues

1 Western language ideologies and small-language prospects

NANCY C. DORIAN

Departments of German and Anthropology, Bryn Mawr College

It might be said with a certain metaphoric license that languages are seldom admired to death but are frequently despised to death. That is, it's relatively rare for a language to become so exclusively tied to prestigious persons and high-prestige behaviors that ordinary people become too much in awe of it to use it or are prevented by language custodians from doing so. By contrast, it's fairly common for a language to become so exclusively associated with low-prestige people and their socially disfavored identities that its own potential speakers prefer to distance themselves from it and adopt some other language. Parents in these circumstances will make a conscious or unconscious decision not to transmit the ancestral language to their children, and yet another language will be lost. The power of the social forces involved is evidently considerable, since under better circumstances attachment to an ancestral mother tongue is usually strong. The phenomenon of ancestral-language abandonment is worth looking at, then, precisely because a good many people, especially those who speak unthreatened languages, are likely to have trouble imagining that they themselves could ever be brought to the point of giving up on their own ancestral language and encouraging their children to use some other language instead.

Unless they become fossilized so that they persist in specialized uses without ordinary speakers, as sometimes happens in connection with religious practices (Latin, Sanskrit, Coptic Egyptian, Ge'ez, etc.), languages have the standing that their speakers have. If the people who speak a language have power and prestige, the language they speak will enjoy high prestige as well. If the people who speak a language have little power and

I'm indebted to Christina Bratt Paulston for helpful criticisms of the first draft of this chapter and for suggestions for its improvement.

low prestige, their language is unlikely to be well thought of. Because the standing of a language is so intimately tied to that of its speakers, enormous reversals in the prestige of a language can take place within a very short time span. The arrival of the Spaniards brought about precipitous changes of this kind in the fortunes of two major New World languages, that of the Aztec empire in North America and that of the Inka empire in South America. Both had achieved great dominance, expanding at the expense of neighboring languages for some centuries as the Aztecs and Inkas conquered new territories and made ever more peoples subject to their rule (Heath 1972; Heath and Laprade 1982). In a stunningly short time both empires were brought low by their encounter with the better armed Spanish, who represented an expanding Old World power. Neither imperial language disappeared, but each survived with severely reduced social standing. Today Nahuatl and Quechua are low prestige speech forms within the regions where they are spoken, and each is under some threat from still expanding Spanish.

To be sure, cases exist in which a conquering power has given up its own language and adopted the language of the very people whom it has conquered. The Vikings seem to have been particularly susceptible to this, going over to Romance speech forms in Normandy and Sicily and to a Slavic speech form in Russia. It is not unique to them, however; the western Franks and the Bulgars followed a similar pattern, as did the Normans in England, repeating the pattern of their Viking forebears in Normandy. In such cases the conquering group is usually numerically thin, compared with the size of the conquered population, and it may deliberately intermarry with the indigenous aristocracy (for lack of enough women of its own group or for the sake of adding legitimacy to its seizure of local power and property, or both). Distance from the original homeland probably plays a role in some such cases, as in the Viking kingdoms, all established far from Scandinavia. Military loss of home territories can have the same distancing effect. The anglicization of the Normans in England might have been delayed or even prevented if they had been able to retain control of Normandy; but they lost their Norman territories less than a century and a half after conquering England, and from that time forward their focus was on their English territories.

In any event, these are the unusual cases rather than the norm. In the more usual cases, the group that exercises military or political power over others will establish its own language as the language of governance in its contacts with those others. And when one speech form enjoys a favored position as the language of those who control obvious power positions (as administrators, governors, judicial officers, military officers, religious officials, major landholders, and so forth), it requires no great sagacity, but only common sense, to see that it's likely to be useful to acquire some knowledge of that language. If members of a subordinate population have the opportunity to learn the language of the dominant group, some or all of them will usually do so. They will not necessarily give up their own ancestral language, however. It seems likely that it's not so much the tendency to learn a dominant-group language which has increased a great deal in modern times, but rather the opportunity to do so, and, concomitantly and more importantly for linguistic diversity, the tendency to abandon one's ancestral language entirely in the process. To understand this last phenomenon, it may be necessary to consider what in the last two centuries or so is characteristic of Western (i.e. European-derived) attitudes toward non-standard speech forms, since tendencies towards complete ancestral-language abandonment seem to be very strong in the widely distributed areas of European settlement.

Ruling powers have not always expected subordinate peoples to give up their ancestral languages or encouraged them to adopt the language of the dominant group. The Ottoman Empire encompassed an extraordinary variety of subordinate ethnic groups but permitted them to retain a good deal of their ethnic identity, including native religious and linguistic practices, in the various *milletler* ("nations") within its domains. Even European states were moderately permissive of ethnic languages until relatively recent times. The rise of nationalism in Western Europe at the beginning of the industrial age coincides to a considerable extent with less tolerant attitudes towards subordinate languages. In the present day, for example, France has shown unusual intolerance of ethnic distinctiveness, even for a Western European country (refusing birth certificates and identity cards to children with Breton given names, for example, as recently as the 1970s [New York Times 1975]). Yet cultural and linguistic diversity was an unproblematic fact of life in France until the 1790s, when in the aftermath of the French Revolution a need for a unifying national identity, expressed in part by a single national language, was rather suddenly perceived (Grillo 1989:22–42; Kuter 1989:76).

The fact that powerful pressures for cultural and linguistic unity emerged in France around the time of the Revolution is not accidental from the perspective of some students of nationalism. Rather the pressures emerged at that time because of the particular stage of development the country was reaching and the changes attendant on such a stage. Ernest Gellner identifies a pre-industrial "agro-literate polity" in which the uppermost social strata (e.g. nobility, clergy, merchants) are sharply layered horizontally vis-à-vis one another, with the layers prevailing across the polity as a whole, while a variety of distinct small communities coexist, laterally separate from each other, within the polity and beneath the upper strata. In societies with this sort of social organization, Gellner (1983:10) describes the state as "interested in extracting taxes, maintaining the peace, and not much else, and . . . [with] no interest in promoting lateral communication between its subject communities." In industrial societies, by contrast, conditions are quite different. Industrial means of production require universal literacy and numerical skills such that individuals can communicate immediately and effectively with people previously unknown to them. Forms of communication must therefore be standardized and able to operate free of local or personal context. This in turn places great importance on educational institutions, which must produce individuals with certain generic capacities that permit slotting and re-slotting into a variety of economic roles. The state is the only organizational level at which an educational infrastructure of the necessary size and costliness can be mounted (Gellner 1983:35–38).

France offers a particularly good (and particularly well-studied) example of rising standard-language dominance at the dawn of the industrial age. At the time of the Revolution, France was passing out of the agro-literate stage of development into a pre-industrial stage, and with a new focus on the polity as a totality the fact that a number of sizable subcommunities such as the Bretons, Basques, Alsatians, and Occitanians were incapable of understanding and speaking French became unacceptable. In 1794 the Abbé Gregoire, priest and revolutionary, presented a report to the National Convention in which he detailed this lamentable situation and called for the universalization of the French language. Under the monarchy, as the revolutionaries saw it, linguistic heterogeneity had been useful to the crown as a means of keeping various feudal constituencies from making common cause with one another (Grillo 1989:35). In the revolutionary French state there could be no place for such policies. As part of the social and ideological transformation they were engaged in, the citizens would be unified by common use of a single language, namely the French language (Grillo 1989:30, 34).

Sentiment that could be called nationalistic had grown in France from the mid-fifteenth century onwards, as the French crown increased its geographic domain and its political strength (Joseph 1987:133). Although France had no actual policy of linguistic unification before the Revolution, the prestige of French had been uniquely high nonetheless. The king and his court spoke French, and from that ultimate milieu of power and status the French language gained unrivaled luster (Grillo 1989:29). The championing of French after the Revolution was perfectly in keeping with the usual linkage between high-prestige people and a favored speech form, despite the Revolution's abrupt termination of the French monarchy. So, too, was the disfavoring of speech varieties spoken by the relatively low-prestige peoples of the country. The speech forms of "vulgar" classes of people were tainted by the status of their speakers: they, too, were "vulgar." Already in 1790, when the Abbé Gregoire conducted a survey that included questions about the influence of *patois* (by which he meant both French dialects and non-French vernaculars such as Basque and Breton) and about the consequences of destroying it in the various regions of France, the letters he received in reply to his questions indicated very low opinions of the various regional speech forms, which were labeled coarse and stupid and were considered to keep the people ignorant and superstitious (Grillo 1989:31, 174).

These were in fact commonplace attitudes in European polities.[1] Grillo (1989: 173–74) states bluntly – and accurately, I think – that "an integral feature of the system of linguistic stratification in Europe is an ideology of contempt: subordinate languages are despised languages." This has been true both where regional dialects are concerned and where the languages of subordinate ethnicities are concerned. In his study of the rise of language standards and standard languages, Joseph (1987:31) suggests that language is particularly susceptible to what he calls "prestige transfer":

1 They were not uncommon in non-European contexts either, for that matter. The Aztecs used a variety of unflattering terms for the languages of their subject peoples, some of which stuck and became the name by which the language is still known, at least to outsiders. Derogatory language names deriving from Aztec labels include Chontal "foreigner", Popoloca "unintelligible", and Totonac "rustic" (Heath 1972:3).

.Because the intrinsic worth of dialects and of their component elements and processes is well nigh impossible to determine, language is highly susceptible to prestige transfer. Persons who are prestigious for quantifiable reasons, physical or material, are on this account emulated by the rest of the community. These others cannot obtain the physical or material resources which confer the prestige directly (at least they cannot obtain them easily, or else no prestige would be associated with them). But prestige is transferred to attributes of the prestigious persons other than those on which their prestige is founded, and these prestigious-by-transfer attributes include things which others in the community may more easily imitate and acquire, if they so choose. Language is one of these.

He further considers that "the power which prestigious dialects hold over non-prestigious speakers goes beyond what logic and rationality can predict or account for," and that the prestige-holding segment of a population can use the mechanisms of prestige-language standardization to maintain and increase linguistic differences between themselves and speakers of less prestigious speech forms (*ibid.*). The histories of several of the national languages of Europe, very conspicuously those of French and English (Grillo 1989), are histories of a growing monopoly on legitimacy and prestige by a single dominant speech form, all others being relegated to inferior status. The standard language is typically considered a rich, precise, rationally organized and rationally organizing instrument; dialects and ethnic-minority languages, by contrast, are considered impoverished and crude, most likely inadequate to organize the subordinate world itself and certainly inadequate to organize other worlds.[2] European states such as

2 One result of this is a tendency among other-language speakers in contact with standard-language speakers to consider that any feature in which their own language differs markedly from the standard language must indicate some own-language deficiency. In Scottish Gaelic the adjective normally follows the noun. Unfortunately for Gaelic speakers, the dominant standard language to which they compare their own is English rather than French. In East Sutherland, Gaelic speakers frequently remark that Gaelic "puts the cart before the horse" in this regard, implying a failing on the part of Gaelic (since carts don't belong before horses). That is, they assume that English, which they were taught in school, represents things as they ought to be. Because the ancestral language is measured against dominant-language norms, it's difficult for speakers who have no special training – and often no schooling in the ancestral language at all – to see in a positive light any unique or highly developed features of their own language. Gaelic, for example, has a very rich system of emphatic suffixes which can attach to nouns, adjectives, many pronouns, and a few verbal forms. Although the emphatic suffixes lend Gaelic a distinctive flavor and constitute a rich discourse device, I've never heard an ordinary Gaelic speaker so much as mention the emphatic suffixes, let alone praise them for the subtle effects they make possible in creating discourse tone and expressing point of view and social distance.

France and Great Britain were unusual perhaps chiefly in their determined allocation of unique prestige and legitimacy to a single carefully cultivated supra-local speech variety as the nation's official language. They were not unusual, certainly, in their allocation of higher prestige to a speech variety originally used by a materially more favored group or in their assumption of the superiority of their own mother tongues. Social status, whatever its basis, seems very generally to rub off on language, as Joseph indicates, so that the possession of wealth, however that wealth is calculated, will enhance not only the social position of the wealthy people but also the social position of the language that they speak. In East Africa, where the "cattle complex" prevails and wealth is measured by the size of the cattle herd, the languages of cattle-herding pastoralists have frequently displaced the languages of hunter-gatherers who own no cattle (Dimmendaal 1989: 16–24).

Europeans who came from polities with a history of standardizing and promoting just one high-prestige speech form carried their "ideology of contempt" for subordinate languages with them when they conquered far-flung territories, to the serious detriment of indigenous languages. And in addition to a language ideology favoring a single normalized language, derived from the history of national-language standardization in their homelands, Europeans espoused other ideologies that exacerbated their contempt for whatever unstandardized vernaculars they encountered.[3] They seriously confounded technological and linguistic development, for example. Unable to conceive that a people who lacked a rich material culture might possess a highly developed, richly complex language, they wrongly assumed that primitive technological means implied primitive linguistic means.[4] This misconception condemned most Europeans to total exclusion from the diverse conceptual worlds and rich oral literatures of many peoples whom they encountered; but much more unfortunately, it

3 Language ideologies/linguistic ideologies are defined by Silverstein (1979:173) as "sets of beliefs about language articulated by the users as a rationalization or justification of perceived structure and use" and by Rumsey (1990:346) as "shared bodies of commonsense notions about the nature of language in the world" (cited in Kroskrity 1993 and Woolard 1992 respectively).

4 There is no evidence, unfortunately, that much progress has been made on this score. Even today only specialists seem to think otherwise, and when linguists and linguistic anthropologists discuss the language endangerment crisis with non-specialists, it's nearly always necessary to make clear at the very outset that the languages threatened with extinction are fully developed instruments capable of great precision and rich elaboration in cognitive terms.

misled many Europeans into doubting the very humanity of peoples whose languages they mistakenly took to be primitive and undeveloped.

Two other European beliefs about language are also likely to have had an unfavorable impact on the survival of indigenous languages in the very considerable portions of the globe where a standardized European language became the language of the dominant social strata (including previously annexed or conquered regions of the home country itself). Particularly widespread and well established is a belief in a linguistic survival of the fittest, a social Darwinism of language. This belief encourages people of European background to assume a correlation between adaptive and expressive capacity in a language and that language's survival and spread. Since their own languages are prominent among those which have both survived and spread, this is of course a self-serving belief. For obvious reasons it's also a belief more widespread among English, French, and Spanish speakers than among Czechs or Icelanders, but even among speakers of the smaller standardized and state-promoted languages of Europe there often lurks a notion that the general Indo-European type of language is exceptionally well suited to clear thinking and precise expression.[5] Difficult as it often is to convince non-specialists of the full grammatical and expressive development of all natural languages, it can be even more difficult (without delivering a lecture on the structural properties of the world's languages, assuming an audience willing to sit still for such a lecture) to persuade them of the extremely useful features of many non-Indo-European language structures, such as, for example, obligatory evidential markers in the verbal system. (Evidentials are discussed in detail in Mithun's chapter in this volume.)

Notions about the "natural" ability of certain languages to thrive and the "natural" inability of others to do so can be seriously entertained only by people who are not aware of the sudden reversals of linguistic fortune that have occurred when polities have fallen on hard times. Sumerian and Akkadian, two spectacularly successful Mesopotamian languages in

5 There is no general awareness of such problems as the poor fit between spoken language and orthography which makes English and French such unnecessarily difficult languages in which to become literate, and there is also no general awareness of such difficulties as phonologically non-unique morphological elements (e.g. the same sibilant suffixes to express both possessive and plural in most English nouns, the same final vowel for infinitive, second-person plural, and past participle in many French verbs).

their time (roughly the first two-thirds and the last third of the third millennium BCE respectively), not only waned after the falls of Sumer and Akkad but became entirely extinct in the end. Greek, if it crashed less drastically, is today more often learned by non-Greeks in a form that has not been spoken for 2,000 years than in its contemporary form as the living language of a small and not especially prosperous European country.[6] Quechua and Nahuatl, the proud languages of once-thriving New World empires, still have strong representation in sheer numbers of speakers but each has poor social standing. Quechua has official-language status in Bolivia and (since 1975 only) in Peru, but not in Ecuador or Chile. Nahuatl has no official status and is seriously threatened in certain Mexican regions where few if any children are acquiring it. The existence of a writing system and even the existence of a notable literature do not necessarily ensure that a language will survive as a living speech form, much less thrive. Hittite has left us copious written materials, yet it is extinct. Irish was one of the earliest northern European languages to be written, and the literature and learning of early Irish are quite distinguished; but as a naturally acquired mother tongue it had declined to the status of a peasant language before late nineteenth-century Irish nationalism encouraged its cultivation once again in literary and expository forms.

The second of the additional beliefs disadvantageous to indigenous languages in regions dominated by speakers of European languages may actually be more characteristic of Anglophones than of speakers of other European languages. Anglophones however are particularly thickly distributed in regions that once had large numbers of indigenous languages, so English single-handedly threatens a disproportionate number of other languages. The belief in question is that bilingualism (and by extension multilingualism, all the more so) is onerous, even on the individual level. This belief is so widespread, in fact, that it can be detected even among linguists. Not long ago in reviewing a collection of linguistic papers about first-language attrition I was startled to find that the editors saw bilingualism above all as "a natural setting for the unraveling of native language abilities" (Seliger and Vago 1991:1). The model of bilingual capacity that

---

6 A given language has a distinct market value that can be calculated by various objective measures. See the useful chapter on "The value of a language: factors of an economic profile of languages" in Coulmas 1992.

underlay the volume was subtractive: the bilingual's two languages were said to compete – "metaphorically," said the editors – "for a finite amount of memory and processing space"; the possibility of a full and richly developed bilingualism was acknowledged only by a single reference to "the so-called balanced bilingual" (p. 2). There were no tempering statements about the enrichment potential of bilingualism, nor was first-language attrition, the official subject of the book, distinguished from convergence phenomena. Attrition in language contact implies loss and incompleteness, while convergence implies mutual influence. The latter can reasonably be considered a normal manifestation of bilingualism, on both the individual and the societal level, but it does not by any means constitute an "unraveling," at least to my mind. It often represents the regional norm, in fact, deviant only when matched against the standard language, and purely in the abstract at that (since the actual performance of even those who claim to be standard-language speakers usually diverges from book and classroom norms).

The cumulative effect of the "ideology of contempt," of ignorance about the complexity and expressivity of indigenous languages, of a belief in linguistic social Darwinism, and of a belief in the onerousness of bi- or multilingualism converge to bear down most of the languages spoken by populations without wealth or power. They are heavy weights for small populations in particular to cast off, and few have so far been able to do so.

In the most general terms, a linguistically distinctive population which has come to have poor standing needs to discover or develop some basis for increased self-regard in order to withstand pressures for ancestral-language abandonment and shift to a dominant-group language. Several possible sources of such self-regard can be identified, at least tentatively. Rising prosperity, as an indicator of increasing economic success, can be an effective counterpoise to the social disfavor that typically accompanies a subsistence-level economy. Provided it does not burst suddenly upon a population with no prior experience of it,[7] prosperity can boost social self-confidence while also providing the resources for institutional language-maintenance efforts that might otherwise seem prohibitively expensive.

---

7 The history of the Osage tribe after sudden oil wealth illustrates some of the problems associated with abrupt and unexpected wealth.

The Ayas Valley, in the Autonomous Aosta Valley Region within the Italian Republic, moved in recent decades from an economy based on agriculture and stock-rearing to one based on tourism. The resulting prosperity of the region supports a trilingual pre-school program for children from 3 to 5. Despite the small size of the population served, five schools deliver a carefully designed and executed program that provides support for local Franco-provençal as well as for Italian and Standard French (Decime 1994). A similar economic transition has changed the outlook for tiny Ladin, spoken in three small and discontinuous districts in the South Tyrol region of Italy (Markey 1988). The development of a booming tourist industry, geared in good part to luxury-level skiing, has been the most conspicuous change in local conditions. The seasonal nature of the tourist industry and the fact that the tourists represent no single dominant language, plus the isolation of the districts at other times of the year, perhaps operate to safeguard the ancestral-language base, which has been strengthening in recent decades.

Where prosperity grows less suddenly and dramatically, it may be that its usefulness lies above all in the fostering of a middle class with the social self-confidence to insist on traditional identity and heritage. Catalan speakers, in a region with a strong economic base and a self-confident tradition, emerged from the severe suppression of the Franco years and were soon able to begin once again attracting new speakers to their language in Castilian-dominated Spain (Woolard & Gahng 1990).[8]

Wales is considerably less prosperous overall than Catalonia, the Ayas Valley, or the Ladin districts of the South Tyrol. Within the ranks of an established middle class, however, social self-confidence can seemingly emerge despite economic weakness if educational achievement permits marked social mobility. In nineteenth-century Wales in-migration of large numbers of English coal-industry workers originally posed a severe threat to the survival of Welsh. Yet in the longer run the coal industry helped to

---

8 Catalan can be considered a "small" language in the context of Spain, since it is spoken by a much smaller number of people than Spanish and is found chiefly in a single region of the country. By comparison with minority languages in many other settings, however, it is extremely well represented. Numbers as such form an uncertain measure of linguistic security, of course; some of the distinctly precarious languages of Central India have over a million speakers, e.g. Kurux (Abbi 1995), and so did beleaguered Breton, in France, as recently as 1926 (Timm 1973:289, citing Meillet 1928:380).

produce a middle class which in the twentieth century has provided much of the impetus for revitalization of Welsh. Khleif, studying the successful growth of Welsh-medium education, identified the "new middle class" in Wales as the chief factor in the turn-around (1980:77–78):

> The current leaders of Welsh opinion are overwhelmingly sons and daughters of coal miners, agricultural workers, steel workers, shop keepers, and minor civil servants, but especially of coal miners . . . They are all Welsh-speaking and, in a small country such as Wales, know each other very well. Their Welshness sets them apart, for to have spoken Welsh at home, a generation ago, meant that the person by definition was working-class. They are very proud of their Welshness, of their ability to speak Welsh, of their ability to "live a full Welsh life". They consider their knowledge of Welsh a badge of achievement, for it differentiates them from other middle-class people as well as working-class people who are English monoglots . . .
>
> Sons and daughters of the new Welsh-speaking middle class are more self-assured, many informants remarked. Welsh-medium schools impart self-confidence to the new generation.

The speakers of Ladin, Catalan, and Welsh are themselves Europeans, of course, and as such they may have been at least conceptually less distant to begin with from envisioning their own linguistic success (and less distant, no less significantly, from outside investment capital and the like). Most small-language communities cannot realistically look to rapidly spurting prosperity to reinforce their standing, unfortunately.

Occasionally more accessible as a socially and psychologically invigorating factor may be progress towards political autonomy, preceding or accompanying the rise of a middle class and of a native intelligentsia. In Greenland, for example, after a period of intense Danicization that accompanied a drive toward modernization, reaction set in and pressure for greater autonomy resulted in Home Rule for Greenland in 1979. Prior to that year Greenlandic had been considered a threatened language, with considerable justification in view of the rise in the number of Danish monolinguals during the preceding quarter-century. Since that year Greenlandic has been supported and promoted to an increasing degree, and bilingual Greenlanders have increasingly replaced monolingual Danes in the top institutional and organizational positions (Langgaard 1992).

It would be difficult, or more likely impossible, to identify a precise cause-and-effect sequence in most of the cases mentioned so far, since the factors involved frequently intermesh. Rising prosperity and an emerging middle class often coincide. A native intelligentsia is likely to appear in conjunction with an emerging middle class, and any or all of these factors may either precede or accompany movement towards greater political autonomy.

While these factors appear to enhance the chances of ancestral-language maintenance, their absence need not doom a small language to rapid disappearance. The case of the Arizona Tewa, still in possession of their ancestral language even though long enclaved among the Hopi, suggests a different sort of counterpoise to the negative effects of European-derived linguistic ideologies. On the basis of long-term work among the Arizona Tewa, Kroskrity proposes that in the theocratic Pueblo societies, where political and religious authority are fused, ceremonial speech has a position analogous to that of the standard language in a nation-state. The highly regarded ceremonial speech variety called *te'e hi:li* 'kiva talk' is of critical importance to the Arizona Tewa, and the rigorous standards applied to its maintenance spill over into attitudes towards Arizona Tewa generally (Kroskrity 1993:37–39):

> Their concern is with maintaining and delimiting a distinctive and appropriate linguistic variety, or vocabulary, for religious expression . . . The strong sanctions against foreign expressions in ceremonial speech – violations of which are physically punished – are motivated not by the linguistic expression of xenophobia or extreme ethnocentrism but by the need for stylistic consistency in a highly conventionalized liturgical speech level. Similarly, the negative evaluation of code-mixing in everyday speech by members of the Arizona Tewa speech community does not reflect attitudes about these other languages but rather the functioning of ceremonial speech as a local model of linguistic prestige . . . Just as ceremonial practitioners can neither mix linguistic codes nor use them outside of their circumscribed contexts, Tewa people should observe comparable compartmentalization of their various languages and linguistic levels in their everyday speech.

The Arizona Tewa have maintained their ancestral language for 300 years, despite enclavement within a Hopi environment, despite considerable intermarriage with the Hopi, and despite a small population base. There may well be a variety of elements in their success: they pride themselves on their skill at languages, for example, and they consider their bilingualism in Hopi, while the Hopi do not control Tewa, a form of cultural victory (Kroskrity 1993:23, 218).[9] The centrality of religious ceremony has been a factor in some other cases of unexpectedly sustained language maintenance in seemingly adverse circumstances, however (cf. Hohenthal & McCorkle 1955; Barber 1973), and a strong religious base certainly cannot be overlooked as a source of the psychosocial confidence necessary for language maintenance in the face of considerable social pressure for shift.

Despite the fact that peoples speaking a variety of small local languages have followed similar paths to a decrease in speaker numbers and to an eventual language shift, the path in question is neither inevitable nor perfectly predictable. Even the prospect of material well-being, for example, seductively associated with Westernization during the long period over which European (and more recently American) power has expanded, does not invariably lure a population away from its traditional culture and traditional language. Natives of Pulap Island in the Western Island group of the Carolines (Micronesia) have proved unusually resistant, during the half-century of US dominance in their region since World War II, to American individualistic and materialistic values, which they consider selfish and greedy. While modern opportunities for wage-earning work away from the home island have produced welcome material rewards for some Pulap Islanders, indigenous values have led to the sharing of those rewards among extended kin groups at home. Many traditional practices reflecting persisting traditional values still prevail among the Pulapese, not only on Pulap Island itself but also on Moen, the capital of Chuuk State, where land purchases by some Pulap Islanders in the 1950s have come to serve as a more centrally located and urbanized extension of Pulap Island:

> The art of [traditional] navigation, production and exchange of local foods, respect behavior toward kin, and traditional dress are the major traits that Pulapese invoke to conceptualize their culture, and this process appears in its most pronounced form on Moen. Pulapese present these cultural characteristics as evidence of their worth in a context in which others are abandoning tradition. (FLINN 1990:123)

9 Compare the Emenyo of New Guinea, who likewise consider bilingualism an accomplishment and feel superior to less frequently bilingual Dene-speaking neighbors in whose language they are commonly bilingual (Salisbury 1962:4). This is the antithesis of the widespread anglophone notion that bilingualism is damaging to the bilingual because the two languages inevitably compete for limited cognitive space.

Navigating by traditional means is more difficult than navigation using modern techniques, and traditional food preparation is relatively slow and laborious. Traditional clothing permits body parts now normally covered elsewhere in the region to go uncovered, and respect behavior requires women to stoop in the presence of their older brothers, among other things. Pulapese cultural conservatism is overt and obvious, therefore, and is acknowledged by other islanders. By laying claim in clearly identifiable fashion to greater traditional "purity," the Pulapese present themselves as superior in a cultural sense, creatively compensating for a lesser material well-being. And as might be expected, given the other conservative Pulapese behaviors, Pulap Islanders on Moen, even the secondary-school pupils whose education on Moen is entirely in English, maintain the use of their Pulap dialect in the home setting (Flinn 1992:156).

The existence of resistant groups such as the Arizona Tewa and the Pulap Islanders (and of others as well, such as the mountain Kwaio of the Solomon Islands [Keesing 1992]) indicates that one of our particularly acute needs is more in-depth studies of linguistic and cultural persistence in small communities. Except in cases of great geographical or social isolation, the long-term maintenance of a small language implies not just the persistence of one language but the enduring coexistence of two or more. Currently we understand the motivating factors in language shift far better than we understand the psychosocial underpinnings of long-sustained language maintenance. We need to understand not just the staying power of the Arizona Tewa (illuminated both by Yava 1978 and by Kroskrity 1993), but the tolerance of the Hopi, who have permitted long-term Tewa–Hopi bilingualism in their midst while remaining largely without knowledge of Tewa themselves. In similar fashion, Moen natives apparently exert no pressure on the Pulap Islanders on Moen to abandon their somewhat archaic behaviors or to give up their home-island speech variety. Another case of seemingly unproblematic coexistence is to be found in the Circassians who fled to the Middle East in the nineteenth century, with 120 years of persistence in what is now Israel, and Israeli acceptance of them. They are reported to cultivate bi- and trilingualism as a matter of course and to show no signs of incipient language shift (Stern 1990).[10]

---

10 There are other cases of great potential interest. English is said to be the language of all monetary rewards for the Koasati of Texas, who number under 200. The children attend English-language

In an ironic turn of events, the excesses of nationalism itself may have begun to effect a change in thinking that could conceivably, if it were to catch hold, lead to an improved outlook for small-language communities submerged in, or under the control of, contemporary nation-states. Recent prime ministers of Ireland and the United Kingdom, recognizing that irreconcilable nationalist aspirations will never offer a basis for peaceful solutions to the problems of Northern Ireland, came forward with the proposal that what they term "multiple allegiances" be recognized. The Irish prime minister, in a talk before the National Press Club in Washington, DC (Bruton 1995), pointed out that land ownership is no longer the basis of real wealth in modern economies, so that discrete assignment of all land to mutually exclusive nations does not have the urgency it once had. So long as no flags are run up the pole (i.e. so long as certain traditional emblems of purely political allegiance are avoided), individuals with different sets of multiple allegiances should reasonably be able to co-exist in one region. He is so much persuaded of the power of this concept that he recommends it as a potential solution in other ethnically and linguistically complex regions of Europe such as Latvia and Catalonia.

Multiple allegiances in this sense might be seen as an extension into the sphere of political organization of the sociologist's status sets, the totality of all the statuses one occupies (not always entirely congruently) in one's social life. In the political sphere this suggestion is to some extent "post-nationalist" and to that degree perhaps an escape hatch from the demands of mutually exclusive nationalisms.[11] The fact that recognition of multiple allegiances is being recommended as a solution for otherwise irresolvable nationalist conflicts precisely in Europe could be especially helpful, since it is the concept of the nation-state coupled with its official standard language, developed in modern Europe and extended to the many once-colonial territories of European states, that has in modern times posed the keenest threat to both the identities and the languages of small communities. Outside the modern European sphere of interest the same problem of insistent single-language dominance coupled with hostility to

schools, furthermore, and yet the ancestral language is successfully transmitted, with "monolingual Alabama-Koasati speakers … still present in each generation of children" (Saville-Troike 1989:215).

11 "What we are trying to do in Ireland is to redefine the concept of nationality, so that it suits the realities of the 21st century, and isn't mired in the concepts that were the cause of so much war in Europe in the 19th and 20th centuries" (Bruton 1995:6).

minority languages has not necessarily arisen.[12] The Ottoman Empire was largely free of it over most of its long history, and the 300-year coexistence of the Arizona Tewa with the First Mesa Hopi indicates that both ethnic and linguistic persistence are feasible over long time spans without fatal ethnic hostility on either side. Thailand, with a stable hierarchical social structure until very recently, is said to have had minimal ethnolinguistic conflict over the six and a half centuries of its monarchy despite the presence of a variety of ethnicities within the national borders (Smalley 1994).

In yet another ironic development, there has been a good deal of consciousness-raising within the European Community recently in connection with small languages and minority languages. The EC member states have not been willing to yield to economic pressures and permit the use of some one or two languages as the Community's official working languages (English and French being the chief candidates). Instead they have insisted on the national-language principle and have accepted the enormous costs of mounting interpretation services and document-translation services for each of the individual national languages. This unyielding adherence to the national-language ideology has given rise to unprecedented European support for multilingualism, and in an overspill of protective enthusiasm for smaller languages, even minority languages within the EC countries have gained a certain increased recognition and at least a few economic benefits (Coulmas 1992:116–117). This recent development shows a language ideology which has previously worked *against* small languages beginning to work *for* them instead: if all nations, no matter how small, have a right to the use of their own language, then by extension other small-language populations, with or without a nation-state of their own, can with some justice claim the right to the use of their own languages as well. In time some of this change of attitude could conceivably be generalized into wider European spheres of influence.

Popular opinion in the United States and other European-settled parts of the world is unfortunately still largely infected with earlier European language ideologies of the types discussed above, all unfavorable to

---

12 This is not to suggest that enforced use of a dominant-group language and intolerance of subordinate languages were unknown outside Europe, since that is clearly not the case. Heath and Laprade describe Inka policies designed to erase both the histories and the languages of conquered tribes, including "a program to spread their language, Quechua, and to prohibit use of the languages of subjugated tribes" (1982:123).

the survival of smaller indigenous languages. The emergence of government-level initiatives to counter some of the negative aspects of nationalism (in the form of the new "multiple allegiances" discussion), the stirrings of a new legitimacy for small languages, and perhaps also the growing acknowledgement in recent decades (in the United States at any rate) of the value for the health of individual and planet of at least some non-Western, small-society forms of religious or spiritual world-view, conceivably offer a small window of opportunity to make the case for the wisdom of preserving linguistic and cultural diversity.

Still, recent concerns about loss of linguistic and cultural diversity, together with new recognition of the possibilities of multiple sociopolitical allegiances and of the legitimacy of ethnic languages and of multilingualism, come very late in the day for most small languages. Material well-being has been intimately linked to the adoption of dominant languages for a very long time, and the reality of that linkage is undeniable. It requires enormous social and psychological self-confidence for any small group to insist on the importance of ancestral-language retention. (Consider, for example, the case of the English-monolingual speakers who can claim Tlingit ethnicity, as discussed in Dauenhauer and Dauenhauer, this volume.) Precisely that sort of self-confidence is hard to come by in communities which have suffered the penalties of an ideology of contempt over a long period.

Special problems can arise, furthermore, if language shift is already well underway. Even in settings where remaining fluent speakers of the ancestral language may sense that their culture is deeply bound up with their language (and it is surely germane to the durability of Arizona Tewa that its speakers frequently state "Our language is our history" [Kroskrity 1993:44]), it becomes impossible to insist on that linkage if a large part of the social group that identities itself by the ancestral-language label no longer speaks that language. In such cases, defining identity in terms of language would define out of membership most of the younger people whose retention is vital to continued existence as a group. And those without the language will resist the linkage, if my experience in the Scottish Highlands is any indication. I found that when I asked speakers of Scottish Gaelic whether a knowledge of Gaelic was necessary to being a "true Highlander," they said it was; when I asked people of Highland birth and ancestry who did not speak Gaelic the same question, they said it wasn't. This is not a surprising division of opinion, but it does greatly complicate the situation for small communities where ancestral-language loss is already well advanced. The question of a linkage between a language and the culture it's associated with becomes so delicate a matter that it's almost easier to insist on the importance of language to heritage and identity in settings where the ancestral language is entirely lost than in settings where it's retained by a relatively small number. Among the Echota Cherokee of Alabama, for example, strong sentiment attaches across various age groups to the Cherokee language and great longing for a lost heritage is expressed in connection with the possibility of introducing it into selected Alabama schools (Sabino 1994:5); but this outpouring of fervor is for a vanished language that none of the Echota currently speaks.

Joshua Fishman points out that language "always exists in a cultural matrix" and that the matrix rather than the language is the point at which support is most needed (1989:399). He calls attention to the power of "Zeitgeist trends that can contribute as much or even more to [language] spread than language policy per se," and to a momentum generated by "mobility aspirations" and "the apparent stylishness of the pursuit of modernity itself" (1989:390). He recognizes (1989:399) that the staying power of endangered languages "must be intimately tied to a thousand intimate or small-scale network processes, processes too gratifying and rewarding to surrender even if they do not quite amount to the pursuit of the higher reaches of power and modernity." Such rewards cannot be supplied from the outside. They are to be had from within the social web of the community itself or not at all. For this reason it is extraordinarily difficult for even the most sympathetic outsiders to provide useful support for endangered small languages, most especially for non-European small languages within a Euro-American sphere of influence. Moral support and technical expertise, including linguistic expertise, can and should be offered, certainly, but acceptance or rejection will necessarily lie with individual communities. Even in the event of acceptance, effective leadership can only come from inside the community.

One role that knowledgeable outsiders have sometimes usefully played is that of information-disseminator and consciousness-raiser, helping to make a wider public aware of the looming threats to a local language's survival. This process has only recently begun on a scale more appropriate to the size of the problem, however, and time has grown desperately short for many local languages. Having waited too long before undertaking to rally support for threatened languages, we may find ourselves eulogizing extinct languages whose living uniqueness we had hoped instead to celebrate.

2 Toward a typology of language endangerment

LENORE A. GRENOBLE AND LINDSAY J. WHALEY
Program in Linguistics and Cognitive Science, Dartmouth College

The fundamental cause for the disappearance of a human language is well known. Speakers abandon their native tongue in adaptation to an environment where use of that language is no longer advantageous to them.[1] This much about language death is simple and uncontroversial. The more complex, and thus obscure, issue is *"What* brings about the decreased efficacy of a language in a community?"* A sufficient answer involves outlining an intricate matrix of variables dealing with the community's self-identity, its relationship with other groups, the degree of political autonomy of the group, its access to avenues of material prosperity, etc. Due to the complexities of the issue, most comparative work on threatened languages seeks out general points of commonality between situations, rather than distinctness, and rightly so. By identifying recurrent patterns in the causes of language decline, such work has helped make manifest those characteristics of speech communities which leave them most susceptible to language loss.

However, the focus on shared characteristics often masks the fact that there are intriguing divergences from the typical scenario for language loss: individual speech communities which have resisted language shift against all expectations, as well as regions of the world which do not fit smoothly into the general picture which has been drawn for language endangerment. The focus on similarities also begs important questions such as: why do linguistically related groups with similar histories and demographics manifest significantly different rates of language obsolescence? Why do linguistically related groups whose histories contrast in obvious ways nevertheless show the same rate of language decline? Why are some

We would like to thank Barry Scherr, Vjacheslav Ivanov, and two anonymous referees for comments on earlier versions of this chapter.

1 There are, of course, dramatic exceptions in which entire speech communities are eliminated through war, disease, or genocide, such as Tasmanian, Lenca, and Cacaopera (Campbell and Muntzel 1989). In such instances, one could hardly identify the cause of language loss to the shifting attitudes of its speakers.

groups able to reverse the process of language shift successfully, whereas others are not?

These and related issues have not been explored satisfactorily in the growing corpus of research on endangered languages, yet until they are adequately addressed, a comprehensive model of language loss is not possible. Indeed, one of the most useful resources the scholarly community can supply is a thorough typology of endangerment situations, one which captures both the homogeneity and the heterogeneity of these situations. Such a typology will allow improved predictive power over the future of threatened languages and furnish an additional tool for the planning of effective language maintenance and revival programs.

In this chapter, we discuss a model of minority-language situations advanced by Edwards (1992), which we believe represents a promising approach to typologizing threatened languages. We highlight certain key aspects of the architecture of this model in section 2. In section 3, we identify several ways in which his model must be adjusted in order to improve its predictive power. In section 4, we justify these suggestions by examining several "anomalous" instances of language shift: the general pattern of language endangerment in sub-Saharan Africa, the decline of Evenki in Siberia, and the revitalization of Maori.

1   Toward a typology of language endangerment

The idea of developing an explicit schema for typing minority-language situations is certainly not new. However, the goal of such work is often more narrowly construed than what we have in mind. Fishman (1985: 158–160), Krauss (1992), and Kibrik (1991), for instance, have each developed methods to rank the relative vitality of languages based on information such as the demographics of speech communities, the political status of languages, and the nature of the language's transmission to the youngest generation in the speech groups. This kind of work has been instrumental in raising awareness about the startling loss in linguistic diversity and in providing a convenient way to prioritize the response of the linguistic community. However, these rating scales do not attempt to identify the full matrix of variables affecting threatened languages.

Operating from an "ecolinguistic" perspective, Haugen (1971), Haarmann (1986), and others have designed approaches to discovering the interaction between languages and their environments. The aim of this work is to identify the status of a language in a *typology of ecological classification*, which will "tell us something about where it stands and where it is going in comparison with the other languages of the world" (Haugen 1971:25). However, this work is typically intended for application to any language, large or small, threatened or not, and consequently it often neglects variables which are obviously relevant to language endangerment. For example, Smalley (1994) notes Haugen's inattention to the historical processes that bring about the ecolinguistic status of a language in the first place. Another shortcoming has been the general bias toward objective measurements of language groups to the exclusion of more subjective (and less readily quantifiable) variables (Giles, Bourhis, and Taylor 1977; Foster 1980; Haarmann 1986). Arguably, the subjective attitudes of a speech community towards its own and other languages are paramount for predicting language shift. Finally, we may note that most work from the ecolinguistic perspective is designed for broad classification, and so is not equipped to account for the often subtle influences on language groups which cause them to maintain or lose a language, especially for those groups which are moving contrary to normal patterns.

In view of these shortcomings, an adequate typology of threatened languages requires a model that takes into account the entirety of variables which can interact to sap the vitality of a language, or alternatively, to bolster it. One model which is quite promising in this regard has been laid out in Edwards (1992).

The basic premise of Edwards' model is that the plethora of variables which are relevant to minority-language situations[2] can be grouped along two parameters. The first, which he simply calls "Categorization A," consists of different perspectives by which human groups can be characterized: Geography, Psychology, Religion, and the like. The second parameter, "Categorization B," identifies the scope over which the A-variables can be applied: Speaker,[3] Language, and Setting. These two parameters

2 It should be highlighted that the model is not exclusively applicable to threatened languages, but minority speech communities generally; thus, one could examine, say individual Spanish-speaking communities in the United States, which are usually under heavy pressure to shift to English use. In the present chapter we focus specifically on its relevance to language endangerment and small speech communities.

3 This label is somewhat misleading in that it suggests the domain of a single speaker. Note that Edwards uses it to refer to groups of speakers rather than individual speakers.

Table 2.1 Edwards' (1992) framework for the typology of minority languages

Categorization A	Categorization B		
	Speaker	Language	Setting
Demography	1	2	3
Sociology	4	5	6
Linguistics	7	8	9
Psychology	10	11	12
History	13	14	15
Political[4]	16	17	18
Geography	19	20	21
Education	22	23	24
Religion	25	26	27
Economics	28	29	30
Technology[5]	31	32	33

generate a table with thirty-three cells (see table 2.1). A set of specific questions is then associated with each of the cells in the table. The result is a relatively thorough overview of those features which are relevant to assessing language vitality. In the case of endangered languages, the model is useful in compiling a prognosis for the continued use of the language.

In order to elucidate the individual cells in table 2.1, we repeat Edwards' sample questions in table 2.2. The number of the questions corresponds to the cell number in table 2.1. Given the range of information Edwards has in view, objections could easily be raised concerning the content of individual questions. At this point, however, we simply offer the questions in table 2.2 as an aid to better understand the spirit of Edwards' model.

Edwards' scheme is very much a work in progress, and for that reason, it is quite susceptible to the criticism that it is still not comprehensive

---

4 This category appears as "Political/law/ government" in Edwards 1992.

5 This category appears as "The media" in Edwards 1992. However, given the generality of most of the A-variables in the table, this misses the important point that communicative media is only one aspect of technology which can dramatically influence language attitudes.

Table 2.2 Edwards' (1992) sample questions

1	Numbers and concentration of speakers?
2	Extent of the language (see also geography)?
3	Rural–urban nature of the setting?
4	Socioeconomic status of speakers?
5	Degree and type of language transmission?
6	Nature of previous/current maintenance and revival efforts?
7	Linguistic capabilities of speakers?
8	Degree of language standardization?
9	Nature of in- and out-migration?
10	Language attitudes of speakers?
11	Aspects of the language-identity relationship?
12	Attitudes of the majority group towards minority?
13	History and background of the group?
14	History of the language?
15	History of the area in which the group now lives?
16	Rights and recognition of speakers?
17	Degree and extent of official recognition of the language?
18	Degree of autonomy or "special status" of the area?
19–21	Basic facts about geography?
22	Speaker's attitudes and involvement regarding education?
23	Type of school support for language?
24	State of education in the area?
25	Religion of speakers?
26	Type and strength of association between language and religion?
27	Importance of religion in the area?
28	Economic health of the speaker group?
29	Association between language(s) and economic success/mobility?
30	Economic health of the region?
31	Group representation in the media?
32	Language representation in the media?
33	General public awareness of area?

enough to generate a full typology of endangerment situations. We return to this, as well as other more substantive criticisms, in the next section. However, it is important to highlight some strengths of Edwards' model which make his general approach well suited for evaluating threatened languages.[6]

First, Edwards' model makes an explicit distinction between features of an individual speech community (the Speaker and Language columns) and features of the broader context (the Setting column) in which that community is located. We refer to these features as *micro-variables* and *macro-variables* respectively. Since language loss always involves contact between at least two communities, a comprehensive typology must identify the properties of an endangerment situation which are internal to the group speaking the threatened language, as opposed to those which exist externally to it (see Sasse 1992; Brenzinger, Heine, and Sommer 1991; and others who make the same point).

Macro-variables are most useful as broad indicators of the potential threat that exists to minority languages in a given region of the world. Whether or not there exists an actual threat depends on the circumstances of individual communities (i.e. it is a function of micro-variables). Consider the United States as an example of a region where macro-variables are clearly at play. A compelling pattern of language loss is easy to detect among the abundant Native communities despite the fact there are prominent differences at the level of micro-variables. The structural features of individual languages differ, the length of contact with English speakers differs, only some groups had sustained contact with other European languages (particularly Spanish and French), the size and traditional social structure of groups differ, etc. However, the vast majority of Native languages in the United States have suffered the same fate: in this century they have either become extinct or moribund. Why is this generally true when

6 At the same time we echo Fishman's cautions that predictive typologies can at best make informed postulates about the future course of language maintenance and attrition because of the potential impact of shifts in societal attitudes and beliefs on language. Fishman's own model (1985:156–172) is proposed to predict trends in "community" (i.e. immigrant) languages of the United States, such as Greek, Italian, Spanish, and Japanese. Accordingly, the future of such languages on US territory depends upon immigration patterns not predictable from a linguistic model. The criteria Fishman proposes are specifically geared to the demographics of the United States, producing a more finely tuned model than that of Edwards (1992), but one which needs to be expanded to be applicable to forecast language loss globally.

unique properties which *might* have led languages down different courses can be identified? Because certain powerful macro-variables are involved in each case. Among them one could include what might be called a "European" attitude toward indigenous languages (see Dorian, this volume), national educational policies which were designed for aggressive Americanization of Native populations, economic development which has marginalized Native peoples, the emergence of telecommunications technology which tends to negate the conservative effects of geographic isolation, and so on.

Whereas macro-variables are indicative of features which are shared across large numbers of endangerment situations, micro-variables are characteristics which are unique to specific speech communities.[7] It is at the level of micro-variables where one can account for how differences in the rate, outcome, and reversibility of language-shift cases come about. Ugong (Bradley 1989) in Thailand offers a nice example. Ugong has disappeared from or become moribund in several communities, but still remains as a first language in others. Why should this be, given that the macro-variables relevant to the Ugong communities are essentially the same? Bradley identifies several micro-variables which account for this fact. First, in the areas where Ugong has been maintained, an Ugong headman held some measure of political control until relatively recently, and "an Ugong headman provides prestige for the group and maintains an Ugong focus for his village or township" (Bradley 1989:34). Another significant variable is access to education. In those regions where Ugong is no longer spoken, there has been access to Thai-based education since the 1930s. In contrast, in those areas where Ugong remains, no schools have appeared until recently. Finally, those regions where Ugong is still found have been more geographically isolated. The result has been to force a certain economic self-sufficiency, to prevent a high degree of exogamy, and to restrict contact with non-Ugong people. All of these features have had the consequence of maintaining Ugong.[8] Thus, the Ugong case usefully depicts the importance of maintaining a distinction between macro- and micro-variables.

7 In theory, no two language communities will be identical with respect to a given micro-variable, yet there may be a high degree of similarity. In developing a typology, one issue which must eventually be addressed is just how similar two groups have to be in order to categorize them together.

8 Bradley also notes that these features have all changed, so the outlook for the continued use of Ugong is not good.

A second notable feature of Edwards' model, one which approaches the level of conceptual necessity for a model of endangerment, is that it maintains an association between micro-variables and macro-variables. Referring back to table 2.1, each Categorization A property (Demography, Sociology, etc.) must be calculated for each Categorization B column. This organization reflects the fact that the import of micro-variables for language endangerment is often determined by the corresponding macro-variable for a given domain.

This point is best elucidated by means of an example. One micro-variable which has been noted for some instances of language loss is the economic organization which a given speech community employs as a means of subsistence for the group. Possibilities include nomadic-pastoralist, sedentary-pastoralist, hunter-gatherer, agriculturalist, and urban-industrial, to name but a few general categories. Without any reference to the broader contexts in which a group finds itself, this particular micro-variable is of limited value in predicting the likelihood of language shift. Knowing the economic organization of a community will generally allow one to predict certain demographic features such as the size of the population – e.g. hunter-gatherer populations are by necessity small. However, there is nothing inherent in any particular form of economic organization or corresponding demographic properties which leaves one group more susceptible to language loss than another. It is only when this information is placed in a context (that is, viewed in relationship to macro-variables) that such information becomes useful in determining the language vitality of the community.

Take, for instance, the general fate of the languages of hunter-gathers in Africa. These languages are generally more threatened than those of groups which are involved in other sorts of socioeconomic organization.[9] This is in part due to the small populations of these groups. However, the more imminent threat is the extreme pressure on them to shift to the pastoralist or agriculturally based economies of the groups they are in contact with. African hunter-gatherers are particularly vulnerable to this pressure for a number of reasons. Often, the habitat they use for hunting and gathering is being co-opted for agricultural use. In the colonial period, game-hunting,

9 Some case studies include Rottland 1982 on Ariek, Heine and Möhlig 1980 on Omotik, Spencer 1973 on Lorkoti, Tosco 1992 on Dahalo, Brenzinger 1992 on Yaaku, Dimmendal 1989 on Kmegu, and Heine 1982 on Boni.

which was classified as poaching, was outlawed in some areas. More causative of language shift is the relative social status of groups from varying
types of economic organization. Hunters are generally the most despised
groups in Africa. They constitute the poorest African people and their lifestyle is often viewed as "animal-like." Accordingly, there is tremendous
motivation for such low-status groups to throw off symbols of traditional
identity in order to assimilate more smoothly into more prestigious groups.
In East Africa, Brenzinger (1993:9) notes that hunter-gatherers

> were attracted by the pastoralists and their way of life for a long time. But
> only with the Pax Britannica did it become feasible for them to acquire and
> (more importantly) keep cattle . . . By securing rights of possession, the
> British allowed hunter-gather groups to become economically pastoralist,
> and many of those groups decided to abandon their former language in
> favor of the pastoralist one.

Although the fate of the languages of African hunter-gatherers has
been recounted here only in cursory fashion, the crucial interaction of
micro- and macro-variables is clear. It is not hunter-gathering per se which
has an effect on the long-term viability of the languages spoken by these
groups, but certain consequences of hunter-gathering within the African
context.

A final important aspect of the organization of Edwards' model is
the distinction he makes between ethnicity (his Speaker column) and language use (his Language column) (see Appel and Myusken 1987). As others
have done, we note for present purposes that a shared language is often not
a guarantee of shared sense of identity. Consider the Twa of Rwanda. Like
the Hutu and Tutsi, the other two major ethnic groups in the country, the
Twa speak Kinyarwanda, but they remain (somewhat) culturally distinct
and socially isolated. Tradition holds that they are dirty and backward,
most likely because of their traditional nomadic way of life in the forests of
Rwanda and because they are economically marginalized in the country.
The tradition is so powerful that access to everything from public education to communal wells is denied to the Twa. It is quite clear that their
fluency in Kinyarwanda is irrelevant for solidarity with other Rwandans[10]
and equally clear that it has little to do with Twa group identity.

---

10 The lack of sociopolitical unity among
Kinyarwanda speakers was even more dramati-
cally displayed in the genocide which took place in
Rwanda in 1994. In this incident, it was the Hutu

In this section, we have identified three strengths of the architecture of Edwards' model: it draws a distinction between micro-variables and macro-variables; it forces one to see a direct association between these two levels of variables; and it separates the notions of ethnicity and language use. Any predictive model of language maintenance and shift must also minimally incorporate these aspects. In addition, we should note that Edwards generally takes a more discriminatory view of the variables involved in minority-language situations than others have. That is, the complexity of describing speech communities is brought to the fore since the model is devised to characterize a minority-language situation from at least thirty-three different perspectives. This fine-grained approach also is, in our opinion, the most useful means to developing a better understanding of language endangerment. Nonetheless, there are still some major lacunae in Edwards' model. We turn to this problem and other shortcomings in the next section.

2   **Extensions to the typological model of language endangerment**

It is noted above that Edwards is aware his model (given in table 2.1 above) does not cover all issues relevant to minority-language situations, let alone language endangerment. Yet we do not find the general criticism that he fails to be completely comprehensive in his coverage of the issues to be an argument against his approach, but a challenge to develop it further. In this section, we propose three such extensions. We discuss one area, literacy, which is not obviously represented in table 2.1, although literacy is generally agreed to play a significant role in speech communities and in the relative vitality of threatened languages. Second, we propose that the macro-variable column be further refined to make a distinction among broad areal settings, national settings, regional settings, and local settings. Finally, we argue that the variables in Edwards' model need to be hierarchically arranged. In particular, we suggest that for endangered languages one must to take into account the potential of economic issues to outweigh all others combined, although this is a potential, not an absolute: ranking

---

and Tutsi who were involved, though the mass murder which occurred was not completely based on ethnicity. Prunier (1995) provides an excellent overview of the historical and social circumstances which led to this catastrophe.

economic concerns higher than other variables is not tantamount to assigning economic factors complete primacy.

2.1   *Literacy*

The role of literacy in language endangerment is one of the more controversial issues today. On the one hand, many linguists see literacy as a crucial step in ensuring a particular language's continued use (see Craig and England, this volume, for representative statements about the role of literacy and written materials in preservation programs). The strong view argues that literacy is essential to nationalism (Gellner 1983) and language survival in the modern world. On the other hand, others (e.g. Mülhäusler 1990) argue that literacy actually facilitates language loss. We will argue that while literacy can be expected to have a certain effect at a macro-level, its effect on language vitality is primarily the result of micro-variables, which are in turn assessable only within the larger macro-situation.

These complications stem from the fact that literacy involves far more than simply whether or not a community has access to and utilizes a written form of language. Rather, literacy occurs in a social context and is best defined as a set of socially organized practices. This may be obscured by the fact that in many cases literacy is implemented at a macro-level, with a federal or regional government determining the nature of language-planning programs, and allocating financial resources for education and publishing materials in the indigenous language.

The necessity of defining different interpretations of literacy at different geographic levels is argued by Okedara and Okedara (1992), with Nigeria as the illustrative example. Nigeria has approximately 413 languages; 198 of these have no existing orthography. Only 4.5 percent of known Nigerian languages are official literacy languages, taught in the schools and used in public and private offices, and in the media. These include English, which is spoken by less than 10 percent of the entire Nigerian population, and which serves as a national language. In addition, Hausa, Yoruba, and Igbo are regional languages for the northern, western and eastern regions of the country. Beyond these four "major" languages, note that there are an additional 409 other languages spoken in Nigeria.

The general failure of literacy in most Nigerian languages can be explained in part by the country's multilingualism: people in regions of very high language density are educated in the regional language, which is used as the language of education, while English remains the lingua franca for the entire country. Since literacy in these languages is sufficient for participating in education, politics, and regional economics, there exists little practical incentive for the development of literacy using the languages of smaller communities.

At the same time, literacy programs may make use of a group's knowledge of the non-indigenous language in order to hasten acquisition of literacy in the native language. This is the basis of a promising literacy project called CELIAC (Centro Editorial en Lenguas Indígenas, AC, or the Indian Language Publishing Center), based in Oaxaca, Mexico. As of 1992, a total of 52 people had been trained in 12 different Mexican languages (Bernard 1992). Working largely through their existing knowledge of Spanish and using computers to create the necessary characters, bilingual trainees were able to quickly implement writing systems for their own indigenous languages. The result has been the relatively rapid and inexpensive production of texts and dictionaries in such languages as Mixe, Zapotec, and Chinantec.

Because of the initial success of programs such as CELIAC, one must be careful not to assume that literacy in a regional or national language is at all times detrimental to developing literacy in minority languages. Rather the full set of consequences must be measured on a case-by-case basis. Clearly, though, the differing impacts of literacy on a society stem from its social functions within the individual community, or what is referred to as its *social meaning*.

Social meaning encompasses a set of micro-variables which involve the attitudes, beliefs, and values of a community. The application of this term to literacy originates with Szwed (1981) and is further developed by Reder and Reed Wikelund (1993) to include a community's assessment of when and where specific literary practices are appropriate. Although this aspect of literacy is less rigorously measurable than its mechanics, it has been shown to be a crucial component in the impact of literacy on a language.

As an example, Reder and Reed Wikelund (1993) point to the role of social meaning in the literacy development of an Alaskan village, where two well established written languages, Russian and English, compete with each other as well as with the native Aleut of the village. They argue that literacy within the community has developed into the two distinct and conflicting concepts of "village" literacy and "outside" literacy. Writing systems were originally introduced into the community by the Russian American Company, which brought a more colloquial style of Russian, and by the Russian Orthodox Church, which brought a more liturgical style of written language. (The Church introduced written language in Cyrillic script; the oral service relies on both Church Slavic and Aleut.) Although both these varieties were introduced by foreign groups, these writing traditions have since been incorporated into village life such that they are seen to be a part of native identity. In contrast, "outside" literacy is in English, which was originally introduced through the US school system and then later reinforced through increasing contact between the native population and US governmental officials. What is interesting in this case is that although each literary language was introduced by outsiders to the local community, it is the Church Slavic that has become identified by community members as part of their native (Aleut) culture. Thus it can be seen that the social interpretation of literacy is a function of micro-variables.

From these three brief discussions of the role of literacy in Nigeria, in CELIAC, and in an Alaskan village, it becomes clear that the interplay between literacy and language viability is a rather complex matter. We cannot begin to explore these complexities in any depth here, but it is worth noting some particularly key issues relating to the impact of literacy on endangered languages.

The majority of endangered languages come from oral cultures, where converting the language to a written form poses certain consequences for the continued use of these languages. It is often argued that any change from an oral to a literate society creates major changes in that society. (See Jocks, this volume, for a discussion of language and religion in Mohawk society.) At the same time, communities with long-standing written traditions may be in a stronger position to hold on to a language despite reduced numbers of speakers, and certainly are in a stronger position for revitalizing a language which may in part need to be reconstructed on the basis of written records. This is arguably the case of Maori (New Zealand), as we will discuss in section 3.3.

At the level of macro-variables, the attitude towards multilingualism, multiliteracy, and multiculturalism which is held by a regionally dominant culture is crucial for minority-language survival. Strong pressures to assimilate to the majority culture may be difficult for minority

communities to oppose, especially when their own children aspire to conform to the majority norm. Moreover, majority cultures tend to control
financial resources needed for mass publication of materials, and tend to
control policy issues, such as determining the language of education, the
ratification and enforcement of laws which permit or restrict access to the
indigenous language, and most often control access to the press. For these
reasons, it is not just the social meaning of literacy within a speech community which determines its success or failure, but external attitudes as well.

Finally, the selection of the specific dialect or form of the language
which will serve as the basis of the literary language may doom the literary
language to obsolescence if the selected dialect is one which the majority of
speakers reject for linguistic or social reasons. The choice of orthography
is also relevant to whether literacy in one's native tongue serves as a boon
to literacy in another language. If the two scripts are similar in design, for
instance both being based on the Latin alphabet and employing many of
the same sound–grapheme correspondences, then literacy in one script
should greatly facilitate literacy in the second.[11]

The question of whether literacy in the native language fosters literacy in the majority language is crucial. There is ample evidence that literacy in one's native language does in fact facilitate the acquisition of literacy
in a second, non-native language (Okedara and Okedara 1992:93). The
extent to which biliteracy facilitates a shift toward the majority language
and culture and away from the indigenous one stems from the role of literacy in the individual community.

We have, of course, only touched here on the intricate association
between literacy and the maintenance or loss of an endangered language.
Our modest aim has been to highlight the necessity of incorporating issues
of literacy into a typological model of endangerment situations. Literacy is
thus understood to be a bundle of interrelated factors, which include at
least the following features, given in table 2.3.[12]

If we consider cases where a written form of native language has
been implemented, we see that the impact of any literacy program in terms

11 As discussed in section 3.2, a concrete example
is provided by the former Soviet Union. The
Soviet government imposed the use of the Cyrillic
alphabet for writing minority languages, thereby
facilitating the acquisition of Russian.

12 *Role of literacy* and *acquisition of literacy* are
adapted from Scribner and Cole 1981:50. Bowers
1968 provides an earlier overview and discussion of
some of the main issues involved in literacy; Goody
1968 includes a number of specific case studies.

Table 2.3 Literacy variables

MACRO-VARIABLES	
Education	Language(s) of instruction, level of multilingualism in school, etc.
Language planning	Nature of goals, input from native community, role of majority culture, financial resources available from majority culture, etc.
Regional attitudes towards multilingualism, multiliteracy, multiculturalism	
Regional languages and orthographies	Relation to minority languages, degree of prestige
Types of readily available printed materials	Religious, pedagogical, instruction manuals, political, literature, etc.
MICRO-VARIABLES	
Role of literacy in community	Education, religion, laws, literature, histories, personal records and correspondence, public records, technical diagrams and instructions, etc.
Acquisition of literacy	Motivation, learning environment, teachers, pedagogical methods and materials, nature of sessions, numbers of participants, etc.
Standardization issues	Which dialect is basis for literary language, prestige, intelligibility, learnability, orthography
Nature of indigenous community	History, language density, levels of multilingualism, multiliteracy, education, prestige factors, etc.

of fostering or hindering depends primarily upon three micro-variables. These are: (1) issues of standardization, including the relative compatibility of the new literary dialect with the speech form of any given community, as well as further orthographic issues; (2) the financial resources available to produce written materials in the indigenous language; and (3) the role of literacy in a given community.

There is obvious and necessary overlap among these categories, as well as the others in table 2.3. For example, the function of literacy in the community and the kinds of printed materials available are directly related, although the latter is usually determined by economic factors as well. Similarly, there is a direct correlation between the language of education and the kinds of pedagogical materials available, or between the social functions of literacy and language prestige.

2.2   *Arranging variables hierarchically*

As we have noted above, one highly commendable aspect of Edwards' model of minority-language situations is the degree to which it compels the analyst to recognize the multiplicity of issues relevant to describing the nature of such situations. Recalling table 2.1 from above, we find thirty-three separate cells used in typing minority-language communities. One deficiency in the layout of this table in its application to endangered languages, however, is that all thirty-three cells appear to have equal significance. Intuitively, though, some of these variables have greater weight in determining the viability of the languages than others. Moreover, certain variables are likely to determine the value of others. To take just one example, whether a group and the language of a group is portrayed positively in the media (cells 31 and 32 in Edwards' model) is largely dependent on the combination of other variables such as socioeconomic status of the speakers (cell 4), the historical relationship between the speakers and larger culture or cultures which engulf them (cells 13 and 15), and most directly the attitudes of the majority culture toward the speakers (cell 12).

In view of such considerations, one way in which Edwards' model must be adjusted, particularly for application to endangered-language situations, is to explicitly capture the direction of the relationship between variables (i.e. which cells tend to determine the value of others) and to rank variables in terms of their importance for predicting language viability. This is no small task, of course. To discover the actual relationship among variables and their relative weights will require a great deal of scrutiny of existing case studies of endangered languages, and it will require much new research. Furthermore, the relationship between variables may vary from one language community to another.

It seems likely, however, that such work will reveal a priority of economically based variables over most others. Over and over again, one finds the relinquishing of a native tongue is tied in part to the belief that success in a non-native language is crucial to economic advantage (see, in this volume, Dauenhaeur and Dauenhauer, for example). Language planning and

literacy decisions are often developed with economic concerns at the forefront. Fishman (1968:56–57), citing Banks and Textor (1965), points out that
linguistically homogenous states tend to have at least a "medium" per capita
gross national product, which in the mid-sixties was defined as at least
$300 per month. This is in contrast to linguistically heterogeneous polities,
which tend in the opposite direction: they are more likely to be characterized by a relatively *low* to *very low* per capita GNP and range economically
from "underdeveloped" to "very underdeveloped." The lack of prestige
assigned to a great many minority groups and the corresponding prestige
tied to larger groups is frequently grounded in relative economic prosperity. Patterns of in- and out-migration are often a function of economic
concerns. Taken together, such issues suggest that for many cultures, the
reality of current economic pressures has the potential to override all other
variables.

2.3   *Levels of macro-variables*

While the direct determinant for language shift is a modification
in the attitude which a speech community holds toward its traditional
language (thus, it is an operation of micro-variables), the impetus for
this modification invariably is external to the speech community (thus,
an operation of macro-variables). This verity is incorporated into a model
of endangerment situations easily enough as long as the value ascribed
to micro-variables is recognized in part to be a function of the relevant
macro-variables.

Edwards' model provides for information about the broader setting
in which a speech community is located. A key theoretical issue, however,
is completely ignored. How broadly is setting to be understood? From
Edwards' questions in table 2.2 above, it is difficult to identify what he
means by the term since he employs vague expressions such as "economic
health of the region" and "state of education in the area." By *region* and
area he may intend the immediate geographic domain contiguous to the
speech community under investigation, or the regional polity, or the nation,
or some combination thereof.

We propose that the external forces which impinge on the language attitudes of a speech community originate at a number of levels:
Local, Regional, National, and *Extra-National*. By Local, we understand
the immediate context of a speech community. Among other things, the

Local domain is comprised of those groups with which a speech community comes into frequent contact, whether it be through trade, cultural exchange, formal education, or the media/communications. Since contact via media/communications does not require physical interaction, the Local context is not entirely a geographic domain. For example, the geographic isolation of the Totonac community of Santo Domingo in central Mexico serves as a partial obstacle to direct contact with monolingual Spanish-speaking Mexicans. However, battery-operated radios carry Spanish into the village on a daily basis. Consequently, Spanish forms part of the Local context for the community.

The Regional and National contexts are both political constructs. By Regional, we mean a geographic region which has some degree of political autonomy within a larger National domain. The significance of these domains is dependent upon the type of language-planning policies instituted in the respective polities, the amount of congruence between them, and how aggressively their policies are advanced.

By the Extra-National context, we mean a region, usually but not necessarily a geographic one, with shared cultural characteristics and/ or histories which transcend any national boundaries. Dorian (this volume), for example, identifies a Western-language ideology which was/is shared by Europeans. The fact that this ideology was shared by the European conquerors of Australia and the Americas can partly account for the remarkable similarities in the patterns of language loss found on these three continents. More strikingly, the lack of a continent-wide Western-language ideology can be seen in Africa, where indigenous languages give way to other indigenous languages, with only isolated exceptions (such as Dutch-based Afrikaans).

The relationship between these levels of context for a speech community is complex and the relative impact that they have on a speech community varies from case to case. This is particularly true for the Regional and National levels. The significance of a Regional domain depends on the degree of autonomy that it has from the nation that contains it. If there is a high degree of autonomy, then decisions about official-language status and the use of language in the courts, the media, and education can all be made and enforced on this level making it highly significant for a speech community. The influence of the National context can also vary. In countries where the national government has a high degree of control, its impact on speech communities is potentially massive. However, in some regions of the world, individual communities exist largely independent from the dictates of the national government, usually due to geographic isolation.

The significance of differentiating between the various levels is dependent upon the speech community being examined. For many indigenous languages of the United States, for instance, the Local, Regional, National, and Extra-National domains are essentially congruent. That is to say that the Local context is usually, if not always, comprised of an Anglo-centered English speaking community. Generally speaking, the same attitudes about minority groups, education, and language issues held by the local community are represented in the policies at the state level, and these policies are not substantively different from the corresponding national policies. Thus, while one can still recognize that a minority speech community is being influenced at each of these levels, the influence is mostly the same – to relinquish the traditional language in favor of English – and the collective nature of the influence is greater than in a situation where the Local, Regional, and National domains are at odds.

In other cases, the various levels bear strikingly different influences upon a speech community. Take, as one example, the case of Basari, a Northern Niger-Congo language of west Africa. The largest concentration of speakers spans the border between Senegal and Guinea (Vanderaa 1991). The prognosis for the language is not good, though there are currently 15,000 or more Basari speakers. At the Local level, Basari is impacted greatly by Fulbe for two reasons. First, there is a great deal of trading between the Basari and the Fulbe; and second, Basari women intermarry with the Fulbe. Notably, the children of these marital unions become Fulbe. At the Regional level, Basari is at a distinct disadvantage to Malinke, which has official status in the south-eastern portion of the country. As an official language of this region, Malinke is used in the primary schools, is actively promoted for literacy, and is used in the media (CONFEMEN 1986). At the National level, Basari speakers are under pressure to achieve competence in Wolof and French. Wolof generally serves as a lingua franca in most urban areas of Senegal and is spoken by a majority of Senegalese. As a result, it is widely regarded as the true national language of the country. French, for its part, enjoys high prestige, and fluency in the language is still necessary for participation in higher education and many aspects of government.

The import of Extra-National variables for Basari is less obvious. It is certainly relevant that the language transcends national borders. Under the reign of Sékou Touré in Guinea, indigenous languages were promoted. The country was sectioned into minute administrative units, and at least in principle, the administrative unit dominated by Basari speakers might have established a strong foothold for the language which in turn would bolster the Basari community in Senegal. After Touré's death in 1984, however, the military regime which seized power promptly identified Touré's promotion of indigenous languages as a major cause of the educational and economic woes of the country (Treffgarne 1986). The current attitude towards indigenous languages in Guinea must be identified as one Extra-National variable which negatively influences the Basari of Senegal.

Two other Extra-National variables should be noted as having a potentially negative effect on Basari. First, at least six other languages[13] are spoken by communities in the immediate vicinity. Second, the Basari were traditionally hunter-gatherers, a form of social organization which is viewed negatively across all of sub-Saharan Africa.

Basari speakers, then, are under pressure at each level to shift to the use of another language: Local, Regional, National, and Extra-National. However, the pressure exerted varies in intensity and in the language towards which the Basari are being moved. This has consequences distinct from the US situation where the various levels are roughly aligned in their force on Native languages. Barring any changes in the current situation, Basari will become moribund, but there will not be a single language which replaces it. Rather some members of the community will take Fulbe as a first language, others Wolof, and still others different languages. Also, it is likely that in the short term, the most pervasive influence will come from Fulbe, but in the long run Regional or National influences will prevail, and the majority of individuals coming out of a Basari-speaking heritage will adopt Malinke or Wolof.

2.4   *Summary*

In section 2, we have discussed three ways in which Edwards' model must be developed in order to better fit the needs of typologizing endangered language situations: it must incorporate issues of literacy more

13 These languages are: Fulacunda, Badyara, Malinke, Budik, Konyagi, and Yalunka.

explicitly; it must allow for ranking of some variables over others; and it must distinguish between various levels of macro-variables. Our proposals here are rather broad, and as such remain largely programmatic. In the next section, we provide three case studies on certain language-endangerment situations which serve to justify the proposals of this section more fully.

3   Sample cases

In this section we present three sample cases so as to illustrate the complex ways in which the macro- and micro-variables impact individual communities. Rather than provide a comprehensive discussion of each endangerment situation, we attempt to show how the typology presented here can be usefully applied. Accordingly, the scope and focus of our discussion varies with each area addressed.

3.1   *Case no. 1: endangered languages in sub-Saharan Africa*

The general pattern of language endangerment in sub-Saharan Africa is rather distinct from much of the rest of the world. Unlike Australia, northern Asia, and the Americas, the most immediate threat to indigenous languages in Africa is not the language of European conquerors but other indigenous languages (Brenzinger, Heine, and Sommer 1991). In fact, to our knowledge the only reported instance of a speech community[14] giving up the language of its heritage in favor of a European language of former colonial overlords is supplied by the Khoisan languages of South Africa: the Kheokoe began shifting to Dutch as early as 1700, with a variety of Afrikaans eventually developing from Khoi-Dutch (Traill 1995:5–7). This example is striking in its singularity and stands in sharp contrast to the tenacity of most African indigenous languages, which is in turn particularly surprising in the case of the former French and Portuguese colonies. Unlike the British, who encouraged social diversity and the use of indigenous

14 Djité (1985) notes that certain elite families in the Ivory Coast have relinquished the language of their ethnic group in favor of French, and this may be true in other countries of Africa as well. However, there have been no reported instances of an entire speech community shifting allegiance to an Indo-European language. The situation in northern Africa appears to be much different. Though information on the use of indigenous languages is hard to come by, many may be seriously threatened by the spread of Arabic, which is promoted strongly on the national level and is tightly linked to Islam.

languages in education, the French and Portuguese actively suppressed African languages.[15]

At a superficial level, all the variables are in place which should lead to the widespread replacement of indigenous languages with European languages. The European languages are firmly entrenched as prestige speech varieties. They are used by the ruling elite and in higher education and politics. In many regions, there has been a long history of the suppression of African languages. In most regions, few resources are employed for the maintenance of indigenous cultures or languages. How can it be, then, that the European languages do not represent an imminent threat to the survival of minority languages in Africa?

This question has been framed over a vast geographical area and is cast at a general level, which suggests that the answer lies at the macrovariable level. We will suggest five Extra-National variables, often interrelated, which are relevant to describing the unique nature of endangerment patterns in Africa. None of the variables is independently sufficient to account for the uniqueness of the African situation, but their combined effect has been to generate a pattern of endangerment which differs significantly from other areas of European colonization.

First, the colonial legacy of Africa is distinct from the Americas, Australia, and northern Asia in one crucial way. Although there was a great influx of Europeans into most parts of Africa in the late nineteenth and early twentieth century, they represented a very small proportion of the overall population. They were and are simply unable to dominate numerically, and for this reason colonial languages do not constitute significant aspects of Local or Regional contexts in many parts of Africa.

Second, the language density in Africa is quite high. By most estimates, Africa contains over one third of extant human languages. These languages are of course not evenly distributed over the face of the continent, so there are certain areas in which the language density is remarkably high. As noted earlier, Nigeria alone has over 400 languages with most of these languages clustering in the eastern half of the country. Regardless of

15 Laitin 1992 has a useful summary of the differences between British and French/Portuguese language policy. See Turcotte 1983 for a more detailed look at French policy and Bender 1978 for comments on Portuguese policy. Collier 1982 explores the different approaches to governance by the British and French in their African colonies, and the eventual effect this had on political development after independence.

offical-language or educational policies, there generally exists constant contact with other indigenous languages. This all but guarantees that the Local contexts for threatened languages will be influencing them in different ways than the National contexts.

Third, perhaps as a consequence of the language density, multilingualism is the norm in Africa and has been for a long time. The expectation of multilingualism forms a notable part of the "African language ideology." The two or more languages in one's repertoire are generally assigned to different social contexts. Therefore, the acquisition of a regionally or nationally promoted language does not pose an imminent threat to a native tongue. However, another indigenous language, which is more likely to fill the same ecolinguistic niche, does.

Fourth, though subtle and somewhat unpredictable, there is a pan-African spirit, perhaps also part of the sub-Saharan African language ideology, which often unites Africans in different nations in a common cause. In the realm of language, this plays out practically in a conscious willingness to shift one's speech toward another African language while resisting use of colonial languages or Arabic (see for instance Kapanga 1990). On a related note, indigenous languages of Africa are not necessarily strong symbols of ethnic identity (Dimmendaal 1983, 1989). Hence, there is often less resistence to the adoption of another African language over a traditional tongue than doing so in favor of a colonial tongue. Note also that the structural similarities between most sub-Saharan languages facilitates shifts between them.

Finally, the disastrous economic situation which has dominated sub-Saharan Africa over the past thirty years has left most national governments unable to instantiate educational systems which uniformly promote a single national language to the exclusion of all others such as exists in North America and northern Asia. One potential exception is Tanzania, which has managed to promote Swahili with some effectiveness, but this case is also the exception which proves the rule. The spread of Swahili as the lingua franca of the country and the primary language of many groups had begun well before independence, bolstered by the numerous trade routes crossing the region. During the colonial period, Swahili was widely used for administrative purposes. Once independence was achieved, the government then successfully used Swahili, which has enjoyed prestige in Tanzania for some time, as a symbol of national unity, a symbol which was effective because it represented something native to the area rather than something brought there by the German and British colonists. Thus, despite lacking substantial economic resources to cultivate Swahili throughout the country, the government was able to make large steps in that direction. A favorable compilation of just the right set of factors is not present in most African nations, however. Therefore, the scarcity of resources presents a much more formidable obstacle to promoting a single national language.

In this section, we have suggested five macro-variables which partly account for the unique pattern of endangerment in sub-Saharan Africa. This underscores the utility of having a distinct level of macro-variables in a typology of language endangerment. This level allows the analyst to create a broad context in which to then examine individual communities. When exceptions to the overall trends do arise (like Kheokoe mentioned at the outset of this section), the typological scheme suggests that remarkable micro-variables are at work.

3.2   *Case no. 2: the former Soviet Union*

Of all regions in the world, the former Soviet Union (FSU) offers perhaps the most comprehensive illustration of the complex interplay of conflicting factors in language maintenance and attrition. With its strong centralized government, it enacted some of the most extensive and conscious language policies known. As a truly multilingual, multi-ethnic state, the FSU shows the impact of sweeping macro-variables against the local-level conditions influenced by micro-variables. While its multilingualism might at first suggest that it be likened to Africa, in fact the situation stands in sharp contrast: a large number of genetically and typologically diverse languages are being replaced by Russian.

The territory of the FSU included over 200 different languages. While some of these have large numbers of speakers (e.g. Russian, Ukrainian, Uzbekh, and Kazakh) a large number are minority languages. "The red book of indigenous languages of Russia" (Neroznak 1994) lists a total of 63 endangered languages. The threat to these languages presents a potentially very serious blow to our knowledge of linguistic diversity, as the number includes a number of language isolates (Yukaghir, Nivkh, Ket, and Yug) as well as entire language families, such as the Chukotko-Kamchatkan languages of Siberia, all of the Samoyedic languages, several dozen of the Nakh-Daghestanian (Caucasian) languages, and large numbers of the Manchu-Tungusic and Balto-Finnic languages. This constitutes a large group of both genetically and, crucially, typologically diverse languages. Many of these languages are sufficiently understudied that their classification remains controversial. The situation is muddled by problems in the identification of language versus dialect, and by the fact that the census tradition both in the FSU and Russia today refers to ethnic groups as opposed to languages. The result is that there may be no information about those languages which do not correspond to any ethnic group (see Comrie 1981:5).

The current situation is the result of a number of macro-variables and micro-variables. At the macro-level are the language-planning policies enacted by the strong centralized Soviet government and a combination of economic and political pressures to conform to the Russian-language norms of the ruling population. Statistics for this period and subsequent years alike are extremely unreliable, making it difficult to assess the situation fully. Nonetheless, there is general agreement that there was widespread illiteracy in the newly formed Soviet Union (with sharp distinctions between the rural and urban populations): in 1897 a figure of only 28.4% literacy was reported for the population of the then Russian Empire (Comrie 1981:28), while an illiteracy rate of 95.5% was reported for Azerbaijan at the time of the Bolshevik Revolution (Isaev 1982:69). This dropped markedly due to the Bolshevik literacy campaigns and more recent figures estimated an illiteracy rate of only 2% for the USSR as a whole (Lewis 1972:57).

Following the general goals of the new communist regime, an extensive literacy campaign was undertaken in the 1920s. This campaign had several key elements, including the codification of a literary language for each of the "major" languages of the country, and a regularization of the orthography for those languages which already had a script. Both of these processes had an impact on the future of the individual languages. All new orthographies were initially established in a Latin script, which was seen to be the alphabet of the revolution and of the global communist community (Isaev 1982:78). In addition, a number of communities which had already established writing systems were forced to switch to a Latin-based script. The notorious cases of this include the Turkic languages of central Asia, which prior to the Bolshevik Revolution used an Arabic-based script. The official justification for the change is a letter from Engels to Marx, in which Engels complains of the difficulty the proletariat faces in mastering the

Arabic script. We will note however, that this move effectively limited communication between the Muslims of central Asia and those of the rest of the world.

More detrimental to the smaller populations of speakers was the standardization process that accompanies the establishment of a literary language. Comrie (1981:24) points to such cases as the Ossete language, where the dialect chosen for the new written language was not the dialect of the majority of speakers, and cases where the mutual intelligibility of dialects is low. Such is the case with the Dolgan dialect of Yakut, as written Yakut can be understood only with difficulty by a Dolgan speaker.

The 1930s saw a shift in Soviet language-planning policies, and a change away from Latin-based scripts to Russian-based Cyrillic. Putting questions of Marxist ideology aside, this shift facilitated acquisition of Russian by non-native speakers, who now no longer needed to master two alphabets to acquire literacy. Consider the case of the Tungusic languages of Siberia, which had no literary form at the time of the revolution. Written languages for several of these (Evenki, Even, Nanai, and Udege) were created at the end of 1920s using a Latin alphabet as part of the Bolsheviks' literacy campaign. The first Evenki textbook was published in 1935, and at the end of 1936 the Latin alphabet was reformed to Russian Cyrillic. Textbooks, social-political works/propaganda and literature (both translated from Russian and original, including oral, literature) were published. That this bilingualism facilitated acquisition of Russian was explicitly recognized by Soviet language planners and was used as justification for bilingual education: "the necessity of parallel education in two languages was dictated by the fact that education in the native tongue was justly seen as an important stage which prepares children for the switch to Russian" (Onenko 1966:28).

In its early years, the Soviet Union had a language policy which at least in theory made attempts to recognize the non-majority languages spoken on its territory. However, beginning in the 1950s Soviet language planners actively and systematically promoted the acquisition of Russian by the non-Slavic peoples of the FSU as part of a campaign to establish "national–Russian bilingualism" (Haarmann 1985:323). This notion of national–Russian bilingualism is a National level macro-variable, extending to virtually all ethnic groups of the FSU; only isolated groups do not have any knowledge of Russian (Haarmann 1985:326–327). Predictably, pressures to acquire Russian as a second language are greatest for urban populations, and more restricted for rural populations and those on peripheral territories bordering other nations. Nonetheless, Russian bilingualism is found here as well. Furthermore, in Siberia as elsewhere in FSU, Russian bilingualism was also promoted as the means of communication at the workplace (Haarmann 1985:336).

Although state policy granted official status to a range of languages, Russian became the sole language of government and largely of education. All official business was conducted in Russian. Bilingualism rates are particularly telling: of the 137.2 million *Russians* of the 1979 census, only 0.2 million report knowledge of a second language. (Significantly, a large percentage of these know a second major Indo-European language, most frequently English, but also French or German, but do not know another "Soviet" language.) This is all the more striking if compared to the statistics of bilingualism *nationwide*: 42 percent of the total population of over 153 million was reported as bi- or multilingual (Haarmann 1985:323). In other words, a relatively small percentage of the Russian population is bilingual, while a much higher percentage of the non-Russian population is bi- or multilingual.

An additional stress on native-language use, at the macro-variable level, appears in certain areas of relatively high language density such as with the Evenki-Yakut in Yakut ASSR. The resulting multilingualism has led to the rapid loss of Evenki, the largest of the Tungusic languages, with a population of nearly 30,000 according to the 1989 statistics (Bulatova 1994:69). While no clear statistics are available, the overwhelming majority of the population is at least bilingual, and often multilingual, speaking Russian, Yakut, and Evenki. Of these three languages, it seems that it is Evenki which is the first to leave a speaker's repertoire. Indeed, statistics show a steady decrease in the numbers of speakers who claim to know their indigenous language as a first language, such that by 1989 only 29.5 percent of Evenki considered Evenki to be their first or primary language (Bulatova 1994:69), while a mere 4 percent of Udege speakers, a closely related Tungusic language, have native command of their language (Girfanova 1994:57).

In order to account for the motivation to learn Russian, often at the expense of the native language, we must turn to *micro-variables*. Mixal'chenko (1994:181) points to the low prestige of the native language in face of the high prestige of Russian during the communist regime. This prestige factor is accentuated by such forces as the fact that Russian is the lingua franca and serves for interethnic communication and that one can receive higher education in Russian but not in the local indigenous language. Speaker gender appears to be a relevant variable as well: there is a direct correlation between the rate of Russian as a second language and lower native-language retention among the males of many ethnic groups (Haarmann 1985:332–333).

The loss of indigenous languages is clearly the direct result of policies implemented by Soviet language planners which created macro-level factors favoring acquisition of Russian at the expense of the native tongue. Nonetheless, the actual viability of each individual language can also be seen as a consequence of Local-level variables and to be the result of micro-variables.

3.3   *Case no. 3: Maori*

New Zealand illustrates another facet of the complex interaction between macro- and micro-level variables, but as an island with only two contact languages in play, it presents a situation markedly different from that of Africa or the former Soviet Union. Initially it bears the rubber stamp of a prototypical case of language attrition: the indigenous Maori (a Polynesian language) has been gradually replaced by the language of the island's colonizers, English. This replacement stems from a combination of macro-level factors, including governmental and educational policies, and the attitude of majority speakers to the indigenous population (Karetu 1994). At the same time, despite these relatively powerful macro-level variables, it is home to one of the most vigorous and seemingly successful revitalization programs today. This success can be accounted for in terms of the relative strength of two other variables: on the macro-level, the issue of language density and a shift of governmental educational policy; and on the micro-level, the strong commitment among the community to its language and culture. As with case study no. 2, the situation of Maori is also instructive for the potential impact of literacy on the maintenance of a native language.

We can first examine the case of Maori from a historical perspective, as it provides an illustration of the long-term impact of literacy. Literacy was introduced to the Maori by missionaries, who established an alphabet and then published the New Testament in its entirety in 1837. Crosby

(1986:246) reports that by 1845 there was at least one copy of the New Testament for every two Maori in New Zealand. Literacy spread rapidly, and by 1856 an estimated 90 percent of the population was literate (Hohepa 1984:1, cited in Mühlhäusler 1990:193).

Despite the widespread literacy at this early point, it conflicted with the language-planning goals of those in power. Consequently, there was a remarkably rapid shift from a predominantly Maori-speaking population to a predominantly English-speaking one: in 1913, 90% of Maori children entering school reported knowing the language, while this figure dropped to 26% in the years 1953 to 1958 (Metge 1976:96). This shift was at least in part due to educational policies which increasingly stressed an English-based curriculum. As early as 1847, a governmental decree stipulated that all schools must offer instruction in both Maori and English in order to receive subsidies (Biggs 1968:73). As early as 1853, English was the preferred language of education. By 1867, an all-English education program was institutionalized by the government.

Mühlhäusler (1990) argues that the shift from Maori to English was facilitated by the large degree of native literacy already present in the Maori communities, concluding that vernacular literacy is often a "transitional" literacy, citing analogous evidence from Hawaiian and from the Melanesian and Papuan languages of Papua New Guinea as well.[16] Accordingly, in his view literacy has had only a negative impact on the preservation of native language and culture.

By the 1970s the number of children learning Maori was so drastically reduced that prospects for its future were dim. A revitalization program was begun, initiated in part by a Maori youth movement in 1971 which solicited some 30,000 signatures on a petition to the government requesting courses in Maori language and culture in all schools with large Maori enrollments (Metge 1976:99). This revitalization program has led to a reintroduction of Maori into the schools and daycares, a general high-profile

16 Note that we might a priori anticipate these linguistic situations to differ, in as much as they differ in terms of a number of key micro- and macro-variables (Mühlhäusler 1990:195–196). Specifically, on a micro-level the languages of Papua New Guinea are represented by fewer speakers than the Polynesian Maori and Hawaiian, and are more localized geographically. On a macro-level, in the case of Papua New Guinea the "encroaching" languages are two highly developed pidgins. Furthermore, literacy in most cases came earlier to the Polynesian populations and later to the indigenous Melanesian and Papuan.

program aimed at increasing language prestige, and ultimately an increase in the number of children speaking Maori (Dixon 1991:249; but see also Fishman 1991 for a different interpretation). Te Kohanga Reo, which began as a movement per se in 1982, is a total immersion program in Maori language and culture.[17] At last count (Karetu 1994:218) there were over 13,000 children enrolled in 710 immersion programs throughout New Zealand. Dixon attributes at least some of the success of this revitalization program to the fact that Maori is the only indigenous language in New Zealand, i.e. it is not competing with other languages. This underscores the relevance of the language density, a Local macro-level variable, on micro-level variables.

Despite these many efforts there were reported to be some 10,000 fewer speakers of Maori in 1989 than at the end of the previous decade (Nicholson and Garland 1991:393). While this is in large part due to the age structure of the population, with about 80 percent of the populus over the age of 25 in 1976 (Benton 1991:17), several key macro-variables have had a significant impact on the loss of Maori, including the all-English media, large-scale migration to cities which resulted in the destruction of Maori communities, governmental policy, and economic necessity. Thus the long-term viability of Maori is far from guaranteed, and it remains largely a second language for many speakers.

An additional micro-level factor which is crucial and yet difficult to measure is motivation of the population to maintain or to revive a language. Initial attempts by the government to replace Maori with English were slow in gaining momentum, surprising officials by the people's reluctance to give up their own language (Biggs 1968:74). Note furthermore that the movement to reintroduce Maori into the schools was initiated and moved forward by large parts of the population itself. Keys to the thinking underlying this movement can be found in an introductory language textbook, whose author argues that learning Maori helps one to "enter into the thought patterns and cultural experiences of the Maori people . . . To me the Maori world has many values which the Pakeha world has lost; tolerant relationships, mutual support, ways of working together, and strong

---

17 See also excerpts from the submissions of the Waitangi Tribunal in response to objections to Maori as an official language of New Zealand (Skutnabb-Kangas and Phillipson 1994:403–405). Karetu (1994) discusses the manifesto itself.

family ties, to mention but a few. These are all part of the Maori world and language is a feature of that world" (Ryan 1978: n.p. [intro.]). It is this sense of commitment of the Maori themselves to their language and culture that has helped the revitalization program gain momentum. It may well be the only factor which can give real power to any revitalization program. Even with such community-level commitment, revitalization is not completely independent from the attitudes of the majority culture.

3.4   *Summary*

In comparing these three separate cases, certain factors contrast. Africa has a high language density, whereas New Zealand very low language density. Siberia presents a middle ground, where multilingualism is common but contrasts with much of Russia proper. In all territories of the FSU, ethnic Russians are strikingly not multilingual. Thus while in Africa one can speak of pan-African identity, in New Zealand and in the FSU there is a sharp division between the Maori and *Pakeha*, or the non-Russian and the Russian.

4   Conclusion

In this chapter we have promoted a schema for typing endangered languages based on Edwards (1992). The crucial characteristics of our schema are: (1) it identifies a multiplicity of variables that are crucial to predicting likely patterns of language loss or maintenance; (2) it distinguishes between micro-level (community-internal) variables and macro-level (community-external) variables; (3) it further organizes macro-variables at a number of levels: Local, Regional, National, and Extra-National; and (4) it ranks the influence of certain variables more highly than others. Due to the breadth of the discussion, most of these proposals are left in a largely impressionistic form. Before such a typological scheme can be applied consistently, many details must be filled in, e.g. precisely which variables should be ranked most highly and how their degree of influence is to be formally marked in the model.

Irrespective of the structure of the model presented here, three crucial issues emerge. The first is *economics*, which may be the single strongest force influencing the fate of endangered languages. (See also Hale, this volume, which argues that "economic" factors should be broadly interpreted to include the pressure to assimilate to the economically dominant culture.) Not only is economic advancement a key motivation to relinquish a minority language in favor of the majority, but economics drives such things as the availability of published materials, schools, teachers, and, significantly, radio and television broadcasting. The realities of the modern day global economy place unprecedented financial pressures on minority languages. Producers of television, movie and video entertainment will continue to prefer to mass-produce materials in a given few languages. The technological boom of computing programs and the internet also involves the allocation of financial resources. While developing computer programs in indigenous languages may seem to be financially reasonable, the economic pressure will always be to limit the number of (human) languages used in computing. Last, it is worthwhile to mention that economics is a key factor in literacy issues, for literacy is dependent upon the writing and production of textbook materials, references, and teacher training, all of which are costly. In sum, economic factors are a driving force behind much of language attrition and may override other factors which support maintenance of the indigenous language.

The second issue, related in part to economics, is *access*. Access should be understood in broad terms to include a community's access to the indigenous language and culture, as well as its access to the majority language. Understood in these broad terms, access encompasses such variables as language density, isolation of the population, age and numbers of native speakers of the language and, in particular, access to media. Media is relevant in terms of the language of broadcasts, i.e. indigenous versus majority language. As the results of the CELIAC project show, media can be used to create access for minority groups and can facilitate communication in the indigenous language. At the same time a lack of access to the indigenous language, and a media devoted to the majority language, will act negatively toward indigenous language retention. Economics enters as a central factor in determining the kinds of linguistic access a community may claim.

Third is the factor of *motivation*. Motivation can sway an entire community toward or away from its native language in favor of the majority language. Citing Fishman (1991), Dauenhauer and Dauenhauer (this volume) point to the necessity of "ideological clarification" in designing revitalization programs, arguing that personal and community attitudes are at least as important as the technical aspects of any such program. In fact, community motivation to maintain a language and, accordingly, a culture, is a crucial factor in preventing language obsolescence. A full-fledged commitment of financial resources and manpower can help offset the trends toward monolingualism and mass culture which are so prevalent now at the end of this century. The cases of such languages as Hebrew (Saulson 1979; Nahir 1983), Irish (Maguire 1991) or Mohawk (as amply discussed in this volume in the chapters by Jacobs, Jocks, and Mithun) provide evidence that a strong commitment to revitalization will have an impact on the viability of a language.

Part II Language-community responses

3 Technical, emotional, and ideological issues in reversing language shift: examples from Southeast Alaska

NORA MARKS DAUENHAUER AND RICHARD DAUENHAUER
Sealaska Heritage Foundation, Juneau

1 Introduction

Native American people across the nation have expressed concern over the loss of indigenous languages, and they have expressed a desire to do something to prevent it. The loss of small, tribal languages is a world-wide phenomenon and an international concern. In Alaska, only two of the twenty Native languages are now being learned by children in the traditional way of parents speaking to children (Krauss 1995b:2–3). If this trend continues, the other eighteen languages will eventually die. Unfortunately, it is not easy to understand and appreciate the process by which languages are lost, the actions we must take to prevent such loss, or the actions we must take to preserve and/or restore endangered languages.

This has been a difficult chapter to write because most of the examples are of failures: things that have gone wrong or that have not worked. We have been personally involved in the dynamics described in this chapter in language research, teacher training, and materials development. As part of that picture, we have contributed to the failures as well as the successes in the general language-restoration effort of the last quarter century. But this chapter is composed in the spirit of optimism. Its goal is to involve all of us in values clarification and to unite us in making informed choices and in taking timely and appropriate action. Hopefully, we all can learn through our mistakes and realign our courses while there is still time.[1]

---

[1] Nora Marks Dauenhauer is a Native speaker of Tlingit. In adult life (in the late 1960s) she became interested in working with Tlingit language and oral literature, and undertook academic pursuits in that regard. Richard Dauenhauer is of German-Irish ancestry, with academic training in European languages and literature. He began work with Tlingit peripherally in 1965, and permanently in 1970. Our professional collaboration dates from 1971. The present chapter is the most recent of several essays we have written over the last few years on the topic of language survival: Dauenhauer and Dauenhauer 1992, 1995; and R. Dauenhauer 1994.

1.1   Background: the Southeast Alaska situation

The Tlingit Indians live in Southeast Alaska from Yakutat to Dixon Entrance, primarily on the coast, but with inland communities along the Chilkat and Stikine rivers in Alaska, and in southwest Yukon and northwest British Columbia. A variety of evidence as well as Tlingit tradition suggests that the Tlingits migrated to the coast at a very early date and spread along the coast from the southern range of their territory to the north, where they were expanding toward the Copper River at the time of European contact. This part of Alaska is an archipelago roughly the same size and shape as Florida, with few communities connected by road, so that contact is primarily by ferry or air.

Native people live in scattered, predominantly Native villages of several hundred people, and also in larger cities such as Juneau, Ketchikan, and Sitka. In the last one hundred years there has been significant intermarriage with other Native people and with non-Natives. The Haida homeland is on the Queen Charlotte Islands of British Columbia, but around the time of European contact some northern Haidas had also settled in southernmost Alaska. The Tsimshian homeland is on the BC mainland, and in 1887 a group migrated to southern Alaska and formed the new community of Metlakatla. The coastal Tlingit, Haida, and Tsimshian live in and on the edge of a rain forest – the most extensive temperate rain forest in the world, extending from Puget Sound to Kodiak Island – and this environment has shaped their lifestyle and material culture. Native American culture of the Northwest Coast has captured the imagination of explorers since first contact. These are the people of totem poles, elaborately carved wooden hats, bowls, and bentwood boxes; plank houses, ocean-going canoes, Chilkat robes woven of goat wool and cedar bark, felt button-blankets, and other well known cultural features, especially the ceremony known in English as "potlatch."

Tlingit, Haida, and Tsimshian comprise a northern subgroup of Northwest Coast culture. Although they are culturally similar, they are linguistically distinct. Tsimshian is unrelated to Haida or Tlingit, and is

We further direct readers to the introduction to our most recent book, especially sections IV, V, and VI (Dauenhauer and Dauenhauer 1994: 30–121), which provides an overview to Tlingit sociopolitical history, and goes into considerable detail on missionaries and their conflicting visions of language, culture, and education. It also examines ethnic process and the Native reaction to Euro-American culture pressure.

generally grouped with the Penutian phylum. Tlingit is related to Eyak and the Athabaskan family, to which its grammar is remarkably parallel, although lexical cognates are more difficult to prove. The relationship between Haida and Tlingit is a topic of continuing debate among linguists, with Heinz-Jürgen Pinnow being the most ardent supporter of a genetic connection to Na-Dene, and Michael Krauss disagreeing.

1.2   Language loss in Alaska

Michael Krauss has published frequently on the linguistic situation in Alaska (1992, 1995a, 1995b), pointing out:

> Of the 20 Alaska Native languages alive today, only two – Siberian Yup'ik and Central Yup'ik – are still being learned in the traditional way, of parents speaking to children. One language, Eyak, has left only one speaker, and she is in her 70s. Two languages, Tsimshian and Haida, have no speakers in Alaska younger than 60. Eleven languages have no speakers younger than 40; they are Aleut, Alutiiq, Tlingit, and seven of the 11 Athabaskan languages: Ahtna, Tanaina, Ingalik, Holikachuk, Koyukon, Tanana, and Han. Three Athabaskan languages, Upper Kuskokwim, Upper Tanana, and Tanacross Athabaskan, may still be spoken by younger adults in their 20s or 30s. Younger adults or teenagers in a few isolated communities speak Aleut at Atka, Alutiiq at English Bay, Inupiaq on the Upper Kobuk, Tanaina at Lime Village, and Kutchin at Arctic Village and Venetie. With just two languages being passed on in the traditional way, 90 percent of the Native languages of Alaska are no longer spoken by children. Without radical change, these languages will be extinct or have no native speakers left some time during the first half of the century nearly upon us.   (KRAUSS 1995b:1–3)

Bauman (1980) identified five categories of language status, with matching strategies for retention. These are: flourishing, enduring, declining, obsolescent, and extinct, with strategies of prevention, expansion, fortification, restoration, and revival (p. 6). Tlingit, Haida, and Tsimshian fit the obsolescent category, as characterized by the following factors: (1) an age gradient of speakers that terminates in the adult population; (2) the language is not taught to children in the home; (3) the number of speakers declines very rapidly; (4) the entire (speaking) population is bilingual and English is preferred in essentially all situations; (5) the language is inflexible, it no longer adapts to new situations; (6) there is no literacy. He stresses the difficulty of restoration, pointing out that only the community as a whole can create the kind of setting prerequisite to fostering fluency in the language.

Bauman emphasizes the urgency with which linguistic information should be gathered and studied while speakers are still available. He underscores the need to record oral histories, folklore and other stories, to create word lists and dictionaries, and to analyze grammar (1980: 11–12).

The loss of Native American languages is directly connected to laws, policies, and practices of European Americans. (See Dorian, this volume, for a discussion of European language attitudes.) The era of military campaigns was followed by an era of educational campaigns in which policies and tactics of replacing Indian language and culture with English and Anglo-American values were strictly enforced. To the extent that it is still not widely known or appreciated by the general public, and to the extent that Native American intellectual content still struggles for a place in the academic canon and curriculum, this history unfortunately continues. For Southeast Alaska, we can appreciate why the English-only language policies were also adopted by the founders of the Alaska Native Brotherhood in 1912. At that time, assimilation and mastery of the English language and Anglo-American culture were the only weapons left to Native people for fighting back and for pursuing the legal struggles for citizenship, integrated schools, and compensation for traditional lands removed from Native ownership and use. The tragedy is that bilingualism has never been the viable educational option for the Anglo-Americans that it successfully was during the Russian–American period (Dauenhauer and Dauenhauer 1994; see also Grenoble and Whaley, this volume).

All of us now inherit the legacy of this unpleasant and even genocidal history, one component of which is that the Native languages of Southeast Alaska are on the verge of extinction. With the battles for civil rights and land claims long won, loss of traditional language and culture loom more central in the awareness of the younger generation, and many of them want "the language and culture" back.[2] And at this point we ask, in the words of the poet Robert Frost, "What to make of a diminished thing?"

2   Reversing language shift

Language shift, a term taken from Fishman (1991), refers to the fact that over the last two or more generations, language use in most Native

---

2 This pattern appears to be common around the world, with the youngest members of the ethnic group berating the elders for choosing not to transmit the language and so allowing it to die; see Dorian, this volume.

Table 3.1 Steps in reversing language shift: severity of intergenerational dislocation

---

I. RLS to attain diglossia (assuming prior ideological clarification)

1 Reconstructing Tlingit and adult acquisition of Tlingit as a second language.

2 Cultural interaction in Tlingit primarily involving the community-based older generation.

3 The intergenerational and demographically concentrated home–family–neighborhood: the basis of mother-tongue transmission.

4 Schools for literacy acquisition, for the old and for the young, and not in lieu of compulsory education.

II. RLS to transcend diglossia, subsequent to its attainment

5a Schools in lieu of compulsory education and substantially under Tlingit curricular and staffing control.

5b Public schools for Tlingit children, offering some instruction via Tlingit, but substantially under Anglo-American curricular and staffing control.

6 The local/regional (i.e. non-neighborhood) work sphere, both among Tlingit and among Anglo-Americans.

7 Local/regional mass media and governmental services.

8 Education, work sphere, mass media and governmental operations at higher and nationwide levels.

---

communities has shifted, and the shift is toward loss of the indigenous, tribal language in favor of national and world languages. Thus, Native American languages are being replaced by English; Native languages of Siberia by Russian; other indigenous languages by Spanish, Arabic, etc. The shift is toward loss of tribal languages. *Reversing language shift* (RLS) means to alter the current trend toward loss by taking decisive and appropriate action. If the current trend in Southeast Alaska continues and is not slowed down or reversed, Alaskan Haida and Alaskan Tsimshian will probably die out within the next fifteen to twenty years, and Tlingit will probably become extinct within the next forty or fifty years. Reversing language shift is not easy, and the obvious question is: how do we do this? Fishman identifies eight "stages of reversing language shift" depending on the "severity of intergenerational dislocation" (1991:395; see table 3.1).[3]

---

3 We have adapted Fishman's table by reversing its order, i.e. Fishman's step 8 is our step 1. The hierarchy is preserved, beginning with reconstruction and aiming toward maximum public and

2.1   *Intergenerational dislocation*

In Southeast Alaska, the "intergenerational dislocation" is extreme: no children are now learning the languages naturally at home from their parents. Moreover, only a few persons in the parent generation learned the language from their parents (the grandparent generation). Tlingit, Haida, and Tsimshian are no longer used as a home language by parents under the age of 40 and were only rarely used as a home language by the previous generation of parents. We do not know of any woman of normal childbearing age who speaks Tlingit, Haida, or Tsimshian. Most speakers of Tlingit are age 50 and above; of Haida and Tsimshian 70 and above. These languages fall solidly within Bauman's (1980:6,11) category of "obsolescent" (the category before "extinct") and requiring a strategy of "restoration" if the languages are to survive.

2.2   *Prior clarification*

Prior to reconstructing the languages, with adults learning them as a second language, we must consider "prior ideological clarification." We have realized that we, our colleagues, and our clients, have been assuming "prior ideological clarification" for the last twenty-five years, where, in fact, it now seems there really has been little or none at all. This has created a situation in most communities where a broad gap and disparity have developed between verbally expressed goals on the one hand (generally advocating language and cultural preservation) and unstated but deeply felt emotions and anxieties on the other (generally advocating or contributing to abandonment). Instructional programs continue to be designed according to the expressed desires of the community, but are implemented according to these unstated anxieties and emotions. The result has been failure, but the reasons for the failure remain difficult to explain. Most often, the perception is a need to re-examine the technical aspects of the program design, develop more materials, change the alphabet, or find a different teacher who speaks a "better" dialect or whose blood quantum is more politically correct.

institutional use. We regionalized his generic terms "Xmen" and "Ymen" as Tlingit and Anglo-American. For the sake of space and simplicity, we mention only Tlingit on the chart, but it should be understood here and elsewhere in the chapter as standing for and including Haida, Tsimshian, and other Native American languages in the same situation.

Rarely do the popularly perceived causes of failure include what Fishman calls "prior ideological clarification." But this is the essential beginning for any program dealing with language and cultural preservation. This calls for an open, honest assessment of the state of the language and how people really feel about using and preserving it, replacing wishful thinking and denial of reality with an honest evaluation leading to realistic recommendations. Personal and community attitude are as important as – if not more important than – the technical aspects that are less emotional.

For Southeast Alaska, "prior ideological clarification" means, in its simplest form, an answer to the question: "Do we *really* want to preserve the Tlingit, Haida, or Tsimshian language or culture?" While it is generally politically and emotionally correct to proclaim resoundingly, "Yes!," the underlying and lingering fears, anxieties, and insecurities over traditional language and culture suggest that the answer may really be, "No." What does a "Yes" answer mean? We often find that those who vote "Yes" to "save the language and culture" expect someone else to "save" it for others, with no personal effort, commitment, or involvement of the voter. But language and culture do not exist in the abstract, as alienable "products." They exist as active processes in the here and now (Dauenhauer and Dauenhauer 1995; Kan 1989). We find a widespread pattern of people expressing or voting for the concept and the "product" but declining to become involved personally in the process. In theory, at least, calling to awareness some of the attitudinal dimensions that have contributed to confusion and failure in the past may be a first step toward the prerequisite open, honest assessment and ideological clarification.

3   Emotional and psychological aspects of achieving ideological clarification

Certainly in Alaska, and probably throughout the United States and Canada, Native American individuals and communities are plagued and haunted with anxieties, insecurities, and hesitations about the value of their indigenous language and culture. These insecurities must be addressed and resolved as an initial step before any meaningful action can be taken on a personal, family, or community level. In identifying some of the emotional problems surrounding Native-language use, and in trying to understand where they came from in the past, and where they are coming from at present, a pattern emerges over the last one hundred years, of how some schools and some churches have been sending negative messages regarding the value of Tlingit. In reviewing the sources of fears and fallacies regarding Native language survival, we begin at the top, with God.

3.1   *Does God like Tlingit and Haida?*

Among the most enduring and powerful anxieties is the feeling that God does not like Native American language and culture. Most Christian churches no longer believe, practice, or teach this; some Christian churches never did, but a few still do – and in highly vocal and politically active ways. Most Christians would consider it absurd to suggest that God does not like Hebrew or Greek, but many are convinced (or at least afraid) that God does not like Haida or Tlingit. It would be equally absurd to suggest that God does not like English, but many of the arguments used against fostering Native American languages may be applied to English and European languages as well. This is, of course, not a rational issue; but, rationally, one can apply the same anti-Native arguments against the ancient English words now used to express key Christian concepts. "God" and "Lord" are both pagan, pre-Christian words which were given new meaning with the new religion. American English language and culture retain pagan names for days of the week, not to mention many popular customs associated with Christmas, Easter, and All Saints' Day. Yet none of this suggests that we denounce the contemporary English language as demonic. Still, some Christian churches remain very outspoken in their condemnation of Tlingit language and culture as "demonic" and in their opposition to public practice or performance, or to school instruction.

This appears to be a global phenomenon (Zepeda and Hill 1991:139–140), and some communities in Southeast Alaska remain bitterly divided over this issue. With difficult problems to resolve, each person must sort these things out for himself or herself. One of our favorite quotes is from a staunch Pentecostal Tlingit elder, who said, "God made us with our language and culture. How can it be bad?"

3.2   *Unpleasant memories and fears*

Another enduring legacy of suppression shared by most middle-aged Native Americans is the memory of being punished physically and psychologically for speaking their Native language in school. These negative associations can be painful. One Tlingit man commented, "Whenever I speak Tlingit, I can still taste the soap." Most elders have similar stories of humiliation and physical punishment. It is not easy to overcome this pain. Many potential language teachers have commented with bitterness, "They beat the language out of us in school, and now the schools want to teach it."

In many communities, there was a blanket condemnation of everything Native as evil. In one village, all totem poles were cut and burned, and a symbolic spike was driven in the boardwalk, vampire-like, to suppress the past forever. For people raised in this religious and social context, language instruction is equated with unearthing demonic evils of the past. We can appreciate the sincerity and intensity of the emotion, although we consider it a fallacy to equate the language intrinsically with particular historical events and social conditions. English-speaking countries have abandoned witch trials, slavery, and other cultural features without abandoning the English language.

In reality, many people are afraid of the traditional language. It is alien, unknown, and difficult to learn. It can be a constant reminder of a deficiency and a nagging threat to one's image of cultural competence. For others, the mere thought of the language stimulates a fear of unplugging evils of the past, real or imagined. While we consider such lines of reasoning to be fallacies, some people are clearly tormented by them as real or potential.

3.3   *Shame and embarrassment*

Closely related is the sense of shame and embarrassment felt by many Native people about their language and culture. "I'm just a dumb Native," many remark. The enduring message of the government and public schools has been that Native American students are of the wrong color, the wrong religion, the wrong language, and the wrong culture. In some Alaskan communities the European-American government officials punished even adults for speaking the Native language in public, and in other communities the Native people themselves passed regulations against use of their indigenous language.

There is often a stigma attached by school systems to Native speech. In general, American schools have viewed bilingualism and Native-language ability as a deficit or detriment. Many Native parents have come to agree, believing that learning Tlingit will hurt the students' development in English. (See Garzon 1992:63 for a Mayan parallel.) In general, bilingual programs tend to have assimilation into English as a goal; maintenance and restoration of Native languages is explicitly discouraged in most districts. School administrators continue to debate the value and wisdom of allowing Native languages in the curriculum, let alone encouraging or requiring them. Regardless of the outcome, such debate in itself sends the message that the Native languages are questionable at best and probably not worth being taught. In contrast to such debate over the value of Native languages, as school systems continue to exclude Tlingit, they extend French and Spanish to ever lower grades, and scramble to offer Russian and Japanese.

Until recently in Juneau, Tlingit children were routinely placed in special education and speech-therapy classes to correct their regional accent in English, a practice which is unprofessional and is deplored by speech therapists. In 1995 this was halted by the US Office for Civil Rights. It is significant that persons such as Bill Clinton, Ted Kennedy, and Henry Kissinger are not recommended for speech therapy on the basis of regional or national accent. All of this can create a feeling of fear about learning Tlingit. Shame, guilt, and fear are important emotions controlling the survival of Tlingit. Administrative prejudice too easily goes hand in hand with Native anxiety about the value of the intellectual heritage of Native American language, culture, history, and literature. It is difficult to fight these patterns of administrative exclusion from the curriculum; it becomes deadly and suicidal when members of the Native community themselves subscribe to it.

As painful and intense as these experiences may be at the personal and community levels, they are most often local examples of universally reported phenomena of dominated minority groups, including the adoption of negative majority-group attitudes toward minorities by members of the minority group themselves (Lambert 1967).[4]

4 One stunning example of the role of self-esteem in linguistic survival is the history of the Manchu language. Manchu, a language of northern China and Manchuria, related to Mongolian and Turkish, was from 1644 to 1911 an official language of the Chinese empire. It was once the language of diplomacy, and official notices were bilingual as late as 1911, even though the Manchu language was no longer widely spoken. The irony was that, although the Manchu people ruled China, they held Mandarin language and customs in higher esteem than their own. In the course of several generations, they gradually abandoned their ancestral language and replaced it with Mandarin. Now there are more than 4 million ethnic Manchus in China (or Chinese of Manchu ancestry), but the language itself is virtually extinct. One dialect is spoken in the Xibo ethnic enclave in western China (Krauss 1995a; Ramsey 1989:215–217).

3.4   *Conflicting messages*

These experiences and emotions are common to all Native American people. They usually do not surface in open verbal discussion about whether to have a program, but are manifested later through lack of support of the programs. Many Native beginning teachers have expressed to us their surprise, disappointment, and discouragement that Native parents do not support the school programs, but even keep their children out of them, either because of shame or embarrassment, or out of fear that learning Tlingit will cause their children pain, hinder their advancement in English, or make them subject to the same punishments that stigmatized and crippled two or three previous generations. This fear is widespread among Native American parents (Zepeda and Hill 1991:141), but program evaluations generally demonstrate increased self-esteem and improved academic performance by students in bilingual programs. Parents may also fear that learning Tlingit will lessen their children's future earning power. Certainly economic and commercial success can be achieved without the Native language; in fact, the economic and political success of the most acculturated groups and individuals show that Native-language skills and a traditional world-view are not only unnecessary for achieving such success, but may even be barriers to it.

In reality, the Native student is experiencing "mixed messages" about the value of learning Tlingit: on the one hand, it is being taught, and people are saying that it is good to learn it; but on the other hand, the student is aware of the overwhelming anxiety and negative associations surrounding the language, whether spoken or unspoken. Such conflict is difficult to overcome and certainly diminishes whatever enthusiasm or motivation the student may have. Given the deep-rooted anxieties and negative associations described above, it should come as no surprise to discover *a disparity between expressed ideals and actual support*. This disparity between general approval and lack of personal commitment and action, between attitude versus actual language use, is also discussed by Fishman for Irish (1991:124).

3.5   *Pride in singing and dancing versus language*

An exception to the generally negative associations with Native-language use is the dramatic increase in Indian pride as manifested in the many community dance groups that have blossomed in the last twenty years. Very few in number in the early 1970s, more groups formed in the 1980s, and there are now many in the 1990s. In June 1996, over 1,200 Tlingit, Haida, and Tsimshian dancers convened in Juneau for "Celebration '96." This is a positive step although it creates new and subtle cultural complications of performance context not necessary to discuss here (Dauenhauer and Dauenhauer 1990, 1994; Kan 1990).

In contrast, the language effort has never matched the popularity of singing and dancing. There are several possible reasons for this. Singing and dancing are easier, more fun, more tangible, and less threatening than language learning. For learners, traditional regalia and performance are very appealing and are obvious outward manifestations of "the culture" that transcend language skills other than learning the songs. The songs are more easily acquired as "alienable objects" than the language at large, they provide a more convenient "badge of ethnicity," and there are abundant performance opportunities. The songs and dances require virtually no additional training to teach: the local clan leaders recognized for their knowledge and competence as performers are ideally suited as role models and have generally been successful as instructors. There are serious problems with the younger generations learning to pronounce the words of the songs correctly, learning traditional musical style, and appreciating the social and spiritual contexts in which the songs should be performed, but there is no doubt that singing and dancing are popular because they provide what educators call a "success experience" for teachers and students.

Language learning has proven to be less successful during the same period of time, requiring extra teacher training and student motivation, which we will discuss below. But of greater initial importance is the problem of involvement or avoidance discussed above: the idea that preserving language and culture is a good idea, "but not for me." This leads to the heart of the problem: determining who is responsible for the learning and transmission of language and culture, and when to do it.

4   Avoidance strategies

Avoidance strategies usually look for others to solve the problem, using what we could call the "bureaucratic fix" and the "scientific" or "technical fix." Both of these look to a quick solution, in which other people are designated or expected to save the language and culture for yet someone else with no personal effort or involvement. This attitude reflects two serious problems: (1) the perception of culture as alienable, something that one puts on or takes off at will, like a shirt or blanket (Dauenhauer and Dauenhauer 1995);[5] and (2) the failure to see the connection between language use and transmission. This latter is most tragic when young parents who are fluent in a Native American language do not use it in the family with their children, but still assume that somehow the children will magically learn the language through another channel, or that the language will survive because others are still using it elsewhere. This pattern now seems common with languages such as Navajo and Yup'ik, which have the appearance of being strong, but may in fact be being abandoned (Krauss 1995b). For Tlingit, one often hears parents and grandparents say that they'll begin teaching the language "next year."

4.1   *"Bureaucratic fix"*

In the "bureaucratic fix" the pattern is to create some kind of organization to deal with language and cultural preservation. There is nothing wrong with this, providing that all realize that even in organizations, the real work is still done by individuals. Organizations can provide focus and umbrellas of various kinds, but they still require the efforts and co-operation of many individuals. For example, Sealaska Heritage Foundation, where we are employed, can contribute staff expertise in Tlingit literacy, applied folklore and linguistics, and book production; but we still require the talent, cooperation, and good will of the individual tradition bearers. We can provide professional consultation and technical training for communities, but people must want it first. We can document the stories, but

5 There is a danger that the worst aspects of the idea of culture as alienable and objectified may be played out in NAGPRA (Native American Graves Protection and Repatriation Act of 1990) in the form of political in-fighting over now decontextualized physical items whose original spiritual contexts, significance, and function have been lost or become obsolete. It is clear that most objects will function differently than in the past. As decontextualized items that fit well into the perception of culture as alienable, they will probably be recontextualized one way or another as political emblems, as rallying points for opposing groups or factions, or as playing pieces or hostages in the personal power struggles of individuals. The public testimony and behavior of some of those involved suggest that the basic concepts of Tlingit kinship and clan ownership are being confused, such as the difference between matrilineal, patrilineal, and bilateral descent; membership by birth in the mother's clan; ownership by the matrineal clan; and conditions of use of clan property by relatives of other clans.

we cannot create them out of nothing; we can produce grammars and instructional material, but they are nothing unless people actually speak the language to each other in the home and community. Other examples of such organizations are schools and local language-preservation and heritage foundations.

Such organizations are too easily perceived as a place to transfer personal responsibility and to target for blame when things go wrong. At their worst, they become arenas for political grandstanding where personal rivalries, insecurities, and frustrations are acted out in thinly veiled expressions of cultural concern. Problems can also arise when board members vote for a certain activity on an organizational level, but fail to support it through their actions as individuals on the personal and community level. The converse is also true, as when a person demands something in a public meeting but then vetoes it in a closed session. It is false to assume that by passing a resolution or assigning a task to a certain position on a flow chart, the desired activity or goal will become a reality without the active, continuing support of others. All of this has to do with the problem of making agendas for other people.

4.2   *Technical fix: tools versus training*

Another evasive strategy is the demand for "More tools!" This is a variation of the "scientific fix" that places the burden of action on "them" (rather then "me" or "us") to "do something to save the language." When word got out in the early 1980s that we had developed a Tlingit chip for our computer, this was enthusiastically greeted as a "quick fix" and "cure-all" for saving the language. People assumed it would provide automatic computer translation and spell-checking for Tlingit. In reality, it allowed us easier word processing through screen display, printing, and modem transfer in a character set other than standard English. People were very disappointed when we told them that if they could not already write Tlingit with an old-fashioned pencil, the new chip would not work wonders for them. The most recent technical fix is the interactive CD-ROM. These are useful tools, and they greatly change the dimensions and possibilities for documentation and instruction, but they are no substitute for human desire and effort.

There is, of course, a genuine need for materials development (discussed below). The issue is not to allow a perceived need to serve as an excuse for avoidance or procrastination. Certainly we can always use more materials (especially for Haida and Tsimshian), but for Tlingit we have enough materials in hand right now to teach the language for several years at several levels using several approaches, provided that a teacher knows how to use them (Dauenhauer and Dauenhauer 1984, 1987, 1990, 1991, 1994; Nyman and Leer 1993; Story and Naish 1973, 1976; plus numerous local publications of more limited distribution). This requires teacher training. At this point in the history of Native-language survival in Southeast Alaska, training in teaching methods is far more important than developing new teaching materials. What is needed, (but rarely perceived as a need) is training in various teaching methods; in how to use existing materials and adapt them to one's own teaching style, personality, community setting, and grade level. We will have more to say about teacher training below; here we emphasize the contrast between strategies of avoidance that place the responsibility on others in contrast to accepting personal responsibility and taking personal action.

5   Need for assessment

The bottom line in all of this is the need to undertake an open, honest, assessment of the language situation, including not only how many speakers there still are, but what are the attitudes of the speakers and non-speakers toward the language. This will not be easy. For Southeast Alaska, part of this will require an acceptance of the moribund state of Tlingit, Haida, and Tsimshian. At present, many people express denial or anger when the question arises. Facing the loss of language or culture involves the same stages of grief that one experiences in the process of death and dying. This is very important, but because we have dealt with it elsewhere (Dauenhauer and Dauenhauer 1995) we will not repeat it here.

5.1   *Assessing the language: speakers and levels of fluency*

It is not easy in most cases to count the actual speakers and determine their level of fluency. The actual picture is obscured by the reality of people who can speak the language but who choose not to, and by the often large category of people who understand the language but who cannot speak it. Then there are speakers who can handle everyday situations, but who are not literary or ceremonial stylists. Fluency is often a matter of impression or opinion; many non-speaking parents assume their children are fluent in the ancestral language after a few weeks of language instruction or immersion in a culture camp.

As we will discuss at length below, there is no critical mass of speakers for Tlingit, Haida, or Tsimshian. These languages are moribund. This is an extremely emotional issue, with linguists estimating the extinction of the languages (unless some reversal happens), and many Native people objecting violently to such predictions. But, unless current trends slow down or reverse, the lifespan of Tlingit and Haida can be extrapolated. If the youngest speaker of Tlingit is 45, and lives to be 100, the language will be gone is 55 years, or by the year 2050. If the speakers in their forties and fifties should not live to be 100, the language could die sooner, perhaps 2030. If the youngest person (in Alaska) who understands Haida is now 67, and the oldest speakers are in their eighties and late seventies, Alaskan Haida could become extinct as a spoken language within the next 15 or 20 years, and the ability to work with whatever tapes remain could be lost within the next 30 years.

As noted above, all three Native languages of Southeast Alaska are "obsolescent." The most generous estimates we now have for Tlingit, Haida, and Tsimshian are:

Tlingit   500–900 speakers total (95% in Alaska; 5% in Canada)
Haida   60–70 speakers in Alaska
Tsimshian 50–80 speakers in Alaska

More conservative estimates (Krauss 1995a) list Haida with less than 45 fluent speakers total, including Alaska and Canada, with only 15 in Alaska. The Haida ethnic population is approximately 40% in Alaska and 60% in Canada. Tsimshian is stronger in Canada, where 90% of the population and 96% of the speakers reside. Krauss (1995a) estimates Coast Tsimshian as less than 500 speakers total, with 70 in Alaska.

Sealaska Corporation has about 16,000 shareholders, of whom about half are now under the age of 40.[6] In addition, there are at least

---

6 The terms and concepts of Indian political organization in Alaska are historically different from those commonly used elsewhere. Under the Alaska Native Claims Settlement Act (ANCSA) of 1971, profit-making corporations were established for each of the regions of Alaska. Sealaska Corporation is the regional corporation for Southeast Alaska (the name is an acronym for SE Alaska). Tribal members are defined under ANCSA as shareholders; enrollment was based

another 8,000 Natives who are not shareholders because they were born after the December 18, 1971 cut-off date for enrollment. Needless to say, this group will continue to increase. At the most generous estimate only 20% of the shareholders speak Tlingit, Haida, or Tsimshian; 80% speak English only and not a Native language. As the ethnic population grows, the percentage of Tlingit, Haida, and Tsimshian speakers decreases, and the real number of speakers diminishes through the death of elders. In all probability, less than 10% of the ethnic Tlingit population speaks or understands Tlingit.

6   Rhetoric and reality: sacred cows and clichés

When the reality of the language situation becomes clearer, considerable disparity is often disclosed between the reality of the situation and the community rhetoric of Native-language survival. We now examine a few of the attitudes, generally repeated as clichés, and often venerated as rhetorical sacred cows. Most of these cluster around the concept of language and culture being inseparably linked. We hear that "cultural values can only be transmitted in the language"; that something "can only be done in the Native language"; that we "can't save the culture without the language." There is clearly truth to all of this, but the truth is more complicated than the cliché. The fact that 90 percent of ethnically Tlingit people do not speak Tlingit suggests that somehow "the culture" is surviving without "the language." Tlingit culture – at least in some form perceived and accepted by its members as ethnically distinct – is actually functioning without use of the ancestral or heritage language (other than in its most symbolic and decorative forms). Yet important aspects of the traditional culture and world-view are indeed being lost along with traditional fluency in the language and the concepts it expresses.

on blood-quantum and restricted to those alive on December 18, 1971. Corporations were left with the problem of how to treat those born after the cut-off date, sometimes called "New Natives" or "After-borns." As of this writing, Sealaska shareholders are about evenly divided over the question of whether to extend enrollment to the "After-borns" or not. This population of ethnic Tlingits, Haidas, and Tsimshians is steadily increasing, with a population of about 8,000, or equal to one half of the total enrollment of 16,000. Sealaska Heritage Foundation, where we are employed to pursue language and cultural studies research and publication, is a non-profit 501 (c) 3 corporation and an affiliate of Sealaska Corporation.

This suggests that cultures do not really die, but change. Certainly the Anglo-American culture of today is different from 100 and 200 years ago. Language is presumably somehow connected to this, and changes along with the culture. Grammar, vocabulary, and the rules of discourse are different (Carbaugh 1989; Scollon and Scollon 1994). The changes are obviously more dramatic over time, as from Old English to Modern. Native languages, too, have evolved over time, although it is a popular misconception among Native American people that their language has always existed in its present (and unchanged) form for thousands of years; it is an equally popular misconception among non-Natives that Native languages are somehow "primitive" and random inventions of recent origin.

While it can be argued that cultures change but do not necessarily die, languages do in fact die, and this is a different process from a language evolving into a different form. To the extent that a cultural component is linked to the ancestral language, it may pass together, or the cultural component may become obsolete, or begin to function in a new and different way. This is certainly the case with Tlingit concepts of kinship, the clan system, traditional protocol, and reciprocity. For example, Tlingit, Haida, and Tsimshian clan names are being replaced by the English words for their crest animal. This can lead to confusion and misunderstanding, because some crests are shared by two or more clans. *L'uknax̱.ádi* is called "Coho," *Lukaax̱.ádi* "Sockeye," *Teiḵweidí* "Brown Bear," etc. The Native clan names are usually translated as "people of" a certain place, and thus contain a sense of history. It will require great family and community effort to maintain knowledge of indigenous clan and personal names, which are becoming increasingly difficult for younger people to hear and pronounce. Many people no longer understand the basic concepts of the kinship system, and are beginning to confuse matrilineal and patrilineal descent. The potlatch tradition is currently undergoing changes in structure, practice, and significance; oratory is being delivered increasingly in English, although some of the youngest speakers and learners are cultivating the tradition of speech-making in Tlingit (Dauenhauer and Dauenhauer 1990). Stories may survive in English, but the untranslatable elements of style will be lost: the puns, the word plays, some of the concepts, and the language itself. (Concrete examples can be found in the chapters by Jocks [Mohawk], Mithun [Mohawk and Central Pomo], and Woodbury [Yup'ik]; all specifically address the issue of translatability.)

But it is clear that for 90 percent of the Tlingit population, "the culture" is operating in English, and the actual "operating culture" that people live and interact by may be quite different from what is popularly perceived as "the culture," with its variety of "badges" of ethnicity such as songs, dances, visual art, ethnic food, and clan regalia. It can also be argued that as English replaces Tlingit as the first language of the people, so the traditional world-view and many of its concepts are gradually replaced with Western patterns of thought. But because the emblems remain the same, the changes in context and function are often overlooked. This often increases the "rhetoric gap" in which perception and conceptualization of "the culture" differ widely from actual patterns of behavior. In reality, the context, function, and ultimate meaning of the symbols are being renegotiated by successive generations as an ongoing process.

Despite the popular rhetoric of linguistic and cultural preservation, it is an undeniable pattern that those individuals who have benefitted most from corporate employment related to the Alaska Native Claims Settlement Act (ANCSA) are those persons who were raised speaking only English and with European-American cultural and economic values. This is not to suggest that they are any less Tlingit or unrepresentative of the Tlingit population, only to observe that most do not speak Tlingit, but have succeeded quite well in contemporary Tlingit culture without the ancestral language. Like other Tlingits, they identify with certain selected elements of culture as "badges of ethnicity," and do not identify with other components of the culture (such as language). As persons in public view and political office, they are often subject to accusations of co-opting "the culture" for personal political gain. This pattern is also a universal characteristic of politicians and their electorates. At the community level, we know many Tlingit men who speak English only, who are not necessarily skilled in ceremonial protocol, but who participate fully in traditional subsistence activities and who operate within a very traditional Tlingit world-view. All of this demonstrates that language and "culture" are in fact to some extent separable, and that English and Tlingit language use are two of many cultural components that interact in very complex patterns. It also reminds us that culture is not absolute but is dynamic and constantly renegotiated (Dauenhauer and Dauenhauer 1995; Kan 1989).

A common expectation placed on Native American youth is that they should know the ancestral language as part of their person-hood. We heard an extreme example of one elder publically condemning as not being genuinely Tlingit all those young people who don't speak Tlingit. The irony is that the children, grandchildren, and great-grandchildren of this woman do not speak Tlingit. Without thinking, this woman is essentially disowning her own family for an aspect of their ethnic identity she is responsible in part for creating.

We should emphasize here our feeling that it is wrong, unrealistic, and mentally unhealthy to insist or expect that all Native American persons speak and appreciate the ancestral language (and be found wanting if they do not). This is not something generally expected or required of other ethnic groups. German-Americans, Scottish- or Irish-Americans, Norwegian-Americans and others are not expected to be fluent in the languages of their ancestors, although they typically identify with their ethnic heritage through other symbols and behavior. (We realize that this parallelism is imperfect in its comparison of original versus transplanted languages, but it is still helpful.) Just as no one should feel guilty for speaking Tlingit, no one should feel guilty for not speaking it. (But if a person does feel guilty for not speaking Tlingit, he or she should take action and do something about it!) We need to view difference of opinion and linguistic taste with tolerance, and work to accept language as one of the many "badges of ethnicity" available.

7   A possible theoretical framework

None of this is unique to Southeast Alaska, but is well documented in the literature on language extinction.[7] Margolin (1996) presents a multidimensional model for understanding and assessing Native American sociolinguistic identity. He suggest that "one of the frustrating aspects of the study of Native American sociolinguistics and ethnic identity has been the lack of a comprehensive means for relating information from the disparate Indian speech communities in North America" (p. 29). Margolin's thesis is that much of the existing literature is accurate and valuable, but

7 Many of the phenomena, dynamics, and problems described here are not unique to Southeast Alaska, but are also mentioned in other reports of language death and obsolescence, including Craig 1992c; Dorian 1993a, 1995; Garzon 1992; Jeanne 1992; Kinkade 1991; Kwachka 1992; Ladefoged 1992; Pye 1992; Robins and Uhlenbeck 1991; Taylor 1992; Wurm 1991; and additional articles referenced in the course of this chapter.

incomplete, and that "the task of developing an overarching theory of Native American sociolinguistic identity demands a fresh start, a recasting of a number of familiar concepts" (p. 1). Drawing especially on Friedman (1994), Kroskrity (1993), Hill (1983), and "classic" works by Goffman, Gumperz, Cook-Gumperz, and others, Margolin posits a continuum of five identity types ranging from traditional ethnicity to modern citizenry, each type characterized by clusters of attitudes and behavior. His examples, as well as theoretical components, are drawn from the spectrum of sociolinguistic literature. As he suggests in conclusion, "the test of a theory such as this lies in its detailed application to real cases" (p. 29).

The continuum and conceptual framework offered by Margolin apply well to the situation we have observed in Southeast Alaska. The five identity types are: (1) traditional ethnicity, (2) substantial ethnicity, (3) optional ethnicity, (4) civic ethnicity, and (5) post-ethnicity. Because ethnicity, by definition, implies a relationship to other groups in the total society, the purest example of type (1) would be a group with no or limited contact with others. Type (2) is characterized essentially by a genetic or biological ethnicity that contrasts with a dominant society. Types (3) and (4) are continuing degrees of replacement of traditional ethnicity with that of the modern ethnicity and citizenry, so that at type (4), ethnic group membership is voluntary, in sharp contrast to type (1), in which it is the only option available. Type (5) is conceptually located in a different plane from the others, and between (3) and (4), because this state can be accessed either through the process of loss of traditional culture or as the first step in an effort to move beyond (4) and return to ethnic roots (see Margolin 1996:30).

The patterns of attitude and behavior associated with the four identity types as shown in the relative symbolism and structural characteristics of the tribal language and English are most useful for our present discussion. Thus, at phase or type (1), the Native language is spoken by all in-group people, and there is a broad stylistic range or elaboration. English use is minimal and instrumental. Characteristic of type (2) is linguistic opposition: there is bilingualism (with emerging "Indian English"), but choice of language use reflects concepts of ethnic solidarity and power.

For type (3), English is the language used for almost all interactions ("effective"), while the tribal language begins to be associated with positive and personally significant emotions ("affective"). Stylistically, the tribal

language is increasingly "lexicalized" or "phaticized," and formulaic, becoming increasingly a positive marker of group membership used more in
public display and less in domestic settings or for serious communication.
In type (3), individual lifestyle is increasingly on the model of the individual
achievement ethic of modern American society, and is immersed in its
behaviors and symbols. An example of how this carries over to Tlingit is the
conscious creation and use of a Tlingit "National Anthem" to symbolize
an emerging identity level in modern, Western terms different from the
traditional clan and moiety membership.

Type (4) is characterized by total loss of tribal language and use
of regional standard English. Learning the Native language is typically
perceived as "academic" or "irrelevant" in contrast to "practical." As
mentioned above, ethnic membership in type (4) is voluntary; individuals
can choose to abandon, embrace, or ignore their biological ethnic heritage.
Many of the traditional symbols of Tlingit culture begin to reappear in new
contexts and relationships determined not by genealogy and clan membership through birth, but through voluntary community membership. In
terms of this continuum, Tlingit may be identified in general with types
(2) and (3), and Haida and Tsimshian by types (3) and (4). When a generational aspect is factored in, Margolin's types (4) and (5) also enter, with
most of the ethnic population not speaking the heritage language, but some
desiring to regain it.

The paradoxical situation is that the languages will certainly die
unless we do something; but, the reality is that they may also die even if
we do something. Therefore, what do we do? In any case, the alternatives
for action will be clearer after an assessment of the community language
situation.

8   Attaining and transcending diglossia

Having reached some kind of ideological clarification, community
members are now in a position to approach and engage in the steps outlined
by Fishman (1991). He distinguishes two groups: (1) *reversing language shift
to attain diglossia* (assuming prior ideological clarification); and (2) *reversing language shift to transcend diglossia*, subsequent to its attainment.

Diglossia can be understood in several ways. One definition would
be a register variation involving two different languages, one of which is

a socially lower vernacular, the other is a socially higher national language. More specifically, it may be described as two historically related language varieties that stand in the same relationship, such as Classical and vernacular Arabic, or Swiss German. We would suggest for our purposes here that diglossia might be understood in a combination of both definitions, as the kind of Tlingit, Haida, or Tsimshian that could be taught and learned artifically and restored, and used in some settings as an alternative to English, but which would lack the elaborated, full, and creative stylistic variety of the traditional language now commanded by only the oldest speakers, and increasingly represented only in transcribed texts.

The important distinction Fishman makes is between learning or acquiring a second language, and transmitting it, or passing it on to the next generation; between a generation of individuals each learning the language for himself or herself, and that generation collectively passing the language on to the next generation. We are optimistic that limited varieties of Tlingit, Haida, and Tsimshian can be learned indefinitely in artificial settings, but we have no hope that these languages will ever again be transmitted naturally as the language of the home with their former full, elaborated stylistic ranges.

8.1   *Natural and artificial language learning*

Clarification of the distinction between learning and transmitting leads to an awareness of the distinction between artificial and natural language learning. Tlingit, Haida, and Tsimshian can no longer be learned naturally, at home. Instead, these languages must now be learned artificially in some kind of structured setting, whether it is school or language immersion camp or private self-study. This is in sharp contrast to the situation a hundred years ago, when children still learned Tlingit at home and when the language was used to such an extent that outsiders (for example, Interior Athabaskan trading partners or white, Jewish merchants such as Charlie Goldstein) could learn it naturally through social and commercial interaction. The distinction is between the need for the first generation to relearn the traditional language artificially, and then create social and cultural situations in which the language can be transmitted naturally to the next generation. The hard question is whether this is still possible for Southeast Alaska, or how much of it is still possible.

8.2   *Fishman's steps to attain diglossia*

In reversing language shift, we suggest that it is relatively easy to undertake steps 1 and 4 from table 3.1 (step 1: reconstructing Tlingit and adult acquisition of Tlingit as a second language; step 4: creating schools for literacy acquisition for the young and old, not in lieu of compulsory education but in addition to regular school). Whether individuals, families, and communities have the desire, skills, and energy to achieve steps 2 and 3 is more difficult to determine. Step 2 involves cultural interaction in Tlingit primarily involving the community-based older generation. In practical terms, this means maximum interaction with the elders, and doing everything in Tlingit rather than English. Step 3 calls for the establishment of "the intergenerational and demographically concentrated home–family–neighborhood: the basis of mother-tongue transmission." This means that all homes, families, and neighborhoods involved resolve to use only Tlingit so that children hear it again as the first language of the home and neighborhood. In practical terms, this means that all those who can still speak Tlingit resolve to use it exclusively; those who do not know Tlingit will learn it and then use it. Couples will learn and use Tlingit together. Young people will marry other learners and raise the children with the language. Young couples will live next to others who wish to do the same, thus creating a neighborhood.

Steps 2 and 3 are very demanding. They will require a complete change of lifestyle followed by a lifetime commitment. One speaker at the 1994 NALI (Native American Language Issues Institute) conference described how a small group of Irish in Belfast resolved to restore Irish in this way, and have now reached the "critical mass" where children are being raised in Irish, and they have control over community-based, Irish-speaking pre-schools. (Hale, this volume, also mentions Irish in connection with the Shaw's Road Community.) Another speaker, a Maori from New Zealand described how they moved through the second group of steps. A major difference is that Maori is the only Native language of New Zealand, and the language still had a critical mass of speakers. The Maori could take social and political action in time to maintain and expand their language base (Grenoble and Whaley, this volume). This may be still possible for Hawaiian as well. Hawaii is often turned to as a model by Native people of Southeast Alaska, but there are significant differences: Hawaiian is the only Native language of that state, and it has a more romantic and "positive" image than any of the Alaska Native languages. Also, the languages of Southeast Alaska are intrinsically more difficult to learn than Maori or Hawaiian because of their more complex grammars and phonologies. For Southeast Alaska, steps 2 and 3 are probably unrealistic: the intergenerational dislocation is too severe. Haida and Tsimshian in Alaska are too far gone; they have been abandoned beyond the point of having the required critical mass. Tlingit may possibly still have the critical mass of speakers in some places, but even these communities would require enormous demographic reorganization and concentration that is probably beyond the ability or desire of most families and communities to achieve.

Thus, the hopes for natural language transmission in Southeast Alaska are grim. Languages can be learned by individuals, but they are transmitted by groups. There is every reason to be optimistic that Tlingit, Haida, and Tsimshian can be learned with varying degrees of success by present and future generations, but there is little hope that the fruits of any individual effort will be passed on. The languages can be learned in artificial settings designed to duplicate natural conditions, but the natural settings for learning Tlingit, Haida, or Tsimshian as a first language are probably gone forever. They could be reconstructed and restored, but only with a great personal and community effort that it is unrealistic to expect.

8.3   *Differing demands of natural and artificial language learning*

It is important to recognize the distinction between natural and artificial language learning because they have different requirements, and it is easy to confuse or overlook them. In a natural speech community, no parent ever needed teacher training to transmit the language of the home. Children learned the language automatically, by hearing it and using it. In many homes and communities around the world, children and adults learn two or three languages in this way, through natural use, or through artificial instruction combined with travel and living experiences in the natural settings. But artificial situations such as learning a second language in school require very conscious decisions. These are the technical aspects of designing and implementing a program for teaching the Native language as a second language (NSL). As will be seen below, this does not imply that the emotional and psychological aspects discussed above have been resolved: they are commonly present at all stages as barriers to successful implementation of what are theoretically technical issues such as teacher training and materials development.

9   **Program design: matching goals with methods, materials, and motivation**

With all of the above distinctions and possibilities in mind, and with a realistic assessment of the community language situation, we need to decide what kind of program we want to reconstruct for Tlingit and adult acquisition of Tlingit as a second language. Having set the goal, it is important to design the instructional program accordingly, to match the methods and materials with the desired outcome, and to build in adequate teacher training for the methods required. The time devoted should be measured in months and years, not hours and days. If materials development at a local level is desired, then adequate training in materials development should be included. Methods, materials, and motivation are all important. No child or mother ever needed any of these for natural language transmission in the first few years of life; language learning somehow just happens. But they will determine the success or failure of a second language teaching program in any artifical situation. Looking at the importance of methods, materials, and motivation, we would like to examine some of the barriers to success that we have witnessed over the last twenty-five years, and then make recommendations for the future.

9.1   Methods training

Training in the methods of oral language teaching and in language and cultural research is the most critical aspect of program implementation and success at the present time. Our biggest need is to identify, recruit, and train teachers from among the present generation of speakers, and then to train the next generation of teachers from current non-speakers. Some of this teacher training was done through summer-school courses for a few years in the early 1970s, but very little has been done since, and most of that generation of teachers is now retired or departed. Unfortunately, there has always been a common assumption that training in second language teaching methods is unnecessary for native speakers, and there has been an accompanying general attitude of resistance to such training. The confusion here is between (acknowledged) competence in oral fluency and (as yet undetermined) professional competence in ways of transmitting those skills to others in a variety of appropriate situations. The same is true for training in methods of research and documentation.

There are several reasons for this. First is the perception that Native languages are simple. It is a general rule that without special training, people have little or no appreciation for the complexity of their own language. One's first language is learned very early in life and through hearing and use, not conceptualization. Therefore, none of us can recall the process by which we acquired that which we understand most deeply and intuitively, and we have difficulty explaining conceptually how and why we say things. Our conscious attitudes toward language are usually confused, inaccurate, and incomplete. This is why it is very hard for a native speaker of any language to teach it without special training.

Tlingit, Haida, and Tsimshian have some of the most complicated sound systems and grammars of all the languages of the world. Of the three languages, Tlingit has the most complicated phonology, featuring 14 glottalized consonants. (In contrast, Haida has 6 and Tsimshian has 7, but both have other features of glottalization not found in Tlingit.) In addition to more universally occurring glottalized stops (such as *t'* and *k'*) Tlingit has a rare series of glottalized fricatives. Some stops and fricatives also include a velar–uvular contrast, and a contrast between labialized and non-labialized stops and fricatives, both glottalized and non-glottalized, creating a twenty-way phonemic contrast of the *k* and *x* sounds, of which only two are found in English (*k* and *g*). For example, the sound written x̠'w is a glottalized, labialized, uvular fricative. In contrast, x̠' is not labialized, *x'w* is velar and not uvular, k̠'w is a stop, etc. Another un-English phonemic contrast in Tlingit involves the voiceless *l* in the sounds written with *l*, *l'*, *tl* and *tl'*. On the rare side of simplicity, Tlingit is unusual among Alaska Native languages in having only a voiceless *l*. Haida and Tsimshian both have the voiced and voiceless contrast. We should note here that the ethnonym written in English as *Tlingit* actually begins with a voiceless *l*. But, as in the case of the Klingon of Star Trek fame, a language which projects Northwest Coast phonology to an intergalactic high, it is pronounced in English as *klink-it*.

Paired with this intrinsic phonological and grammatical complexity is the failure of most speakers to appreciate this complexity and how difficult it is to teach or learn these languages. Although people resent the term "foreign language" when applied to Native American languages, these languages are typically taken by beginning students as their first foreign language. Generally, the teachers are Native speakers with little or no training in methods of second-language teaching. Add this all together (beginning students, untrained teachers, the world's most complicated languages) and the sum is usually discouragement and failure. A related danger for students is the *genetic fallacy*: the assumption that the ancestral or heritage language will be easier for a person of the same ethnic background: that Polish will be easier for Polish-Americans, Classical Greek for Greek-Americans, etc., and, of course, that Tlingit will come naturally for learners of Tlingit descent. Therefore, the student does not study, and does not succeed. It is a tremendous blow to one's self-esteem to fail the ancestral language. All of this has been going on for twenty-five years, but is avoidable. A corollary to the *genetic fallacy* as it pertains to students is that teachers must also be of the ethnic group.

Pride and ego also play a role in the resistance to professional training, but the causes may run deeper. Many Native people feel that if they already speak their traditional language, they can automatically teach it, and they don't need anybody to teach them how; or if they "know the stories" they can automatically teach Native literature. Part of the problem is failure to distinguish natural transmission from artificial learning situations. The theoretical continuum of identity types (Margolin 1996) is also enlightening here. To the extent that speaking the (naturally acquired) Native language is a strong component of type (2) as a definer of ethnic identity and group membership, it follows that training to teach in academic or artificial settings would be perceived as non-Native activity regarding the language, and therefore conflict and contrast with the basic, defining ethnic behavior.

Race and gender are also involved. Many Natives are reluctant to take advice from white people on Native subjects, and many Native men will refuse to take instruction from a Native woman. Jealousy and rivalry may be involved. People may look at a product done by others and easily say, "I can do that, too" – but denying or failing to consider or appreciate the many years of professional training, preparation, and experience that went into the ability to produce the product. Many community programs have been characterized by rivalry, misdirected energy, and failure. What is required is an ideal combination of attitudes: the energy and optimism of "I can do that, too" combined with the discipline to get the training that can lead to success and satisfaction. The tragedy of such refusal to participate in professional training for whatever reason is that it often involves the last generation of fluent speakers, who with training in applied folklore and linguistics or teaching methods could make a lasting contribution to the survival of the language. (We should note here that there is also a danger of hubris from the non-Native side of denying or underestimating the validity of indigenous methods of and attitudes toward organizing and transmitting traditional knowledge.)

Administrative support is also often lacking in areas of teacher training. While school districts typically require years of course work and certification to teach "regular" subjects, school administrators often fail to appreciate the need to support NSL teachers with the kinds of training that will increase their confidence and skill. Year after year, from college to kindergarden, we see Native speakers hired with little or no training or support and placed directly in a classroom. The administrators are often monolingual speakers of English and have no appreciation of the complexities involved in language teaching in general; for Native languages, they often share the misconception of simplicity described above. (The misconception of simplicity is is also widely encountered as a racial and cultural stereotype of ethnic-minority languages held by speakers of many "major" or "world" languages other than English.) Administrators may be enthusiastic and have all kinds of ideas about teaching Native language and literature, but all too often this energy results in designs of programmatic and institutionalized trivialization.

As a final comment on administrative support, we should note that in one major school district in Southeast Alaska that has not taught Tlingit language for over twenty-two years, a non-Native teacher recently raised money through grants and donations to hire a teacher for a two-week, experimental course in Tlingit. His personal effort is admirable, but we should remember that the French and Spanish ethnic communities of the same city are not responsible for raising the money for Spanish and French instruction. As the district continues to extend instruction in French and Spanish to ever lower grade levels, it continues to exclude Tlingit instruction from all levels of the regular curriculum.

10   Materials development

Fishman's first word in the first step is significant: *reconstructing* the Native language. A problem for teaching all Native American languages is that we lack the choice of instructional materials common and even taken for granted in teaching of Spanish, French, Latin, Greek, and other languages with long histories of literacy and academic instruction. In most cases, Native American teachers create their own materials, working with linguists who are often still analyzing the language. (Jacobs, this volume, makes this point for Mohawk-language instruction as well.) Three barriers to materials development have slowed progress in this effort over the last twenty-five years: attitudes toward Native-language literacy; traditional concepts of clan and tribal ownership of stories, history, and other "intellectual property"; and suspicions of commercial profiteering.

10.1   The role of literacy

Confusion about the role of literacy is common in NSL instruction, and literacy is obviously a component of materials development, even where it is intended for teachers to present materials orally. Many teachers become enthusiastic about literacy after participating in teacher-training workshops and are eager to teach it, but forget that while they already know the language, their students do not. They tend to substitute literacy for building a base in oral fluency. Many well-meaning non-Native advisors to NSL programs have also confused the concepts of "readiness skills" with oral language acquisition, so that many NSL instructional units include numbers and colors translated from English (with confusion where the colors don't culturally match!). One school district had children's classics such as "Brown Bear, Brown Bear, what do you see?" translated into Tlingit for use as supplemental reading because it worked well with Spanish and Tagalog. The problem is that no school-age children spoke or read Tlingit, and the language was not taught anywhere in the school district. A related problem was that none of the rhyme and charm of the original translated. Another community proposed to teach Tlingit by giving all grandparents copies of our *Beginning Tlingit* grammar, have them meet weekly with their grandchildren, and evaluate the success of the program by giving spelling tests from our *Tlingit spelling book*. The concept of re-establishing language contact across the generations is excellent, but the automatic assumption of literacy as the medium of instruction and evaluation is flawed. It is not uncommon to see inexperienced teachers using spellings from two or three different writing systems without being aware of the discrepancies. Materials developers in another part of Alaska seem to be having success using video tapes for teacher training in oral methods, and by simply adding the teacher-literacy component in the form of subtitles, which are less culturally intrusive.

As the above examples show, the role and place of literacy in second-language teaching have been misunderstood. The role of literacy is also poorly understood as a means of documenting oral literature. For the generations steeped in oral composition, the publication of literature, literacy, and reading can add a confusing dimension. We have seen elders aggravated by students who attempted to please them by reading Native-language texts, but who still read imperfectly. We have also seen elders convinced that linguists who knew very little of their language were not only fluent but were excellent stylists as well, simply because they could read back a text transcribed from oral tradition.

Common to literate cultures is the confusion between literacy and spoken language, the misconception that literacy precedes spoken language, and that one's spoken language was learned from a book.[8] Although Tlingit has been written since the 1840s (first in the Cyrillic alphabet, and then in the Roman) there has never been a tradition of widespread popular literacy. The popular orthography currently in use was developed by Summer Institute of Linguistics/Wycliffe Bible Translators in the 1960s. It was modified and accepted as a standard by Tlingit language teachers in 1972, and was overwhelmingly confirmed at a regional conference in 1996. Since 1972 there have been several major publications of grammars, dictionaries, and texts using this spelling system. We should note here that spelling reform is always a lively topic for debate, but that most of the advocates of change are those who are not literate; it would seem that the possibility of changing the spelling system offers a convenient opportunity to procrastinate or postpone learning to read and write the existing standard.

---

8 This mystique of literacy is well illustrated with an example from Tsimshian. One elder and village leader who designed a Tsimshian writing system for his community in opposition to a standard orthography used in other communities argued as follows. One hundred years ago, when Boas wrote Tsimshian using the Boasian spelling system, all Tsimshians spoke the language, and even children were fluent. Now (in the 1970s and 1980s), with the innovation of the new writing system, only the very oldest generation can speak the language, and children are not successfully learning it. The logical conclusion: the death of Tsimshian is related to abandoning the Boasian orthography in favor of the new one. We heard a similar line of reasoning from a Yup'ik elder who observed that children spoke the language better years ago when it was still written in Cyrillic, but speak it poorly now that it is written in "English."

Literacy is most popular among the younger generations of Tlingit who are learning the language and who are more acculturated to books and literacy in English than are the older generations. In the absence of natural oral transmission, a generation is now emerging which has learned most of what Tlingit they know through printed materials. Among the older generations there remains considerable resistance to standardized literacy for a number of understandable reasons both emotional and technical. The emotional side may be partly a reluctance to admit that there is some aspect of the language they do not know so that non-literacy may be perceived as a challenge to their linguistic competence. There is also clan, family, or regional chauvinism: "They can't write my dialect," or "We won't do it that way because X or village Y does it that way." Resistance can be along ethnic lines. One Tlingit woman proudly announced that she refused to learn to read and write Tlingit because she didn't want to learn it from a white person. She would teach herself. (She remains non-literate, and proud of it.) A Tlingit man publicly explained that "Some people speak the language, and some people read and write it. I'm a speaker." The implication is that real Tlingit speakers are not literate, and that literacy and fluency are in conflict. (There is some truth in this equation; but whereas speakers may fear that literacy causes language loss, the opposite seems more accurate: that literacy gains in appeal after language decline or loss as a strategy for restoration.)

Part of the explanation may be found in the observations and suggestions of Scollon and Scollon (1981) and David Margolin (1996). The Scollons describe how literacy in general (especially in English) is perceived by traditional Native people as a non-Native phenomenon so that non-literacy or resistance to literacy becomes part of the Native "badge of ethnicity." Literacy is not a continuum on Margolin's theoretical model in its present stage of development, but certainly could and should be. Plotting the use of and attitudes toward literacy can help conceptualize the phenomena. For identity type (1), literacy is not an issue. Either it does not exist at all, or it may be a variety that is accepted as indigenous, such as the Cherokee system or the Indian and Inupiaq syllabaries of northern Canada; or different types of literacy may exist in the form of complementary varieties used for distinct ethnic functions, as in the widely cited (Scollon and Scollon 1981:46–47) African example first reported by Scribner and Cole (1978) of Arabic used for religious or "Qur'anic" literacy, English literacy used for schooling and other colonial contexts, and a tribal Vai script for domestic purposes. In type (2), literacy does become an issue, and is a feature of the "us versus them" opposition, literacy being identified with the outside. This seems to describe the phenomenon described above for Tlingit of widespread refusal among the last age group of fluent speakers to be involved with literacy. For type (3), literacy is phaticized, lexicalized, and decorative in contrast to communicative.

There is the widespread phenomenon of individuals and organizations that do not speak Tlingit, or speak it marginally, but who use literacy for its decorative and symbolic effect or impression: for example, "Merry Christmas" in Tlingit on corporate windows or Christmas cards, usually in highly idiosyncratic spellings rather than standard orthography. Names of dance groups are typically spelled in non-standard ways, suggesting that the display of literacy is important, but correct spelling and communication through literacy are not, as the idiosyncratic spellings are often incomprehensible. Literacy in Tlingit seems most accepted in type (4), where there is minimal emotional involvement with the spoken language, but an academic effort to learn it. Ironically, literacy begins to function most where the spoken language functions the least.[9] The tragedy for linguistic and cultural documentation for future generations of learners is the widespread emotional reluctance described above to use literacy as a technical tool by the generation most ideally suited to transmit this knowledge, at the same time as the language is no longer being transmitted orally. In this context, we confess envy as we read of communities where the dynamics of literacy have been more fruitful and supportive of language maintenance. Watahomigie and Yamamoto report for Hualapai that "another effect, in some areas at least, is to bring local language literacy to people who have never before experienced it, to enable people to express themselves in

9 There is a fascinating dimension to literacy that is worth mentioning here. As a cultural phenomenon, literacy is associated with English for speakers of Native languages (as noted repeatedly above). In this context, we have observed that for beginning transcribers of all ages and in various languages, it was extremely difficult to transcribe Native-language material directly to the page. At first, all tended to translate into English, write down the English, and then back-translate the written English in their own words into written Native. The resulting text was a paraphrase rather than a transcription. The concept of direct transcription or original written composition in Native was alien. Ralph Maud's recent edition (1993) based on Henry Tate's original manuscripts shows that this process frustrated Boas almost a century ago, and that many of the classic Tsimshian texts were first composed in English and are essentially classics of indigenous creative writing in English!

written form of their own languages, even if only to give voice to feelings of mild despair" (1992:16–17).

It is understandable that beginning teachers with limited training may feel insecure with literacy, but the problem is that rather than use genuinely oral methods of instruction, they almost always end up spelling. One often sees the irony of refusing or denying literacy where it is really needed (as in documentation of names) combined with reverting to literacy when it is not needed or desired (as in oral language instruction). If literacy is taught, we feel it should be standard and consistent. For example, personal or family spellings can also be an extremely emotional issue. Descendants who can no longer pronounce the names of ancestors cling tenaciously to traditional family spellings of the names that in no way represent the actual sounds. If the names are being taught orally and learned accurately, spelling is not critical. But especially where names are being lost orally, they need to be preserved in a correct spelling that allows the present and coming generations to retrieve them. It is probably safe to say that for most Tlingit people, spelling remains highly individual, with each word spelled "phonetically" and "just like it sounds" based on the spelling of a rhyming English word, and without awareness of the many phonemic contrasts of Tlingit that cannot be recorded in such a way.

The technical problem is that Tlingit has about three dozen sounds not shared with English (some of which are described above), so there are no familiar, existing letters with which to spell these sounds. New letters or spelling conventions must be created. Thus, Tlingit spelling can appear intimidating because "regular" English letters need to be modified by accents, underlines, or apostrophes to signify the special sounds of Tlingit. Tlingit is also a tone language, and phonemic tone needs to be indicated, although this would not be strictly necessary if the language were orally thriving. Speakers are aware of these phonemic differences when they hear or say words, but they have difficulty conceptualizing the distinctions in terms of writing. Non-speakers tend to hear and spell about twenty of these phonemic distinctions as *k* or *h* (the closest English sounds). For learners, the problem is twofold: to learn to hear and pronounce the differences, and to learn to read and spell the differences. For the older generations that already speak Tlingit, literacy is not very important; for them the language survived without writing since time immemorial. But for learners of the now moribund language, and for passing on the accurate pronunciation of names and other cultural information, accurate spelling is crucial.

10.2   Ownership

Another barrier to materials development is the Northwest Coast tradition of clan and tribal ownership of stories, history, and other "intellectual property." The system (described at length in N. Dauenhauer 1995; Dauenhauer and Dauenhauer 1987, 1990, 1994) historically functioned to guarantee survival of oral and visual art tradition through fostering stewardship, but many aspects of the concept of ownership are now counterproductive. The system assumes a critical mass of speakers to sustain natural transmission of information, and it operates within a larger system of social structure that assumes understanding of kinship, genealogy, protocol, and reciprocity. Many of these prerequisites are now being lost, but the idea of ownership remains strong. Thus a person may know that his or her clan owns a certain song, story, or design, but he or she may not understand who else might use it and under what conditions, depending on kinship and protocol. Perhaps combined with the rise of the Western concept of individualism, the concept of ownership seems to be evolving in the direction of privacy or secrecy. But such materials were never esoteric or secret. They were known to all, but were treated with deference and respect according to kinship and protocol. In order to operate as a competent clan leader and to interact ceremonially and ritually with clans of the opposite moiety, a person must know not only his or her own clan traditions, but those of others as well.

There is a real and legitimate fear of traditional ethnic materials being appropriated, exploited, trivialized, or desecrated by outsiders, and this fear has led many elders and communities in the direction of secrecy. We respect the right of elders not to transmit oral materials. If tradition bearers decline to work with us, we comply with their wishes. But ownership is only half of the traditional equation; the other half is stewardship and transmission to the next generation and to the grandchildren. An important feature of our publications (acceptable to the storytellers) is that we do not "retell" or "rewrite" stories, but offer the Tlingit text transcribed from their oral performance along with an English translation of the text, and with the tradition bearer clearly identified and featured in a biography that includes photographs.

Often relatives or descendants of elders are more protective than the elders themselves. This happens where elders request that their oral material be recorded for future generations, but family, clan members, or community bureaucracies disagree for various reasons. There have been cases where one relative sabotaged another elder's attempts to have an event video-taped. There have been situations where children interfered with recording sessions, with the result that after the death of the parent, there was no record of what he knew and wanted to preserve for them. Only with the death of the elder did the younger people realize the enormity of their loss. They assumed that "somebody" knew "the stories," but this was not the case. There are also cases in which elders taped stories, but the archives have become part of a community bureaucracy and tribal politics: something to fight over. In one community, access has been repeatedly denied to both Native and non-Native scholars working to produce written instructional and cultural resource materials from the oral tapes. Unless the tapes are worked with, they may soon deteriorate and fade. More tragically, there is a real danger with some languages (such as Haida) that even if the tapes survive physically, there will soon be nobody left alive who can understand what is on them. The tragedy here is that coming generations of such ethnic groups will be left with neither living oral tradition nor audio or written documentation. This is an extreme case of linguistic and cultural suicide.

We appreciate the fear of desecration, but we believe that the risks of sharing information are less dangerous at the present time than the risk that it may otherwise be lost forever. Part of the emotional confusion that individuals and communities must resolve is the increasing sense of personal possession now combined with the rising awareness of loss, not from theft from without, but through lack of transmission within.

Negative resolution to this is common, with people or programs declining to cooperate in materials development in favor of doing it themselves. Fueled by suspicions of profiteering and misconceptions of the economics of materials development, with delusions of the great riches to be obtained from the sale of books, but unaware of the costs and technical requirements of producing them, many of the tendencies described above combine for the worst. Most often the result is that nothing is done at all, which satisfies the desire for secrecy and private ownership, but thwarts the idea of transmission to the next generation. As the language becomes more alienable, objectified, and unknown, materials development and cultural documentation can easily become industries in themselves and something to be fought over or manipulated as part of larger political agendas.

When it works, local production of materials is perhaps the best. There are many benefits, especially the sense of personal pride and local ownership of the final product. People also learn from the process of developing the materials. We encourage local materials development. We also encourage local developers to gain experience in applied folklore and linguistics. Over the last twenty-five years we have seen that local communities tend not to have the skills or resources required for production entirely on their own. One of the frustrations is that materials from which other communities might also benefit are frequently not produced in lasting quality or quantity or with a distribution network.

A related problem is that some communities or programs decline to share materials with others, either through sale or professional exchange. In Southeast Alaska and adjacent Canada, we know of at least five Tlingit, Haida, and Tsimshian communities that have produced excellent and valuable materials, but declined to make them available for use to other communities of the same language. This is very discouraging, as it forces each community, with its very limited resources, to reinvent the wheel. We do not have the luxury of human or financial resources to afford this kind of isolationism, which now seems to coincide with a general movement toward decentralization that is also reflected in funding support for training and materials development.[10]

10.3   *Motivation*

A final barrier to successful language instruction is student motivation. Assuming that we have motivated and well-trained teachers supplied with adequate and acceptable materials, we are still faced with the real and nagging question: why learn Tlingit? Other than a career as Tlingit teacher

---

10 In our case we are salaried by Sealaska Heritage Foundation (SHF) to research, write, and produce camera-ready manuscripts, but we receive no personal profit from sales. Our products are available to all audiences, and are designed for the interested, intelligent reader. They provide documentation for shareholders and their descendants, they help non-Native users gain an understanding and appreciation of Tlingit, and they are models for other programs. Some people resent this, arguing that our efforts and products should be restricted to Sealaska shareholders. We disagree, arguing that SHF cannot assert leadership and be successful in documentation and materials development in a context of suppression and secrecy.

or materials developer, there are no economic benefits. Every year there are fewer people alive to speak it with. All of the speakers already know English better than a learner will ever master Tlingit. Tlingit is neither "practical" nor "relevant," so why bother?

One of our colleagues teaches high-school German and Russian. She promises her German students, "Stick it out for two years of German, and we'll go to Germany for the summer." Spanish is widely heard and spoken in the United States, and there are many opportunities for study in Spanish-speaking countries. But there is no such motivation to offer students of Tlingit, who are already in the homeland. In contrast to immigrant languages in the United States, which have homelands in which the languages grow and develop, the American continent is the homeland of the Native American languages. There is no Germany or Norway, Japan or Vietnam to which one can return to learn it, where movies and television support the language rather than erode it. If Native languages die here, there is no homeland to which one can go and find it living. This is a serious motivational factor, especially when combined with all the negative potential described above. One possible motivation might be a network of exchange programs with reservations in the "Lower 48," or Native communities elsewhere in the world, ideally where the indigenous languages are stronger and where people have managed to impede or reverse language loss (Watahomigie and Yamamoto 1992; Zepeda and Hill 1991: 142–147). Another is a tour of American and/or European museums with Northwest Coast art.

Whatever motivation an individual, family, or community can find, it should be carefully considered. Unrealistic, romantic reactions in support of Native-language instruction can be just as disappointing in the long run as the negative attacks that label it demonic. The ultimate motivation must be spiritual. We can offer no motivation other than satisfaction, that it feels good to learn Tlingit. Or – it could feel good. With so few material rewards to offer, if it doesn't feel spiritually good to study Tlingit, Haida, or Tsimshian, there is little hope that the languages will survive in any form at all. Working with Native American languages can be sad and depressing, stressful, and full of grief. One is always dealing with death and dying, not only of the individual elders, but cumulatively of the language itself.

As noted throughout, little of what we have described here is unique to Tlingit or Southeast Alaska. Many journal articles, books, and chapters have been written describing the experiences of other Native American groups and evaluating the success or failure of their efforts. These can be a source of guidance for local communities.[11] A very important source of information and encouragement is the exchange of energy and information that takes place during conferences such as the annual meetings of the Native American Language Issues Institute (NALI). At the 1994 conference, a number of speakers and participants touched on many topics covered in this chapter. They were unanimous in their acknowledgment of the enduring emotional legacy of the abuses of the past, but they were also unanimous in their insistence on "no more excuses," on taking control, taking action, and taking responsibility for the future of their languages. The problems are the same: "lip service, but no love for it," "cliché but no commitment." All emphasized the importance of personal, positive, self-esteem in all aspects of survival, especially language and culture. Otherwise, the alternatives are shame, guilt, insecurity, anger, and hostility. Some speakers described learning methods (communicative competence versus grammar), others explained program models, such as apprenticeships matching language learners with tradition bearers who are among the last speakers of their languages. There was a general agreement on motive: it is spiritual and psychological; learning the ancestral language gives peace, real identity, and intellectual pleasure. It also provides a vehicle to communicate with the past, with the generations of departed.

There is comfort in reading great literature of the past. The American poet Robinson Jeffers called this feeling "The honey of peace in old poems." We derive pleasure and draw inspiration from literature that may be several hundred or several thousand years old: the Homeric epics, the Epic of Gilgamesh, the Bible, Beowulf, the medieval Icelandic sagas. Part of the greatness of ancient Greek and Hebrew literature is that the oral tradition was flourishing at the same moment in history that literacy entered with the technology to preserve it in writing. It is a humbling experience to read a love poem from the Greek Anthology that was written over 2,000 years ago. It is also humbling and sobering to realize that all of this ancient literature survives partly because someone cared enough to write it down, and partly because of luck that the pieces of paper survived and outlived

11 The Administration for Native Americans (ANA) has distributed copies of some of the most useful of these articles as part of its community grant writing workshops.

the spoken languages. Tlingit and many other Native American languages today have the technical capability to document their oral literature for posterity so that the creative genius will in a very real sense live, even though the spoken languages are moribund and not expected to survive. The great Jewish writer Isaac B. Singer was asked in an interview why he wrote in Yiddish. The interviewer told him Yiddish was a dying language, and would soon be dead. "So," replied Singer, with his characteristic wit, "I like ghost stories. Also, I believe in the resurrection. What will all those Jews have to read when they come back to life if I don't write in Yiddish?"

11   Conclusion: now is the time for action

As a closing frame for this chapter, we would like to turn again to the thoughts of Joshua Fishman, this time from key elements of his address on "Reversing language shift" to a plenary session of the 1994 Native American Language Issues Institute. The dynamics of language restoration are very complicated, and on a worldwide scale there have been more failures than stories of success. The sanctity of one's language is a common feature and attitude around the world. But why is it so hard to reverse the language shift, even with dedicated people? Fishman offers four main reasons, and reviewing them provides a convenient summary for this chapter. First, the odds are not encouraging when a weaker culture takes on a stronger one. There is little margin for error. Each mistake is doubly costly for the minority effort. Second, efforts are often undertaken too late. This is often a combination of denial and procrastination. It may be too late biologically, with no speakers left of childbearing age, and it may be too late ideologically, when it has become more convenient and comfortable to "do it in English." Third, the reversal and restoration effort is often undertaken without clear understanding of the difference between language acquisition and language transmission, between starting from scratch, learning anew by this trick or that, and intergenerational transmission (described above). Fourth, the effort is often introduced in a haphazard way, instead of doing the right thing at the right time.

The reversal effort requires widespread, intense conviction that this is the right thing to do. This ideological clarification must be assumed prior to any successful community effort. The effort requires a community level of commitment, and an awareness that this is a "do-it-yourself" effort.

Language reversal cannot be done *to* one or *for* one by others. It doesn't require a budget. Fishman quoted a Yiddish proverb, " 'To promise' and 'to like' don't cost anything."

Finally, there is a range of tactical problems that must be considered. Most often, people aim too high, too soon, relative to the state the language is in. Fishman emphasizes that the supports of a building are not the same as the foundation, and that we must build the foundation first, then the support structure. The foundation of language reversal is the family and community link. The tactical problems present a number of dilemmas. One of these is the role of schools. Fishman admonishes communities not to entrust their language to an institution not under their control. Schools have their own goals. Language needs to be brought into informal daily life. The problem is, the people don't know how to take it out of school. Somewhere, people need to find a safe place for language in daily life, a place where it isn't always being bombarded, a place where it can expand and grow. The paradox is that the vernacular lives in spontaneity and intimacy, but reversing language shift requires planning. How can you plan intimacy and spontaneity?

The odds are against reversing language shift for Tlingit, Haida, and Alaskan Tsimshian. The anxieties and attitudes that contributed to abandoning the languages still remain stronger in the community and among individuals than the attitudes necessary for restoration of the languages. It is unrealistic to expect the Native languages of Southeast Alaska to recover fully and thrive as they did sixty to a hundred years ago. But they can continue to be used in many ways, both oral and written, that are of enduring spiritual value to the individual and community, even if these new uses are far more limited and restricted than they would have been in the past (Bauman 1980). Until community discussion and dialog such as we have described occurs, we won't know what the final consensus of the Tlingit ethnic community will be. We hope that the deep-rooted emotional issues discussed above can be called to awareness and somehow resolved, and when the question is raised, "Is Tlingit worth learning?" the answer will be "Yes, Tlingit is worth learning!" The reasons will almost certainly not be "practical," but spiritual: because it feels good, because it is satisfying, because it gives intellectual pleasure and spiritual comfort. But this kind of language learning (much less transmission) is not something that can be forced on people. We suspect that the language effort will never be a mass movement, and will never be as popular as singing and dancing. It is more likely that the languages and documentation of traditional culture will be cultivated by a small group of apprentices, each working more or less alone, with older tradition bearers (see Hinton 1994). The mainstream of ever-changing Tlingit culture will continue to bypass the ancestral language and traditional world view, but parts of it will survive through the efforts of dedicated learners. We suspect that living language transmission is now at an end for the Native languages of Southeast Alaska, but that language learning will be one of the many markers or "badges" of ethnicity that members of the culture elect to use as an expression of membership and pride.

4 Mayan efforts toward language preservation

NORA C. ENGLAND

Department of Anthropology, The University of Iowa

1 Introduction

Mayan languages are among the most vigorous of indigenous American languages. They are spoken by over 6 million people in Guatemala alone (Tzian 1994), with significantly large numbers of speakers in southern and central Mexico (Chiapas, Tabasco, Campeche, Yucatán and Quintana Roo, San Luís Potosí, and Veracruz) and Belize. Although Mayas suffered great losses of population and territory as a result of the Spanish invasion of the sixteenth century, their population has largely recovered, and they form absolute majorities in almost all of the communities where they presently live. The great majority of Mayas speak one of the twenty-nine extant Mayan languages, almost always as a first language, and many Mayas are monolingual in a Mayan language, especially among the older population. In spite of these demographic signs of vitality, however, language shift and loss among Mayas is growing at an alarming rate, and Mayan community leaders are increasingly concerned about the future viability of their languages and community structures.

Because of the strengthening of signs of language shift, especially in, but not restricted to, the smaller language communities, Mayan languages must certainly be counted among the world's endangered languages. Mayas in Guatemala have begun to take steps to fortify their language and try to prevent language loss on a grand scale. Whether these efforts will ultimately be successful is of course still unclear, but it may be instructive to examine the measures that are being proposed and followed in a situation where language shift and loss is still in its earlier rather than final stages.

I would like to acknowledge my intellectual debt to the many Mayas I have worked with in Guatemala, especially the past and present members of Oxlajuuj Keej Maya' Ajtz'iib' (Waykan, José Gonzalo Benito Pérez; Saqijix, Candelaria Dominga López Ixcoy; Lolmay, Pedro Oscar García Matzar; Ajpub', Pablo García Ixmatá; Pala's, José Francisco Santos Nicolás; B'aayil, Eduardo Pérez Vail; Pakal, José Obispo Rodríguez Guaján; Nikte', María Juliana Sis Iboy; and Saq Ch'en, Ruperto Montejo Esteban).

2   Background

Mayas live in a complex society. In Guatemala, they speak twenty different languages natively, some with as few as several hundred speakers and others with over a million speakers. These languages are all historically related, but the differences among them are as great and small, roughly, as the differences among European languages. Thus, several languages are mutually intelligible with practice, much like Spanish and Portuguese, or Dutch and Frisian, but others are as distant and incomprehensible to others as are Russian and English. The Guatemalan languages correspond to five of the six different branches of the Mayan language family; the branches are roughly comparable to the European Romance, West Germanic, North Germanic, Slavic, and Baltic branches. The Guatemalan Mayan languages, according to their branches, are given in table 4.1.[1] Of these languages, the largest is K'ichee', with over a million speakers.[2] Q'eqchi', Kaqchikel, and Mam are also very large, with between 400,000 and 700,000 speakers each. The smallest language, and that most in danger of imminent death, is Itzaj, with fewer than 100 older speakers (Hofling

Table 4.1 Mayan languages

Ch'ol	Q'anjob'al	Mam	K'ichee'		Yukatekan (Maya')
Ch'orti'	Q'anjob'al	Mam	K'ichee'	Uspantek	Mopan
	Akatek	Teko	Kaqchikel	Q'eqchi'	Itzaj
	Popti'	Awakatek	Tz'utujiil	Poqomam	
	Chuj	Ixil	Sipakapense	Poqomchi'	
			Sakapultek		

1 I use new spellings for the names of Mayan languages, in which these names are spelled according to Mayan orthographic conventions. The names, in Mayan and traditional spellings are: Akatek = Acatec, Awakatek = Aguacatec, Chuj = Chuj, Ch'orti' = Chorti, Itzaj = Itzá, Ixil = Ixil, Kaqchikel = Cakchiquel, K'ichee' = Quiché, Mam = Mam, Mopan = Mopán, Popti' = Jakaltec, Poqomam = Pocomam/Pokomam, Poqomchi' = Pocomchí/Pokomchí, Q'anjob'al = Kanjobal, Q'eqchi' = Kekchi, Sakapultek = Sacapultec, Sipakapense = Sipacapense/Sipacepeno, Teko = Teco/Tectitec, Tz'utujiil = Tzutujil/Tzutuhil/Zutujil, Uspantek = Uspantec.

2 The figures used here are conservative and are cited from Oxlajuuj Keej Maya' Ajtz'iib' 1993. Other less conservative population projections can be found in Tzian 1994.

1991). Teko and Mopan are also spoken by relatively few people and are gravely endangered, while Poqomam, although not as small or as immediately endangered, has been steadily losing speakers during the past 500 years. Popti' (Jakaltek) is undergoing significant shift, especially in the town center. Uspantek, Sipakapense, Sakapultek, and Awakatek are all spoken in one municipality each, and must be considered to be endangered due to small size alone. The remaining languages, Akatek, Chuj, Poqomchi', Ch'orti', Ixil, Tz'utujiil and Q'anjob'al, have populations that range from around 20,000 to well over 100,000 speakers, and for the moment seem to be viable. However, all Mayan languages, including K'ichee', show signs of active shift, in which an increasing number of children, especially in the urban centers, are not learning the Mayan language as a first language, and in some cases, not at all. Two dissertations (Brown 1991 and Garzon 1991) document various aspects of language shift in Kaqchikel, including prestige factors and language dominance in urban compared to rural schools.

Literacy in a Mayan language is not a widespread tradition in this century. There have been two periods in Mayan history when literacy was common enough for substantial literary production to take place. The first of these was between AD 200 and about 1,200, and saw the development and florescence of Mayan hieroglyphic writing, the only true writing system developed independently in the Americas. An enormous literature was produced, only part of which has survived, due to the Spanish policy of destroying Mayan books in an effort to combat Mayan beliefs. The second period was the sixteenth century, when Mayas learned to read and write using a Spanish-based alphabet and produced such classics as the "Popol Vuh" (K'ichee'), the "Annals of the Cakchiquels" (Kaqchikel), and the "Books of Chilam Balam" (Yukatek Maya'). After the sixteenth century, literacy (and literary production) generally declined, except perhaps in the Yucatán, but there have probably always been at least some individuals who know how to read and write in a Mayan language.

Until recent decades bilingualism in Spanish and a Mayan language was relatively low. As late as the 1970s, there were several areas of Guatemala, most notably Alta Verapaz and Huehuetenango, where monolingualism in a Mayan language typically was greater than 85 percent for the Mayan population. Since the sixteenth century there have always been bilingual individuals, who acted as language and culture brokers for their communities, but their numbers were relatively low. Also typically, the non-Maya population (known locally as *Ladinos*) has been almost universally monolingual in Spanish; thus, the burden of translation and interpretation has been almost entirely borne by bilingual Mayas. Today, bilingualism among Mayas is growing rapidly, especially due to greater educational opportunity and changes in economic structure. In many families an increased attention to the acquisition of Spanish by children has resulted in the emergence, for the first time, of significant numbers of Mayas who do not speak a Mayan language.[3] Language has always been considered to be an immutable marker of identity by Mayas, and for the first time they are being confronted with a situation in which it can no longer be assumed that Mayas speak Mayan.

Social complexity and heterogeneity exist in many spheres besides language. While Mayas have been characterized as being an essentially peasant society that practices subsistence agriculture augmented by plantation wage labor, economic variability is in fact much greater than this characterization would convey (see Smith 1988). There are large numbers of Mayas engaged, as their primary economic activity, in the production of handcrafts, in construction, or in commerce, and smaller but noteworthy numbers who are professionals, especially teachers and governmental or NGO staff. Although all Mayas are "poor" in the national or international economic context, there is measurable wealth differentiation on the basis of land ownership and/or real monetary income. Religious affiliation and practice varies from traditional Mayan to traditional Catholic, to combinations of Mayan and Catholic practice, to fundamentalist and evangelical Christian. Formal educational levels have typically been very low, but are increasing rapidly. Twenty years ago, for instance, it was almost unheard of for a Maya to have any university education, but today there are three Guatemalan Mayas with doctorates, several more studying at the doctoral level, several others with master's degrees, and a quite large number with *licenciaturas* (college degrees). Diversity in educational level has thus increased dramatically as educational opportunities have grown. Mayas have also been characterized as a largely rural population, but in fact large

3 While there were undoubtedly Mayas who did not speak a Mayan language in the past, this usually was accompanied by a shift in identity. There seem to be many young Mayas today, in contrast, who clearly identify as Mayas but who do not speak a Mayan language, or who learn one late, as a second language. For a related situation among the Tlingit, see also Dauenhauer and Dauenhauer; and among the Mohawk, see Jocks, this volume.

numbers live in municipal centers, which are small urban centers, and in the departmental or national capitals. Finally, Mayas have probably always accorded differential status to community members on the basis of age, community service, and leadership capability, but the parameters of status differentiation have increased as people become more diverse in education, work, and experience.

One aspect of the Mayan experience that has remained relatively constant over the last 500 years is that, although a numerical majority in Guatemala, they have been politically, economically, and socially marginalized since Spanish contact. They own and occupy the most marginal lands, they have been subjected to some of the worst discriminatory practices that can be found anywhere in the world, they have almost no voice in formal politics at the state level, they have been ruthlessly exploited for their labor and at the same time accused of being non-productive, and they have been the victims of ethnocidal civil wars at moments of crisis in Guatemala's history, the most recent in 1980–1984. Mayan languages and cultures are customarily regarded as defective by the dominant *Ladino* population, the facts of an extremely illustrious Mayan history that included high levels of artistic, literary, architectural, and scientific achievement are barely mentioned in public education, and popular images of Mayas characterize them as servile, lazy, stupid, and brutish. The prevailing intellectual concept of Mayas, taught in the national university and quoted widely in the press, holds that the "Indians" of Guatemala are not in fact Mayas, who were all dead long before Spanish contact, but instead are some sort of hybrid (and by implication, impure, and valueless) creation of the colonial period. This attempt to deny Mayas their own heritage and a considerable source of cultural pride is being particularly invoked at the present moment, seemingly in reaction against an emerging Mayan intellectual position, led by Demetrio Cojtí (see Cojtí Cuxil 1991, 1994), which clearly states that the "Indians" of Guatemala are Mayas, that while they are in no way the "product" of colonialism, they are still suffering *Ladino* colonialism, that assimilation to a *Ladino* state and *Ladino* cultural ways is not and should not be their collective goal, and that certain measures of political autonomy and control over identity and community are theirs by right.

This position is part of a widespread movement in reaffirmation of Mayan identity and cultural values, a movement with popular, technical, and intellectual aspects. One of the first areas of concern within the movement is language because Mayas consider that language has always been one of their strongest cultural symbols. This perhaps helps explain why Mayas, unlike many other peoples, seem to be concerned about language loss while shift is in its early rather than later stages.

3   Language shift

The signs of language shift and loss among the larger Mayan languages are clear. Many children, especially in the urban centers, no longer speak a Mayan language as their first language. They may have passive knowledge of the language depending on family and playgroup exposure, but they are unable to use the language actively and may exhibit embarrassment and an unwillingness to even try to use it. Some of these children acquire an active knowledge of the local language as they become more fully incorporated into the community (as adolescents or young adults), but it is not at all clear whether this is a general pattern that can be relied on to prevent language loss, or merely a sporadic pattern within some families.

Language loss seems to proceed in a fairly classic manner. Older siblings are more likely to speak a Mayan language than younger siblings. Mothers in families that are undergoing shift usually speak enough Spanish to encourage its use in the household, and seem to be instrumental in the decision to use Spanish rather than a Mayan language in the family. The availability of formal education greatly encourages language shift, because families that are interested in their children receiving the benefits of formal education are concerned that they speak enough Spanish to begin school without a language disadvantage. Older siblings who may have begun school without being able to speak Spanish are particularly instrumental in teaching their younger siblings Spanish, in order to spare them the frequent ridicule that accompanied their own first days in school. Finally, there is a general attitude that Spanish, as a foreign language, requires considerable household attention so that children will learn it well, but Mayan languages will be naturally picked up by Mayan children and therefore need no special attention. The evidence, increasingly, is that Mayan children do not "pick up" a Mayan language naturally when they no longer hear it at home, in school, or even in their playgroups. This is of increasing concern to many Mayan adults.

Language shift and loss have occurred to varying extents in different parts of Guatemala. Factors such as size of the language population, the relative isolation of the community, and differences between rural and urban settings play a large role in determining the pace of language loss. Thus, rural communities are more likely than urban communities to show more language maintenance, small languages have suffered more loss than large languages, and proximity to major urban centers, especially Guatemala City, and to the Mexican border or frontier areas has resulted in greater shift. Therefore, for instance, the large and very important urban center of Quetzaltenango, originally a K'ichee'-speaking city, has many K'ichee' families in which no one speaks the language, going back three generations. In addition, the eastern part of Guatemala, relatively sparsely populated by Mayas, has whole towns that once were "Indian" in the census figures and no longer are, presumably as a result of complete language shift several generations ago, accompanied by a total shift of identity as well. The examples of Quetzaltenango and the east aside, the more usual pattern seems to be that language shift, where it is occurring in large numbers, is a relatively recent phenomenon, affecting mostly children and, in some places, young adults. Most people report that in their home communities the urban centers are undergoing shift, but that the outlying villages show few signs of shift yet.

4   **Cultural reaffirmation and language maintenance**

Guatemalan Mayas are undergoing a quite remarkable renaissance of cultural pride accompanied by the reaffirmation of cultural values. This is a widespread movement which undoubtedly had its roots in the 1970s, but began to flourish and take on a very coherent form in the last decade, following the devastations of the Civil War in the early 1980s. Language is a focal point for cultural revitalization. Mayan languages constitute one of the principal symbols of an unequivocally Mayan identity, they are still spoken by the overwhelming majority of the Mayan population, and they are the principal communicative devices through which Mayan worldview and philosophy are learned and transmitted. As a consequence, Mayas have begun to articulate a program for the reinforcement of their languages. In its most ideal form, that program involves:

1   Mayan control of language decisions;
2   the standardization of Mayan languages in at least their written forms, and
     possibly in their spoken forms as well;
3   the expansion of the domains of usage of Mayan languages to the written, and
     the reinforcement of other domains such as public speech and conversation,
     or use in the home;
4   the use of Mayan languages in the schools as mediums of instruction rather
     than only as instruments for the acquisition of Spanish;
5   the establishment of principles whereby Mayan languages are recognized as
     official regional languages.

The most important concrete event marking the beginning of a program directed toward language maintenance was the establishment of the Academy of Mayan Languages. After a lengthy process the Academy was approved as an autonomous state institution in 1991, the first government approved and funded institution that is wholly directed by Mayas and devoted to Mayan interests. As such, it possesses great symbolic and political value. Four years before its eventual approval, however, in 1987, the unofficially constituted Academy took its first instrumental action, when it convened a meeting to discuss and establish a "unified" alphabet for Mayan languages and then had that alphabet legalized by presidential decree. This event was of great symbolic and practical importance.

Its symbolic value lies in the fact that Mayas were signaling that they would henceforth be in charge of decisions affecting Mayan language use and standards. Official, legally approved alphabets had been established for Mayan languages several times in the past, but their proponents were never Mayas. At the meeting where the new alphabet was discussed and chosen, non-Mayas were allowed to listen and to speak during the proceedings, but were not allowed to vote. The practical importance of establishing a "unified" alphabet, by which Mayas mean both a single way of writing each language and also that the alphabet used for each language should be as similar as possible to the alphabet for every other Mayan language, is closely connected to the goals of standardization and the expansion of domains of usage for Mayan languages. For literacy to be successful, the first requirement is that there be a single convention for the writing of each language. Although conventional agreements about how languages should be written involve more than alphabets, the choice and interpretation of graphemes is the first step.

The goals of the Academy have always been to promote the use and preservation of Mayan languages, in a context that provides for linguistic self-determination of the speakers. Since its legalization at the end of 1991, the Academy has in part struggled with exactly what its mandate is or should be. Almost immediately the goal was expanded to include the promotion of Mayan culture as well as language, which has led inevitably to a certain confusion about where resources should be used and what kinds of projects should be undertaken by the Academy. During 1992 it was severely criticized for expending considerable effort in a reforestation project, which, while it could certainly be argued convincingly that it would have an impact on Mayan life, had a somewhat more tenuous connection to Mayan culture and an even more tenuous connection to Mayan languages. The fact that the Academy is the only state institution devoted to Mayan interests and directed by Mayas encourages its extension into all aspects of Mayan life; what some Mayas have called an overextension. One point of view holds that the Academy must first fulfill its mandate to promote Mayan languages, and then if it still has resources to devote to other projects, well and good. An opposing point of view holds that languages are situated in a cultural matrix, and that all aspects of culture need attention as part of the task of promoting language.

The internal structure of the Academy is interesting. In a deliberate effort to counteract the tendency of state institutions to become unwieldy bureaucracies with low productivity, the designers of the Academy of Mayan Languages chose to follow a populist model for its structure. Speakers of the twenty different Mayan languages[4] were organized into "language communities," each with an elected governing board. The presidents of the twenty language communities form the advisory board of the Academy, and each year they elect from among themselves an administrative board of seven members. In addition there are provisions for hiring staff in the various "departments" of the Academy, such as linguistics, education,

---

4 The Academy recognizes twenty-one languages, because it counts a dialect of K'ichee', called Achi, as a separate language, thereby respecting the separate political traditions of the Achi (Rab'inaleeb') community. One of the recognized languages, Akatek, refused to organize itself into a language community governed by the Academy, on the grounds that their language should not be separated from Q'anjob'al. Linguistically, Akatek and Q'anjob'al are either very closely related languages or very distantly related dialects of the same language, so the point is arguable. They are equally distant from Popti' (Jakaltek), which is always considered to be a separate language.

translation, and so on. This experiment in anti-bureaucratic organization has had mixed results so far. On the one hand, state institutions require a certain weighty bureaucratic apparatus, because of required legal and financial accountability to the state, so it appears to be impossible to avoid all of the bureaucratic pitfalls. In 1994 the Academy had already experienced a major labor dispute and by the end of the year had an almost complete turnover in its technical staff. On the other hand, the populist nature of the community organization and electoral process has resulted, so far, in a situation where the majority of the presidents and board members of the linguistic communities are unsophisticated about the technical aspects of language preservation and promotion. The president of the Academy in 1993, for instance, has been quoted as saying that he did not consider that the Academy's main goal involved linguistic work; it had other, more important things to do. What these community leaders are good at is rallying popular support, which also has its positive and negative sides. Such support will be absolutely necessary for language-preservation measures to reach the communities. However, there is some danger that the leadership will lose sight of the more technical goals of the Academy in pursuing their own political ends, or will compromise certain necessary technical decisions by conceding to popular, but uninformed, opinion.

In addition to conceptual and organizational problems which are still being worked out in the Academy, there is a very grave problem of lack of technically adequate personnel. This reflects, in part, the lack of a sufficient number of such individuals among the general population to fulfill the Academy's needs, but also reflects an unwillingness on the part of those people who are technically capable of doing the work to take an employment chance in a new institution which is not yet organized well and which cannot offer better or more secure employment than they already have elsewhere. Some of those individuals already work for the state in positions where they are unwilling to jeopardize their pensions, others work in situations where they know that they are respected and productive and are unsure about whether they can be equally productive in the Academy, and still others work at higher salaries than the Academy can pay. Reports of labor disputes and quarreling among members of the board have not helped attract new people to the technical positions. As a consequence, the Academy at the present is too woefully understaffed to accomplish most of its linguistic goals.

In spite of criticisms of the Academy on the part of many Mayan leaders, more or less as outlined here, it receives substantial support from those same leaders. Criticism thus far is meant to be constructive and arises from a very real commitment to the goals of the Academy and great enthusiasm for the real possibilities in self-governance and self-determination that the creation of the Academy has opened up. The Mayan leadership hopes to be able to slow language loss measurably, and believes that a language academy is critical to accomplish that.

In addition to the Academy of Mayan Languages, there are a number of other groups and institutions that contribute directly to language preservation. One set of institutions provides linguistic training to Mayas, thereby contributing to the creation of a necessary pool of individuals who will be responsible for the technical decision-making required by standardization. These include principally the Proyecto Lingüístico Francisco Marroquín (PLFM), Oxlajuuj Keej Maya' Ajtz'iib' (OKMA), the Universidad Rafael Landívar (URL), and the Universidad Mariano Gálvez (UMG). The PLFM taught basic descriptive linguistics and dictionary-making procedures to about eighty people between 1972 and 1977, and taught intensive descriptive linguistics and Mayan grammar to about forty more individuals in 1988 and 1989. OKMA is a linguistic research group formed by some of the people who were in the 1988 or 1989 classes at the PLFM, and has continued the intensive study of Mayan linguistics and the production of grammatical and scholarly materials about Mayan languages. Both of the universities have *licenciatura* programs in linguistics or sociolinguistics, in which the great majority of the students are Mayas and the aim is to study linguistics as applied to Mayan languages (see England 1995, for a fuller description of these programs).[5] Both universities publish small journals devoted to linguistics, and the URL has a very active linguistics institute which publishes books in and about Mayan languages, many of them designed for children or secondary-school students. In spite of these programs there is still a dearth of adequately trained linguists in Guatemala, but the situation is greatly improved by comparison with a few years ago.

5 I have been involved as a teacher and technical advisor in all of these programs. I was a linguist at the PLFM between 1971 and 1973, teaching linguistics to speakers of Mam, K'ichee' and Kaqchikel and coordinating the Mam group. I taught the intensive linguistic courses at the PLFM in 1988 and 1989, and have been the technical advisor to OKMA since its inception in 1990. I taught in the Mariano Gálvez in 1990 and in the Landívar in 1990, 1992, 1994 and 1997.

Most languages (but not all) have someone who has received some training in linguistics, and there are now several highly trained linguists.

In education, the National Program in Bilingual Education (PRONEBI, now DIGEBI) was established in 1985. Although often analyzed as an essentially assimilationist program (see Cojtí Cuxil 1991), PRONEBI has produced school materials in Mayan languages and has the potential to reach a very large number of Mayan schoolchildren. The existence of the program means at least that Mayan languages are used by more teachers and heard in school by more children than they were in the past. In an increasing number of communities private "Maya schools" have been established. These schools all have the goal of introducing as much specifically Mayan cultural and language material into the curriculum as feasible. Most of them describe themselves as bilingual, although the actual amount of the curriculum that is taught in a Mayan language is usually minimal. Nonetheless, the Maya schools usually take a positive attitude toward the use of Mayan languages and encourage them to the best of their ability, given the curricular, financial, and pedagogical constraints under which they operate. Finally, the previous administration appointed, for the first time in Guatemala's history, Mayas as the Minister and Vice Minister of Education. The Vice Minister, in particular, was very active in trying to reform the school system so that it takes more account of the educational needs of Mayan children. One of his contributions, for instance, was to establish the principle by which a school district that is primarily Mayan should have a Maya as Supervisor of Education.

There has been an increase in the production of materials in Mayan languages in the last few years. Several regional newspapers that have columns in a Mayan language have been established, the Academy of Mayan Languages for a while had a monthly series of articles in a Mayan language in one of the national newspapers, and several new radio programs in Mayan languages have been initiated. Calendars, appointment books, invitations, posters, and fliers in Mayan languages have been appearing with greater and greater frequency. The URL and PRONEBI have produced some children's literature and school materials in Mayan languages. While there are still almost no basic scholarly materials written in Mayan languages, the publication of grammars and other treatises about Mayan languages has grown, largely due to the efforts of Mayas who have become linguists.

5   Specific successes and problems for language maintenance

Returning to the five points that comprise a Mayan program for reinforcement of their languages, certain successes and problem areas can be identified.

5.1   *Mayan control of language decisions*

The establishment of the unified alphabet in 1987 was a resounding success, in terms of signaling that Mayas would henceforth be in charge of language decision-making. This was not done without some cost; in particular, the Summer Institute of Linguistics (SIL)/Wycliffe Bible Translators mounted an intensive campaign against the alphabet changes. Many evangelical Mayas were mobilized to oppose the new alphabet, and eventually a "human rights" complaint was filed against the Academy of Mayan Languages, to no effect. Although largely dissipated now, the effects of the SIL position are still felt in some language communities where conflict about minor and unimportant alphabet changes still occurs (see also Grinevald, this volume, for a discussion of the comparable situation in Brazil). A more serious deleterious effect was to convince many people that reading and writing in a Mayan language is essentially very difficult, so that any alphabet change would make it impossible. The fundamental issue at stake seemed to be precisely that of control.

Mayas are not yet in agreement about what control of language decisions means. There is considerable discussion, sometimes acrimonious, about who, exactly, should be in charge. The principal points of tension involve:

> The central Academy versus the individual language communities: do the language communities have independent decision-making power or not? If there is a disagreement about a decision between the experts in the central Academy and the members of the community, who prevails? If the level of expertise is greater in either the central Academy or the linguistic community, should that affect the weight of the decision-making power of one or the other?
>
> The central Academy versus other institutions with linguistic, language, or educational expertise: are other institutions required to wait for pressing practical decisions from the Academy? Are they required to abide by those decisions if they are in disagreement? Do other institutions need to be licensed in some way by the Academy? The Academy calls itself the "maximum director" of issues having to do with Mayan languages, what

does this imply regarding the role and independence of other institutions that also work in this field?

Technical expertise versus popular opinion: are language decisions technical or popular? If the decisions involve writing, do people who are unable to write in a Mayan language have a legitimate opinion? Who is able to represent popular opinion?

Descriptive linguistic versus sociolinguistic expertise: given that there are two different university degrees given in linguistics, one a degree in linguistics and the other a degree in sociolinguistics, which kind of degree is more valid for making decisions? Are there real differences in the preparation of people with these two different degrees? Who are the technical experts? Should specific positions be limited to one or the other kind of expertise?

Speakers versus non-speakers, including other Mayas who are not speakers of the language in question but can offer trained linguistic opinion: should linguists who are not speakers of the languages in question be excluded from any decisions about those languages? Does this include technical or board members of the central Academy? Should foreigners be excluded? Should either of these categories of non-speakers be listened to, even if not allowed to vote on decisions?

Part of the lack of agreement stems from the fact that Mayas are in a completely new situation. They have not had a similar opportunity in 500 years to establish language policy at a national level. As a consequence, there is considerable jockeying for political position within this new arena. With time, procedure and lines of authority will doubtless become clearer. If the eventual model for how to handle decisions is collaborative rather than dictatorial, then greater success in establishing a coherent language policy can be anticipated.

5.2   *Standardization of Mayan languages*

The Academy has done almost no work on standardization beyond the establishment of the alphabet. Because of the problems in agreement mentioned previously, the Academy has also been unable, so far, to reform its own alphabet where needed. Two other groups, however, have been making substantial contributions to standardization: the Kaqchikel Linguistic Community and OKMA. The Kaqchikel community publishes a short newsletter in which new vocabulary is introduced; it is involved in a project to create new (largely technical) vocabulary, and also in a two-year project with OKMA to write a complete reference grammar of Kaqchikel which will suggest standard forms beyond the level of writing. The members of OKMA, working in Kaqchikel, K'ichee', Tz'utujiil,

Poqomam, and Q'anjob'al, and with the recent addition of Mam, have written pedagogical grammars with some attention to standardization, and writers' manuals; they also are completing the reference grammar project. Standardization will eventually need much larger teams of investigators than OKMA, with only one or two people per language, can provide, but their work may provide a good model of how to proceed. PRONEBI has made a number of ad hoc standardization decisions which in many instances are inadequately thought through. In addition, because their materials are directed toward children and child-language use, standards from adult language are not always applied.

Standardization is the single most technical issue in language reinforcement. Unless it is accomplished, literary production and the expansion of literacy will always be problematic, because people need both good models and a certain amount of technical reference materials to be comfortable with literacy. The reference materials do not yet exist. These include, minimally, complete monolingual dictionaries and reference grammars for each language. Bilingual dictionaries, writers' guides, specialized vocabularies, and so on are also helpful. So far, one monolingual dictionary (K'ichee') and five reference grammars (K'ichee', Kaqchikel, Mam, Tz'utujiil, and Poqomam) are being written. They will not yet be totally standardized because not enough research about specific dialect differences has been done. Writing dictionaries and grammars is hard, and very few people have the technical expertise to embark on these projects. Furthermore, they require a long time to complete. The level of technical competence required frightens many people, including leaders in the Academy of Mayan Languages, so it often seems more feasible to do something else, something less demanding. If, however, sufficient Mayas are not provided with the necessary training and opportunities to make these materials and make rational decisions about standard forms of their languages, standardization and the expansion of literacy will not occur.

5.3   *Expansion of domains of use*

As mentioned, there are considerably more sources for published material in Mayan languages than previously, although the quantity is still not great and literary production has not by any means reached the level of the sixteenth century. Similarly, more Mayan is being heard in public events, beginning to reverse a trend toward exclusive use of Spanish publicly. Impressionistically, it seems that more Mayas are willing to speak in a

Mayan language in informal public settings, such as on the street or in the bus. Another rather interesting phenomenon is that Mayan leaders, whose families have often been the worst examples of language loss because of higher levels of education and similar social factors that promote language loss, have begun to reassess language use in their homes. Some have children who are too old to benefit greatly from this reassessment, but others, with younger children, have in some cases reversed the trend toward language loss in their own families. This is still an individual phenomenon and cannot be evaluated yet as a general tendency, but there may be significant positive effects for language retention if it can be seen that some of the children of major leaders, most of whom receive high levels of formal education and enjoy a relatively high economic status, are good speakers of a Mayan language as well as Spanish. Another factor that compounds the problem of language maintenance for many leaders is that there is a growing tendency for them to marry spouses from other language groups.

The extent to which the promotion of expanded domains of usage for Mayan languages is reaching ordinary community members is still unclear. Many Mayas are still more concerned about the acquisition of Spanish by their children than the maintenance of Mayan languages. It is still too early to know to what extent the position taken by Maya leadership has real impact in the communities, or to know to what extent community members share that position.

5.4   *Mayan languages in the schools*

The existence of PRONEBI and the Maya schools have ensured that Mayan languages are being used more in the schools than previously. In addition, there are several normal schools with specifically bilingual teacher certification, and there are several other normal schools that attempt to incorporate some material about Mayan languages or courses in a Mayan language into their curriculums. School materials in or about Mayan languages are still much too scarce, so all schools suffer from a lack of adequate materials to meet their needs. PRONEBI schools also have a significant problem promoting their programs to their teachers and parents. Many teachers are highly resistant to using the new materials that PRONEBI provides, often because they are then required to teach something that they have little or no competence in. Most teachers are unable to read and write in a Mayan language, even if they are Mayas. Parents are often unconvinced that Mayan language should be part of the curriculum; they send their children to school principally to acquire Spanish. Parents of children in Maya schools are typically not as skeptical about the benefits of Mayan language for their children, but then they are preselected for their interest in a specifically Mayan cultural content in the schools.

5.5   *The recognition of official regional languages*

For the first time, the idea of officializing Mayan languages at the regional level is being discussed among national political leaders, especially in the context of the Peace Accords signed by the government and the guerrilla leaders. Mayan leaders find the idea tremendously attractive, but also somewhat daunting. If Mayan languages were to be recognized in any official capacity, it would imply an even greater urgency to the problem of standardization, still in its initial stages. Official scribes, writers, interpreters, and translators would all be necessary, and there is almost no one, at present, who can fulfill these functions. If regionalization should occur in the near future, the entire process of adjustment to its role that the Academy is going through would inevitably be cut very short, because the demands on it for both clear decisions and concrete products would increase dramatically. If it were to prove incapable of meeting the legal demands of regionalization, then Mayan capacity for autonomy and leadership would be severely challenged.

6   Conclusions

Mayas have in place programs or models for meeting almost any requirement for language maintenance. They have a clearly articulated program devoted to the reinforcement of Mayan languages. There is an official state institution with some funding dedicated to the task of language promotion. There are individuals with the expertise for making the technical decisions required in standardization and language promotion. Several institutions are producing school materials. There are efforts toward increasing the production of literature. There is a heightened level of consciousness about language maintenance and loss among the leadership and possibly in the general population as well. Bilingual teachers are receiving some training in language. There are university programs for the preparation of linguists.

Problems can be divided into two major areas. First, resources are severely limited, so all of the institutions and groups that are currently working for language preservation are understaffed and much less productive than is needed. Serious linguistic research is only taking place in one quarter of the languages, school materials are limited or unavailable, the technical staff in the Academy is miniscule, very few teachers ever receive in-service training in literacy, and so on. With the approval and funding of the Academy, the Guatemalan government supported Mayan languages for the first time, but the resources are still much too limited to accomplish much. This problem is being partially alleviated by the willingness of European governments and the European Economic Community to invest in programs that promote indigenous cultural reinforcement.

Second, the complexity of embarking on a totally new effort in a large and diverse society is overwhelming. Mayas are not in agreement about exactly how to proceed in the formal tasks necessary for language promotion. The process of working out procedures can be very healthy and positive, but there are also risks involved. The risks that seem most salient at the moment are the risk of losing sight of the goals of language preservation in political bickering, and the risk of losing credibility through an inability to produce, especially on the part of the Academy of Mayan Languages. The problems of complexity must be solved by Mayas themselves. There is ample talent among Mayas to meet all of the challenges they face, but it has been repressed so brutally for so long that it requires time to be brought forth.

5 A chronology of Mohawk language instruction at Kahnawà:ke

KAIA'TITAHKHE ANNETTE JACOBS
Karonhianónhnha Ionterihwaienstáhkhwa, Quebec

The following is a chronology of developments since the inception of the Kanien'kéha (Mohawk) language instruction program into our school system in Kahnawà:ke, Quebec, the mistakes we made, and also the status of the program today.

1 The development of the Kanien'kéha program

Prior to 1970, the only thing native in our schools was the children. There were no native teachers, no native content, no relevant history, no stories, no songs, no pictures, and least of all, there was no Mohawk language. This had a very negative impact on our self-identity and our self-image, so one of the goals of our program today is to reverse this by immersing children not only in Mohawk language, but also by surrounding them with native teachers, content, history, culture, pictures, and stories.

In September, 1970, due to the efforts of a small group of parents and a sympathetic non-native principal, the Mohawk language was introduced into our schools for fifteen minutes every day for every grade. Three courageous people from the community were asked to take on this challenge and teach. They applied for and received a small grant from the Federal Department of Cultural Affairs to cover a small salary. These people had no training and no materials, but what they did have was the conviction that this was something that had to be done. They also planted a seed: the daily instruction increased from fifteen minutes a day to a half hour over the next several years.

1972 was a milestone year. At this time the University of Quebec began offering a teacher-training program, initiated by our Combined Schools Committee and funded by the Quebec office of the Federal Department of Indian Affairs. Five people from the community enrolled to receive what was originally designed as a specialized teaching certificate. This eventually changed to offer those who wished to continue their education the possibility of working toward a bachelor of education degree. The program also expanded to include not only those people who wished to specialize in Native-language teaching, but also those who wished to train for regular English language classroom teaching.

Pedagogical materials for our school were initially developed by the teachers themselves. In the summer of 1972 linguistic students worked with people from Kahnawà:ke and produced a grammar workbook entitled "She:kon Wa:ri" as a summer project. In 1973 a standard orthography for the Mohawk language was established for use in the schools by the five student teachers as part of a course taught by Marianne Mithun. The writing system that was used prior to this was based on a method of writing established by Jesuit priests in the 1700s. There were few conventions in place for those using the Jesuit system. If there were four teachers in a classroom, there would be four different ways of writing the same word. Such confusion made it clear that the standard orthography developed by Mithun and the student teachers was needed.

Another important step in the evolution of the Kahnawà:ke school system came in 1976. A survey was conducted by the National Museum of Man in Ottawa, Canada, that showed the Mohawk language was endangered.[1] I know from personal experience that the Mohawk language was very much taken for granted in my community. The general perception was that the language was still being learned and used widely, so the results of the survey came as a surprise. For this reason, the survey motivated people who were interested in the preservation of the Mohawk language. As a result, in the following year our own college and university students on a summer project developed a collection of Mohawk materials: primers, charts, games, legends, and a calendar, all under the direction of one of the teachers, who is named Karihwénhawe Dorothy Lagare.

However, it became increasingly evident that our goal of teaching our children to communicate in Mohawk would not be achieved with the program that was in place. Accordingly, in September, 1979, a pilot project using a total-immersion nursery was initiated. This was a half-day program sponsored by our own Kanien'kéhàka Raotitióhkwa Cultural Center. Thirty

---

1 Some of the results of this survey, as well as a great deal of other information regarding the indigenous languages of Canada can be found in *The national atlas of Canada* (1980).

students applied. The following year the students who had completed the total-immersion nursery continued on to a total-immersion kindergarten. This was also a half-day program. The next year fifteen of the thirty students went on to a partial-immersion grade 1. Teaching materials for the partial-immersion first grade and subsequently for the other grades were prepared by parent volunteers, and supervised and coordinated by the teacher. These students continued in a partial-immersion setting until grade 4.[2]

Further, we received a grant for curriculum development from the Federal secretary of state and hired a curriculum coordinator from the community. Many textbooks and other materials were produced during this period although, unfortunately, many were directly translated from English textbooks and workbooks; consequently, they were not very useful in the immersion study. In 1983 a permanent Kanien'kéha language curriculum office was established as part of our education center. Some funding was received through a "NEED" program. This was a Canada Man-Power make-work project which enabled us to hire a staff. Later, in 1991 the Kanien'kéha Owén:na Curriculum Center, with its permanent staff of seven people, was moved permanently to Karonhianónhnha Ionterihwaienstáhkhwa. This staff of seven consisted of a coordinator, two writers/translators, one artist, one editor, and two production people. The two writers/translators were retired teachers who we also considered to be our resident elders.

In September, 1984, we came to another milestone. Total-immersion Kanien'kéha was established at three levels: nursery, kindergarten, and grade 1. Over time, the immersion was extended through grade 3, and partial immersion through grades 4, 5, and 6. In the latter grades, the students receive their first formal English instruction for 50 percent of their day. At this point they also start studying French. By June of 1989, the first graduates of the Mohawk total-immersion program completed grade 6.

Other initiatives were also undertaken during this time period. For instance, Kanien'kéha language immersion summer camp was initiated

---

2 At McGill University, Doctors Lambert and Genesee conducted a study on the effectivenss of our partial-immersion program. The study showed that English learning was not harmed by Mohawk immersion. (These findings are more than supported by my own observations.) However, the Mohawk skills were far from satisfactory. The children acquired some comprehension, but very little fluency.

and sponsored by our own Kanien'kéhaka Raotitióhkwa Cultural Center. Beginning in September, 1994, we extensively reorganized our schools. In order to maximize our resources, the kindergarten and fourth grade were increased to full-day language-immersion programs, while we decreased the fifth and sixth grade partial programs to maintenance-level programs. Part of the motivation for the overhaul was that we no longer had a staff of seven in our curriculum department. Crucially, one of our writers passed away. Although the loss of this staff member meant added strain on the curriculum department, it also served to reaffirm our commitment to Mohawk-language training. When a person with such knowledge of the culture and language passes away, it leads you to understand what you're going to lose if you lose your language.[3]

2   **Pedagogical materials**

Throughout the development of the language program at Kahnawà: ke, one of the biggest challenges we faced was the lack of any kind of pedagogical materials in Mohawk.[4] Therefore, I would like to explain a little about how we generate curricular tools in our immersion school. Developing these materials has required the time and effort of professional educators as well as community members. As mentioned above, the initial work began in the early 1970s with the codification of Mohawk based on Marianne Mithun's work and advice, and the writing of a linguistically sound grammar workbook that has become a reliable teacher resource (Deering and Delisle 1976). Since that time, both the curriculum and the teaching materials have steadily been developed. For example, in 1986 another teacher and I were released from classroom duties to develop social studies, science, and language arts objectives in Mohawk. Also, a collaborative effort began in 1992 with our sister community, Kanehsata:ke, to write and publish books. To date we have published five books as the result of this joint venture. In addition, a math program, *Exploring mathematics*

3 On a happier note we have three young student teachers in our schools who are studying to become full-time teachers who are fluent and one who is studying to become fluent.

4 This is a general problem for many endangered languages. In this volume, Dauenhauer and Dauenhauer discuss the problems and potential solutions for developing materials for Southeast Alaskan languages, and England summarizes the approaches put forth by the Maya of Guatemala.

(1991) published by Gage, is currently being translated into Mohawk. (Here I use the term "translation" very loosely because the person who does the work transposes the ideas rather than strictly translating.)

We have used every available resource to create relevant materials for the students. We have looked at guidelines, textbooks, and workbooks. We have consulted with professional people. We have consulted with teachers and with community people, especially elders. After these efforts, we adapt what is adaptable, borrow what we can, and we create the rest. An excellent example of how we adapt is the use of the Quebec Education Curriculum Guide, especially in the area of social studies. This guide lent itself very well to our needs and situation because of its focus on the community and its people. It is divided into three components of study: time, space, and social realities. We kept what was usable, deleted what we thought was irrelevant, and added what we thought was important such as our own stories, traditions, legends, dances, and songs.

The burden of providing proper educational materials belongs to the curriculum center. With input from the teachers, the members of the center produce everything needed for instruction, from the less tangible necessities such as pedagogical objectives and strategies, games and songs, to the more tangible checklists, charts, posters, flashcards, maps, text-books, workbooks, videos, slide presentations, and film strips. Often, they are called upon to create materials using our own legends and stories. For example, one of our writers has written a series of humorous stories on a mischievous mythical creature *skakotinenióia'ks*.

3   Conclusion

There are two schools in our community. One is an English-speaking school, and one is the Mohawk immersion school. Parents choose which of the two schools to send their children to. Approximately 50 percent opt for the Mohawk immersion and 50 percent for the English school. We see a significant difference between children in the immersion program and those not enrolled in it with regard to the way they live their lives and relate to their families. After all, there is something about being reprimanded in Mohawk that seems to be a little bit stronger than in English! Though I'm being facetious, there is an intangible but powerful difference between using Mohawk and using English in teaching our children.

Thanks to the Mohawk language immersion program the children learn many of the positive facets of Mohawk culture beyond the sounds and phrases of the Mohawk language. Emphasis is also placed on traditional spirituality and respect for teachers and elders. The children can identify with Mohawk role models. Along with completing all that is required academically, the children have a feeling of pride of knowing their own language, the feeling of security of knowing their heritage and culture, and the confidence of a strong identity. It has taken us twenty-five years to arrive at where we are now. It has been a struggle, but tremendously satisfying. We still have to contend with getting the community more involved, so we are far from being able to sit back on our laurels.

Our school is founded on the belief that our children have the right and responsibility to learn through a culturally based education that promotes understanding and pride in being Kanien'kéhà:ka. The success of the program depends greatly on the support and participation of parents, grandparents, extended family, community leaders, and the whole community. Parents who enroll their children in our school, Karonhianónhnha Ionterihwaienstáhkhwa, are required to sign an agreement to participate actively in the program and in the activities of the school. They commit to reinforce the language at home by speaking with the children, to call the children by their Kanien'kéha name at all times, to make a sincere long-term commitment to the program, to enroll in Kanien'kéha evening language courses, and to make sure their children attend school every school day to increase and to retain the Kanien'kéha that is taught.

Perhaps the most fitting conclusion to this outline of the Mohawk immersion program at Kahnawà:ke is to summarize our objectives as they appear in the literature the parents receive:

Goals of Kahnawà:ke Education
(from the school calendar, distributed to parents)
- To develop an understanding of self through the learning of Kanien'kéha language and the culture of Kanien'kéhà:ka.
- To develop respect and appreciation for the gifts of the Creator and to acknowledge thankfulness through the Ohén:ton Karihwatéhkwen ["thanksgiving address"].
- To develop values of respect, trust, sharing, peace, brotherhood, harmony and justice.
- To learn, appreciate and use the French language as a necessary means of communication with people of neighboring communities.

- To develop a mastery of mathematic skills to solve problems to deal with daily situations.
- To understand and appreciate the achievements of all peoples in the natural sciences, the social sciences, and the arts.
- To develop and promote creativity through a variety of activities and experiences.
- To develop a cooperative attitude toward learning, working and living in a group and in a community.
- To develop an ability to examine and evaluate constructively the opinions and situations of other peoples.
- To nurture independent and responsible behavior.
- To promote self-sufficiency and self-determination through academic, recreational and vocational orientation and training.

6 Language endangerment in South America: a programmatic approach

COLETTE GRINEVALD
Université Lumière-Lyon

1 Introduction

I will approach the task of talking of language endangerment in the context of South America from two angles. The first one is a geographic and linguistic approach that aims at providing an overview of the situation of the indigenous languages of the region, without encyclopedic ambition but with an eye toward the big picture for those unfamiliar with the specifics of that continent. The second one is a strategic approach that aims at sketching a possible agenda for the linguistic profession in the face of the endangerment situation of South American indigenous languages, taking into account some of the sociopolitical and academic developments of the region in recent times.

2 The indigenous languages of South America

By South America, I mean the continental part of Latin America south of Panama.[1] For the purpose of this overview I have collated information from some of the most reliable sources on the region, which I have amplified with notes from my recent personal exploration of the situation in countries such as Colombia, Brazil, Ecuador, and Bolivia, and with generous comments from South American specialists.[2]

This chapter has benefited greatly from generous comments by South American language specialists gathered at the International Conference on "The indigenous languages of Amazonia in science and society" (March, 1996) in Belem, Brazil. I would like to thank in particular Aryon Rodrigues, Wilem Adelaar, Luis Enrique Lopez, Mauricio Gnerre, and Francisco Queixalos for their careful reading of the manuscript and generous comments and corrections. All remaining inaccuracies and errors of judgment are mine to be accountable for.

1 Although the Caribbean islands are usually included in South America, they will not be considered here since all their Arawakan and Cariban languages are now extinct. The chapter will not consider either the Creoles and immigrant languages of South America.

2 My experience includes personal contact with the Centro Colombiano de Lenguas Aborígenes of Bogotá, Colombia, the Museu Goeldi of Belem, Brazil, the Vernacular Language Program of the Museum of Anthropology of the Central Bank of

Adelaar (1991) is the most comprehensive work on the situation of endangerment of the South American indigenous languages. It provides a thorough countrywide treatment based on sources available up to 1988. For the most updated work on the classification, location, and population estimates of the South American languages, the best reference is T. Kaufman (1990, 1994). There are also collections such as Pottier (1983), and Klein and Stark (1985); as well as recent surveys such as Moore (1990), Moore and Storto (1994) and Rodrigues (1986) for Brazil; Cole, Hermon and Martin (1994) for the Andes; and Albó (1995) for Bolivia.

2.1   *Some basic facts and figures*

By basic facts and figures, I mean the number of indigenous languages still spoken today and their genetic affiliation, as well as the regional linguistic situations in which they are found. The presentation is admittedly biased toward a national-boundary approach, in part because that is how most of the available information is presented. In addition, it would eventually be the approach one would have to take if one were to consider doing fieldwork on any of these languages. From a strictly linguistic point of view, it would be preferable to ignore political boundaries since a significant number of languages are spread across borders. This is true both of the major indigenous languages of South America (Quechua across five countries, Aymara three, Guarani three, and Mapuche two), and of the smaller Amazonian languages whose surviving speakers tend to be found in the border areas of the nine countries of the Amazon basin.[3]

2.2   *Number of languages involved*

As expected, no exact figures are available on the number of indigenous languages in South America; much work remains to be done in some regions to assess accurately the existence and status of some of the reported languages. All figures given below are necessarily approximative,

Ecuador in Guayaquil, and being hired recently as a consultant for the Educational Reform of Bolivia to prepare documentation on the Amazonian languages of the country. I have also been working in recent years at the University of Oregon with Latin American students from Argentina (Pilaga), Peru (Shipibo), Ecuador (Quechua and Ecuadorian Spanish), and Brazil (Nheengatu and Apurina).

3 See Grenand and Grenand 1993:95 for a map of the largest zones of indigenous settlements today in Amazonia. The issue of border languages was one of the most debated during the recent Belem conference on Amazonian languages which gathered representatives of all nine countries involved.

Table 6.1 Number of South American languages by country

Countries	Number per country
Brazil	170
Colombia, Peru	60
Bolivia, Venezuela	35
Ecuador, Argentina, Paraguay and Guyana	12
Chile, French Guyana, Surinam	6
Uruguay	0

although it is easy to state with relative certainty an order of magnitude. In terms of the number of languages identified and recognized today by each one of the South American countries, the situations vary from the one of Brazil, which has by far the highest number of indigenous languages (170), to that of Chile which has many fewer (6), to the extreme of Uruguay with none today. Table 6.1 offers an overview of distribution of indigenous languages by country.[4]

The number of languages is not related to the proportion of Indian population per country. There the situations vary from countries with high proportions (Indians constitute the majority of the population in the Central Andean countries) to countries where geographically and politically very marginalized Indian populations represent a small percentage of the total population, such as Argentina. The situation of languages spread across borders also means that the same linguistic group can be a large minority in one country and a much smaller one in another, as is the case of Aymara, for instance, which numbers between 2 and 2.5 million speakers between Peru and Bolivia but only 30,000 in Chile.

To put it in world context, the total number of South American indigenous languages is in the range of over 400 languages. This is not very

4 This is meant to give a range of number of languages spoken in each country for comparative purposes. Assessing the exact number of languages is no easier for South America than for any other part of the world, with the issue of what is considered a language versus a dialect (e.g. Quechua is usually treated as one language, although linguistically it is a complex of several languages) and the lack of documentation of some of the languages (especially the heart of Amazonia which is still in places a linguistic black box).

high for a whole continent when compared to some other parts of the world, such as India, or the Australia–Indonesia–Oceania complex, but larger than the rest of the Americas combined.[5]

2.3   *Genetic variety*

There are two interesting facts about the genetic relations of South American languages: their extreme genetic variety and the high number of isolates. As pointed out by Adelaar (1991:45), South America represents "a situation of unsurpassed genetic variety," only comparable to the linguistic variety of New Guinea.[6] T. Kaufman (1990, 1994) recognizes 118 families. Linguistic diversity in South America correlates partly to the ruggedness of the terrain; for instance, the 13 minority languages of western Paraguay belong to 5 different families, and the 30 languages of the Amazonian region of Bolivia belong to 15 different families (including 6 isolates).[7]

---

5 Consider the official count of 1,683 "mother tongues" in India of which 850 are in daily use (figures given by Matisoff 1991:205); the numbers of languages given by Dixon (1991:229) are 250 for Australia, 550 for Indonesia, 160 for the Philippines, 760 for Papua New Guinea, and 260 for the Pacific Islands. The figures for the Americas are 95 languages for Mexico and Central America (Garza Cuaròn and Lastra 1991:120), a high figure of 213 for the United States, Alaska, and Canada (from Chafe 1962), which included then 51 languages with 1–10 speakers which are probably extinct by now (Zepeda and Hill 1991:136).

6 Kaufman's 118 families do not exactly correspond to Louktaka's 117 (Adelaar 1991:46). For a critique of Greenberg's (1987) claim that all South American languages are ultimately related, see Campbell (1988).

Kaufman (1994) introduces new terminology for linguistic units that may become a guideline for future handling of the languages and language families of South America. "The terms used to name groups of communities speaking genetically related forms of speech are ranked in decreasing order of inclusiveness: phylum (or superstock), stock, family, branch (or division), group, sub-group, language complex, language areas, language, virtual language, emergent language,

dialect area (or division), or group, dialect, variety." Language complex "refers to a geographically continuous zone that contains linguistic diversity greater than found within a single language (between 1,000 and 1,500 years) but where internal linguistic boundaries similar to those that separate clearly discrete languages are lacking ([e.g.] Gallo-Romance: Catalan, Provençal, Franco-Provençal, French . . .). The divisions of a language complex are 'virtual languages'. Language area refers to a situation where there is a good amount of internal diversity (600–900 years), clear-cut linguistic division or boundaries, but a good deal of mutual intelligibility within the whole area. The components of a language area are 'emergent languages'." In addition, one of the challenges of accounting for the languages of Latin America is "that speakers of different dialects of what is obviously the same language (to a linguist) often consider themselves to be ethnically distinct" (1994:31).

7 South America is, with Papua New Guinea, the poorest documented part of the world, and has not seen yet the kind of "fairly systematic efforts [that] were launched in Papua New Guinea in the early 1960s" (Kaufman 1994:46). This is not to say that recent efforts have not been set in motion in South America, as discussed in section 5.

Behind the fact of this extreme genetic variety lies another interesting fact: a very large number of the languages in South America (70 of the 118 language families) are considered isolates, genetic units of one language. The highest concentration of such languages is found in northeastern Brazil, where the 10 languages of the region are all listed by Kaufman as isolates (1994:51). The question remains open, of course, as to whether some of those languages have remained unclassified for lack of data and might not come to fall into some classification as better documentation becomes available.[8]

2.4   Large and small minority languages

As a general rule, the indigenous languages of South America are being dominated and pushed out of existence by the official Indo-European languages which were the languages of the conquest and colonization of the continent: Spanish, Portuguese, French, English, and Dutch. It is striking, however, that there is a handful of indigenous languages with large speaker populations, by far the largest of the Americas: Quechua, Aymara, Guarani, and Mapudungu.

QUECHUA has more speakers than any indigenous language of the Americas. Estimates of Quechua speakers vary, from a high of 12 million (Kaufman 1994:64) to 8–8.5 million (Parker 1969; Cerrón-Palomino 1987; Adelaar 1991), the major populations being distributed as follows:

Ecuador	2 m
Peru	4.5 m
Bolivia	1.5 m

Large numbers of previously unknown languages have been discovered in this century. Kaufman mentions about 50 new groups having been contacted since last century, with their language identified (1994:51). Moore and Storto (1994:1) cite the examples of a new Tupi-Guarani language discovered in 1987 and a language called Kujubim being discovered in 1991 by researchers of the Museu Goeldi of Belem. Grenand and Grenand (1993:109–114) list 52 groups of Amazonia that have not had contacts yet with outsiders, 10 of which are of unknown linguistic affiliations, although most of which are likely to speak yet undescribed variants of languages that have been at least identified.

New linguistic families have been identified as well, as shown in the changes in the figures given by Loukotka: 77 families in the 1934 publication, but 117 in the 1968 one.

8 The extreme linguistic diversity of South American indigenous languages, especially those of the Amazonian region at the foot of the Andes, was the theme of Adelaar's plenary session of the Belem conference already mentioned. He compared it to the linguistic situation in California and the northwest of the United States, and speculated on the possible scenarios that would account for such diversity, such as a very early settlement in the region, by very slow migrations.

Notably, Quechua was the lingua franca of the Inka colonization, and later continued expanding as the lingua franca of Christianization in colonial times.[9] The spread of the Quechua language has led to the disappearance of all but very few of the original languages of the Andean region.

Quechua is actually a cover term for a number of languages. Kaufman claims, in purely linguistic terms, that Quechua represents 17 different constituent "emergent" languages (languages with 3–5 centuries of diversification). In terms of internal diversification, then, the Quechuan linguistic unit is comparable to the language complex of Romance languages.[10]

A measure of the importance of Quechua is that it is the South American indigenous language most frequently taught as a second language in the various contexts of universities, religious missions, and development programs.[11] More for its symbolic value maybe than its real impact, it is also worth mentioning the creation of an Academy of the Quechua Language in Peru in 1953, whose proclaimed activities include teaching Quechua to non-Quechua speakers, publishing books and journals in Quechua and sponsoring annual competitions of literary works (Hornberger 1989:76). In its efforts at emulating its model, the Royal Academy of the Spanish language, the Quechua academy is of a rather different nature from that of the recently created Academy of Mayan languages of Guatemala, or the Basque Academy of Spain and may not be set up in a way which will have significant impact on the future maintenance of the language.

Also representative of the importance of Quechua is that the language was declared one of the official languages of Peru, the country with most

9 See Mannheim 1985a, for instance for a discussion of those two stages of language spread of Quechua.

10 The established tradition of Quechuan linguistics recognizes two branches: Quechua I (also called Quechua B) which includes the languages of Central Peru, and Quechua II (or Quechua A) which includes the dialects of Cuzco (the general Inka language) in southern Peru, the varieties of Quechua in Bolivia, Chile, and Argentina, as well as the varieties spoken much to the north, in Ecuador. The language is called Quichua for the varieties spoken in Ecuador, Argentina and parts of Peru. The naming of Quechua I and II is from Torero 1964, and that of Quechua A and B from Parker 1963 (in Stark 1985:444).

11 It is taught in regular courses at the Instituto Pastoral Andina in Sicuani (Cuzco, Peru), at the language institute of the Maryknoll order in Cochabamba (Bolivia), in several universities of Peru and Bolivia (e.g. in majors such as nursing, medicine, agronomy, veterinary studies), as well as at various US universities (e.g. Cornell, Illinois at Urbana-Champaign, Minnesota) and European universities (e.g. Bonn, Hamburg, Berlin, Liverpool, Saint Andrews, London). Teaching materials include a computerized course at Cornell and multimedia in CD-ROM at Liverpool (Luis Enrique Lopez p.c.).

speakers, in 1975.[12] When officialization occurred, the policy was not to give preference to one of the many dialects in existence, but to recognize at least six of the principal dialectal variations and to give them equal status. However, only one official alphabet of Quechua was established, one with which all of the six dialects could be written (Adelaar 1991:77; Lopez p.c.).

Finally, in recent decades Quechua has been the object of major bilingual education experiments, some of which turned into regular school programs in three of the Andean countries in which it is spoken.[13] Language planning involving Quechua has included efforts at standardizing the language in all three countries where it is spoken.

AYMARA has 2 million speakers, the majority of whom live in Bolivia. Its homeland is the Collao altiplano, around Lake Titicaca which extends into the three countries of Bolivia, Peru, and Chile. There are 350,000 speakers in Peru and 25,000 in Chile (Briggs 1985:546). Aymara also functioned and still functions as a lingua franca and has been the object of standardization and bilingual education programs, as well as of teacher-training university programs in both Bolivia and Chile.

The claim has been that, unlike Quechua, Aymara exhibits relative regularity and little diversification which does not impede mutual intelligibility, as described in Briggs (1985, 1993 [based on her 1976 Ph.D. dissertation]). One factor in the modern homogeneity of the language may be attributed to the impact of the radio programs in that language (on the air since the 1950s on Radio San Gabriel de la Paz) that reach out to speakers of a very large area. However, more recent studies of more divergent dialects are pointing to more language diversity than originally claimed (Lopez p.c.).

MAPUDUNGU is the name of the language of the Mapuche people (Araucanians) and is often cited in the literature under the names of

12 Discussions of the officialization of Quechua in the other countries have included concerns about declaring the language official before enough language planning had been done and before there existed some infrastructure to implement the functioning of the language as official. Efforts have been aimed at groundwork to prepare for the officialization (Haboud p.c.).

13 In Peru it started with the Ayacucho bilingual education experiment in the 1960s, followed in the 1970s by the Puno and Cuzco experiments, leading in the 1980s to a department-wide implementation in rural Quechua-speaking communities of southern Peru (Hornberger 1989). Ecuador was the site of the pilot program for Latin America and the Caribbean started in 1982 (Haboud 1995). Other bilingual education projects (Proyecto Educativo Rural I, II) took place in Bolivia in the 1970s. See Amadio and Lopez 1993 for a comprehensive bibliography of Bilingual Intercultural Education in Latin America.

Araucanian or Mapuche (*mapuche* means "earth people" and *mapudungu* "earth language"). The language is spoken principally in Chile where it may have between 200 and 500,000 speakers distributed across some 2,000 small reservations. Mapudungu may have up to a million speakers, including 300,000 in Santiago de Chile alone, according to Chilean sources (Lopez p.c.). The whole ethnic group is presently very politically mobilized, fighting for its land rights and the maintenance and development of its language. There are also Mapudungu speakers in the southwest of Argentina who have emigrated from Chile in recent times. Mapudungu is said to have great linguistic uniformity (Croese 1985:786), although Huilliche in the south is said to exhibit more variation (Adelaar p.c.).

GUARANI represents a unique case in the whole of the Americas in that the majority of its 3 million speakers, who live in the country of Paraguay, are *mestizo* (Spanish-speaking) rather than indigenous people. There are at least five Guarani languages which are spoken in Paraguay, Bolivia, Argentina, and Brazil.

Paraguayan Guarani, which had long been recognized as a national language (i.e. the language of the majority of the population of the nation) was recognized as an official language of that country in 1992. The new Paraguayan Constitution of 1994 confirms its official status and endorses new educational legislation which includes bilingual education (Guarani–Spanish) for the Spanish-speaking population. This standardized Paraguayan Guarani of an urban and non-indigenous population bears the mark of being the language of bilinguals. It exhibits heavy relexification (Rubin 1985:428 calculates 28–54 percent of Spanish loanwords in its vocabulary) and is also said to have been expurgated of religious and cultural vocabulary that still remains in the indigenous vernaculars (Adelaar 1991:74). This Paraguayan type of Guarani is also spoken in northeastern Argentina.

The other Guarani languages consist of the varieties spoken as native languages by largely rural indigenous populations in the eastern parts of Paraguay, the southwest of Brazil and the southeastern part of Bolivia.[14] In Bolivia, where Guarani is spoken by about 50,000 people,

---

14 Rodrigues (p.c.) identifies at least the following four Guarani languages: (a) Mbyá in SE Paraguay, NE Argentina and S Brazil; (b) Nhandeva in Brazil, or Chiripá in E Paraguay and S Brazil; (c) Kayvá in Brazil, or Pau in E Paraguay and SW Brazil; (d) Bolivian Guarani, with its dialects: Chiriguano, Izoceño and Tapieté (also spoken in NE Paraguay and N Argentina).

community-based efforts have been under way in the last decade to stand-
ardize the local variety and to have it officially recognized (Gustafson 1995;
Lopez 1997).

The existence in South America of large minority languages such as
Quechua, Aymara, Mapudungu, and Guarani is to be put in contrast with
the fact that the largest indigenous language of the United States–Canada–
Alaska combined is Navajo, with 140,000 speakers (Broadwell 1995).
Only one other language of the Americas has beyond a million speakers:
Nahuatl of Mexico, with 1.4 million. Two other Amerindian languages rise
above the 500,000 speaker mark; both Mayan languages, Yucatec (Mexico)
and Quiche (Guatemala).

Rather more like other indigenous American languages are the
abundant small minority languages, most of which are spoken by populations in the thousands or hundreds. Consider for example the language situation of Brazil (Rodrigues 1985b; Moore 1990; Moore and Storto 1994).
On one hand the whole country has only around 150,000 speakers of
indigenous languages, which is a very small number for the vast expanse
of territory, but on the other hand it has 170 languages, a relatively high
language density. (Grenoble and Whaley, this volume, discuss the impact
of language density on language endangerment.) Although this means on
average a thousand speakers per language, the reality is a range from 18,000
for Tikuna to those with almost no speakers left.[15]

Although this presentation opposes large and small indigenous
languages, the issues involved in the maintenance and development of
both types of languages to be considered later may well be only a matter

---

15 Consider for instance the Carib family where one language has 15,000 speakers (Makushi), and the
others have the following populations of speakers:

Waiwai	922	Kalapalo	191
Ingarikó	459	Apalaí	135
Bakarií	409	Wayana	125
Atroarí	350	Txikáo	107
Hixkaryana	308	Nahukwá	83
Warikyana	300	Arara do Pará	72
Tirió	264	Matipú	40
Kuikuru	221	Amapá	37
Taulipáng	220	Waimirí	no data
Mayongóng	200		(Adelaar 1991:60)
Kaxuyana	198		

of different magnitude and urgency. All indigenous languages of South America must be considered when assessing levels of vitality and endangerment, since the large number of speakers of some of them today is in fact no guarantee that they are not becoming endangered.

3   Types of situations: regional patterns

Depending on the proportion of the Indian population, and the number and type of indigenous languages, the following patterns of linguistic situations can be found in South America.

Colombia and Venezuela have small indigenous populations, although a significant number of languages, and, in contrast to the southern Andean countries, no indigenous language larger than Paez in the south, with 60 to 80,000 speakers. Colombia is characterized by its great variety of indigenous habitats and indigenous languages. Indigenous populations are found in the north and south of the Andean highlands, the two coastal regions (Caribbean and Pacific), the *llano* (the lowland that is not Amazonian) and the Amazonian region. The country has an interesting situation of multilingualism (documented by Sorensen 1985) due to a high degree of mixing and intermarriage among the eastern Tukano and Arawak people of the Vaupes region shared by south Colombia and northwest Brazil.

Venezuela's indigenous languages are found in the eastern and western edges of the country. The majority of the languages of the Amazonian part of the country spill across the borders of Brazil and Colombia.[16]

The three Andean countries of Ecuador, Peru, and Bolivia, constitute the region of the continent with the highest concentration and highest proportion of Indian population. That population is unevenly distributed between large highland Quechua–Aymara populations and small but very varied Amazonian lowland populations. The whole region is characterized by two factors. One is the phenomenon of the spread of Quechua over a vast geographic expanse, causing over time the loss of many local

16 Grenand and Grenand (1993:96–98) give 19 languages for the Amazonian region of Venezuela, of which 4 are shared with Colombia (Sikuani/ Guajibo, Piapoko, Piaroa, and Puinave), 6 are shared at least with Brazil (Akawayo, Bariwa, Bare, Karib, Pemon, and Yanomami), and one with both (Kuripako).

languages. The other is the intensive language planning for Quechua and Aymara, the two major languages of the area, that has taken place in the last two decades (reviewed in Moya 1987; Chiodi 1990; and Amadio and Lopez 1993).

In Ecuador the majority of the Quichua population lives in the highlands which are also the area where major Spanish-speaking urban centers are found, including the capital, Quito. Pre-Inkaic languages have survived only in the lowlands of the country, on the coast to the west, and in the Amazon region to the east where Quichua is still spreading. Noteworthy is the high level of organization of the Shuars in that region.

Peru has the largest Quechua-speaking population of the three countries, with 4 million, and a well-documented history of language policy and language planning dealing with this language (Cerrón-Palomino 1989; and Mannheim 1984, 1985b). The population pattern of Peru is unlike that of Ecuador in that the Quechua population was traditionally concentrated in the southern highlands while the *mestizo* population is concentrated in the coastal lowland.[17] Peru also has the largest indigenous population in the lowlands of South America, with an estimated 300,000 indigenous people from about 45 ethnic groups in the Amazonian region.

Bolivia has two of the largest indigenous languages of the Americas living side by side – Quechua and Aymara, for which it is now the main homeland. A characteristic of the Quechua of southern Bolivia up until the 1952 revolution was its being spoken by many strata of the society, including *mestizo* families in contact with their Quechua-speaking workers (Stark 1985:533–540). But unlike the situation of Guarani in Paraguay, the *mestizo* population is no longer learning the language today. Bolivia also has some of the very few surviving pre-Inkaic indigenous languages of the Andean highlands. One is the Chipaya-Uru complex, of which Uru had been reported extinct although a language revitalization project is presently underway by the community.[18] The other, Machaj Juyai, is a language

17 There is no coastal indigenous population left. The last died by the middle of this century (Adelaar 1991:77). But the effect of the violence of the Shining Path has been massive migration of highland Quechua people towards Lima, which is said to have at least 500,000 Quechua speakers today (Lopez p.c.).

18 The Chipaya-Uru people have actually shifted to the Aymara language for primary language, not Quechua. The Chipaya language is better preserved than the Uru one, which has only two native and fluent speakers left (a brother–sister team, 85 and 87 years old). The Uru community calls its ethnic language Uchhumataqu.

of an interesting sociologuistic and linguistic nature. It is the professional secret language of Callahuaya herb doctors north of Lake Titicaca. It is known to have survived as a men's language of mixed linguistic nature: lexical roots from the extinct Pukina language and affixes from Quechua (Adelaar 1991:56; Stark 1985:529).

The languages of the Bolivian Amazonian lowland, which were among the least documented of the Amazonian basin, are now receiving attention following the proclamation of the 1994 Constitution, which acknowledges the multilingual and pluricultural nature of Bolivia. An extensive educational reform has been set in motion, which includes plans for bilingual education programs for those previously ignored languages.[19] Let it be noted here that in Bolivia the indigenous languages are being referred to as *lenguas originarias*.

Brazil is a world by itself, an immense open space where large areas, mostly in the east, have no indigenous populations left. It is within the borders of Brazil that the largest part of the Amazon basin lies. There live 150,000 speakers of indigenous languages in small communities representing the major South American language families and stocks such as Tupi-Guarani, Macro-gê, Carib and Arawakan. Of the 170 languages of Brazil, 36 have fewer than 100 speakers, of which 14 have fewer than 50 speakers. (Rodrigues 1985b:406). The new Constitution of 1988 included in its chapter on education the right of the indigenous people to be taught in their native languages as well as in Portuguese.

Chile and Argentina, the countries of the Southern Cone, are the most Europeanized countries, countries in which the native population has been largely decimated. Chile still has a large population of Mapuche Indians in the south, in what is now a very reduced territory compared to

---

19 The author is presently coordinating a documentation project for these languages, as linguistic consultant for the Ministry of Ethnic Affairs and the Ministry of Education (UNSTP), with the assistance of Pilar Valenzuela and Alejandra Vidal from the University of Oregon. In a first phase in the fall of 1995, the writing systems for ten of the twenty-nine languages of the region were revised and teams of native speakers began training to become the language specialists for the future bilingual education programs. In the second phase in the summer of 1996, an additional ten alphabets were attended to and the first course in linguistics was offered. A five-year plan for training language specialists and coordinating the linguistic documentation of these languages is underway. The project is funded by DANIDA of Denmark (Ministry of Ethnic Affairs), the World Bank (Ministry of Education), the Harvard Institute for International Development through UDAPSO of Bolivia, and UNICEF.

the original land they occupied. There is a pocket of Aymara speakers in the north, and very threatened or extinct languages in the south (Adelaar 1991:64). Argentina still has thirteen small linguistic communities which are scattered at the edges of the country. Due to their geographic location, they are hard to reach and are, therefore, understudied.[20]

Paraguay constitutes a unique situation in which an originally indigenous language has acquired the status of an official language and is spoken by more than 90 percent of the population of the country. Rubin (1968, 1985) describes Paraguay as a case of a Guarani-speaking country with a high level of bilingualism in Spanish. The striking fact of a standardized variety of "Paraguayan Guarani" being spoken by a large *mestizo* population has a great impact on the vitality of the language, as will be discussed in section 5.2. below. The original indigenous varieties of Guarani are still spoken by a small population in the southeastern edge of the country, where other small indigenous languages still remain.

Surinam, Guyana, and French Guyana have been colonized by non-Romance language speaking countries: Surinam is Dutch-speaking, Guyana English-speaking, and French Guyana French-speaking. All three countries have low proportions of indigenous populations, from 3–7 percent, and a majority of languages lying across national borders. Of the 6 languages of French Guyana for instance, only one is contained entirely within the borders, the Tupi language Emerillon, with 200 speakers.

This presentation has briefly considered indigenous settlements in South America on a countrywide basis. The major features discussed were the proportion of the Indian population to the general population, and the nature of the languages as larger linguistic minorities which, to a certain extent, determine the identity of a country. For example, the Andean countries are known for the presence of large Quechua and Aymara populations, whereas other countries are known for the multiplicity of small linguistic communities whose existence is only beginning to receive official recognition.

20 The languages of Argentina include Quechua dialects in the northwest, 3 languages related to Paraguayan Guarani together with languages of 3 other families in the Gran Chaco in the northeast, Mapudungu speakers from Chile in the Southwest, and extinct or near extinct languages in the south (Adelaar 1991:55–56).

4   **Language death and language endangerment in South America**

Beyond the facts and figures presented above lie the same tales of death and endangerment that prevail in all of the Americas. The number of ethnic and linguistic groups that became extinct during the colonial period is estimated to be in the hundreds, and the endangerment of the surviving languages, whether large or small, is an ongoing concern.

4.1   Three types of language death

The relatively low number of indigenous languages spoken in South America today is due to various situations of language death. Many cases of language death came during the period of colonization through a drastic decimation of the indigenous population, particularly in eastern Brazil and Argentina. For instance, estimates are that the greater Amazonian region had about 6.8 million people in the sixteenth century, and only about 700,000 by 1992 (Grenand and Grenand 1993:94). This loss of language by loss of the people is unfortunately still a factor, as physical violence against indigenous people of South America continues.[21]

A second factor that has caused language loss is the spread of lingua francas, in particular in the Andean countries of Ecuador, Peru, and Bolivia, where Quechua principally, but Aymara too, have erased practically all the local indigenous languages. The practice of forced displacement of local populations by the colonizing indigenous powers turned out to be quite effective to achieve the aim of ethnic and linguistic mixing and language replacement. The adoption of Quechua by speakers of smaller

---

21 See for instance various accounts from Colombia, such as the cases of relatively recent massacres mentioned in several of the papers from the 1994 CCELA symposium on language revitalization efforts (Pabón Triana 1995), or the mention of the decimation of the Andoke people which went from a population of 10,000 in 1908 to 100 bilingual individuals as a consequence of the atrocities that accompanied the exploitation of wild rubber earlier in the century (Landaburu 1979).

  Grenand and Grenand (1993:109–1100) mention recent massacres of at least three groups that had remained out of contact (Mamainde, Marima, Miqueleno). Other recent cases include the threats to the survival of the Yanomami people of Brazil, and the indigenous casualties of the border wars of 1982 and 1995 between Peru and Ecuador, where indigenous people of the same ethnic groups, some of them relatives, were made to fight each other on both sides of the border. Needing to be mentioned also is the state of violence created by the confrontation between the Shining Path and the army as well as the local populations which prevailed in much of the indigenous highlands of Peru in the last decade, paralyzing most of the government educational and economic development programs and creating a massive exodus of the indigenous population.

minority languages is still going on. A case in point is the reported shift of Zaparo to Quechua by the Zaparo population of the western lowland of Ecuador: of the 20,000 speakers of Zaparo that are claimed to have existed 135 years ago (Stark 1985:184) only 7 speakers of Zaparo were left in the early 1980s (or maybe still 24 speakers, Gnerre p.c.).[22]

There have also been shifts from one indigenous language to another, not considered lingua franca. This is the case for instance in Bolivia where some of the communities of Guarani and Chiquitano speakers today are descendants of local populations which adopted those relatively more dominant languages (Lopez p.c.; Rodrigues p.c.).

The third factor contributing to the loss of indigenous languages is the phenomenon of shift to the major European colonizing languages that has taken place in the midst of the steady increase in urbanization of the rural population of South America. The massive urban shift is affecting the vitality of even the larger indigenous languages such as Quechua, a general matter of concern in all Quechua-speaking countries.[23] Urbanization is accompanied by the process known as *mestizaje* (abandonment of indigenous traits to assimilate to the dominant *mestizo* culture), a process which is accelerated by interracial mixing and the unrelenting pressure of socio-economic discrimination.[24]

In terms of overall language extinction the figures are high for some of the larger families of South America: of the 65 members of the Arawakan family, 31 are extinct today; of the 43 languages of the Cariban family, 19 are extinct; of the 24 members of the Chibchan family, 6 are extinct (including the Chibcha language itself). Similarly the rates of extinction are drastic in many areas. For example, in Ecuador, only 12 of the 30 languages known to have been spoken at the time of the Conquest have survived into this century (Klein and Stark 1985:5).

22 Other cases of lingua francas in South America include Tupi, the lingua franca of Brazil of the colonial time, also referred to as Lingua Geral, Nheengatu or Ienkatu (Adelaar 1991:59). Nheengatu has only 3,000 speakers today and has been characterized as a possible creolized language (Moore, Facundes, and Pires 1991). Tukano in central NW Amazon also functions today as a local lingua franca in a situation of high level of multilingualism (Sorensen 1985:142).

23 Consider for instance the figures of the recent urbanization trend of Ecuador: from 20% in 1950 to 60% in 1995 and a projected 70% in 2000, or the fact that there are more than a half million Quechua in Lima (Peru) alone, and 300,000 Mapuche in Santiago (Chile).

24 While one speaks of *mestizo* Spanish-speaking culture, the term is *caboclo* for the Portuguese-speaking culture (Rodrigues p.c.).

4.2   Vitality of the large indigenous languages

Although the large indigenous languages of South America would seem relatively safe from the point of view of the sheer number of speakers, their maintenance into the future is not necessarily assured. The situation of Quechua and Guarani will be considered below; they are the two largest and best documented indigenous languages, both in terms of linguistic documentation and documentation of language-planning efforts (including corpus and status planning).

The situation of Quechua varies with the regions. Evidence has been gathered to show that it is vulnerable in some regions to a language shift to Spanish that could endanger it earlier than expected. One such region is Central Peru, where the local varieties of Quechua are said to be at the verge of a shift phenomenon (Adelaar 1991:50–51). Similarly, a recent extensive sociolinguistic survey of Quichua speakers in Ecuador reveals a trend toward language shift (Haboud 1991, 1995). In the survey, there were telling differences between two types of measurements taken, one being the linguistic preference (Quichua, Spanish, both) expressed by native speakers of Quichua to the interviewers, and the other being the actual use observed by the fieldworkers, themselves native speakers of Quichua.[25] Even when native Quichua speakers expressed a strong preference for Quichua, they were observed to use more Spanish than they acknowledged.

The trend toward bilingualism and declining use of the Quechua/Quichua language in these areas could portend a relatively sudden shift to Spanish in the next generations. This would constitute another instance of the phenomenon of "language tip" – a rapid shift to the dominant language after a long period of gestation not recognized by the speaker population itself (see the discussion in Dorian 1986).

The bilingual education projects which started in the 1960s have not appeared to temper the shift from Quechua/Quichua to Spanish, amply demonstrating what is already well known about such programs: corpus planning (standardization of orthography, lexicon, and grammar, production of pedagogical materials) without status planning (creation of opportunities for public and official use of the language in all spheres of political

---

25 One of the characteristics of this sociolinguistic survey is that it was carried out by trained Quichua native speakers, an example of collaborative fieldwork framework of the type discussed in sections 5 and 6 below (Haboud 1994).

and economic life) will not ensure the maintenance of a language. The decline in the vitality of the language is linked to the pervasive negative socioeconomic incentives and the rampant social discrimination that the native speakers of indigenous languages have to endure.[26]

The overall vulnerability of a large language such as Quechua, at least in some areas, is not unlike the situation of the majority indigenous languages of Guatemala, as discussed by England (this volume). The situation of Guarani on the other hand appears to be very different.

Guarani is probably the healthiest indigenous language of the Americas, particularly in its Paraguayan variety. Its vitality is due to several factors – in great part to the sheer bulk of the speaker population (3.5 million speakers representing over 90 percent of the population), but just as importantly to the status it enjoys, which is one of prestige and strong language loyalty. Indeed, it represents a case of an indigenous language which has been appropriated as a symbol of ethnic identity by a non-indigenous *mestizo* population. Speaking Guarani is what makes Paraguay – a small landlocked country with a history of isolation and extensive *mestizaje* – different from any other South American country. The kind of prestige and language loyalty Guarani enjoys leads to its use in public life by presidential candidates in their electoral campaigns on one hand, while being the intimate language of songs, love, and poetry (Rubin 1968).

4.3   *Vitality of small indigenous languages*

It is a fact that most of the small indigenous languages are endangered, even those that have survived so far in enough isolation to maintain vitality.[27] These last vital linguistic communities are likely targets of swift shifts, as it does not take long for a language to become threatened once encroachment from the dominant culture and language starts, through road-building and the introduction of electricity (hence television). Various types

---

26 In defense of bilingual education, one must recognize that if it can be made to function also as status planning, it can also generate new linguistic needs and language awareness that spurn dynamics of language revitalization. This has been the case with Bolivian Guarani, for instance, as documented in Lopez 1995, as well as in Ecuador, and Peru (Puno and Alto Napo in the Amazonian region) (Lopez p.c.).

27 Traditionally, indigenous lowland communities were small to maximize survival in the ecological conditions of their environment. Historical studies show that it is improbable that ethnic groups of less than 500 existed in the sixteenth and seventeenth centuries (see Grenand and Grenand 1993:100).

Table 6.2 Number of Brazilian languages by
population of speakers

Number of speakers	Number of languages
> 10,000	4
5,001–10,000	4
3,001–5,000	4
2,001–3,000	8
1,001–2,000	6
601–1,000	12
401–600	18
201–400	29
101–200	31
1–100	50

of sedentarization programs for otherwise nomadic populations, including religious and schooling pressures, also generally contribute to a shift towards the dominant language.

One way to look at endangerment is to consider the figures of speakers. The detailed account of the speaker populations of the languages of Brazil given in Rodrigues (1993) shows the vulnerability of the languages of those populations in simple numerical terms (table 6.2).[28] Not indicated by these numbers is the fact that there exist cases of populations that are small but where the whole population speaks the language, including all the children. Such is the case of Daw of the Maku family for instance, where all 70–80 members are speakers (Aikhenvald p.c.). In a sense those languages are not presently endangered, to the extent that the survival of the whole ethnic group is not immediately endangered, but there is no guarantee for the future, as circumstances can change quickly.

Dwindling speaker populations are to be put in contrast with an overall trend of increase of indigenous populations. Figures for the Amazonian

28 Another source of figures for the indigenous languages of South America is Wise (1994), although the figures look inflated. For Brazil she gives for instance 247 languages, while Rodrigues gives 170, for Colombia 99 languages when Landaburu (1979) gives 60, and for Bolivia 46 languages, when the figure handled these days in the country is 32.

region show that 87 percent of the ethnic groups have increased in population since 1970 and only 6 percent are suffering demographic decline (Grenand and Grenand 1993:105). Language loss is therefore mostly a matter of shift of language loyalty.

What is noteworthy is how such widespread situation of language endangerment is being perceived today by many communities and what this means in terms of linguistic fieldwork and interaction between linguists and communities. Many communities are indeed interested in the revitalization/maintenance of their language and expect to interact with linguists interested in the documentation of their language. See section 5.3 on the nature of work on endangered languages.

The mobilization of the indigenous people of South America in defense of their threatened languages, from the largest to the smallest linguistic communities, would appear to be a trait of the recent history of the Americas. In Latin America in general, and very certainly in South America, the last decades have been a time of extensive indigenous organizing which acquired a special momentum around the time of the 1992 quincentennial commemoration of the arrival of the Spaniards in the continent. While Spain was celebrating the so-called "discovery" of America, the indigenous communities organized multi-ethnic encounters at a continental level and orchestrated successive declarations of indigenous rights. Such declarations always included as a high priority the maintenance, protection, and development of their native languages, just after the securing of land, and the demands were primarily for changes in the educational system, away from a system of monolingual education in the dominant language. Local indigenous organizations have intensified their networking at a national and international level, articulating demands that are now recognized in the International Labor Organization Decree 169 and the declaration by the United Nations of this being the decade of the indigenous people.[29]

The issue of the revitalization and maintenance of the smaller languages is a relatively new challenge for both the speakers' communities and the linguistic profession. There is no simple or obvious answer, as the strictly linguistic issue is embedded in the much larger challenge of the

---

29 A World Conference on Linguistic Rights was held in Barcelona, Spain, in June, 1996 during which a Universal Declaration of Linguistic Rights was proclaimed by representatives of all the continents.

survival of viable indigenous communities as such (principally a matter of securing enough of a land base and self-determination for the communities). So far little collective wisdom has been shared within the community of linguists, although linguists are being confronted with such challenges in the field at an increasing rate. Much remains to be done at the conceptualizing as well as the strategic and practical level. Bridging the gap between academic linguistics and community wants and efforts is surely one of the major challenges of the linguistic profession as it faces the situation of endangered languages at the turn of the new century. Sections 5 and 6 below are an attempt at addressing some of these conceptualizing and strategizing needs, more specifically the issue of preparing linguistically trained manpower to deal with the situation of the widespread endangerment of South American languages.

5   The linguistic study of the indigenous languages of South America

While the previous section offered an overview of the situation of indigenous languages of South America for readers unfamiliar with this region of the world, the goal of this section is to assess the present situation in terms of linguistic work being done or to be done, with the idea that, besides Guarani, all indigenous languages of South America can be considered at some point of endangerment. This assessment is offered from the point of view of a foreign linguist working in the region, and is addressed primarily to fellow foreign linguists with little familiarity with the region. This section will consider what linguistic work needs doing, what has been done and is being done by foreign missionaries and by nationals at local institutions. It will conclude with some food for thought offered primarily to foreign linguists eventually interested in becoming involved in work on the languages of the region.

5.1   *An overview of the linguistic work needing to be done*

As of today relatively few languages remain completely undocumented, but comprehensive language documentation is still an exception. No attempt will be made here to set priorities between the different kinds of linguistic research that are needed, and no specific recommendations will be given on which languages or language families represent the most urgent situations to be considered. Such information is partly supplied by Adelaar (1991) in an explicit way and is partly retrievable from the major publications mentioned at the beginning of this paper, particularly Pottier (1983), Klein and Stark (1985), Rodrigues (1985b), T. Kaufman (1990, 1994), and Moore and Storto (1994).

Specific needs include an exact inventory of languages, modern grammar documentation, basic documentation for comparative purposes, substratum research, archival work, and applied linguistics (for educational linguistics and revitalization projects, at least). Exactly how many languages there are and how many speakers they have, particularly in the black hole of the Amazon, is still not known. One of the major problems in this area is that languages have been given different names, and we still need to sort through names of people and names for dialects and languages. In terms of grammatical descriptions, there is some documentation on most languages of South America, but there are very few comprehensive grammatical studies set within modern linguistic frameworks and useful to the field of general linguistics (although some existing grammars can provide models for what can be done).[30]

The issue of so many languages being considered as isolates may be the product of linguists missing clues due to a lack of information. Basic documentation of languages is needed in general to complete the classification schemas proposed and to study the actual history of those families. An example of a linguistic project addressing this need is the Kariban comparative project of the Museu Goeldi of Belem. This project aims at providing linguistic descriptions of Kariban languages done by affiliates of the Museu (including Brazilian graduate students in training) with the ultimate goal of studying family-wide processes of grammaticalization and rechecking classification proposals.[31]

---

30 See for instance the grammars of Yagua (D. Payne 1985; T. Payne 1985; Payne and Payne 1990), Sikuani (Queixalós 1995) or Andoke (Landaburu 1979).

31 This is a National Science Foundation funded project (S. Gildea from Rice University as P.I). This project represents a model of collaborative research project in which a foreign linguist is working closely with a local institution and contributing directly to the training of local Brazilian linguists. See section 5.3 below for more detail and section 5.4 for a discussion of such collaborative research project design.

Other work of a comparative nature includes the work of Rodrigues on the Tupi-Guarani languages and the work of Aikhenvald on Arawakan languages (Aikhenvald 1995, 1996).

In order to retrieve some information on the extinct languages of South American, particularly those of the highlands that were lost due to the spread of the lingua francas of the area several approaches can be taken. As advocated by Adelaar, who himself did such work (Adelaar 1988), a thorough study of the toponomy of the highlands may yield some information on extinct languages of the region. An additional source of information on substratum languages is the study of the local varieties of Spanish and Portuguese (a reality with which fieldworkers must reckon as they seek to establish a working language with the native speakers of their field projects!).

For the purpose of historical linguistic studies, much work could still be done on archival material, both in the archives of Spain and the local ones, although access to local materials is not always easy due to lack of funding to establish and maintain archives in South America and to the complexities of local politics.[32]

The gaps are serious too in the area of applied linguistics, as native speakers' communities become actively involved in language-maintenance and revitalization projects. The needs include in particular applied linguistics aimed at educational programs, from bilingual education with the indigenous languages as first or second language to general literacy programs for the communities. Development of the languages to facilitate the translation of the new constitutions and new legislation concerning the welfare of the indigenous populations are also needed.

5.2   *Missionary documentation of South American indigenous languages*

Although South America may still stand as one of the most under-documented parts of the world at this point in time, systematic efforts have been orchestrated at different times by different entities to remedy this situation.

There exists an important documentation of the major languages from the time of the colonization produced by catholic missionaries from the sixteenth and seventeenth centuries. They include, *inter alia*, grammars for Tupi (1595), Quechua (1560), Aymara (1603), Chibcha (1619, extinct today), and Guarani (1620), some of which are considered to be admirably

---

32 Such is the case of the materials from Jijón y Camaño in Ecuador (Haboud p.c.).

accurate considering the times (Adelaar 1991:47).[33] This colonial documentation is an important resource which is still available for a modern review of its contents and which provides invaluable information from a historical perspective.

In the last several decades, the Summer Institute of Linguistics (SIL) has been the major source of linguistic documentation of the South American indigenous languages, in particular the documentation of the smaller lowland languages. The only South American countries in which SIL has not established any presence are Paraguay and Venezuela, and they are officially no longer in Bolivia or Colombia.

SIL linguists have therefore produced the vast majority of the publications on South American languages. The quantity and usefulness of the linguistic documentation available for any one language attended to by SIL missionaries varies greatly depending on the linguistic sophistication of the individual missionaries involved. Professional linguists from SIL such as D. Derbyshire, D. Everett, David Payne, Doris Payne, and Thomas Payne, for instance, have been important contributors to the linguistic documentation of the lowland Amazonian languages, with some of their more theoretically oriented work having an impact on the field of linguistics at large.[34]

The vast majority of SIL members, however, are missionaries whose primary interest is evangelization work and whose fieldwork goal in terms of language work is the translation of the Bible.[35] For this work they train native speakers in translation work. Many of the missions also promote literacy programs in native languages aimed primarily at being able to read the translations of the Bible. They often run in addition their own bilingual education programs at the elementary level, for which they train local bilingual teachers. All languages on which SIL missionaries have worked will have at least publications of educational material produced for these

33 See Adelaar (1991:47) and his bibliography for exact references for the colonial documentation mentioned here.

34 See for instance the contribution of SIL linguists to the National Science Foundation and National Endowment for the Humanities sponsored Working Conference on Amazonian Languages that took place at the University of Oregon in 1988 and the publication which resulted from it (D. Payne 1990).

35 SIL is associated with Wycliffe Bible Translators. The focus on Bible translation work as a goal probably accounts for the fact that the SIL twenty- or thirty-year presence has not resulted in the training of professional native or national linguists, one of the main complaints leveled against the organization by South American academics.

literacy programs; many have in addition more or less sophisticated grammatical sketches and word lists or dictionaries.[36]

Although SIL missionaries are the most numerous and the better known of the linguistic profession because of their extensive publications, smaller missions are also working with indigenous languages and occasionally contributing to the description of the languages. For instance, in the Amazon region of Bolivia, which SIL left more than ten years ago, the team of linguists working on the standardization of the alphabets of nine Amazonian languages in the fall of 1995 encountered a Catholic mission running a Guarayu language program, a Franciscan priest who had just written a grammar of Chiquitano (Besɨro), a North American New Tribes mission running a Tsimane' (Chimane) bilingual education program, a Swiss mission a Bia Yë (Yuqui) program, and a Swedish mission a Weenhayek (Mataco) program.

5.3   *Institutionalized linguistic work on indigenous languages in South America*

The longest tradition of work on indigenous languages in South America is that of the study of the Andean languages, Quechua and Aymara. The Chair of Quechua studies at the University of San Marcos, Lima, dates back more than four hundred years, for instance. The first generations of South American Andean linguists began to appear in the mid-1960s, among them native speakers of those languages. The University of San Marcos has been offering an undergraduate linguistics degree (*licenciatura*) in Andean, Amazonian and Spanish linguistics for thirty years, and a master's degree in the same for over fifteen years now.[37]

36 SIL members are trained at SIL "summer institutes of linguistics" (literally) and receive linguistic mentoring in the field from SIL linguists stationed in each country. Much of the linguistic descriptive work available has been cast into a structuralist framework which was popular at the time of SIL's major expansion. One may consider unfortunate also the centralized decision in some countries to cast all grammars in a particular framework, such as the tagmemic framework developed by SIL linguists. This is the case of the two volumes of Bolivian grammars (Matteson

1965), the usefulness of which in strictly descriptive terms is severely reduced, the information being extremely tedious to retrieve and the data on which the analysis was done largely unavailable.
37 The original degree program was partly funded by the Ford Foundation as part of a plan of Linguistic Development (Plan de Fomento Lingüístico), which also sponsored the experimental educational projects of Ayacucho and one of the first sociolinguistic surveys of the Quechua world (Lopez p.c.).

Various training programs with emphasis on the study of indigenous languages of South America have been developing in the last decades, in Colombia and Brazil in particular. For example, the Centro Colombiano de Estudios en Lenguas Aborígenes (CCELA) was founded in 1987 and is associated with the Universidad de los Andes in Bogotá.[38] Its goal is to train linguists of Colombian origin, including native speakers of Colombian languages, and to prepare them to do a comprehensive study of both languages and linguistic communities, within a framework of collaboration with linguistic community efforts. The Center has established several series of publications: grammatical descriptions, dictionaries, and publications of conference proceedings.[39]

The first graduating class of 1987 was working on sixteen languages. By the third graduating class of 1995, graduates of the program were working on thirty-nine languages of Colombia (including coastal Creole). A total of twelve indigenous native speakers have graduated from the program, all with a monograph on their language. As of today, two-thirds of the graduates of the program are employed in linguistics.[40]

Another country offering advanced training programs for the study of indigenous languages is Brazil. The conditions for the study of indigenous languages changed drastically in Brazil in 1987, after a coalition of all the institutions where indigenous languages were being researched or taught submitted a research and action program to CNPq, the national research outfit.[41] Although the program was not actually funded, its definition of priorities and lines of action opened the doors of CNPq for linguistic projects concerning indigenous languages.

38 Teaching team and funds have been provided by the French Centre National de Recherche Scientifique.

39 The publications to date include eight descriptive grammars (*descripciones*), one Dictionary and three conference proceedings, the most recent and most relevant here being Pabón Triana (1995) mentioned earlier. The quality of the grammatical descriptions is uneven, as could be expected of such an effort, and has concentrated on basic descriptions of grammar and phonology, with so far no discourse or pragmatics work. A data base to include all information gathered by the members of the program is being set up (Landaburu p.c.).

40 Information from Jon Landaburu, director of CCELA (p.c.). The National University in Bogotá has a master's degree in Indigenous linguistics and has had three promotions too, but very few have actually graduated.

41 The program is called PPCLIB: Programa de Pesquisa Cientifica des Linguas Indigenas Brasileiras. All information on Brazil is from Rodrigues, Moore and Franchetto p.c.

Three other institutions are worth mentioning for their focus on indigenous languages. The first two are departments of linguistics, the third a research institute with no university affiliation. UNICAMP (Universidad Estatal de Campinas) has the longest record of training students for fieldwork on indigenous languages since its start in 1977. It has awarded so far twenty-seven master's degrees and ten Ph.D.s.[42] The linguistics program at UnB (Universidad de Brasilia) has been offering a master's degree in indigenous linguistics since 1988 and so far has graduated thirteen students.[43]

The linguistics branch of the Museu Goeldi of Belem is the most recent institution to enter into the study of indigenous languages. It is a Brazilian federal research institute with a focus on the languages of the Amazon. It provides research opportunities to local and foreign linguists, and training and assistance in gaining entrance to graduate schools to a limited number of selected students, many of whom are from Amazonia. The goal is to increase the number of highly qualified Ph.D.s in Brazil, preferably people of the region, who will have the appropriate field skills and theoretical background to carry out the needed descriptive and practical assistance work in the Brazilian Amazon.[44] A number of these students are studying abroad and many of them are already involved in literacy and language revitalization projects.[45] The staff of the Linguistics Division is partly foreign and partly Brazilian, as is the funding.

While the programs considered so far emphasize university-level linguistic research, several important programs are addressing the linguistic needs of the native communities themselves. The program in Puno (Peru) started in 1985 and offers training in Andean linguistics and education at two levels: a two-year master's degree with thesis and a one-year diploma of secondary specialization for teachers already working within the bilingual education system which is more oriented towards pedagogical issues.

---

42 It hosts the Documentation project of the languages of the Indigenous Park of Xingu, coordinated by Lucy Seki.

43 This is the home institution of Aryon Rodrigues.

44 They plan a comprehensive audio-/video-documentation program for the indigenous languages and an expansion of the training program, which may be extended to students of other Amazonian countries.

45 By the academic year 1995–96 Museu Goeldi linguistics graduate students will be found at UC-Santa Barbara, the University of Oregon, Rice University, the University of Chicago, MIT and the University of Paris and soon the first Ph.D. graduate will return to train the next generation.

The training program for bilingual teachers of the Peruvian Amazon region located in Iquitos was started in 1988 and deals presently with ten languages. It includes a linguistics component in which native speakers study their own languages under the supervision of professional linguists. Other teacher-training programs for indigenous people include the programs in Quichua applied linguistics of the University of Cuenca (Ecuador), the Bolivian normal school of Camiri for Guarani speakers (with another one projected for Tumichucua for other Amazonian languages of the region).

The most recent efforts at developing local linguistic resources are efforts at sharing manpower regionally, to combat the state focus of established institutions and respond more directly to the actual needs of the population of speakers involved. Two instances of such efforts can be mentioned. One is centered on the highlands: it is a new Andean program, a regional training center established in Cochabamba (Bolivia) for Quechua, Aymara, and Guarani speakers with the goal of providing the manpower for the educational reforms underway in those languages in Bolivia, Peru, Chile, Columbia, and Ecuador.[46] The other is the creation of a network of parties involved with the study, maintenance, and development of the languages of the Amazonian basin. It began following an international gathering of representatives of native-speaker communities and of institutions as well as individual academics from all the nine countries of the Amazon.[47]

5.4   *Food for thought for foreign linguists*

The existing work being carried out presently in South America through local institutions was presented first to put the role of foreign linguists in South America in perspective. The point to be made is that foreign linguists interested in contributing to the linguistic work that remains to be done on South American indigenous languages would do well to take stock of what is happening in South America and reflect on the kinds of relations they might establish in the region. Fieldwork relations are simply not what they used to be when most of present-day practicing linguists were in training or beginning their careers, at least. The dynamics are

---

46 This new program will combine documentation, archiving, teacher training and research. It is funded by the German government (GTZ) (Lopez, director, p.c.).

47 See the recently started Bulletin LINDA (Línguas Indígenas da Amazônia), to be produced at the Museu Goeldi in Belem, Brazil for its first two years.

shifting at this point in time, and it is useful to make some aspects of that shift explicit.

The reality is that there are very strong feelings South American academic and linguistic circles about the necessity to develop linguistics done by Latin Americans, and to establish the institutional base that is needed for it. There is a widespread sentiment that foreign linguists who help these efforts, in a genuine and effective way, are very welcome, while others who continue to function on an individual(istic) basis, mostly concerned with furthering their own career in foreign universities, are not so.

To accept the fact that South American linguistics should be carried out as much as possible by South Americans has in fact deep implications for the way we conduct our business and the way we basically conceive of our role as linguists.[48] The reality of South American academic life is that, due to the absence of doctoral programs in linguistics in South America until recently, most prominent linguists from South America have been trained abroad, in the United States and in Europe, and are therefore familiar with the teaching and research facilities that exist there. When they return to their country, they are faced with difficult professional conditions. The general lack of resources for research on indigenous languages is prevalent in local state universities and has hampered the development of local linguistic manpower. Academics in South America lack the resources available to outside linguists, such as library resources, research funding, capacity to offer advanced training to graduate students, or to provide graduates with employment.

In addition, the linguists established in South America who work on indigenous languages (both native South Americans and foreign linguists) and have received training abroad, tend to find themselves in a minority in the linguistic profession of their own country. This is because whatever linguistics has developed recently in South America has been more along the lines of formal linguistics focused on the major colonial languages

---

48 The original spoken version of this paper delivered at the Dartmouth conference was blunt, in the way one can get away with saying things one is not as comfortable putting down in writing for publication, but I think it is worth tucking away in a footnote for people to see and reflect on what I actually said. The message was, in plain language: "Beware of gringo imperialism," i.e. beware of the multiple ways it is easy for us foreign-based linguists to plan research projects, obtain funding for them, and carry them out from our home-base institutions without regard for local needs or potential collaboration.

or applied linguistics focused on the acquisition of English as a foreign language.[49]

It derives from all of the above that our South American colleagues are expecting from us collaborative work which will contribute to the strengthening of indigenous linguistics locally. Examples of such collaborative work are the programs of CCELA in Bogota (with French support) and the Museu Goeldi in Belem (with US and French support) mentioned earlier.[50] Professional collaboration with South American counterparts includes contributing to the training of local manpower, which has to happen at two levels. One is training the future linguists of South America to become the academic manpower at local universities and research centers. While most of them will be non-indigenous nationals in the majority, means should also be found whenever possible to provide the opportunity to native speakers of indigenous languages to become the linguists of their languages.

The other training effort must happen at a more local level and address the needs of the native speakers who are or will be the bilingual school teachers and other local linguistic resources for the communities. This second line of work and training has not been an integral part of traditional academic research projects of the first world. It is however a preoccupation and priority of most linguistic field-research projects of local institutions, where interest in indigenous cultures and languages in general, and the discipline of linguistics in particular, are conceived within the broader context of concern for the survival and empowerment of the indigenous communities. This is the framework within which the CCELA center of Colombia and the Museo Goeldi of Belem, Brazil, function.

In the case of South America, there is in addition another delicate issue to be faced by any linguistic fieldworker, which is that of the presence of SIL missionary linguists in most countries. It is part of the reality of South America that in the local world of linguistics, affiliation or non-affiliation with SIL is always a variable to be factored in, whether one wants to think about it or not. One needs to know that such affiliation matters in

49 Consider for instance the popularity and predominance of formal linguistics of the Chomskian variety in Brazil today, or the fact that the only Ph.D. in linguistics of Bolivia is a linguist trained in the Government and Binding Theory tradition with no connection to the issue of documenting the indigenous languages of the country.

50 An earlier program was the one for Aymara founded by Mary Hartman in La Paz.

some circles and that, as a foreign linguist, one is primarily defined as being or not being associated with SIL.[51] Therefore some of the major tenets of US culture and academic life are likely to be seriously challenged in the field in South America where academic work is divorced neither from "politics" nor from "religion."

Strengthening local research efforts on indigenous languages will therefore mean refraining from involvement in projects proposed by non-local groups and institutions, which all too often become influenced by the requirements and interests of a foreign-based academic community.[52] Indeed, much would need to be reconsidered in the way we foreign academics conduct our business in general if we profess to be concerned with the fate of endangered indigenous languages, in South America or anywhere else in the world for that matter.

6   General issues about linguistic work on endangered languages

The focus so far has been on the specifics of the situation of endangered indigenous languages of South America, with a consideration of the attitudes of local indigenous populations towards their languages, as well as the interest of South American academics, leading to a reflection of the implications of such interests for how to conceive of the role of foreign linguists in the region. But the issues raised reach much beyond South America. In this section, and by way of conclusion, I would like to consider some of the wider implications for the linguistic profession as it is practiced today in the United States or Europe for those of us concerned with the situation of endangered languages. As a senior linguist engaged in the business

51 This is another reality of South America. The risk in the field of being taken for a CIA agent varies with the countries and the particular times and circumstances, but the burden of proof will always be on any "gringo" linguist to prove that he or she is not a member of the CIA, if that is the case and if that matters to the individual. Whereas US academia tends to blur the interconnection of academia and politics and to ignore for the most part the ideological underpinnings of its enterprise, Latin American academia does not separate academia and politics. As I stated earlier, this is a reality check, of the kind that is very important to do if one contemplates working in or sending a student to work in South America.

52 From my twenty-five years experience in US academia, I realize that what I am saying here goes against some of the most cherished values of its culture, such as a cultivated inclination for individualistic enterprise, a deeply ingrained devotion to a certain sense of freedom, and a strong pull towards insulating academia and the research enterprise from its sociopolitical context. This needs to be said if we are truly to contemplate the situation of endangered languages in South America in its actual context.

of fieldwork on endangered languages, I would like to offer three lines of thought to help see our way through the enormity of the task ahead of us.

There is no doubt that what I am about to say has been shaped by my experience in Latin America, although I would assume that much of it is generally relevant to the situation in any part of the world.[53] I will develop three points: first how the business of endangered languages is the business of the whole profession; second what some of the specifics of doing field-work on endangered languages are; and third what those specifics mean in terms of preparation and training of future fieldworkers.

6.1   Concern of the whole profession

As concern over the fate of endangered languages has been growing steadily in the last few years, catching media attention and being brought to the attention of the whole profession as well as the general public, there is no way to escape wondering what we linguists can/should do about en-dangered languages. There is a need, as Fishman stated appropriately, to "intellectualize" the field, to make it a legitimate concern of the academic profession of linguists.[54]

One issue worth clarifying is how the business of endangered lan-guages, whether in Latin America or somewhere else, is the business of the whole profession, not just the responsibility of or limited to the interests of, the fieldworkers. The fact is, the whole linguistic profession can help the situation with endangered languages.[55]

There are multiple ways of confronting the situation, and linguists can all do what they are best at: we need descriptive linguists, historical lin-guists, sociolinguists, psycholinguists, and theoreticians with a taste for data. The work involved includes desk/archive work, fieldwork, training of fieldworkers, professional support for the work in the form of grant reviews, hiring decisions, promotion and tenure decisions, and other forms

53 Contents of this sections were first presented at the 1992 International Congress of linguistics in Quebec (Craig 1993) and the first Endangered Language symposium of the LSA (Craig 1995; Craig and Hale 1995).
54 I will not argue here for why linguists and the world at large should be concerned with the fate of endangered languages, convinced as I am, as Fishman (1991) points out, that it is a question not really amenable to rational thinking, and more a matter of ideology than many want to admit, and in any case beyond the scope of this chapter.
55 I am aware that this attitude is not as widespread attitude as it could be, in spite of the Linguistic Society of America declarations and the activities of the Committee on Endangered Languages it sponsors.

of reward decisions. And I would add to these tasks one specifically linked to the issue of training national and local linguists: it is the issue of admissions, and the mentoring and training of those future linguists once admitted. In these times when the concept of affirmative action is being attacked, it needs saying that the enterprise of training national linguists at North American or European centers to return to their country and work on the local endangered languages requires a commitment to some form of affirmative action. And as it can be a serious burden on the faculty sponsoring such students, acknowledgement of that work by the community of linguists would be a form of support.

6.2   *Understanding the nature of work on endangered languages*

Some of the characteristics of fieldwork on endangered languages which are rarely made explicit, but are part of the experience of fieldworkers engaged in that line of work, will be considered here.[56] They include linguistic and sociolinguistic characteristics of such languages; the need to deal with the indigenous communities and their needs; and the potential dissonance between the demands of the field and the demands of an academic career.

The strictly linguistic issue is that of the challenge of describing decaying languages. There are the frustrations and limitations of working with the only speakers available, with little choice in the matter, and the added difficulty of dealing with the very complex attitudes speakers have toward those languages, often based on their own linguistic insecurities. The work is often emotionally stressful, and the bewilderment of the linguist trained in a tradition that only considers the description of vital languages with healthy native speakers is great. Fieldwork on unwritten and non-standardized languages is no easy task, but the twist of the language being in a state of decay is an added layer of challenge. For one thing, the standard field method of direct elicitation becomes particularly impracticable; if it is already a dangerous method of data gathering that needs great care and control in normal field situations, it becomes often useless in the case of work with semi-speakers typical of situations of endangered languages.

For the documentation of endangered languages, one must also take into account in all seriousness and great detail the sociolinguistic

56 See Craig (1997) for a survey of the research and fieldwork issues linked to language obsolescence.

dimensions of the situation, when graduate training and professional specialization emphasize a narrow focus on grammatical description. And independent of the variations of a sociolinguistic origin, one must deal with a frustrating situation of pervasive speaker variation due to incomplete learning and lack of reinforcement of norms which has been eloquently described by Dorian (1993b).

In addition to these linguistic issues is the fact that it is more and more common for the linguistic community involved to place some demands on the linguist to meet some of their needs. One way to think about this issue is to consider the evolution of the concept of fieldwork framework over the last decades and to be conscious of which framework one espouses. For this exercise, I find the approach to the concept of fieldwork frameworks developed in Cameron *et al.* (1993) helpful. Moving away from the traditional "ethical" fieldwork framework that has prevailed in academia – which Cameron *et al.* characterize as work *on* the language and for the sake of science – and rethinking the "advocate" framework of the late sixties and seventies – which they label as work *on* the language and *for* the people, we need to situate ourselves within the type of negotiated and collaborative fieldwork framework that is becoming the dominant one in the field, in South America at least, and which consists of a multidimensional framework of work *on* a language, *for* its speakers and *with* its speakers.[57] Although the ultimate goal would be to promote work *on* the language *by* the speakers, such a goal is generally unobtainable in a situation of extreme endangerment.

If one espouses an empowering framework of fieldwork that acknowledges the needs of the speakers' community, one is immediately challenged to types of work that one is unprepared for and feels little competence for. The point is to realize that there is no division of labor in the field, that the linguists, with their formal education are the main – supposedly expert – resource for whatever project is wanted, from literacy programs to bilingual education programs, to revitalization programs, to translation of legal texts.

A third critical aspect of work on endangered languages is that it aggravates the dissonance that generally develops between the values

57 For an account of a salvage linguistics/language revitalization project in this framework see the case of Rama described in Craig 1992a, 1992b.

and goals of academia and the values and goals encountered in the field situation. What are still most valued in the profession are theoretical pronouncements that will advance our understanding of the nature of language, with one of the measures of one's contribution to the field being publications. This goal is easier to meet when the data are abundant, verifiable and quantifiable, as with work on official/healthy/vital languages, which typically have a written tradition. But the reality of work on endangered languages is that old and last speakers are often hard to find, and hard to work with; that the data collected from them seem inconsistent and come in a trickle; that the enterprise is time consuming and can be expensive. These may not be safe situations for producing a doctoral dissertation, or publications to secure tenure, except in unusual circumstances (of previous documentation, of available and sophisticated speakers). So, of particular concern to me is the liability such work represents for the career of graduate students and junior faculty, unless the profession as a whole understands the difficulty of the work and appreciates the accomplishments for what they are.

6.3   *Appropriate training*

There are those who believe that the best training for fieldworkers is still the sink-and-swim approach, although this is certainly not the attitude of other disciplines which rely on fieldwork, such as anthropology or sociology.

The fact is that we can hardly afford to send the wrong people, unprepared people, into the sensitive and complex situations that most of these endangered language situations are. There are linguistic fieldwork issues to handle, and there are also much larger ethical/sociopolitical issues that make sheer survival of a research project a difficult endeavor.

We must rethink the issue of the training of fieldworkers beyond our traditional field-methods courses. Linguistic elicitation in the field with unsophisticated speakers carries little resemblance to the usual situation of field-methods course taught on campuses with fairly acculturated "informant" speakers. For one thing, there will always be the difficulty of handling the working language. On campus the burden is more on the linguistic consultant to adjust to the language of the linguist, but the situation changes drastically in the field. Difficulties with the working language common to native speaker and linguist, the lack of formal education of the native speaker, and the nature of the different relations speakers of languages with oral and written traditions hold toward their language make the kind of direct elicitation practiced in standard field methods courses a gambling game. One must rely on textual material, which is time consuming and itself a challenge to gather, if much safer as a source of data. But what if none of the last speakers is a "story teller," and no coherent texts can be gathered?

The technicalities of linguistic elicitation methodologies must be supplemented with a component of ethical/sociopolitical contextualization of the enterprise of fieldwork. Although there are no available fieldwork recipes, each situation being a unique configuration of circumstances and personalities that need to be handled on a case-by-case approach, we need to sensitize fieldworkers to the major components of the situations they are likely to walk into.

As already mentioned on several occasions, the fieldworkers may well be asked to respond to some of the needs of community linguistics, for example, the need for programs in language revitalization and in language maintenance, either through official bilingual educational projects or on a more ad hoc basis. Therefore it would seem judicious to include as part of the training for work on endangered languages the areas of applied linguistics which may be of some use. It is true that, for this, a curriculum still needs to be designed, as established programs of applied linguistics are not equipped to deal with the specific challenges of such populations. But the need is there, and some intellectualizing needs to happen at the university level, particularly within departments of linguistics that sponsor work on endangered languages. Language-revitalization projects need to be recognized as a special area of second-language acquisition and second-language teaching. It is not enough for "straight" linguists to think that such projects are the domain of educators and applied linguists; on one hand, manpower is much too scarce, and the reality is that the linguist is a one-person orchestra in the field. On the other hand, the linguists could be the ones most able to comprehend the linguistic situation of endangered languages.

There have been encouraging signs in recent years that the concern for endangered languages is becoming a shared concern within the profession of linguists. The above thoughts are just meant to point to some of the challenges we face as we try to understand better what the enterprise of work on endangered languages means. Hopefully they also make it clear that there is no discussion of work on endangered languages without taking into consideration the perceived needs of the communities of speakers involved. This calls for a reassessment of the kind of fieldwork framework one works within, a reassessment which challenges some of the basic premises of first-world academic circles. For those of us already involved in negotiated collaborative linguistic-documentation and language-revitalization projects with speakers of endangered languages, the intellectual as well as human rewards are real. It is only hoped that the profession sees it for the opportunity it is and the responsibility it means, at the dawn of the century beyond which little may be left of these endangered languages for ever.

Part III What is lost: language diversity

7 The significance of diversity in language endangerment and preservation

MARIANNE MITHUN

Department of Linguistics, University of California, Santa Barbara

At long last the tragedy of language loss worldwide has begun to enter the public conscious. In the past, individual communities and linguists have grieved over the disappearance of particular languages, but until recently the general public has been unaware of the accelerating loss of one our most valuable human intellectual resources. As the drama is repeated over and over around the world, it is easy to forget a crucial feature of the phenomenon: the very diversity that makes the loss irreversible. A great variety of languages are being threatened by a multiplicity of factors, in a wide range of community situations. Attitudes toward the impending loss differ both across and within communities. The human and material resources available to those hoping to work toward revitalization and documentation are similarly varied. Because of this diversity, the kinds of goals that are envisioned and feasible differ as well. What these communities do share is the significance of the moment: what they choose to do now, as well as what they fail to do, will have irrevocable consequences for future generations. With business as usual, all will be lost to the descendants of current speakers.

1 The diversity of languages

Many modern residents of North America are themselves unaware of the phenomenally rich linguistic diversity indigenous to their continent. We will never know exactly how many languages were once spoken in North America, but documentation survives of around 270 distinct, mutually unintelligible languages north of Mexico, and there were once many more. A third of the known languages are already gone, and most of the others are in grave danger. Only a handful will survive far into the next century.

The loss of these languages is not a monolithic one. Some notion of its scope can be grasped by considering the genetic relationships among the languages involved. Languages are considered genetically related, that is members of the same language family, if they are descended from a single ancestral language. Genetically related languages typically share certain vocabulary and structural characteristics inherited from their common parent. Most of the languages of Europe, for example, belong to a single family known as Indo-European, which includes not only English and other languages of the Germanic branch of the family, but also languages of the Romance, Celtic, Baltic, Slavic, Greek, Albanian, Armenian, Indic, Iranian, Tocharian, and Anatolian branches. Native American languages, by contrast, are generally considered to constitute over fifty distinct families. The families are of all sizes, from the Athapaskan-Eyak-Tlingit family with around forty languages, down to many single-member "isolates," languages that show no demonstrable genetic relationship to any other, such as Zuni. This genetic diversity is matched by tremendous structural diversity. North America is home to an extraordinary variety of languages, as different from each other as they are from European languages, each with unique potential contributions to our understanding of the possibilities of the human mind and spirit.

2   **A glimpse of linguistic diversity: Central Pomo words**

A small sample of the kinds of differences found among North American languages can be glimpsed in some examples from Central Pomo, a Pomoan language of California. The Pomoan family consists of seven mutually unintelligible languages. Central Pomo is spoken approximately 100 miles north of San Francisco in three communities: Point Arena-Manchester Rancheria on the Pacific Coast and the Hopland and Yokaya Rancherias 40 miles inland. Examples cited here come primarily from conversations recorded over a 9-year period among most of the remaining speakers: Jesse Frank, Winifred Leal, and Eileen Oropeza of the Point Arena Rancheria; Frances Jack and Kate Daniels of the Hopland Rancheria; and Salome Alcantra and Florence Paoli of the Yokaya Rancheria. The recordings were transcribed, translated, and analyzed with the help of Mrs. Jack. Mrs. Jack, Mr. Frank, Mrs. Alcantra, and Mrs. Paoli have since passed away.

2.1   *The segmentation of experience into words*

Most people who know two languages realize that all words in one may not have perfect equivalents in the next. This lack of isomorphism can be seen by comparing the Central Pomo words in (1) with their English translations.

(1)   Central Pomo–English translation equivalents: many to one

čá:ʔwan	"run around"	*čʰmáw*	"sit"
hé:ʔwačʼ	"run around"	*bamáw*	"sit"
mó:ʔwan	"run around"	*ʔčʰá:w*	"sit"
mó:ʔwačʼ	"run around"	*napʰów*	"sit"
čá:ʔwačʼ	"run around"	*čóm*	"sit"

As might be expected, the Central Pomo words for "run around" are not equivalent to each other. When just one person is running around, the verb *čá:ʔwan* is used, but if there is more than one, *hé:ʔwačʼ* is used; running around alone is portrayed as a different activity from running in a group. When the runner is a coyote, deer, or dog, the verb *mó:ʔwan* is used, indicating locomotion on all fours. The same verb is used for an older person, particularly a parent-in-law, as a sign of respect. A pack of running dogs (or several parents-in-law) would be described with a slightly different word, *mó:ʔwačʼ*. A group of people travelling around in a car are described with still another word: *čá:ʔwačʼ*. Verbs for "sit" show similar distinctions. For one person sitting on a chair alone or a bird perched on a branch, the term *čʰmáw* is appropriate. For a group sitting together on a bench or a row of birds on a wire, the term *bamáw* is used. A person sitting on the ground may be described with the verb *ʔčʰá:w*, but a group sitting on the ground would be described with the verb *napʰów*. For a container of liquid sitting on a table, the verb *čóm* is used.

From these examples it might be hypothesized either that Central Pomo allows finer distinctions than English (sitting on the ground versus sitting up off the ground), or that it prohibits generalization (general sitting). Of course neither hypothesis is correct. The categories delineated by Central Pomo words are simply different from those in English. Just as multiple Central Pomo words may correspond to a single English one, a single Central Pomo word may correspond to a whole set of English ones. The verb *napʰów*, used for a group sitting on the ground, is also used for a group camped together or settled, as well as to mean "marry," but only for women. If a man marries, an entirely different verb is used: *ʔdúw*. Marriage is expressed as a different event for a woman than for a man. Many other single Central Pomo terms also correspond to sets of English ones.

(2)   Central Pomo–English translation equivalents: one to many
  šyéw "stop picking fruit/collecting seaweed/weaving"
  šdíw "carry something in a bag"/"string beads"/"pull bucket out of a well"

2.2   *The segmentation of words into morphemes*

The alert reader may have noticed that some of the Central Pomo words seen so far share certain elements. English shows the same phenomenon. An English word like *unknowingly*, for example, consists of several meaningful parts, termed "morphemes." The root *know* forms the basis of the word, the suffix *-ing* converts the verb *know* to an adjective *know-ing*, the suffix *-ly* converts the adjective to an adverb *knowing-ly*, and the prefix *un-* contributes the meaning "not."

(3)   English *un**know**ingly*
  un- **know-** *ing-* *ly*
  prefix- **root-** suffix- suffix

Each of these morphemes also appears in other English words. The prefix *un-* also appears in *un-happy*, the root *know* also appears in *knowledge*, the suffix *-ing* also appears in *becom-ing*, and *-ly* also appears in *quick-ly*.

  The root of a word serves as its foundation, the morpheme generally considered to contribute its central meaning. The Central Pomo verbs in (1) are based on the roots *čà-* "run" (said of one person), *hé-* "run" (said of more), and *mó-* "crawl." The prefixes and suffixes attached to roots, collectively known as affixes, generally modify the roots in some way. All of the Central Pomo verbs in (1) for "run around" contain a suffix *-:ʔw-* "around," which qualifies the kind of running expressed. All of those verbs also contain an imperfective aspect suffix that qualifies the action as having internal temporal texture, here continuing activity. The Central Pomo imperfective suffix has two different forms, depending on how many individuals are involved: *-an* for one, *-ač'* for more. The verb *cá:ʔwač'* "group riding around in a car" is interesting in this regard. The root *čá-* "(for one to) run" is used because there is a single running activity, but the imperfective suffix shows the plural form because there are multiple participants. The verb describes a group of people running as one.

(4)   Central Pomo morphemes
       čá-:ʔw-an   *čá-:ʔw-ač̓*
       root-suffix-suffix   **root**-suffix-suffix
       one.run-around-imperf.sg   **pl.run**-around-imperf.pl
       "run around" (said of one person)   "run around" (group in a car)

2.3   Roots and affixes

An intriguing difference that can sometimes be seen among languages is in the distribution of meaning between roots and affixes. The picking motion in the Central Pomo verb *šyéw* "stop picking," for example, is indicated by a prefix, *š-* "pulling, dragging, manipulating by a handle." A pulling/dragging/handling motion similar to that involved in picking hops or cherries is involved in collecting seaweed and weaving. The root *yé-* contributes the meaning "stop."

(5)   Central Pomo roots and affixes
       š-yé-w
       prefix-**root**-suffix
       by.pulling-**stop**-perf
       "stop picking fruit off branch/collecting seaweed/weaving"

Carrying a bag or purse, stringing beads, and pulling a bucket or dipper from a well, are seen to involve the same kind of pulling motion as hoppicking. The verb *šdíw* "carry a bag," "string beads," "pull a bucket from a well" thus contains the same prefix *š-*. The meaning of the root *dí-* is quite general: "move or be in a location."

(6)   Central Pomo roots and affixes
       š-dí-w
       by.pulling-**move**-perf
       "carry something in a bag"/"string beads"/"pull bucket out of a well"

The roots *yé-* and *dí-* both appear in a number of other words with different prefixes. The verb *hyéw* "stop pounding acorns on a rock/poking someone in the ribs," for example, contains the prefix *h-* "by poking/thrusting/jabbing," and the root *čͪyéw* "stop cracking acorns" contains the prefix *čͪ-* "with full body weight/heavy mass/pressure."

2.4   Denotation and connotation

Such translations raise the question of just how specific the meanings of these verbs actually are. When a speaker hears the verb *šyéw*, for example, does he or she think "stop picking fruit or stop gathering seaweed or stop weaving" or simply "stop pulling"? The answer seems to be a bit of both.

Children learn words as wholes, in real-world contexts. A word like *šyéw* might first be heard while picking pepperwood nuts or gathering seaweed, but certainly not as part of a lesson from a parent explaining the semantic features of the prefix *š-*. Images of the situations in which words are used invariably become associated with them. When adult speakers discuss the meanings of words like *šyéw*, they refer to the contexts in which the words are used. Mrs. Jack never characterized the meaning of *šyéw* as "stop pulling," but rather as "stop picking fruit, . . . or stop gathering seaweed, . . . or stop weaving," adding new uses one by one as they occurred to her.

At the same time, there is evidence that speakers can become aware on some level of the internal structure of words such as these, although they may not be conscious of this knowledge. The extent of such awareness varies to some degree with the language and the individual. The internal structure of words in some languages is simply more transparent than in others, and some persons reflect on such issues more than others. Mrs. Jack first became conscious of Central Pomo prefixes like *š-* only after concentrated collaboration on linguistic analysis, when similar forms were juxtaposed. Throughout most of her lifetime, however, her unconscious knowledge of such morphemes allowed her to understand new words containing them and to produce neologisms of her own. She recounted an anecdote told many years earlier by a friend who had been offered a particularly juicy peach. The friend had declared with a grin:

(7)   Central Pomo: extension of existing morphemes
       slápčiwla
       s-láp-či-w=la
       sucking-lap-at.once-perf=performative.evidence
       "I just lapped it right up!"

The word is clearly an innovation: it was produced by combining the Central Pomo prefix *s-* "by sucking" with the English verb *lap*, then adding Central Pomo suffixes. It could not have been created if the speaker had not recognized on some level the elements of Central Pomo words. Mrs. Jack clearly shared this knowledge; she knew she had never heard the word before, but she understood it immediately, appreciated the image it created, and remembered it for years afterward.

2.5   *Does internal morphological structure matter?*

If speakers learn, store, and select words as wholes, we might assume that cross-linguistic differences in their internal structures are ultimately of little importance. The Central Pomo verb *baʔól*, for example, seems to have approximately the same range of meanings as its English translation "call." The Central Pomo verb is structurally complex (*ba-ʔól* = "orally-summon"), while the English verb *call* is not, but both words label the same action.

There is evidence, however, that the internal structures of words can in fact have subtle effects in several domains. One is in the resources offered by the language for the naming of new concepts. Speakers tend to exploit their existing grammars for new labels, rather than inventing words out of whole cloth. The features they abstract from new situations are shaped by the grammatical tools already present in the language. When Central Pomo speakers invent verbs for new kinds of activities, they often cite the kind of motion involved, "pulling," "poking," "sucking," "orally," etc. Speakers of English and other languages without such prefixes generally do not. They typically focus on other aspects of the situation, those for which resources already exist in their languages.

Such differences can also affect the ways in which concepts are linked. The actions represented by the words in (8), for example, might not be grouped conceptually by an English speaker, but they are all based on the same Central Pomo root.

(8)   Central Pomo: relations among concepts
       bayól   "while humming a song, suddenly put in words"
       syól   "wash down cookies/doughnuts with coffee or tea"
       šyól   "stir with a spoon"

All are based on the root *yól* "mix."

(9)   Central Pomo: relations among concepts
       yól "mix"   *ba-yól*   "orally-mix"
                            s-yól   "sucking-mix"
                            š-yól   "by.handle-mix"

A number of other verbs are also based on the same root. Many could be translated "mix," but they are not interchangeable in context.

(10)   Central Pomo *yól* "mix"

    čayól   "chop several things together, as onions and celery for stew"
          (*ča-* "by sawing or slicing")

    čʰyól   "plant things close together, such as melon and pumpkin, with the result that the flavors meld"
          (*čʰ-* "by vegetative growth"/"by pressure or mass")

    dayól   "add dry ingredients one at a time while baking"
          (*da-* "by pushing, especially with palm of hands")

    hyól   "add salt or pepper"
          (*h-* "by poking/jabbing/thrusting")

    myól   "throw various ingredients together into pot"
          (*m-* "by heat")

    mayól   "mix, as shortening with flour to make pie crust"
          (*ma-* "by stepping or twisting wrist")

    qayól   "eat several things together, as meat and potatoes, bread and jam"
          (*qa-* "by biting, pinching")

    šayól   "sift dry ingredients"
          (*ša-* "by shaking, moving long object lengthwise")

    yól   "throw various ingredients into a bowl with fingers"
          (*ʔ-* "by fine hand action, especially fingers")

Similarly, verbs meaning "call," "comb," "dig for," "peek at," "shake," and "set fishing line" might not seem to form a semantically coherent set, but their Central Pomo equivalents share a common basis, the root *-ʔól*.

(11)   Central Pomo *-ʔól* "summon"

    baʔól   "call"
          (*ba-* "orally")

    čʰʔól   "comb hair"
          (*čʰ-* "involving vegetative growth or flowing motion")

    daʔól   "dig for"
          (*da-* "by pushing, digging")

    hʔól   "probe with stick to see whether something is hiding"
          (*h-* "by poking")

    maʔól   "reach for something with the foot"
          (*ma-* "by stepping")

    pʰól   "peek at someone"
          (*pʰ-* "visually")

    pʼʔól   "shake something to see if there is dirt on it"
          (*p-* "encircling")

    šʔól   "set fishing line"/"check for fish"
          (*š-* "hanging/dangling/manipulating by handle")

2.6 *The legacy of the lexicon: possible words versus actual words*

A sample of the rich repertoire of Central Pomo prefixes can be seen in (10) and (11) above. There are more. These prefixes are pervasive in Central Pomo speech: a substantial proportion of events and states are characterized according to the kind of motion or medium involved. The prefixes are in fact so pervasive that it may at first seem that all can be combined with any root. In fact not all combinations of prefixes, roots, and suffixes necessarily occur as words in the language, even when they make sense. Words are created for a purpose, as labels for recurring, nameworthy concepts. Part of speaker competence involves knowing which combinations could exist as words in the language and which could not because they would violate the regular grammatical patterns. Speakers also know, however, which words could exist but simply do not because there has not been sufficient need for them. The verb *lót's* "be slick," for example, appears in combinations with some instrumental prefixes, among them *ča-* "by sitting," *da-* "by pushing," *qa-* "by biting," and *ʔ-* "by finger action," but not with others, such as *čʰ-*, *h-*, *m-*, *pʰ-*, *s-*, and *ša-*. Some of these combinations would make sense, such as *čʰlót's* "with.pressure-be.slick." It could conceivably be used to describe a slick object that slips when one tries to hit it with a heavy instrument. Speakers have simply not felt a need to express this property sufficiently often to devise a label for it. They are, furthermore, aware of that fact.

(12)   Central Pomo actual versus possible words

Actual, existing words		Possible but not actual words		
lót's	"be slick"	*čʰlót's*	*čʰ-*	"with heavy mass/pressure"
čalót's	"be slick to sit on"	*hlót's*	*h-*	"by poking/thrusting"
dalót's	"be slick to the palm of the hand, like a hard surface"	*mlót's*	*m-*	"by heating"
		pʰlót's	*pʰ-*	"by swinging/seeing"
qalót's	"be slimy to eat"	*slót's*	*s-*	"by sucking"
ʔlót's	"be slimy to the fingers, like a fruit"	*šalót's*	*ša-*	"by shaking"

The words that exist in a language thus provide a special legacy to new generations of language learners. They provide a view of the concepts speakers have chosen to label over the centuries during which the language has evolved, those that have been expressed sufficiently often to be considered nameworthy.

2.7   *The legacy of the grammar: origins of grammatical categories*

One of the ways that languages can vary the most saliently is in their grammatical categories, the distinctions that are typically or even obligatorily expressed. An important aspect of these differences is that they are neither arbitrary nor accidental.

Within most languages, the majority of grammatical categories have been part of the language for such a long time that their historical origins have become obscure. It has been possible in a number of cases, however, to trace their development so that much is now understood about the kinds of origins that underlie them. The evolution of some categories can be traced through written records. The origin of certain Modern French affixes can be seen in Latin documents, for example, and the origin of certain Modern English forms can be traced from Old English.

The most common source of affixes is in independent words. The *Oxford English Dictionary* (1971) tells us, for example, that the English suffix *-dom* in such words as *kingdom, freedom*, and *wisdom* developed from an Old English noun *dóm* meaning "jurisdiction" or "position" among other things. It was combined with certain other nouns in recurring phrases. As the phrases were used over and over, they came to be interpreted as lexical units, single words referring to single concepts: *cyningdóm* "royal or kingly dominion," *fréodóm* "the condition or state of being free," and *wisdóm* "the condition or fact of being wise." The element *dóm* lost its stress and was reinterpreted as a suffix. It continues as a productive suffix in Modern English meaning "condition/state/dignity/domain/realm," even though the noun *dóm* from which it originated has disappeared.

Sometimes the original source of a modern grammatical affix has remained in the language as a separate word. The Modern English suffix *-ful* of *faithful*, for example, originated from the Old English adjective *full* (*Oxford English Dictionary* 1971). The adjective typically appeared adjacent to nouns. Over time, some of these noun-adjective phrases melded into single words with a single primary stress, and the element *-ful* was reinterpreted as a suffix. It is now highly productive, frequently used to form new adjectives. Its ancestor, the adjective *full*, has remained in the language as a separate adjective alongside the suffix.

Although we have no written records through which to trace the historical sources of Modern Central Pomo prefixes and suffixes, some can still be detected because the sources have remained in the language.

Central Pomo contains a set of suffixes that indicate the direction of motion. Examples of them can be seen in (13) with the verb root *čá-* "run."

(13)   Central Pomo position and direction: suffixes
    čá-   "run"

čá:ʔwan	"run around/here and there"	*-aʔw-*	"here and there"
čámliw	"run around something"	*-mli-*	"around a point"
čá:qʼ	"run by"/"run south"	*-aq*	"south/on level/by"
čá:qač	"run uphill"	*-aqač*	"upward" ·
čá:law	"run downhill"	*-ala*	"downward"
čáway	"come running up to/against"	*-way*	"up to/against"
čàčʼ	"run away/escape"	*-čʼ*	"away"
čám	"run over/across something"	*-m*	"over/on/across"
čámač	"run northward"	*-mač*	"northward"

The historical origins of most of these suffixes have been clouded by time, but a few can still be detected because their sources have remained in the language. One of these is *-m* "over, on, across."

(14)   Central Pomo suffix *-m* "over"/"on or onto a surface"/"across"
    a. *pʰ-dí-**m***   *pʰ-dí-w*
       swinging-be/move-**over**   swinging-be/move-perf
       "(S/he) jumped **onto/over/across** (it)"   "(S/he) jumped"

    b. *tá:sa mčá-**m***   *mčá-w*
       dish set.pl-**onto**   set.pl-perf
       "(S/he) set the table"   "(S/he) set them down"

In certain contexts this suffix has the shape *-ma*.

(15)   Central Pomo suffix
    *tá:sa mčá-**ma**-m!*
    dish set.pl-**onto**-imp
    "Set the table!"

The historical source of the suffix is the verb root *ma-* "be over," "cross," which still survives in the language.

(16)   Central Pomo verb root *ma-* "be over," "cross"
    má-w   *čʰ-**má**-w*
    be.over-perf   sitting-**be.over**-perf
    "He went over it (a bridge)"   "He is sitting (up off of the ground)"

The development of the suffix probably began when speakers juxtaposed verbs such as "jump" and "cross" to yield "jump across." As the combination was used more and more frequently, speakers began to consider it a single word referring to a single event rather two separate actions. The element *má* lost its status as an independent word and its primary stress. Over time, its form has further eroded with use, so that it is most often just *-m*.

The source of another directional suffix is also still recoverable. The suffix *-mač* means "northward," "upstream," "upward," or "into." Its range of meanings reflects the fact that the Russian River, along which the Central Pomo live, flows from north to south.

(17)   Central Pomo suffix *-ma:č* "northward," "upstream," "upward," "into"
       *pʰa-dí-**mač**ʾ*   *pʰa-dí-w*
       flowing-be/move-**upstream**   flowing-be/move-perf
       "It (a fish) swam upstream"   "It (a fish) swam"

An independent verb root *máč-* "go north" also still survives in the language.

(18)   Central Pomo verb *máč-* "go north"
       *Mí=da **máč**=ya*
       that=at **go.north**=perceptual
       "He went thataway (northward)"

This verb is presumably the source of the modern suffix.

An important principle that comes from our understanding of the processes of grammaticization is that the grammatical categories we find in languages are not random. They represent those distinctions that speakers of the language have expressed the most often, over centuries or millennia. Some grammatical distinctions are quite common cross-linguistically, because they express concepts shared by much of humankind. Some differences can be related to the environment in which the languages have been spoken, such as the suffix *-máč* "go northward, uphill," where the river was a basis of orientation. Even today Central Pomo speakers indicate location and motion in terms of cardinal directions in natural speech more often than do English speakers.

Other differences in grammatical categories are more subtle, reflecting the many possibilities of expression and interpretation open to the human mind. Much can be learned about traditional patterns of expression in these domains as well from the grammatical distinctions available to modern speakers. Central Pomo, for example, contains a rich repertoire of morphemes (clitics) for indicating the nature of the evidence on which statements are based. Examples of their use can be seen in (19).

(19)   Central Pomo specification of evidence

    a. =*do:* quotative evidence (speaker was told by a specific person)

        Mu:l=do: *qó   tʰí-n*

        that=**quotative** what not-imperf

        "**According to him**, there's nothing wrong with that"

    b. =*ʔdo:* hearsay evidence (speaker has heard tell)

        Bal=ʔdo   masá:n ʔ=mú:tuya me:n dó-č-ma-w

        this=**hearsay** white   it.is=they   such do-semlf-multiple.agent-perf

        "**They say** white people do this"

    c. =*ya* perceptual evidence (known from direct personal observation)

        ʔúl   ʔe   qó=ča-m-ma=ya

        already it.is toward=run-multiple.event-multiple.agent=**perceptual**

        "They're here!" (speaker is standing on porch as they drive up)

    d. =*nme:* auditory evidence (speaker has heard evidence)

        *ʔúl   ʔe   qó=ča-m-ma-**nme:***

        already it.is toward=run-multiple.event-multiple.agent=**perceptual**

        "They're here!" (speaker hears the crunch of gravel from indoors)

    e. =*la* performative evidence (speaker is/was responsible)

        qʰawé: qa-dó-:n=la

        gum   biting-do-imperf=**performative**

        "I'm chewing gum"

    f. =*wiya* affective evidence (event affected the speaker)

        qʰawé: qa-dó-:n   s-dí-:q=wiya

        gum   biting-do-imperf sucking-be/move-levelly-**affective**

        "I swallowed my chewing gum (accidentally)"

    g. =*ka* inferential evidence (speaker has deduced or surmised)

        Mé:n ya-l   qadál-maq-ač=ka   mu:l šé:mi.

        so   we-patient hate-multiple.agent-imperf.pl=**inferential** that long.ago

        "They **must** hate us from way back"

The use of the evidentials illustrates another difference that morphological structure can make. Two languages may both contain devices
for specifying a certain distinction, but differ in the frequency with which
they are used. English speakers can of course specify their source of information if they wish, as can be seen in the translations of the Central Pomo sentences in (19). To do so, however, they must resort to a full word or phrase

(*apparently, so they say, according to him*). These devices, which involve a certain focus of attention, tend to be used more rarely than their pervasive Central Pomo counterparts. The Central Pomo evidentials have eroded through use to just one or two unstressed syllables that do not interrupt the flow of speech or thought. The difference in use appears even in translations by bilinguals. When Central Pomo is translated into English, speakers usually omit the evidentials.

The evidential examples illustrate another related point. What is asserted in one language may be only implied in another, and vice versa. Sentences (19e) and (19f) above contain no overt pronoun referring to the speaker corresponding to the "I" of the English translation. Yet reference can be inferred from the evidentials. In (19e), the speaker indicated with the evidential =*la* that her statement was based on evidence of personal experience in carrying out the action herself. In (19f) the statement with =*wiya* is based on the speaker's experience of having been affected by the event.

This brief sample of Central Pomo words and grammatical categories provides just a glimpse of some of the subtle but pervasive ways in which languages can differ. Glimpses of other kinds of differences can be seen in a language from the other side of the continent, one which differs as much from Central Pomo as it does from English.

3   Further glimpses of linguistic diversity: a Mohawk anecdote

Mohawk is a language of the Iroquoian family, spoken primarily in Quebec, Ontario, and New York State. Mohawk speakers have been recognized for centuries for their skillful use of language and their rich repertoires of oratorical styles. It would be impossible to do justice to this virtuosity within the space of a short chapter, but a few features of the language can be seen in the anecdote in (20), told by Karihwénhawe' Lazore, originally of Ahkwesáhsne. The top line shows the words as spoken. (In this orthography, currently in use in community schools, vowels *i, e, a, o* are essentially as in French, *en* represents the nasalized vowel of French *en, on* the nasalized vowel of English *noon*, and ' glottal stop.) The second line shows a segmentation of each word into its meaningful parts or morphemes. The third line provides the meaning of each morpheme. The fourth line is a free translation, composed by the speaker.

(20)   Mohawk: Karihwénhawe' Lazore, speaker
        Ake'nisténha   ó:nen kwáh kén' náhe' ionkkaratón:ni.
        ake-'nisten-ha   ó:nen kwáh kén' náhe' ionk-karat-onni
        my-mother-little now   just   a.bit ago   one/me-tell-to
        "My mother told me that a while ago,

        Kanáthen   ne tsi   kaná:taien
        ka-nat-h-en   ne tsi   ka-nat-i-en
        it-town-divided-is the that it-town-lie-s
        she was crossing the street

        ia'teiakohahahiia'konhákie'.
        ia'-te-iako-hah-hiia'k-onhakie'
        there-two-one-road-cross-ing
        in downtown Cornwall.

        Tha'kié:ro'k iá:ken' ísi'   na'oháhati   iakothón:te'
        tha'-kiero'k iá:ken' ísi'   na'-o-hah-ati   iako-at-hont-e'
        suddenly-X hearsay yonder so-it-road-beyond.is one-own-ear-goes
        All of a sudden, she heard

        ónhka'k   khe tontahohén:rehte',
        ónhka'-k   khe t-onta-ho-henre-ht-e'
        who-only just back-toward-he-shout-cause-perf
        someone give a yell from across the street.

        "Se'nikòn:rarak   wáts ensákwahte'   thi kà:sere."
        se-'nikonhr-ra-k   wats en-sa-kwa-ht-e'   thi ka-'ser-e
        you-mind-set-cont later will-it/you-get-cause-perf that it-drag-s
        "Watch out for that car!"

        Tánon' iá:ken' tontahohahahiia'konhákie'.
        tánon' iá:ken' t-onta-ho-hah-hiia'k-onhakie'
        and   hearsay back-toward-he-road-cross-ing
        The fellow who had issued the warning crossed the road,

        Tsi wa'thiátera'ne'
        tsi wa'-t-hi-ate-ra-'-ne'
        as factual-two-they.two-each.other-reach-come.to-perf
        and as she met him,

        ne ake'nisténha   wa'è:ron,
        ne ake-'nisten-ha   wa'-e-ihron
        the my-mother-little factual-one-say
        my mother replied,

        ["If the car hit me, it would be no loss to you." After he had walked on a bit,
        her protector turned and yelled back, "But the car would be demolished!"]

3.1   *The length of words*

Even the short passage in (20) illustrates a number of ways in which Mohawk differs from both Central Pomo and English. One of the most obvious ways is the length of words: Mohawk words tend to be longer, on the average, than Central Pomo or English words. They can consist of a large number of morphemes (meaningful parts), a characteristic known as "polysynthesis."

(21)   Mohawk polysynthesis
       wa'-t-hi-áte-ra-'-ne'
       factual-two-they.two-each.other-reach-come.to-perf
       "they two met each other" = "she met him"

An English speaker might well wonder whether the Mohawk in (21) is indeed just one word. A number of facts confirm that it is. The most important is that speakers know it is just one word, whether or not they have ever thought about grammar. If asked to repeat a sentence word by word, they do not hesitate. A second is that speakers do not pause in the middle of words like these any more than English speak . . . ers pause in the mid . . . dle of Engl . . . ish words. A third is that none of the parts would be identifiable to a speaker in isolation. A Mohawk speaker would not recognize the segment *-ate-* or *-ra-* any more readily than an English speaker would recognize the segment *-t* in isolation (the past tense of *feel* in *fel-t*). A Mohawk word has only one primary stress, one syllable that is stronger than the others. The stressed syllable in (21) is on the middle *á*. Additional facts confirm the fact that it is a single word.

Does this word-hood matter? In fact it does. Words express a single conceptual unit, here a single event of meeting. If the speaker had wanted to say that she had met a policeman she would have used at least two words, one for the meeting and one for the policeman; policeman-meeting is not a simplex idea. If she had wanted to draw special attention to the fact that there were just two who met, she would have emphasized the number with a separate word "two" in addition to the verb "meet" above.

3.2   *Nouns and verbs*

A second difference between the Mohawk passage and its English equivalent is the relative proportions of nouns and verbs in each. It might be thought that although the words of one language might not have perfect equivalents in the next, at least where speakers of one use nouns, speakers of the other will also use nouns. In the English version of (21) the proportion of nouns and verbs is equal: 9 nouns, 9 verbs (1:1). (Pronouns are not included in the count.) The Mohawk version of the same anecdote contains 2 nouns and 14 verbs (1:7). Such a proportion is not untypical of Mohawk. Mohawk speakers generally use a much higher proportion of verbs than either English or Central Pomo speakers do. Several factors contribute to this discrepancy, most related to the richness of Mohawk verbal morphology.

Many objects labeled by nouns in English or Central Pomo are labeled by verbs in Mohawk. The verb may characterize the object by describing its appearance, behavior, or function. These descriptive verbs are then used as if they were nouns, although their literal meanings are still verbal.

(22)   Mohawk verbal descriptions of objects
  kà:sere   *kaná:taien*
  ka-'ser-e   *ka-nat-i-en*
  it-drag-s   it-town-lie-s
  "car"   "(lying) town"

Relationships are often described with verbs rather than prepositions.

(23)   Mohawk verbal descriptions of relations
  na'oháhati   *kanátthen*
  na'-o-hah-ati   *ka-nat-th-en*
  so-it-road-beyond.is   it-town-divided-is
  "(it is) across the road"   "(it is) in the middle of the town"

Finally, nouns are often incorporated into Mohawk verbs.

(24)   Mohawk noun incorporation: noun-verb compounds for unitary concepts
  se'nikòn:rarak   *ia'teiakohahahiia'konhákie'*
  se-'nikonhr-ra-k   *ia'-te-iako-hah-hiia'k-onhakie'*
  you-mind-set-continuative   there-two-one-road-cross-ing
  "Watch out!"   "She was crossing the street"

Noun incorporation is done for a purpose. It creates single words for what are portrayed as single concepts or events. The construction offers speakers options. If they would like to put separate emphasis on an entity, the noun referring to it is expressed as a separate word. In the anecdote in (21), the speaker's mother had said "If the car hit me, it would be no loss to you." The man replied, "But *the car* would be demolished," contrasting the car with the woman. The focus of contrast, the car, is a separate word.

(25)   Mohawk focus of contrast: no incorporation
        Kà:sere *ki' wáhe'   enkarihwén:ta'ne'*
        car   just certainly it will break to pieces
        "But **the car** would be demolished"

3.3   *The ordering of ideas*

A third difference between Mohawk and English speech is in the order of words. As can be seen by comparing the Mohawk in (20) with its translation, words do not appear in the same order in the two languages. The basic order of words in English sentences is Subject–Predicate–Object:

(26)   English word order
        The fellow crossed   the street.
        subject   predicate object

Mohawk word order differs in a fundamental way. It has little to do with the syntactic status of words as subjects, predicates, or objects. In (25) above, for example, the car, which is the subject of the sentence in the English translation, appears at the beginning of the Mohawk sentence. But in (27), the car, again the subject in the English translation, appears at the end of the Mohawk sentence.

(27)   Mohawk word order
        Ensákwahte'   **thi   kà:sere.**
        en-sa-kwa-ht-e'   thi   ka-'ser-e
        will-it/you-get-cause-perf that it-drag-s
        "**That car** will get you"

Words are ordered in Mohawk according to their relative newsworthiness at the moment. Items which are particularly significant, because they are new and important, or they introduce a new topic, or they highlight a focus of contrast, appear early in the sentence. Those that express more predictable or peripheral information appear later. The most newsworthy element of the warning in (27) is the possibility of being hit, so the verb appears first and the "car" appears later. In (25) the car is more newsworthy, because it represents the focus of a contrast with the mother. This time it appears first in the sentence, before the verb "break."

3.4   *Text-structuring through particles*

In addition to the nouns and pervasive verbs, Mohawk contains a third kind of word termed "particles." These words, which have no internal morphological structure, are often notoriously difficult to translate. Many particles serve an important but subtle role in regulating the flow of information, the rhythm of the discourse. A minor example of such textual structuring can be seen in the use of the hearsay particle *iá:ken'* "it is said" in (20). Mohawk speakers, like Central Pomo speakers, systematically identify information they have heard from others. If identifying the source of information were the sole function of *iá:ken'*, however, it should appear only once in an anecdote like that above, perhaps at the beginning. Yet it appears twice just within the short passage cited in (20), even though the original teller of the tale, the speaker's mother, had just been specifically identified two lines before. The particle serves another more subtle secondary function, structuring the narrative by highlighting significant shifts in the flow of the action.

(28)   Mohawk text-structuring through particles
   "My mother told me that a while ago
   she was crossing the street
   in downtown Cornwall.
      *Tha'kié:ro'k **iá:ken'***
      suddenly   **hearsay**
      All of a sudden, **it seems**,
   she heard someone yell from across the street.
   'Watch out for that car!'
      *Tánon' **iá:ken'** tontahohahahiia'konhákie'.*
      and   **hearsay** back-toward-he-road-cross-ing
      And **it seems** that he crossed the road,
   and as she met him,
   my mother replied, . . ."

The examples cited here in sections 2 and 3 have provided just a glimpse of some of the ways in which Central Pomo and Mohawk contrast with English and with each other. Each shows us alternative ways of structuring perceptions of the world, of making sense of experience. Most people who speak more than one language well have noticed that they not only use different words in each, they also say different things. Both Central Pomo and Mohawk speakers comment that they "think differently" when they speak their first and second languages. The differing vocabularies of each language may lead them to package concepts differently. The grammatical categories of each may lead them to single out different aspects of situations under discussion, and relate ideas in different ways. Languages are constantly evolving to meet the needs of their speakers as they are shaped by use, but they are not created overnight. They reflect what a people has chosen to say most often over millennia. A lost language cannot be replaced.

4   The diversity of community contexts

Just as the languages indigenous to North America differ substantially from one community to the next, so do the situations in which they are disappearing. Over the course of history and before, languages have disappeared for a variety of reasons. Some languages died abruptly with the premature deaths of their speakers. In North America, diseases brought by Europeans often preceded direct contact with the Europeans themselves. In many areas heavy losses resulted from warfare. These factors, combined with the sudden loss of land needed for subsistence, destroyed already small communities. The Yana of Northern California, for example, were reduced from approximately 1,900 to under 100 within twenty years of the arrival of white settlers in 1846 (Johnson 1978:362–363). The Yahi dialect of Yana was assumed to have been extinct by the 1860s, until a lone Yahi man, later known as Ishi, emerged in 1911 after decades of hiding. His language came to an abrupt end when he died of tuberculosis in 1916.

More common in recent times has been the loss of traditional languages through language shift, as people used the language of the dominant society in place of their mother tongue in more and more situations. A major contributor to the current decline of languages all over North America was the institution of formal education, particularly in boarding schools designed to separate children from the influence of their homes and families during their formative years. In community after community, elders now recall the pain of this separation, of being forbidden to speak their languages or observe their traditions, and of their resolve never to put children of their own through the hardship of being unable to speak the dominant language. It was a time when the strength of their own cultures and the intellectual value of bilingualism were little understood or appreciated. Strong pressures against the maintenance of traditional languages persist to this day. In most areas, children continue to be educated in the outside language, and success in life is often equated with the ability to conform. The ubiquitous presence of television in the dominant language also sends a strong message to children and young people.

Even processes of language shift have not been uniform across the continent, however. Obviously more remote communities, such as those of the Yup'ik in Alaska and the Inuktitut in the Canadian north, were not subject to outside pressures as early as those near centers of European settlement, such as the Powhatan of Virginia or the Esselen south of San Francisco. Community size has also played a role. Navajo and Cree are spoken not only in relatively remote areas, they are also used by relatively large numbers of people. Both languages are still being learned as a mother tongue by children, though the proportion of children learning them is diminishing every year.

In a number of cases what has been remarkable is the impressive strength of linguistic traditions under highly unfavorable circumstances. In the west, the Barbareno Chumash were nearly all taken into the Franciscan mission at Santa Barbara within a few years of its founding in 1786. With a few exceptions, the Franciscans seem to have had scant interest in the language or culture of their converts. Little attempt was made to learn or even record the language. The Chumash were immediately put to work learning European occupations and Spanish. Yet the Chumash languages persisted miraculously for generations, over nearly two centuries. The last speaker of Barbareno Chumash, Mary Yee, was highly skilled in the language right up until her death in 1965. She commanded a massive, intricate vocabulary and a full, elaborate repertoire of grammatical and stylistic categories and constructions. Several factors can be seen to underlie her skill. She was in daily contact with at least one other fully fluent speaker throughout most of her lifetime. She thought about her language and its structure, recording and analyzing it over three decades of work with linguists. She was also an intelligent, articulate individual, fully fluent and literate in three languages: Barbareno Chumash, Spanish, and English.

A second impressive example of the strength of linguistic tradition comes out of a different kind of history, this time in the East. The Mohawks encountered Europeans quite early, at the beginning of the seventeenth century, and contact has continued to the present. Mohawk communities have been characterized by neither the geographic isolation nor the very large numbers of the Navajo or the Cree. The community at Kahnawà:ke has been situated on the south bank of the St. Lawrence River, directly across from Montreal, for three centuries. Residents have long gone outside the community for work; particularly their steel work as far away as Boston, New York, Detroit, and even Dallas. Yet the Mohawk language is still spoken skillfully, after nearly four centuries of contact. What is the key to its strength? There are probably nearly as many answers as speakers, but certain factors stand out. The Mohawk communities have always been strong ones, in which individuals are respected and relations among members valued. Mohawk speakers have always appreciated their language and cultivated skillful use of it. Unfortunately, even here few children are now learning Mohawk as a first language. Perhaps the most important ingredient in the current vitality of the language is the dedication of a core of individuals who have worked tirelessly and selflessly for over twenty-five years to give their children the gift of their own heritage in Mohawk immersion schools and language classes (see Jacobs, this volume, for details).

4.1   *The diversity of attitudes*

Even in the face of language endangerment, heroism like that of the Native teachers and curriculum specialists at Kahnawà:ke and elsewhere is not uniformly acclaimed. Attitudes toward language and its preservation vary both across and within communities. In parts of California, for example, where communities have always been relatively small, people could often expect to marry someone with a different language, and thus to use several languages during their lifetimes. Multilingualism was a norm, and a pragmatic view of language often prevailed; language was seen first as a practical tool of communication. Learning a new language was not viewed as a sign of disloyalty to the old. In other areas, or among other individuals, there is stronger consciousness of the social meaning and cultural connections of specific languages. Some of the most salient forms of culture are expressed linguistically. Special ceremonial language cannot be easily replaced with a translation into a new language; jokes no longer have the same zip; stories no longer convey the same spirit or warmth. People interact with each other in different ways.

Current attitudes toward the perpetuation of the traditional language vary as well. In some communities, elders realize that the maintenance of language is crucial to the retention of culture in its full form. Considerable effort is being devoted to language instruction. Young people are searching the historical, anthropological, and linguistic literature for any information they can find about their cultures and languages. Yet in other communities, such pursuits are viewed with little enthusiasm, for several reasons.

It is felt by some that if the traditional language is to die, it is not up to human beings to interfere with this natural process. The kinds of measures that preservation might entail, such as formal teaching, recording and writing, are seen as conflicting with the nature of the language itself, which has always been an oral organism. At present, the majority of active language programs involve writing, even where students are not taught to read and write themselves. Writing has allowed curriculum planners and teachers to become conscious of the structures unique to their languages and allowed them to plan lessons accordingly. Of course successful language curricula depend on strong documentation of the language. For documentation, writing is even more central: audio or even video recordings alone will be of little use to future generations who do not control the language. Yet, for understandable reasons, some community members feel that "reducing the language to writing" would do violence to it, destroying its integrity and strength. There are fears that once it is written, this most intimate cultural inheritance will no longer be uniquely theirs but, like so many other aspects of their heritage, become accessible to any passersby, people who may not accord it appropriate respect.

In many communities not all parents are convinced that retention of the traditional language is best for their children. Perhaps they or their parents suffered through the pain of boarding school, of being criticized and punished for using their mother tongue. Perhaps they are simply considering the economic fate of their children in a world that requires competence in one or even two major languages as a prerequisite for employment. If an English-speaking Mohawk child in Quebec needs to know French to find work, whether it be clerking in a drugstore or presiding over a bank, parents may hesitate to force the child to learn Mohawk first, and to dedicate scarce human and economic resources to a Mohawk language program.

4.2   *The diversity of available resources*

Tremendous differences exist across communities in the resources available to those concerned with language preservation, differences in linguistic resources, in human resources, and in economic resources.

In some communities, the traditional language can be heard everywhere, while in others, it is used only rarely. In a few areas people of all ages still speak the traditional language well, and children are still learning it as a mother tongue. In others, parents are fluent but young people have only a passive understanding. In many, a strong core of middle-aged people speak the language well, although younger adults have only a rudimentary or passive knowledge. In still others, only elders command the language fully. Finally, in a number of communities, no speakers remain. Such differences necessarily affect the kinds of preservation efforts that are possible.

Probably the most crucial ingredient in the success of language programs over the past several decades has been the attitudes and talents of community members. The creation of Native-language programs requires extraordinary vision, determination, and industry. In many communities, knowledgeable speakers with unending dedication are few, and potential language students have other priorities. As more and more communities have developed language programs, however, more curriculum ideas are becoming available for sharing. Techniques devised for one language in one community may not always be appropriate for the next, but in many cases they can stimulate new ideas, a valuable commodity for teachers who have no textbooks for their subject matter but who must produce classes that will hold their students' attention day in and day out. For most speakers, language is a relatively unconscious phenomenon. Few speakers are aware of the tremendous complexity or harmony of the tool they use constantly. A good linguist can help a community discover what is special about their linguistic heritage and how to understand it in its own terms, rather than those of the dominant outside language. Most successful programs have in fact involved collaboration between community members, who set the goals and provide language expertise, and linguists, who can provide technical support in such areas as orthography construction, curriculum design, language-teaching techniques, and procedures for language documentation.

Finally, in the closing years of the twentieth century when it is almost too late, certain practical resources are slowly becoming more accessible. In the United States, an evolving respect for Native languages and awareness of their impending loss are leading to increased funding for community projects. Conferences, workshops, and summer courses specifically designed for communities developing Native-language programs are now taking place in a variety of locations throughout North America. These gatherings are providing a forum for the sharing of ideas, expertise, solutions to problems, and enthusiasm. Communities no longer need work in complete isolation.

4.3   *The diversity of goals*

Because of the diversity of the language structures involved, of the patterns of language use, of attitudes toward traditional languages, and of human and material resources available, no single goal is appropriate for all situations, nor is there a single formula for success. One response to impending language loss is to do nothing and let the process run its course unimpeded. Such a decision is of course the privilege of local communities, to whom the languages belong. Such a decision should of course be made only with full awareness of its effect not only on current community members but also on their descendants, who will not be in a position to make the decision for themselves.

In some communities, the perpetuation of native bilingualism is a desired and even attainable goal. Where children are still learning the traditional language as a mother tongue, as in Greenland, maintenance may be primarily a matter of ensuring that it remains a part of their daily lives, that it is in constant use around them even if they are bilingual in the dominant language, and that it is enjoyed and respected. Special linguistic training may not be necessary in such a situation; strong personal commitment may be sufficient.

Where the youngest speakers are parents of young children, as in some Yup'ik communities in Alaska, now is the time for communities to discuss their priorities. If they value the traditional language, it may still be possible to pass it on to their children with concentrated efforts at constant use. If adults who know the language always choose to use it with each other and with the children, the children will have a much better chance at remaining bilingual.

Where most of the younger speakers are middle-aged, vital language programs are still possible, as has been demonstrated at Kahnawà:ke and elsewhere. The commitment of Mohawk speakers at Kahnawà:ke has brought about a tremendous change over the past twenty years. In the early 1970s, the language was rarely heard in public. There was no reason for children to consider it a viable part of their heritage. Once they realized the consequences of their daily use of English, however, a substantial number of Mohawk speakers simply resolved to speak Mohawk to each other. The community has transformed itself. The sound of the language and the usual accompanying laughter is everywhere; it is a visible presence as well, appearing in places of all kinds, from signs on buildings to bank statements. Children growing up now are being given a strong, positive sense of their special heritage, but their English has not suffered at all. Decisions such as this do not necessarily require great financial resources, although they may involve substantial personal effort. Where active speakers remain, a number of such options remain possible. Grandparents may resolve to speak only the traditional language to their grandchildren. Simply gathering fluent speakers together with semi-speakers (those with basic but limited native competence) for daily gossip sessions can foster tremendous growth, allowing them to widen their vocabulary and augment their mastery of idiomatic expressions, complex structures and stylistic options. Language classes and even immersion programs remain possible. Speakers past their childrearing years often provide the most valuable human resources of all, combining vigor and commitment with knowledge and experience. Master/apprentice projects like those in California described by Leanne Hinton could be especially successful in such situations, where energetic masters are available and apprentices already possess native command of the basic sounds and structures of the traditional language.

Where the only speakers are too elderly to teach, as among the Hupa of California, they can still serve as a vital resource for language programs, as models for semi-speakers, as resources for curriculum construction, and as the basis for documentation of the language. Because it is extremely difficult to teach full fluency if one is not fluent oneself, appropriate goals in such situations may be more modest, but still extremely important. Even limited familiarity with the language can have strong symbolic value for both children and adults, providing a link with their own heritage and a crucial sense of self.

Where no native speakers remain, as among the Chumash in California, it may be too late to create new ones, but if good documentation of the language exists, it may still be possible to instill an appreciation of the special richness and power of the traditional language. The extensive field-notes of John Peabody Harrington on Barbareno Chumash, for example, have provided an irreplaceable resource for descendants of speakers to discover their own heritage. There is not a language in North America that fails to offer breathtakingly beautiful intricacy. For descendants of speakers to discover this beauty can profoundly enrich their lives, much like the discovery of music, literature, or art, if not more.

Although the diversity of community settings, attitudes, and resources necessitates a diversity of goals among language programs, efforts in the face of severe endangerment must differ in a fundamental way from those meant to prepare American tourists for a week in Paris, or allow Japanese students to read American computer manuals. The ultimate aim of Yup'ik, Mohawk, Hupa, or Chumash language programs is not rudimentary communication or comprehension. Most speakers of endangered languages in North America also know English, French, or Spanish, so their children and grandchildren need not learn the traditional language to speak with them. The purpose of the work is to understand and preserve what is special about the tradition itself. The loss of languages is tragic precisely because they are not interchangeable, precisely because they represent the distillation of the thoughts and communication of a people over their entire history. Language instruction and documentation that is limited to translations of English words or even English sentences misses the point entirely. It must capture not just how things are said, but also what people choose to say, not only in ceremonies and narrative, but in daily conversation as well.

5   Conclusion

Language represents the most creative, pervasive aspect of culture, the most intimate side of the mind. The loss of language diversity will mean that we will never even have the opportunity to appreciate the full creative capacities of the human mind. The hundreds of North American languages that are currently disappearing or that have already disappeared differ in a vast variety of ways, some fundamental, some subtle, many both. Just a few of these ways have been illustrated with examples from Central Pomo, a language of the west, and Mohawk, a language of the east. We have seen differences in the segmentation of experience into word-sized categories: languages do not contain perfectly equivalent vocabularies. We have seen differences in the features selected as most salient to describe certain concepts: languages differ in their repertoires of grammatical categories. What is packaged in one language as a root, the primary foundation of a word, may be packaged as a prefix or suffix in another, a qualification of the core concept. What speakers of one language express primarily with nouns, speakers of another may convey with verbs. Distinctions expressed routinely in one language may be expressed only rarely in another. We have seen, furthermore, that such differences are neither random nor arbitrary. Vocabulary and grammar are shaped by use. The lexicon of a language reflects those concepts that speakers have referred to often enough to consider nameworthy. The grammatical categories of the language represent those features of situations that speakers have specified so often that they have become routinized. It is this diversity, the result of millennia of development, that makes the loss of these languages irreparable.

The circumstances under which the languages are disappearing differ as well. Some of the languages are spoken in large communities, some in small ones; some are spoken in remote areas, others under conditions of heavy contact. Some of the languages are still used daily by large numbers of people of all ages, while others are only dimly remembered by a few elders. Among some groups the traditional language is highly valued and preservation is greatly desired, while among others alternative values have priority. Some communities have, through great effort, been able to secure certain human and financial resources for language projects, while others have few resources at all. Such variables mean that no single goal can be appropriate for all situations, nor can there be a single formula for success. Results of one program cannot be judged against those of any other.

Because of the urgency of the situation, however, now is the time for general awareness of the consequences of both action and inaction. Now is also the time for the sharing of experiences, expertise, and solutions to similar problems. Although the same strategies and techniques may not be equally applicable to all programs, ongoing communication can provide useful ideas and encouragement in the face of a demanding task.

For those communities committed to language revitalization, preservation, and appreciation projects, it is worthwhile to take time to consider the ultimate goal of the work. If the intent is simply to equip descendants with a short list of basic words to use as symbols of their heritage, the task is a relatively minor one. If it is to capture the uniqueness of their heritage, however, this specialness must be respected in both teaching and documentation. Simply eliciting vocabulary and basic paradigms will not be enough; speakers must be allowed to speak for themselves. It is crucial to record how good speakers use their language, what they choose to say in the multitude of settings that constitute their daily lives, how they describe their own experiences, how they provide explanations, and especially how they interact with each other. Such a record will lay a foundation for their descendants to discover the intricate beauty of a system unlike any other, and a chance for us all to appreciate some of the capacities of the human spirit.

8 On endangered languages and the importance of linguistic diversity

KEN HALE

Linguistics Program, MIT

1 Introduction

During the coming century, according to some informed estimates, 3,000 of the existing 6,000 languages will perish and another 2,400 will come near to extinction. This leaves just 600 languages in the "safe" category, assuming that category to be languages having 100,000 speakers or more. Thus, 90 percent of the world's languages are imperiled (cf. Krauss, in Hale *et al.* 1992). Languages in this situation are typically "local" languages, as opposed to national or international languages, and in the minds of many people, both linguists and non-linguists, their endangerment and progressive extinction amount to a catastrophe for human intellectual and cultural diversity, a disaster comparable in its extent to losses in other aspects of our environment.

The loss of linguistic diversity is a loss to scholarship and science. The scientific study of the mind is a venerable pursuit in human intellectual history, and the human capacity for language is the human mind's most prominent feature. While a major goal of linguistic science is to define universal grammar, i.e. to determine what is constant and invariant in the grammars of all natural languages, attainment of that goal is severely hampered, some would say impossible, in the absence of linguistic diversity. If English were the only language on the face of the earth, we could not know literally hundreds of things which are permitted, even predicted, by universal grammar and accidentally missing in English, or any other single language. We would not know, for example, that Modern Irish audibly instantiates a theoretical chain of connections between successively embedded clauses in complex relative clauses like "the novel that I thought I understood GAP" (*an t-úrscéal a mheas mé a thuig mé*). As demonstrated by the Irish linguist James McCloskey (1979), the leniting particle *a* appearing at the head of each clause marks a *path*, so to speak, between the head of the relative clause "the novel" (*an t-úrscéal*) and its corresponding (empty) position, symbolized GAP, in the lower clause. The existence of such a path was suspected for many years, but evidence from English alone was of the most indirect sort. The Irish evidence is of enormous importance to our understanding of these matters (see below for further discussion of this example). Our experience tells us that *every* language adds something to the general program of the scientific study of grammar. The loss of a language is a loss indeed, and the loss of many is a disaster.

There is a more urgent concern, and that is the effect of language loss on human intellectual life. At least this is so for those who believe that linguistic and cultural diversity is the enabling condition for the maximal production of intellectual wealth of all kinds and in all fields. The fact is, an enormous body of cultural and intellectual wealth was lost irretrievably in the course of the European colonization of the New World and the South. It was lost utterly and without being noticed, primarily because it was *mental* wealth, appreciable only through the language which was lost with it. Only by accident do we know the extent of the loss. The Damin auxiliary language of the Lardil people of Mornington Island, North Queensland, was lost during the decade just past; only fragmentary accounts of it remain – it is a serious loss, as it embodied the only known strictly oral account of the semantic structure of the vocabulary of an entire language, a worthy product of human intellectual labor.

2   Linguistic diversity and the scientific study of language

I will begin with a consideration of the importance of diversity for the science of linguistics, a legitimate consideration given the admitted legitimacy of the study of human mental capacities. It is a fact, I believe, that without linguistic diversity it will be impossible for us to perform the central task of linguistic science, i.e. the task of developing a realistic theory of human linguistic competence, realistic in the sense that it properly reflects not only the limits on the manner in which grammatical structure is determined by the properties of lexical items, for example, but also the impressive diversity of surface form in the observable structures of natural languages. The truth of this, i.e. of our dependence upon linguistic diversity, can be appreciated by performing a simple mental experiment. Imagine that English was the only language. What would we know about universal grammar and about the potential diversity of surface form? We would know a lot, to be sure, since the observed form of English is *determined* by universal grammar. We would know a lot, and of what we did not know we would be *blissfully* ignorant, since we would not, and could not, know. But fortunately, English is not the only language. So we can perform another experiment. We can ask ourselves what each language adds to what we know, say, from the study of English. When we do this, the role of diversity in linguistic science becomes explosively obvious. At this point in the history of linguistics, at least, *each* language offering testimony for linguistic theory brings something important, and heretofore not known or not yet integrated into the theory. In many cases, data from a "new" language forces changes in the developing theory, and in some cases, linguistic diversity sets an entirely new agenda. Diversity gives us the visibility that results from "movement," as a tiger against a jungle backdrop becomes visible when it moves, to use Kiparsky's simile in defense of the study of language change as a way of learning about synchronic grammar. To look at two, or three, or more, languages is to see "movement" or "slippage," it is to see how *one and the same mental organ* functions to produce forms which are systematically different, in the manner which leads us to say that we are dealing with different languages or different dialects. The effort to understand how this can be, how there can be such differences, has been one of the most important driving forces in theoretical linguistics. For example, it took French and English together, not just French and not just English, to make Pollock (1989) and Chomsky (1991) see the principles which have been so important in the development of the *minimalist* theory of grammar.

The role of Modern Irish in contemporary linguistic theory is an excellent example of the point I have been trying to make. In the space of one minute, I was able to think of fifteen examples of Irish contributions to our understanding of the principles of grammar. The example already cited is one – here, what Irish gives us is (possible) confirmation of a theory based on rather indirect evidence from English. It is the idea that "extraction" must "obey subjacency." In the English translation of the Irish relative clause (1a), the head nominal *the novel* is separated from the GAP at the end of the sentence by two clause boundaries (signaled by the English complementizer *that*). This is "too much distance," and the theory of "subjacency" holds that it is possible because the relationship between the head nominal and the GAP is established in stages, in shorter steps; first, you establish a link between the GAP and the rightmost *that* and then you establish a link between the two *thats*. So each link is short, and obeys subjacency. Now Irish helps to confirm this stepwise process of linking the head nominal to the GAP. Compare the words corresponding to English *that* in the two sentences of (1) below. Look first at (1b). Here there is no GAP, and the ordinary Irish complementizer *go* (*gur*) is used. But when there is a GAP, as in (1a), the complementizer changes to *a*. This happens at each step, suggesting – to some linguists, at least – that the complementizer change is a reflex of the stepwise process which, by hypothesis, establishes the link between the GAP and the head nominal. If this is true, then Irish is the linguistic equivalent here of the cloud chamber which permits an observer to see the movement of otherwise invisible charged particles. The path of movement is visible in Irish, invisible in English, and most other languages.

(1)   a. *an t-úrscéal a   mheas mé a   thuig   mé* GAP
            the novel   that thought I   that understood I
            "the novel that I thought that I understood GAP"

    b. *(Dúirt mé) gur mheas mé gur thuig   mé an t-úrscéal.*
            (said I)   that thought I   that understood I   the novel
            "(I said) that I thought that I understood the novel"

    c. *an t-úrscéal ar mheas mé ar thuig   mé é*
            the novel   that thought I   that understood I   it
            "the novel that I thought that I understood it"

The second version of the relative clause – i.e. (1c) – is the so-called "indirect form." It does not involve movement; instead, a resumptive pronoun (here *é*, referring to the head nominal *an t-úrscéal* "the novel") appears in place of the GAP used in (1a), the "direct relative." These forms are cited and discussed in McCloskey (1979:155, *et passim*).

The next example I would like to present is one which, so far, remains a challenge to linguistic theory. It involves a structure which the existing perception of universal grammar, literally, rules out as impossible, or appears to. This sort of example represents the "gold" of linguistic diversity, since its accommodation will almost certainly tell us something very important about universal grammar, forcing a reconsideration of certain assumptions now held.

In order to discuss the example, it is necessary first to introduce another grammatical system, one which is relatively widespread but one which would be a part of our blissful ignorance if the only language were English, or even if the only languages were those of Europe and most of Asia and Africa – this is the system of "track keeping" known as "switch-reference." Our example comes from the small Misumalpan language family of the Atlantic Coast of Nicaragua and Honduras.

Sentences (2a–b), illustrating the Misumalpan switch-reference system, are from Ulwa (also called Southern Sumu):

(2)   a. *yang nawah tal-i   îr-ikda.*
          I   tiger   see-PROX run-PAST.1sg
          "On seeing the tiger, I ran away."

        b. *yang nawah tal-ing   îr-ida.*
           I   tiger   see-OBV.1sg run-PAST.3sg
           "Upon my seeing the tiger, it ran away."

In each case, the inflection of the first verb (*tal-* "see") indicates two things, (i) that the verb is subordinate, and (ii) the switch-reference value. In relation to the latter, (2a) represents the "same-subject" relation, while (2b) indicates the "different-subject" relation. That is to say, in (2a) the two clauses have the same subject (I . . . I), while in (2b), the two clauses have distinct subjects (I . . . it).

Now consider the causative construction in Ulwa; this is the construction which has a surprise for any complacent linguist. As (3) shows, it uses the switch-reference clause-sequencing pattern just illustrated:

(3)   *yang nawah ât-ing   îr-ida.*
        I   tiger   cause-OBV.1sg run-PAST.3sg
        "I made the tiger run."

And in this very respect, it differs markedly from the familiar causative construction in relation to the relative subordination of the substructures corresponding to the "cause" and the "effect" – in the familiar type, the cause is expressed in the main clause, the effect in the subordinate. The reverse is true in the Misumalpan construction. This follows directly from the fact that the favorite Misumalpan clause-sequencing pattern is used, putting the main verb to the right in this head-final language, plus the fact that the iconic "cause–effect" order is reflected in the construction. Thus, while the English construction has *make* as the main verb and *run* as the subordinate, just the reverse is true in Ulwa.

One could imagine, of course, that the Ulwa "translates" the English causative but that it is not really the same thing – instead of saying "I made the tiger run," Ulwa says something like "Because I did something to the tiger, it ran." The English here achieves the same subordination effect as the Ulwa. If this were true, then there would be nothing left to say. However, there is evidence suggesting that (3) is a true causative and that the syntactic "insubordination" of the causative verb actually presents us with a contradiction when other constructions are considered in interaction with the causative – this is our surprise. For example, by contrast with what the switch-reference system and inflection indicate, the controlled infinitive construction illustrated in (4) treats the causative verb as the main verb:

(4)   *yang walta-yang*   [*nawah ât-ing   îra-naka*]
       I   want-PRES.1sg tiger   cause-OBV.1sg run-INF.3sg
       "I want to make the tiger run."

The infinitive is required by the verb *walta-* "want" when its subject is identical to that of its complement. In (4), the relevant subject is that of the *causative* verb, not that of the verb identified *morphologically* as the main verb. This holds in spite of the switch-reference morphology which indicates the reverse pattern of subordination. The imperative, not exemplified here, exhibits the same contradictory pattern.

While these superficially contradictory phenomena remind us to keep our theoretical guard up, it is likely that they can be understood within existing theoretical frameworks, though this is not altogether obvious. This particular constellation is almost certainly made possible by the conjunction of predominant Misumalpan features – clause chaining with switch-reference morphology (forcing adjunct to precede main clause), and SOV syntax, together with expression of iconic cause–effect order.

I would like now to turn to another area, morphosyntax, and look briefly at the phenomenon sometimes called "concord," whereby the sub-parts of a phrase are marked for some grammatical category pertaining to the phrase as a whole. Case concord is in fact familiar to us, since many Indo-European languages show it. The example in (5) below is from Lardil, an endangered Australian Aboriginal language of North Queensland. In Lardil plain non-future transitive clauses, the object of the verb is marked for accusative case. And if the object is complex, involving, for example, a demonstrative and a modifying adjective, as well as the head noun, each of these subconstituents will bear the accusative ending. This is exemplified in (5), a nominal phrase in the accusative case (glossed ACC):

(5)   *diin-in   karnan-in maarn-in*
       this-ACC long-ACC spear-ACC
       "this long spear"

(5′)

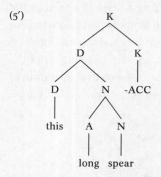

This behavior is altogether familiar, from Latin, German, or Russian, for example. The principle is rather simple, reflecting a universal and favored option among languages with suffixal case inflection: attach suffixal K to the head of the phrase it locally governs, where "head" is *each* head in the minimal domain locally governed by K.

In Lardil, and most other Australian languages, a possessor phrase (or genitive, glossed GEN) also acquires the case inflection of the accusative object of which it is a part, as in (6), corresponding to the structure given informally as (6′):

(6)   *kantha-kan-in   karnan-in maarn-in*
       father-GEN-ACC long-ACC spear-ACC
       "father's long spear"

(6′)

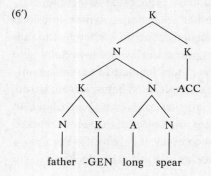

However, there are limitations on concord, evidently. Not every word is properly "in the domain" of an accusative case governing the nominal as a whole. Thus ACC does not attach to a genitive which is itself contained within a larger genitive constituent. Thus, there are limits on "how far down" case marking can extend, as seen in (7) and its informal structural representation (7'). This sort of limitation is also quite familiar, of course, being a reflection of the general structural relation of locality:

(7)   *marun-ngan kantha-kan-in   karnan-in maarn-in*
       boy-GEN   father-GEN-ACC long-ACC spear-ACC
       "the boy's father's long spear"

(7')

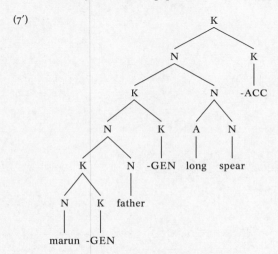

In short, most of what we see here (apart from the details of morphology) belongs to the realm of that which does not have to be *learned* in the course of first-language acquisition. It is part and parcel of universal grammar. We are not surprised.

But given the principles of case concord, there is much more that we would be surprised *not* to find. If suffixes can attach to the head (i.e. *any head*) in the domain they locally govern, then it is natural to expect, for example, that overt suffixal *tense* (T) would also exhibit concord, spreading on to the heads in the verb phrase it locally governs. But we have something to learn here, for this behavior is the exception, not the rule. Lardil, and its sister Wellesley Island languages Kayardild and Yangkaal, belong to the exceptional class of what might be termed tense- (or modality-)

concord languages. Thus, while the non-suffixal perfective of (8a) does not participate in tense concord, the suffixal future (FUT) tense of (8b) does undergo spreading of the type we might expect to be possible, despite its rarity among languages of the world:

(8)   a. *Ngada yuurr-were   kiin-in   karnan-in maarn-in.*
        I   PERF-throw that-ACC long-ACC spear-ACC
        "I threw that long spear."

       b. *Ngada were-th-ur   kiin-kur karnan-kur maarn-kur.*
        I   throw-*th*-FUT   that-FUT long-FUT   spear-FUT
       "I will throw that long spear."

(8′)

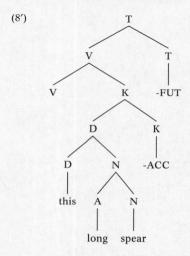

The question is, why is tense concord of the type represented by (8b) so rare? But, on second thought, perhaps the *real* question should be, why is it possible at all? If (8′) is in fact the correct representation of the abstract syntactic structure of the tense phrase (TP) of (8b), then concord into the nominal should be impossible, since it invades a subordinate domain (that of case, K), violating the principle of locality. This would certainly account for its rarity. So what accounts for its occasional possibility, as in the Wellesley Island languages of North Queensland?

We do not really have the answer to this, just as we do not have the answer to hundreds of puzzles which the world's linguistic diversity offers to us. This is precisely why linguistic diversity is so important to the discipline. While we do not have a fully satisfactory account of tense concord in

Lardil, there is at least one avenue of inquiry which could be explored. Notice that the future suffix (-FUT) *replaces* the accusative (-ACC). Suppose, therefore, that the structure present at the time concord is realized is not (8′) but, rather, a structure at which the case and tense are merged into a single element. If K and T were merged in this way, they would not define distinct domains, and the single ending could then be realized in the manner which is normal for Lardil inflections, i.e. as suffixed to each head in the relevant domain. What is special about Lardil is not that it permits a violation of locality – in theory, no language does that – rather, it possesses a merging process which results in the circumstance that tense *appears* to undergo concord, like case, and in the process to invade a subordinate, non-local domain. It must be said, however, that the putative merger itself is not unproblematic; it must involve local processes, e.g. attachment of T (= -FUT) to V and K, fusion by replacement of K by T, and then subsequent reattachment of the fused K-T to the constituents of D. But we cannot say as yet that we fully understand these processes. In any event, if all of this comes together in a manner similar to what has been suggested here, then the existence of tense concord is to be expected. But its rarity is also to be expected, since it is a *marked* phenomenon whose occurrence requires a constellation of factors, each unremarkable in itself, but marked in concert.

Are there any true surprises in case and tense concord? Let us continue looking at the domains into which concord can penetrate. If what we have suggested so far is correct, concord cannot really violate the locality condition. But consider the following sentences:

(9)   a. *Ngada yuurr-kurri maa-n#nanga-n*
           I   PERF-see   child-ACC#person-ACC
           "I saw the child." (cf. *mangarda* "child")

        b. *Ngada kurri-th-ur mang-kur#dangka-r*
           I   see-*th*-FUT child-FUT#person-FUT
           "I will see the child."

The Lardil word *mangarda* (= *manga#da* < *mang#dangka*) "child" is a compound, one member of an impressively large inventory of nominal compounds, some rather opaque and eroded (like this one) and some relatively transparent. The sentences in (9) illustrate the fact that Lardil concord does not respect the integrity of compounds. It treats the parts of a compound as if they were separate words – the relevant suffix attaches to each component, not merely to the whole (as it would in German, or Irish, say). This is a surprise if lexical integrity is the general rule in morphology. Why is the Lardil pattern possible in that language, but not in another, even one which generally exhibits concord? Lardil, and its Wellesley Island sisters, force this question upon us, another benefit from linguistic diversity.

I would like to look at concord now from a more globally syntactic perspective. From the examples we have observed in what precedes, it would appear that concord, so to speak, "works downward," not "upward" – a suffix spreads on to material which is in some abstract structural sense "at or below" the level of its own base position. This would follow, of course, if concord were defined in terms of "local government," as we have suggested. Since a suffix attaches to the head it locally governs, it follows that it attaches to an element at or lower than its base position, assuming the government relation involved here implies c-command.

We expect, therefore, that tense concord should pattern as it does in in the Lardil sentences (8b) and (9b). Specifically, we expect the tense to spread onto the object, but not onto the subject. And this is what we see in (8b) and (9b) – the subject *ngada* "I" is in the nominative case and it is unmarked for tense; only the object bears tense morphology. This is not surprising, since the subject is an *external* argument, external to the verb phrase. In English, at least, the subject is normally held to be in the specifier of Infl (= TP) and hence not c-commanded, and not locally governed (in the intended sense), by the functional head T (tense). And if local government, with c-command, is required for concord, then we do not expect an external subject to be inflected for tense. The Lardil subject is evidently external in the conventional sense, as it does not show tense concord.

But what of the VP-internal Subject Hypothesis? Strong arguments have been given in favor of the view that the *basic* position of the subject is internal to, or at least adjoined to, the verb phrase. For English, and a large number of other languages in which this is evidently not the case superficially, it is argued that the subject raises to its observed external position. For others, there is reason to believe that the subject remains in its lower VP-internal (or VP-adjoined) position.

The diversity found in systems of tense inflection could have something to offer here, obviously. Consider a language with suffixal tense, like Lardil, in which the subject remains in the hypothetical lower position, c-commanded by the functional head T. If this were suffixal, it would not be impossible for it to be realized on the subject. This expectation is fulfilled by the future tense in Pittapitta (Blake 1979), another language of Queensland, as illustrated in (10b), corresponding to the structure set out in (10'):

(10)   a. *Majumpa-lu   pukarra-nha thaji-ka.*
             kangaroo-ERG grass-ACC   eat-PAST
             "The kangaroo ate the grass."

        b. *Majumpa-ngu pukarra-nha/-ku   thaji.*
             kangaroo-FUT grass-ACC/-ACC.FUT eat.FUT
             "The kangaroo will eat the grass."

(10')

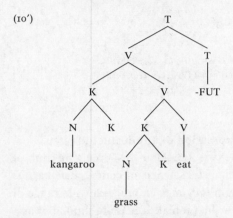

Past tense (and present tense, not shown here) follow the more usual pattern found in languages of the world, according to which just the verb inflects for tense. In the future tense, however, the subject regularly inflects for that category, whether the clause is transitive, as here, or intransitive. In modern Pittapitta, the object is not inflected for future as regularly as it was in the nineteenth century when the language was first described, hence the second option for the object of a future clause is now the least frequent.

Before leaving the system of concord represented by these languages, I would like to consider one additional fact, both surprising and not surprising. In these languages, concord is a matter of suffixes. In addition to the locality requirement, an element undergoing concord, or "spreading," must be an affix. It is worth asking whether there are any limits on the *nature* of the affix. We know, for example, that verbs can be affixes – the causative, for example, or the host of an incorporated nominal. It is natural to ask whether a suffixal verb, for example, could participate in concord.

This might be seen as surprising, since a lexical (as opposed to functional) category is at issue; but it would not be surprising from the strictly morphological point of view, where the category *suffix* is the relevant one. The Wellesley Island languages, including Lardil, possess a set of semantically "case-like" suffixal verbs. Perhaps it is not too surprising that these participate in the concord system:

(11)　　a. *Ngada ketharr-iya-th-ur.*
　　　　　I　　　river-GO-*th*-FUT
　　　　　"I will go to the river."

　　　　b. *Ngada kiin-kiya-th-ur　ketharr-iya-th-ur.*
　　　　　I　　　that-GO-*th*-FUT river-GO-*th*-FUT
　　　　　"I will go to that river."

　　　　c. *Ngada kiin-kiya-th-ur　mutha-ya-th-ur ketharr-iya-th-ur.*
　　　　　I　　　that-GO-*th*-FUT big-GO-*th*-FUT river-GO-*th*-FUT
　　　　　"I will go to that big river."

3　　Local languages and the expression of intellectual life

The world's linguistic diversity is a precious resource. The truth of this does not derive solely from linguistic science, of course. Language is much more than grammar. The term *language* embraces a wide range of human capacities, and it is not clear that it makes sense to think of it as a single entity.

Of supreme significance in relation to linguistic diversity, and to local languages in particular, is the simple truth that language – in the general, multifaceted sense – embodies the intellectual wealth of the people who use it. A language and the intellectual productions of its speakers are often inseparable, in fact. Some forms of verbal art – verse, song, or chant – depend crucially on morphological and phonological, even syntactic, properties of the language in which it is formed. In such cases, the art could not exist without the language, quite literally. Even where the dependency is not so organic as this, an intellectual tradition may be so thoroughly a part of a people's linguistic ethnography as to be, in effect, inseparable from the language.

The loss of local languages, and of the cultural systems which they express, has meant irretrievable loss of diverse and interesting intellectual wealth, the priceless products of human mental industry. The process of language loss is ongoing. Many linguistic fieldworkers have had, and will continue to have, the experience of bearing witness to the loss, for all time, of a language and of the cultural products which the language served to express for the intellectual nourishment of its speakers.

In this section, I would like to describe one such product of a people's intellectual work. This is a tradition whose decline and virtual disappearance I witnessed in the course of fieldwork in Australia. It was the treasure of a small group of Australian Aboriginal people, the Lardil, living on Mornington Island in North Queensland.

While working on the syntax and lexicon of Lardil in 1960, I heard of the existence of an auxiliary language, called Damin, which some initiated men in the community could still use. Most men could not, since the missionaries who were in power on Mornington Island during the early decades of this century had forbidden the practice of initiation many years earlier, and it was in the context of initiation that Damin was learned. Only men initiated before the mission was established had the opportunity to learn Damin, and only a few of those men were still living in 1960.

I was not able to work on Damin until 1967. An anthropologist working with the Lardil people sent me a tape of Damin while I was working in another community farther south. When I heard the tape, I knew that Damin was something very special, so I arranged to visit Mornington Island again. The feature of Damin which first caught my attention was its phonology. It departs drastically from the phonology of Lardil, and it has sounds in it which do not exist in any other Australian language. For example, it has click consonants, otherwise found only in Africa – in the Khoisan languages, for example, and in the Nguni languages of the Bantu family. There is no historical connection between the Lardil and these African languages. The use of clicks in Damin developed locally. Damin has the appearance of an invented language, and it is attributed, in fact, to a legendary figure named Kalthad (Yellow Trevally). If it was invented, then it is a clever invention, indeed, because it is almost unheard of for an invented language to depart radically from the phonological constraints of the ordinary language of the inventor. The impression that Damin is an invention is strengthened by the fact that it not only has sounds absent elsewhere in Australia, but it also has sounds found nowhere else in the world – as true phonological segments, that is. These include an ingressive voiceless lateral and a labiovelar lingual ejective.

Although its sound system is spectacular, the extraordinary genius of Damin is to be found in its lexicon. In its original purpose, Damin was an "auxiliary language," in the sense that it was used in place of Lardil when this was necessary for ritual reasons. An idea of its nature can be gained from a consideration of how it was learned and used. According to the accounts of surviving *Demiinkurlda*, or "Damin-possessors," as they were called, Damin was learned by novices in the advanced phase of men's initiation. Men who went through this stage were called *Warama*, and in theory, only Warama learned Damin. In practice, however, since it was used in public, many people who were not Warama, both men and women, had passive knowledge of it. Its purpose, apart from the intellectual pleasure it gave, was to serve as a vehicle of communication between Warama and all individuals involved in their initiation. The use of ordinary Lardil with these people was forbidden, until they had been repaid the ritual debt owed to them by the Warama as a result of initiation. Damin is a lexicon, not an entire language. The rule in using Damin correctly is this: each lexical item of Lardil must be replaced by a Damin item; the inflectional morphology and syntax of Lardil remains intact. An example of this lexical replacement procedure can be seen in (12) below, in which the first line is in Lardil, the second is the Damin equivalent, and the third is a literal gloss of the morphemes in the sentence:

(12)   *Ngithun dunji-kan   ngawa   waang-kur werneng-kiyath-ur.*
        n!aa   n!n!a-kan   nh!nh!u tiitith-ur   m!ii-ngkiyath-ur.
        (my   WiYBro-GEN dog   go-FUT   food-GO-FUT)
        "My wife's younger brother's dog is going hunting (lit. going for food)."

As this example shows, the syntax and morphology of Damin and Lardil are the same. Both use the same case system. The genitive (glossed GEN) is exemplified here, as well as the nominative, which is not overtly marked – *ngawa, nh!nh!u* "dog" is in the nominative. And the two share the same system of verbal tenses – the future, glossed FUT, is seen here. And finally, they use the same system of derivational morphology, exemplified here by the verb-forming allative ending -*(ng)kiya-* (glossed GO). This element converts the noun *werne, m!ii* "food" into a verb meaning "to go after food, to hunt."

While the morphology is the same for Lardil and Damin, the lexicon is totally different. Thus, each noun, verb, or pronoun in the Lardil of (12) matches a distinct item in Damin. It is the nature of this replacement lexicon which is extraordinary. It is constructed in such a way that, in principle, it can be learned in one day. It can be learned in one day, yet, in combination with Lardil syntax and morphology, it can be used to express virtually any idea. How can a lexicon be *small* enough to learn in one day and, at the same time, be *rich* enough to express all ideas? A moment's reflection on this question can only inspire admiration, in my judgment.

The answer, of course, is abstractness. The Damin lexicon cannot be rich in the usual sense of having large numbers of lexical items denoting concepts of great specificity (like the ordinary Lardil or English vocabularies, for example). Rather, the richness of Damin is of a different sort, the opposite of this in fact. Damin lexical items are abstract names for logically cohesive families of concepts. The richness of Damin resides in the semantic breadth of its lexical items, permitting a small inventory (less than 200 items) to accommodate the same range of concepts as does the much larger ordinary vocabulary (of unknown size).

The example given in (12) above can be used to illustrate the basic point of Damin abstractness. Consider the first word of that sentence. In Lardil, this is a form of the first-person singular pronoun, and, as such, it is involved in a rich complex of oppositions expressed by a set of nineteen distinct pronouns. There are three persons, three numbers (singular, dual, plural), an inclusive–exclusive distinction in the first-person dual and plural, and in all non-singular pronouns there is a two-way distinction among the pronouns for generation harmony. There can be little doubt that ordinary Lardil is rich, in the sense of highly specific, in this domain. By contrast, Damin reduces all of this to a single binary opposition:

(13)   a. *n!aa* "ego"
        b. *n!uu* "alter"

The first of these is used to refer to any set which includes the speaker, including the set which includes only the speaker. The second refers to any set which does not include the speaker. Incidentally, these two forms illustrate one of the click consonants of Damin. All Damin clicks are nasalized. That is to say, the velar occlusion associated with the production of clicks is released as a velar nasal. In this case, the click articulation itself (symbolized!) is in the alveopalatal position (symbolized by using [n] for the nasal component). The other clicks are the dental [nh!], as in the word for "dog", and the bilabial [m!], as in the word for "food." In some items, the click is reduplicated, as in the words for "dog" and "wife's younger brother."

The abstraction represented by (13) is actually greater than I have indicated, since the entire set of determiners (i.e. demonstratives, as well as pronouns) is subsumed in this opposition. This means that each of (13a) and (13b) is more abstract that any of the actual Lardil words which it covers. There is, in ordinary Lardil, no single word which corresponds either to (13a) or to (13b). Nor is it likely that there is any such word in English, or any other language, for that matter, setting aside the highly technical vocabularies of fields in which deictic reference is of central importance (e.g. *ego* and *alter* of kinship studies, a close, but not exact correspondence).

The domain of time is analyzed in the same fashion. Thus temporal reference, like pronominal reference, employs a fundamental binary classification, opposing the present to all other times:

(14)   a. *kaa* "present, now"
       b. *kaawi* "other than present, other than now"

The first of these terms is used in place of Lardil words such as *yanda* "now, today" and *ngardu* "presently," while the second corresponds to such words as *bilaa* "recently (in the past)," *bilaanku* "tomorrow," and *diwarrku* "yesterday." Again, the terminology here involves an abstract classification of the domain, and each of the terms is more abstract than any Lardil lexical item.

Our example sentence (12) contains further examples of abstraction. The term *nh!nh!u* "dog," is one of the few terms in Damin that refers to a narrow class of entities (the class of canines, dingos and dogs). It would appear to be a counterexample to the general principle of abstraction. However, the term is, in fact, used to refer to an abstract set, that of domestic animals – it combines with *ngaa*, a term refering generally to animate beings, especially humans, and to mortality, to form *ngaa-nh!nh!u* "horse," and it combines with *wiijburr*, a term referring to wooded plants, to form *wiijburr-nh!nh!u* "cattle." The study of the semantics of Damin compounds is in its infancy, I am afraid, and it is not clear how the components of the compounds just cited yield the meanings given. It is clear, however, that *nh!nh!u* refers to domestic animals in general. And, as usual, this usage is not matched by that of any Lardil lexical item.

Sentence (12) also illustrates the most abstract of the Damin verbal lexical items, *tiiti* "act." This is the generalized active verb in Damin. It corresponds to both transitive and intransitive verbs of Lardil – e.g. *jitha* "eat," *jidma* "lift," *kirrkala* "put," *matha* "get, take," *murrwa* "follow," *wutha* "give," *wungi* "steal," *jatha* "enter," *kangka* "speak," *lerri* "drip," *waa* "go." The Damin verb is used in reference to activities other than those resulting in harmful effects. Verbs of harmful effect are represented in Damin by *titi*, with a short initial syllable, rather than the long syllable of the generalized activity verb. However slight this phonological difference might seem to be, it is real and rigidly observed in Damin usage – *titi* corresponds to such Lardil verbs as *barrki* "chop," *betha* "bite," *bunbe* "shoot," *derlde* "break," *kele* "cut," *netha* "hit." This does not exhaust the verbal inventory of Damin, but it covers the vast majority of active verbs in Lardil. And each of these Damin verbs is, as expected, more abstract than any Lardil verb.

While abstraction is the general rule in Damin, exceeding that of Lardil lexical items, in some cases the Damin terminology corresponds to abstract terms in Lardil itself. This is particularly true in certain domains having to do with foods. Thus, the Damin term *m!ii* applies to foods in general, particularly vegetable foods, and corresponds closely to the Lardil term *werne* "food." Likewise, certain seafoods are classed in the Lardil manner – thus, *l*ii* "boney fishes" (with *l** representing the ingressive lateral consonant) corresponds to Lardil *yaka*; Damin *thii* "cartilaginous fishes, sharks and stingrays" corresponds to Lardil *thurarra*; and Damin *thuu* corresponds to the interesting heterogenous Lardil class *kendabal* "sea turtles and dugongs."

The Damin lexicon must achieve a balance between abstraction and expressive power, since it must satisfy two essentially contradictory requirements. It must be such that it can be learned quickly and, at the same time, it must be such that it can be used, in cooperation with Lardil inflectional morphology and syntax, to express any idea which Lardil itself can be used to express. It cannot be *too* abstract, therefore.

The extent to which this balance is achieved can be appreciated through an examination of the system to which the Damin kinship term *n!n!a*, also exemplified in (12), belongs. This term is used in (12) to render the Lardil term *dunja* "junior brother-in-law." Of course, as expected, the Damin term is in fact more general than any actual Lardil kinship term. The entire Lardil kinship system – which, like most Australian systems, is terminologically enormous – is reduced to the five Damin terms charted below:

(15)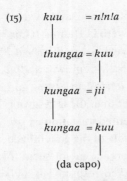

kuu   = n!n!a

thungaa = kuu

kungaa = jii

kungaa = kuu

(da capo)

To understand this system, place yourself in the upper left-hand corner. That is the class to which your siblings belong – thus, you call your brothers and sisters *kuu*. Your spouse and his or her siblings are directly opposite, joined by the symbol =, as usual in kinship charts. Thus, a man calls his wife and her siblings *n!n!a*, and correspondingly, a woman calls her husband and his siblings by the same term. A man calls his children and his father, and his father's siblings, *thungaa*; the bar (|) links father–child connections generally. One's mother is located in the column opposite to one's own (i.e. in the opposite "patrimoiety"), one row down – thus, your mother and her siblings are called *kuu*, the same as your own siblings (corresponding to the fact that you all belong to the same "matrimoiety"). The mother–child links follow this logic generally – opposite column, one row down. Applying this set of principles consistently to the chart in (15), it is possible to assign a Damin term to any person for whom a biological connection can be traced, actually or theoretically, no matter how distant. This terminology is based on an "eight subsection" classificatory system. It uses a biological model for calculation, though the terminology is "classificatory" and is not dependent on actual biological connections – though if these are in fact known, they will be used in determining how the terms should be applied in a given instance. In accordance with the principles inherent in this terminology, one's mother's mother's brother's daughter's child is *n!n!a*, a member of the class to which one's spouse belongs, in the preferred (second cross-cousin) marriage pattern. And one's mother's brother's child is called *jii*, and includes the class of people to which a spouse belongs according to the less favored alternative (first cross-cousin) marriage pattern.

A moment's reflection on this system will probably give rise to the natural question of why the number of Damin kinship terms is five, rather than two, four, or eight. The question is natural because the logic of the system suggests even numbers – four, say, would be appropriately abstract; eight might violate the principle of abstractness. The answer to this question, I believe, reveals the genius of Damin, i.e. the balance between abstractness and expressive adequacy. Reduction to four terms would force a merger in the most important distinction within the kinship system. This is a *subsection* system, containing eight classes of kinsmen. The key ingredient in the subsection system is the distinction between kinsmen related through the second (fourth, sixth, etc.) generation from those related through the first (third, fifth, etc.) generation. That is, it distinguishes kinsmen related through *harmonic* generations from those related through *dysharmonic* generations. Systems which merge this distinction, also widespread in Australia, are called *section* systems. The beauty of Damin is that it expresses generation harmony precisely where it is most important in relation to alliances within the community – i.e. in classifying one's cross-cousins, thereby defining the set of potential spouses in the preferred marriage aliance. The generation-harmony distinctions are merged where they are less crucial to the expressive efficiency of the terminology. Therefore, Damin has fewer terms than the eight implied by the subsection system, in keeping with the principle of abstraction.

The auxiliary language of the Lardil people is an intellectual treasure of enormous worth. It has not been studied in depth, and it is not clear that it will be possible, ever, to give an adequate picture of its structure. It is clear from what we know that it involves a sophisticated semantic analysis of the lexical resources of Lardil. The system of abstractions lays bare aspects of lexical semantic structure to a degree which, quite possibly, is not achieved by any other system of analysis which attempts to accommodate an *entire* vocabulary.

The last fluent user of Damin passed away several years ago. The destruction of this intellectual treasure was carried out, for the most part, by people who were not aware of its existence, coming as they did from a culture in which wealth is physical and visible. Damin was not visible for them, and as far as they were concerned, the Lardil people had no wealth, apart from their land. This visibility problem was overcome only at the last hour, when Doug Belcher, an extremely enlightened superintendent, with great intelligence and at considerable risk to his position at Mornington, struggled valiantly to create an environment in which the Aboriginal wealth of the island could regain its position of dignity in the life of the community. His efforts led eventually to the real possibility of the resumption of initiations and of a role for local languages in the educational system. In the context of the atmosphere which Belcher initiated, efforts were later made to produce tapes for Damin which would be available to Lardil young men, and an elementary dictionary of Lardil, with an appendix on Damin, was produced. It is not yet clear what effect these developments will have in relation to the intellectual traditions of the Lardil people. They have, however, had an important effect on the Kayardilt community, a refugee people from Bentinck Island, whose language is still very strong and whose intellectual traditions can form a central part of the education of the school-age population.

We cannot say that the Damin tradition is utterly lost to the Lardil people. However, it is all but gone, since revival of it would be from recorded sources, and if revival were to be attempted, a *new* Damin tradition would be initiated, necessarily, since the cultural context of the original tradition is irrecoverable – there are no survivors of that period. The development of a new Damin tradition is not a bad thing, of course, in fact it would be an exciting thing. But the old Damin tradition is effectively lost. And the destruction of this tradition must be ranked as a disaster, comparable to the destruction of any human treasure.

It is perhaps of little use simply to bemoan the loss of a treasure. The example of Damin is offered as an instance of the nature of things that have been lost and of what can be lost if linguistic and cultural diversity disappears. In the case of Australia, we cannot know what has been lost in regions where Aboriginal cultures no longer thrive – the wealth there was mental, not physical. But if the remaining diversity in Australia is not safeguarded, we know that we stand to lose a lot, including the language-based traditions of verse, and a living tradition of antonymy in Central Australia embodying a semantic analysis of lexical items along the lines of Damin. The same is true in all areas where local languages are spoken.

4   Concluding remarks

The safeguarding of linguistic and cultural diversity does not guarantee the unchanged perpetuation of existing traditions of intellectual endeavor, of course. In fact, a living tradition implies change. And it is precisely the development of new traditions which is most consonant with the human purpose. And it is precisely where local languages are viable that new traditions develop. Thus, for example, in the southwest of the United States, beside the continuing traditions of sung verse, a new tradition of poetry is developing, in Papago, Pima, Yaqui, and Hualapai, for example, in the context of the growing use of the written form of these languages. Similarly, in Nicaragua, there is an increasing use of Miskitu and Sumu in the writing of prose and in composing lyrics for popular music. And the use of Miskitu in political discourse is contributing to the development of an increasingly effective oratorical style in the language, as well as an impressive body of new terminology, both borrowed and coined. In these regions, and in many others, new traditions of language use are developing and growing. Their success will depend, of course, on a continuing position of strength for the languages involved.

In the preceding sections, I have presented a somewhat self-serving perspective on the human costs of the observed decline in linguistic and cultural diversity. It is the point of view of a person who is professionally involved with language and whose field of study is seriously threatened by language loss. So I have not said anything about the personal costs of language loss, the grief felt by countless numbers of people who have been prevented, for one reason or another, from acquiring the language, or languages, of their parents, or the grief of parents who, for one reason or another, have not been able to give to their children the full portion of linguistic tradition which they themselves possessed. Those who experience this grief are the immediate human victims of language loss. And their experience, as much as any other consideration, is good reason to resist language loss.

To reverse language loss, ultimately, a certain condition must prevail. In a word, people must have the *choice* of learning or transmitting the local language of their family, or other relevant social unit. In some cases, of course, this choice is directly denied to people, by an oppressive authority. Often now, however, the choice is effectively removed by other factors, prominent among them, economic factors (see also Grenoble and Whaley, this volume). Choice is severely reduced where it is not economically feasible for the members of a local language community to stay together. In many cases, this boils down to the simple observation that if you can work where you talk your local language, your choice in the matter of promoting that language is greatly enhanced. Otherwise, your freedom of choice in the matter is virtually nil, except by dint of an extraordinary act of will, sometimes seen in the case of parents who simply insist that their language be used in the nuclear family, in defiance, so to speak, of the otherwise prevailing dominant language. In this connection, it should be mentioned that untold numbers of local communities are exercising this extraordinary will to safeguard, and in some cases, restore their linguistic traditions. These include communities, like the Wampanoag of Southern New England, whose language is known now almost exclusively from seventeenth- and early eighteenth-century written sources (Goddard and Bragdon 1988), substantial enough to permit the development of materials for learning this Algonquian language. They also include examples like the group of eleven families in West Belfast who took it upon themselves to perform a rather remarkable feat, comparable in many ways to the revival of Hebrew in Israel. These young Belfast adults, non-speakers, undertook to learn the language, to form a coherent community by buying houses in the same neighborhood – at considerable personal sacrifice – and to raise their children as true bilinguals. They were

> motivated by the recognition that the creation of a socially cohesive speech community was necessary if they were to have any chance of bringing up Irish-speaking families in Belfast. This project proved successful. Not only did the Community of eleven families survive the pressures of being rooted in an English-speaking society. In addition, it exerted a significant impact upon the surrounding neighborhoods, contributing to a wider shift towards bilingualism. Furthermore, the Shaw's Road Community inspired other community enterprises throughout the North, particularly in the area of Irish-medium education.   (MAGUIRE 1991:2)

In many of the documented cases of language loss, one or another of the factors just mentioned could, arguably, be cited as a factor. Lardil and Damin clearly represent the situation of an oppressive authority which, in this instance, achieved its ends by separating the children from their parents and elders, and brothers from sisters, and by imposing English as the sole language of the school and dormitory. But the economic factor, broadly conceived, combined with the almost overwhelming influence of the dominant language, is perhaps the greatest contributor to language decline now. In many cases, economic considerations have forced individuals and families to separate from their local-language communities, with the result that their descendants have been effectively deprived of the choice of learning the local language of their parents and forebears. This has been the situation of many North American local language communities. The alarming decline of Navajo, still the leader in absolute speaker population for North America, is due in part to this mechanism. By comparison, the relatively greater strength of the numerically much smaller Jemez community, is almost certainly due to the fact that it is possible, economically, for a significant number of Jemez speakers to live together in the same village.

I believe that it is appropriate to extend the term "economic" to cover a situation which may well be just as important in explaining language loss as are the official suppression of linguistic choice and the economically forced emigration of local-language speakers. The situation I have in mind stems from the extraordinary pressure which a dominant language puts on a local language, even where the speakers of the latter are able to live together in the same community. The pressure comes, not, of course, from the dominant language itself, but from the subtle and not-so-subtle propaganda of the associated economically dominant culture and society which encourages speakers of local languages to believe that their futures depend on switching from their native languages to the dominant one. Typically, the propaganda encourages the belief that a choice is not viable – the choice of retaining the local language is thought to be incompatible with the "proper vision" of the future. I am sure that I am not alone in having heard this argument many times in the course of doing fieldwork in local-language communities. The pressure involved here is fundamentally economic pressure, I believe, and its role in language decline belongs, therefore, to the category of economic factors, with economically forced emigration.

Essentially, the factors which I have mentioned here are factors which limit choice – the choice to maintain and propagate one's native language. The condition which must prevail in order to halt language loss is a form of sociopolitical and economic justice in which this choice is *not* limited. This necessary condition does not obtain in any country I know about, certainly not in the United States, where local-language endangerment is an extremely serious matter.

The necessary condition for halting language loss, globally, or in the United States, say, is certainly not something that we will see in our lifetime. But this is just a fact of the world and cannot be allowed to get in the way of efforts on behalf of local languages. The hard work of local-language planning and development must go on, as it has been going on, in the context of the particular, usually unique, situations of local-language communities – like the efforts briefly mentioned earlier and like other established programs of the type represented by the Hualapai bilingual education program, described in the essay by Zepeda and Hill (in Robins and Uhlenbeck 1991), and by Watahomigie and Yamamoto (in Hale *et al.* 1992), or the Mohawk bilingual education program, described by Jacobs (this volume). This kind of work must be done in any event – it amounts to an effort to *resist* language loss, in the absence of the condition which would be necessary to *halt* it utterly. If this work is not done now, all will be lost, I think, well before true advances are made in bringing about the conditions of sociopolitical and economic justice necessary for freedom of choice in maintaining and promoting local languages – the choice will be gone, because the languages will be gone. Work in the effort to resist language loss, it is reasonable to hope, can have the effect of retarding language decline.

9 Living words and cartoon translations: Longhouse "texts" and the limitations of English

CHRISTOPHER JOCKS

Program in Native American Studies and Department of Religion, Dartmouth College

1 Introduction

All across Native North America it is hard not to encounter an almost universal concern over language erosion in relation to Native American languages. In some cases individuals and communities recognize that loss or near-loss of traditional languages has already occurred, and they wrestle with the consequences, as well as with prospects for at least partial restoration. In other cases the threat is more distant but still looming; the issues are framed in terms of saving and revitalizing these languages. Invariably, though, there is a sense that not much time is left.

In many cases the work of professional linguists, including some represented in this collection, has been invaluable in helping these communities to evaluate the extent of language erosion, and to develop practical responses. In the midst of their efforts to understand these situations scientifically, it is equally important to solicit commentary from members of impacted communities who are not linguists. For Native American people these issues are rooted in deep soils of human identity, thus giving them an urgency that is an inseparable quality of the facts we are all trying to understand.

In the several traditional settings I have encountered in Native American communities, knowledge is neither expressed, nor conceived without reference to its background, sources, and affective qualities. The formal "texts" of such expressions are but skeletons around which a body of interpretation – often in terms of personal experience – is hung. It is with this in mind that I have not hestitated to include a first-person dimension to these remarks. Specifically, I will relate and reflect on my own experience in approaching the traditional knowledge of the Mohawk Iroquois Longhouse initially through written texts translated into English. In doing so I do not aim to make broad theoretical claims, linguistic or otherwise, about language erosion or about universal relationships between language and culture. If I refer occasionally to such theories I do so more to raise questions than to assert solutions.

Finally, I must emphasize that I do not write as a representative of the Mohawk people of Kahnawà:ke, traditional[1] or otherwise. The experiences and thoughts I express are my own, however representative or non-representative.

2   Language and knowledge

In the mountains of a western state, a few summers ago I was privileged to be present as a Native community enacted and celebrated a young woman's coming-of-age.[2] The visible, public portion of the ceremony was an intense and beautiful affair of four days and nights, set in an alpine meadow miles from town with more than a hundred friends and relatives witnessing and participating and camping out. It was the crown of years of preparation by the young person and her extended kin. One afternoon during a break in the doings I was relaxing in the camp of the head singer, the man more or less in charge of ceremonial procedures, when the young woman at the center of things approached with her entourage. She had been summoned by the singer, whom I shall call Will. That night would be the last night of the public portion of the ceremony, its culmination, and he wanted to convey certain important instructions to her. He would have to do so in English, as she did not speak her Native language.[3]

I had gotten to know Will over this and other visits and had come to feel not only personal admiration for the man, but a sense of awe over the wide and intricate knowledge he commanded, which was vital to the continuation of the tradition. Hundreds of songs; days and nights of complex procedures; beautiful stories that went with each and interlocked with each other; and a wealth of detailed knowledge about plants, animals, landforms, astronomy, and history, all went into this work. The foundation of this knowledge he had gained in the traditional way, during an entire

1 By "traditional," here and elsewhere, I refer to ideas and practices understood to have strong pre-invasion roots, as well as to people who attempt to ground their daily lives – intellectually, affectively, and otherwise – in these ideas or practices.

2 For reasons of privacy I have chosen not to specify the identity of the community or individuals portrayed here.

3 By "Native language," here and elswhere, I mean the language of her Native American community, not the language she originally spoke. This is how Native people use the phrase.

summer spent in the mountains with his grandfather. Fluent in his Indigenous language, his first and obviously preferred way of thinking and communicating, over the course of his life he had nonetheless gone to school and had lived and worked around and for many English-speaking people, so that his skill in that language was more than adequate as well.

Yet he began to grope for words as he tried to explain important implications of the coming evening to the teenage woman-to-be. There were extended pauses. Frequently the singer lapsed into his own language, then abruptly he stopped, clearly frustrated with the attempt. I remember him staring for a moment into the trees or sky, a look of unmistakable pain in his face. "I can't do it," he said. "I can't say it right in English." I could only guess at the mental work he had been engaged in, crossing back and forth between very different conceptual worlds. He was drained and distraught; there would be much the young woman would have to do without.

As a scholar of religion, a student of the religious life of North American First Peoples in particular, and as a Native person myself, I am deeply concerned about the loss of Native language skills. There is no way to decide which is more devastating: the loss of practical knowledge in such realms as history, natural science, and social organization; the loss of stories and jokes and all the richness of human experience they carry; the loss of skills of perception trained by Indigenous linguistic structures; or the loss of depth in our relationships with Other-than-human beings. According to many Native North American elders, such relationships are only fully maintained through ceremonial work in traditional languages. "If you don't speak the language," Oneida scholar and traditionalist Carol Cornelius remembers her elders saying, "you can't understand the culture" (1994:146). I and most Native people I know hesitate to embrace the radical version of this view – that without our languages we are no longer Native people – but on the other hand, I fear that without our languages it is all too easy for us to become cartoons, caricatures of ourselves. Not only does ceremonial work too easily become rote and formalistic, but when we must depend on English-language contextualization, it becomes easy for us to adopt and incorporate alien images and understandings of ourselves, without knowing it.

Therefore I have chosen to examine what else is threatened when a Native language becomes endangered, by looking at a few examples drawn from the Iroquois Longhouse tradition, and from my experience approaching that tradition as practiced in the Kanien'kehá:ka (Mohawk) community where most of my relatives live: Kahnawà:ke, located near Montreal, Canada. What are the real-life impacts of language erosion? What happens, specifically, when key religious and political ideas become represented by their English translations?[4] What becomes of the relationship between specific utterance, and the extended matrix of meaning – the entire Gestalt of linguistic and paralinguistic structures, from morphology to ontology to history, human and natural – within which both the Native original and the English translation were and continue to be set?

Yet this is not an argument for untranslatability. Instead, it is a small demonstration of the kind of complexity that is too easily left behind in the move from traditional oral expression to translated written text, especially when the original and target languages embody such significant conceptual differences as obtain between, say, English and Mohawk. Thus I am both pointing in the direction of better, fuller translation, and also asserting that living traditional speakers are essential for the kind of translation I am thinking of.

For me these are practical questions more than theoretical ones. Much of this discussion originates in my own experience as a person of Kanien'kehá:ka descent who had, of necessity, to approach traditional knowledge first by means of written documents in the English language. This was necessary because I did not speak Kanien'kéha (Mohawk language), and because I was mostly raised away from the community that could have taught me both the language and the traditional knowledge. Many other Kahnawa'kehró:non (people of Kahnawà:ke) of the past two generations have also had to do so. Some of us know well the "anger, hurt, and frustration" Carol Cornelius describes that come from being two or three generations removed from our Indigenous languages (1994:146). Traditional *identity* has undergone a strong revival, while traditional *knowledge*

---

4 I am very much aware that many First Nation traditionalists refuse to accept the category of "religion" at all in relation to their traditional knowledge and practices. Their point, as I understand it, is that in English usage today the term "religion" signifies certain qualities such as doctrinal dogmatism and institutional compart- mentalization that have never existed in their communities. I agree, and were I writing for a traditional Native audience I would not use the term at all; but since I am not, I use the term in the broader sense of a system of knowledge and practice related to Other-than-human beings.

in Kanien'kéha is harder to locate. Recognizing this, the community has been engaged for more than twenty years in a spirited and diligent effort to restore the language in coming generations, cultivating the significant resources in Kanien'kéha that still remain.[5] It is one issue about which there exists widespread and deeply felt consensus there. Were it not for this work, I and others of my generation would not be able to even begin to grasp what it is that our people are in danger of losing.[6]

3   Myth-history in translation

It has been a mixed blessing for me that the persons at Kahnawà:ke and elsewhere who are most knowledgeable about the Longhouse – the religious, political, and social world of traditional Kanien'kehá:ka and other Iroquois peoples – are bilingual. Because of their capability and often considerable eloquence in English, I have been able to learn a great deal in a relatively short time. For the same reason, however, I was not forced to learn Kanien'kéha before meeting them. Thus, while our conversations almost always make frequent reference to ideas in Kanien'kéha, because of my non-fluency in that language the run of our speech is in English. I have learned enough not to mistake the translation for the original meaning; I have even caught glimpses into what it is that I have been missing; but in public debate – of which there is much these days both within communities such as Kahnawà:ke and between them and their neighbors – it is the English versions that are employed and disputed, and become familiar or at least recognized by a wider population. I maintain that this is a source of significant potential distortion.

At Kahnawà:ke the public debate to which I have alluded has sprung from a growing conviction within the community that some form of

5 The Kanien'kéha immersion program at Karonhianónhnha School in Kahnawà:ke is described in Jacobs, this volume.

6 My own efforts to learn Kanien'kéha began with linguistic study under Marianne Mithun at the University of California, Santa Barbara. Although I visited my Kahnawà:ke relatives from time to time through the years, it was not until my dissertation fieldwork that I began to seriously listen to speakers of the language and attempt to learn from them. Unfortunately that period passed too quickly and subsequent visits have been too sporadic. Over the last two years the duties of a junior tenure-track professor have had a further detrimental effect on my efforts to learn Kanien'kéha. I hope this situation is only temporary; I am convinced that gaining some measure of fluency in Kanien'kéha is the single most important thing I can do to deepen my understanding of traditional Longhouse knowledge.

traditional Iroquois government must replace the current system, which was instituted by Canada and derives its authority from that country's Indian Act. There are distinct variations and trends within this broad movement – some deeply conflicting – based on different interpretations of the tradition and different strategies for its implementation in modern times. In a recent study of the community's political history, Kahnawà:ke political scientist Gerald Alfred characterizes what these variations hold in common:

> Kahnawake Mohawks have shaped a consistent message out of the various elements previously identified . . . as the characteristics of a nascent "nativism" during the 1950s. These have been modernized and consolidated into three core principles: the achievement of sovereignty through the re-implementation of a traditional form of government; the strengthening of an identity of distinct peoplehood through a focus on ancestry; and the redress of historical injustices surrounding the dispossession of Mohawks from their traditional lands.
> (ALFRED 1995:76)

What role has language played in this movement? Elsewhere in his study Alfred mentions that recognition of the decline in Kanien'kéha proficiency was a contributing factor in Kahnawà:ke's push for strengthening distinct identity; yet he does not dwell on, or even mention, the most direct result of that recognition: the community's strong program for Kanien'kéha revival. This may be due to the political as opposed to cultural framework of Alfred's project; a narrowing of focus which non-Native scholarship demands. Yet the *separation* of political analysis from "cultural" factors such as language and religion – not to mention other categories such as gender or science or economy/ecology – is markedly non-traditional. It is not that Longhouse traditionalists make no distinction among these, or live in some kind of primitive-romantic intellectual formlessness. Long-house practice naturally recognizes distinct areas of concern or interest among persons, activities, and expressions, but it also persistently attends to the interconnectedness of these nodes.

Analytically, the relevance of Indigenous language survival and revival is obvious with regard to the second of Alfred's three core principles of Mohawk nationalism, "the strengthening of an identity of distinct peoplehood," despite his reduction of that principle to issues of ancestry and membership. Aside from whatever practical knowledge, mental or perceptive structures, or affective sensibility Kanien'kéha might carry, the mere fact of speaking it even in rudimentary form is a potent source of pride and identity, especially in politically and culturally antagonistic surroundings. This has been a powerful motivation for many Native communities to develop what Carol Cornelius terms "survival curricula," in which basic words and simple everyday phrases in the Native language are taught by rote (Cornelius 1994:147).

Only a little less obvious, however, is the importance of language – in the case of Kahnawà:ke and other Iroquois communities, at least – to Alfred's first principle, that of sovereignty and traditional government. This is because for Longhouse people, traditional government is perennially based on an oral tradition maintained most authentically in its original Iroquoian languages, the tradition known in Kanien'kéha as the Kaianeren'kó:wa, and in English as the "Great Law," or the "Great Peace." Yet public discussions of the Kaianeren'kó:wa, even within Iroquois communities, most often take place in the English language, aside from the small circles of Confederacy elders and other Longhouse people who remain fluent in their Iroquoian languages and traditions. In fact, public discussions often refer in questions of authenticity to turn-of-the-century *written* versions in English, particularly the two collected by Arthur C. Parker and published in 1916.[7]

Scholars, myself included, have studied the background and content of these various written versions; to do so here is unnecessary. For me to go further and to pronounce academic judgment as to which version, English or otherwise, is more or less appropriate or "accurate" for use today, would be the height of arrogance. Rather, I would like simply to reflect on the different contexts and implications of a few key concepts in Iroquoian language versions, written and oral, and their common English translations. Note that these English-translated terms are sometimes the only ones available, not only to outsiders who need or wish to make sense of Longhouse political perspectives, but to many members of Longhouse communities themselves, who are not fluent in their Indigenous language.

7 Other early written sources on the Kaianeren'kó:wa include H. Hale 1881, Hewitt 1892, and the Onondaga text recited by John Arthur Gibson in 1912, recorded by A. A. Goldenweiser, and recently edited and translated by Hanni Woodbury (Gibson 1912/1993). A succinct modern Longhouse version can be found in *Traditional teachings* 1984:15-62.

5.1   Kaianeren'kó:wa, *"Great Law"*

One must begin with the name of the tradition itself. *Kaianeren'kó:wa*, based on the root -*ianer*- "to be good, noble," with the augmentative suffix -*kowa*, seems to describe the manifestation of a "great goodness." In usage today as well as in derivation, it describes a positive, ongoing activity quite different from modern Western notions of law and order as based on the identification of destructive influences through reason, the overpowering of these influences by the use of state-sanctioned force, and their eventual submission as a result of punishment. It is especially important to note that *Kaianeren'kó:wa* – again, both in its derivation and in the way I have heard it used in the Longhouse – refers not only to political harmony or peace or "great goodness," nor only to what in English must be described as religious or spiritual fulfillment: it refers equally to both, and as well to balanced and harmonious social relations, with special attention given to gender and clan, to economy, and to relations between human and Other-than-human beings.

It is remarkable, then, that this profound tradition has been named under such legalistic titles as "The Constitution of the Five Nations," "The Great Binding Law," and "The Great Immutable Law" (Parker 1916:7). This is not in the least to discount the political import of the Kaianeren'kó:wa. In the face of more than a century of determined effort by the governments of both the United States and Canada to supplant traditional Iroquois decision-making and prevent its return, Iroquois nationalist-traditionalists have needed to emphasize and publicize the tradition's political face.[8] Putting upon it the appearance of codification, as if it were indeed a "constitution," has been one strategy in this response. The essential role of Iroquoian language proficiency here is to ensure that *within* Longhouse communities at least, knowledge about the rest of the tradition's field of meaning is not lost amidst the political struggle.

---

8 I cannot agree with the distinction Gerald Alfred maintains between *traditionalists*, who pursue "static interpretations of tradition," and *nationalists*, who promote "a flexible interpretation which jealously guards only the basic principles and values contained in the [Kaianeren'kó:wa] and [allow] for a modification of strategy dependent upon the demands of the political environment" (1995:87–88). Granted, tradition-minded people usually take a more conservative approach to change; the statement is nonetheless far too broad, and does an injustice to the subtlety of traditionalist thought and engagement with the "real world."

3.2   Onhwentisa, *"nation"*

It is easy to observe, again both in derivation and in discourse, that the Kanien'kéha word translated as "nation," as in *wisk nihononhwentisá:ke* "The Five Nations," is rooted in ideas of land, earth, or ground. The noun root, *-onhwentsi-*, is used in many words involving land, topography, and cultivation, conveying the unmistakable impression that in Iroquois tradition, nationhood is an inalienable component of a people's relationship with the land they live upon. Gaining recognition and respect for their "nationhood" has been the overarching mission of Iroquois diplomats since the early seventeenth century, but it is good to keep in mind that for them, this recognition was never sought in order to convey or create the status. Nationhood, for them, is literally rooted in the ground, and is not predicated on the shifting machiavellian sands of the assent of other "nations"!

3.3   Karihwíio, *"Righteousness"*

Every version of the Kaianeren'kó:wa that I have encountered has used the phrase, *skén:nen, ka'shatsténhsera, karihwíio*, or its equivalent, as an epitome of the Kaianeren'kó:wa as a whole, and the title by which it is usually announced. The first and second terms are easily glossed as "peace," and either "power" or "strength," respectively, but the third term is more problematic. "Good message" is the most direct rendering of the word's composition, consisting of the important noun root *-rihw-*, with such meanings as "thing, business, affair, message", and the suffix *-i:io*, "good." Yet a number of translations have preferred the term "righteousness", despite its heavily moralistic connotations by way of the King James version of the Bible. One such version, produced by Longhouse activists in 1984, presents the following commentary:

> This message has three parts: peace, righteousness and power, and each part has two branches. Health means soundness of mind and body. It also means Peace, for that is what comes when minds are sane and bodies cared for. Righteousness means justice practiced between men and between Nations. It means a desire to see justice prevail. It also means religion, for justice enforced is the will of the Creator and has his sanction.
>
> (TRADITIONAL TEACHINGS 1984:18)

I cite this modern exegesis not in order to criticize its accuracy – again, it is up to the practicing community to decide how it shall understand its inherited expressions – but to demonstrate how deeply a tradition in translation may draw from very different realms of discourse in the process of recontextualizing itself in the target language. In this case those different realms seem to include, paradoxically, not only the King James Bible but the discourses of post-Vietnam white American liberalism and social responsibility.

3.4   *Translation and translatability*

These are just a few examples of the way discrete ideas can mutate as they cross from one language to another; there is no limit to the number of others that might be cited. Some of these changes invite historical inquiry: for example, in the story of the origin of the Kaianeren'kó:wa, how did the figure of Tsikonhsáse, "her face is new," a woman who is the first person to accept the Great Peace, and who thus reinforces the primacy of the clan mothers in Longhouse life, come to be known under the titles of "Peace Queen" and "Mother of Nations"? That is, who coined these patently nineteenth-century-style honorifics, and why?

The same could be said of the appellation of the Confederacy chiefs, the *rotiiáner*, as "lords," as in the versions published by Parker. The influence of Lewis Henry Morgan's persistent comparisons of Iroquois society with that of classic Rome, and the entire evolutionary-historical fixation of pre-Boasian thought about Native American peoples as representing early stages of a universal progression of human society, cannot be dismissed. Furthermore, some Iroquois traditionalists of that period seem to have conceived a strategy of portraying their ancient systems of decision-making in terms congruent with those Euro-American systems with which they felt themselves to be in direct competition.

Other lines of inquiry would be more linguistic in nature. What nuances of meaning are necessarily stripped from utterances in Kanien'kéha, for example, when subtle morphological distinctions and structures are left "on the cutting room floor"? And what other nuances are picked up in their place when the translation is re-situated in the context of English? What are the discourse implications of verb predominance and other general features of Kanien'kéha, and how are any such implications lost or transformed in translation? Wallace Chafe has engaged in a marvelous exploration of these kinds of questions and their implications for human cognition, based mostly on discourse in English but with one chapter of comparative analysis based on his long-standing work on Seneca (1994:146–160), an example of insightful theoretical work that only emphasizes the limits of "survival curricula" described above. As Cornelius notes: "In some cases, much of the complexity of the language was diminished because it lost a connection to the earth. For example, the color of the 'inside of rotten logs' might be translated to mean simply 'brown.' The emphasis was on writing and reading the language" (Cornelius 1994:147).

Here an important question arises: why should this Native American etymology of a word perhaps translatable as "brown" claim any more of our attention than the etymology of any word in English? Is the speaker demonstrably more aware of its composition, or is this "brown" matter – as well as the three Kanien'kéha examples (*Kaianeren'kó:wa, onhwentsi-*, and *Karihwíio*) cited above – only of philological or lexicological interest, incapable of sustaining the level of significance I have assigned them?

The difference I am suggesting has less to do with Kanien'kéha versus English than it does with traditional knowledge maintained primarily as oral expression versus knowledge maintained primarily in writing. In the former case, with no written archive to fall back upon, the background and composition of each word, including its relationship with other words, are all part of its "meaning" – part of what one learns in order to use the discourse with authority. It has been my experience that the carriers of these traditions invariably assign great importance to, as well as take pleasure in, reflecting and discussing these relationships.[9] Working at the level of word composition is useful as an initial indicator of what is likely to be missing in English translation, in terms of the thinking that happens in Kanien'kéha. Yet it is only an indicator. It gets me to the threshold of promising doors, but not inside, where this portion of the ongoing creative work of this living intellectual community takes place.

9 The finest illustration I can think of comes from the novelist Leslie Marmon Silko: "The word he chose to express 'fragile' was filled with the intricacies of a continuing process, and with a strength inherent in spider webs woven across paths through sand hills where early in the morning the sun becomes entangled in each filament of web. It took a long time to explain the fragility and intricacy because no word exists alone, and the reason for choosing each word had to be explained with a story about why it must be said this certain way. That was the responsibility that went with being human, old Ku'oosh said, the story behind each word must be told so there could be no mistake in the meaning of what had been said; and this demanded great patience and love" (1977:35–36).

Finally, there are broader issues of local and individual variation, and of genre at stake. English versions of the narrative of the Kaianeren'kó:wa and its founding are usually clearly marked as either myth or history, depending on the prominence or absence of paranormal or "supernatural" events and explanations, but how are their Native language antecedents to be classed when such genres do not even exist as such in Kanien'kéha discourse? The Kaianeren'kó:wa both expresses a political philosophy and delineates a concrete political structure, but usually included with these are also the narrative of Aionwà:tha and procedures for rituals of Condolence, both of which focus intensely on the treatment of grief. Moreover, all Longhouse meetings, whether political, ceremonial, or social, begin with some version of the so-called "Thanksgiving Address," *ohén:ton karihwatéhkewn*, in which the community regenerates its own participation in an entire cosmology infused with power and maintained through reciprocal relations. Thus the enactment of the Kaianeren'kó:wa – as opposed to its textualization – is always framed by something like cosmology, metaphysics, and ethics. How can this kind of complexity survive translation?

4   Learning in English

Although I did not grow up within the Longhouse tradition or even for the most part in the physical community of Kahnawà:ke, when I began to conduct research on the subject of Longhouse religious thought, I had already been convinced that it was time to begin learning about the lives and histories of my relatives there. I no longer question my intangible, organic links with them, yet within the tradition I learned very soon that these links cannot be merely acknowledged. They are relationships that must be actively maintained: "polished," in the old diplomatic usage. Moreover, I began to suspect that the same may be said for other kinds of knowledge as well, even for knowledge itself: that in Longhouse epistemology knowledge is not a thing to be possessed, nor a static condition to be attained, but an activity. It is something you do, something you must maintain, not something you simply store up.

Longhouse people have affirmed this principle to me in different ways. The implications seem revolutionary: ceremonial knowledge itself is useless unless it is taken out and vivified. "Knowing" the elements and procedures of a ceremony is of no worth if one is unable or unwilling to enact them. This further emphasizes how even the best of English translations must seem pale, even vapid, to those truly conversant in the tradition. There is nothing one can *do* with such verbiage, aside from using it to offer pale explanations of what the non-speaker of the Native language is missing.

The language activists at Kahnawà:ke have known this all along, of course, and because of it there are now six-year-olds in Kanien'kéha immersion classes there, learning *ohén:ton karihwatéhkwen* from the ground up, as it were; not just learning what it means, but learning to enact it, in Kanien'kéha. The colorful scenes of these immersion classrooms at Karonhianónhnha School are quite a few steps removed from the chambers of the Six Nations Confederacy chiefs at Ohswé:ken, near Brantford, Ontario, where Seth Newhouse, Kanien'kehá:ka, learned the tradition of the Kaianeren'kó:wa in the late nineteenth century. Some time between 1880 and 1900 he composed his version in "Indian English," in the words of Parker, hoping to regularize and settle disputes over variations. This version was subsequently reviewed, criticized, and corrected by Albert Cusick, an Onondaga-Tuscarora from New York, then apparently collected by J. N. B. Hewitt, but somehow obtained by Parker, who writes that he "found" it on the Six Nations Reserve in 1910, and who went on to publish it six years later.

Interestingly, this "Newhouse version" of the Kaianeren'kó:wa has been the most influential in the rekindling of the drive toward traditional government at Kahnawà:ke. Perhaps this is due in part to its easy availability, thanks to numerous reprintings; perhaps it is also due to Newhouse's tendency where there is latitude to favor the Kanien'kehá:ka chiefs in his version of Confederacy protocol. It is worth noting, however, that Newhouse most likely never imagined his version would have this kind of influence. Its composition was directed toward local and immediate political goals in the midst of an intense struggle between the *rotiiáner* at Ohswé:ken and assimilationist factions and interests seeking to replace the traditional system with a modern elective government. This is not to say that Newhouse altered the basic content of the tradition; however it may help explain some of its details, beginning with the division into 117 articles, sometimes called "wampums."

We see once more, therefore, how the translation and codification of oral tradition into written document can exert unforeseen influences quite different from its original context and motivations, especially in communities where the living oral tradition has been neglected or lost or partially supplanted. In time the living community ought to be able to resolve any anomalies resulting from such an importation, but it would appear unreasonably difficult to do so if the discussion has to take place in an alien language, one vastly different from the tradition's own. The loss of nuance, with only outlines remaining, is what I call the "cartooning" of culture. With it, the link with the living tradition based on enactment is seriously endangered.

5   Conclusion: what is endangered?

Today issues of language, culture and identity are being considered, discussed and argued in Native communities across North America. Neither my opinion nor anyone else's should be read as representative. In traditional circles one frequently hears the assertion that language and culture are inextricably linked, and that loss of an Indigenous language prefigures loss of distinct culture and identity. But one also hears the opposite assertion: that Native people can and do live traditional lives without speaking or understanding their traditional languages. I agree. For one thing, language is not the only carrier of culture. One need not speak a traditional language in order to engage in traditional dance or traditional social exchanges or other non-verbal expressions of culture. For another thing, in places where a sizable number of English-speaking people are nonetheless determined to forge some kind of traditional identity, a body of traditional discourse *in English* can arise that is related – though not identical – to discourse in the original, traditional language.

How close that relationship is, however, depends on the participation of an active community of traditional language speakers – not just the presence of translated texts. It is in this sense that I have sketched out a few of the ways in which language loss is a threat to cultural survival, in two phases: first, Indigenous knowledge, perceptions, and strategies encoded in the language are lost; second, knowledge, perceptions, and strategies dictated by the colonizing language and culture will attempt to fill the vacuum. It can happen on multiple levels, from the loss of subtle shades of meaning when derivations and morphological relationships are forgotten and cease to enliven new forms of speech, to the loss or enfeebling of entire genres of discourse. Humorous devices, encoded references to the community's shared history, and knowledge about local flora and fauna, all stand in danger. In a sense this is not new – as has been said, an oral tradition always stands one generation away from extinction – but the powerful and seductive forces ready to seep through every crack in the Native language have never been as formidable as they are today.

The most dramatic culmination occurs when the ceremonial life of a traditional people is threatened by language erosion. That is, when the most deep- and far-reaching forms of expression the people possess – and the critical relationships they enliven, especially with Other-than-human beings – grow pale, lose significance and coherence, and begin to die. Cartooning. If scholars are around, the knowledge may be preserved in fossil form, in articles and reports and proceedings and field notes, but the loss of performability, from a Native perspective, renders such knowledge moot.

To see this happening, as I have, is to see a people become truly impoverished. They can recover, substitute, rebuild, but some of their loss will be irreplaceable. Encountering such a loss is an experience that has left me uninterested in theories that contest over-abstractions, leaving out practical, human, down-to-earth costs. In theory, perhaps Whorf was in fact wrong: given enough data and enough time for refinement, perhaps the perfect translation could be achieved between two languages. Again, I do not argue for untranslatability. In real life, however, in a kind of conceptual entropy, something significant always seems to be "lost in the translation."

Based on my experience as a young Kanien'kehá:ka man who first began learning about his Longhouse predecessors from Lewis Henry Morgan's *League of the Ho-de-no-sau-nee* (1851/1922), in which Iroquois society is cast in the image of classical Rome, I have learned to approach critically any document purporting to explain Longhouse life in written English. Consider: an event takes place in a Native North American community, and as it happens this event involves some form of expression in the community's own language. (Let's assume Native speakers remain.) It could be a formal, even ceremonial occasion, or it could be a conversation around someone's kitchen table. In any case it is observed and recorded, and eventually a report, a narrative appears in print, in a medium intended not for the community itself but for some broader audience, scholarly or otherwise. If the observer is linguistically competent there may be a "text" of some or all of the Native language expression, but the primary language is English, and some manner of translation into that language will be provided. Few readers will be interested in the Native-language text itself, if it is visible, except as curiosity or as evidence to support the observer's veracity and acumen. The observer's interposition may include more active, substantive interpretation, or it may be limited to the translation itself, and to matters of presentation and descriptive style.

I have been a Native participant in this scenario – albeit, given my lack of fluency in Kanien'kéha, a mostly mute one. I have also played the role of observer and reporter, and further, I have been a reader of the reports of others. Finally, I am a teacher who has attempted to use such reports in a classroom. Students often arrive with no previous experience with, and either no knowledge at all, or worse, a good deal of inaccurate knowledge about, the life of the communities at the source of the reports, so far removed through these layers of presentation and interpretation from my classroom. Because mainstream education reduces learning to the exchange and acquisition of knowledge, information, or "data", and because translation gives the impression of conveying data whose appearance only has changed, but whose essence or integrity has been only incidentally damaged in the process, I must constantly locate new critical approaches to these texts, informed by Indigenous perspectives and Indigenous theory. My students and I try to recognize inaccurate and distorting assumptions on subtler and subtler levels.

The reasons for doing this are not merely intellectual or academic. Not only is uncritical acceptance of translation and presentation a poor basis for interpretation or theory, but in the case of Native North Americans and other Indigenous peoples great harm can result, since hegemonic state powers wielding tremendous power often make far-reaching decisions based on or excused by such interpretative work. As long as there are Native speakers of an Indigenous language remaining, there is a rich source of rebuttal against such initiatives. Whether their wisdom can prevail is another question, but at least it can be heard. Language is not the only critical resource for a community striving to meet modern threats to its identity, existence, and growth, but it is an irreplaceable one.

Another potential that is impaired when language is endangered is the potential of a community to grow, and for its members to find new, creative solutions to the problems they face. Patterns of thinking and perception and prioritization encoded in their original language can easily be lost with that language, making it increasingly difficult to *frame* problems – and so solve them – in any but the dominant culture's terms. Far from being a backward-looking and stultifying drag on a people, I believe these traditional languages offer the strongest source for new, creative thinking: for keeping a critical distance from imposing forces, for prioritizing and strategizing about them, and for imagining new continuities between past and future.

I honor the people of Kahnawà:ke, who have looked over the brink of language loss and worked as hard as anyone could to keep from going over. As well, I honor the linguists who have assisted them, working for their benefit and leaving the ultimate credit for this work with them.[10] I do not know whether they will ultimately succeed, whether Kanien'kéha will merely survive – in which case it will die! – or will live and breathe and change and grow. But there is at least a chance that a new generation of Kahnawa'kehró:non (people of Kahnawà:ke) will know the truth of Carol Cornelius' English words: "In learning native languages we begin to view our world differently; we learn respect for all forms of life and we learn and understand that culture and language are intimately linked" (Cornelius 1994:149).

10 I include especially Marianne Mithun, who introduced me to linguistic study and who was an integral part of this work at Kahnawà:ke, especially in its most difficult, early stages.

10 Documenting rhetorical, aesthetic, and expressive loss in language shift

ANTHONY C. WOODBURY

Department of Linguistics, University of Texas, Austin

1 The maintenance of traditional communicative practices during radical language shift

There has been considerable discussion recently of language endangerment. Language endangerment is a timely issue because, according to Michael Krauss (1992), at least 20 percent – and perhaps as many as 50 percent – of the world's 5,000 to 6,000 languages are already *moribund*, that is, no longer spoken by children and hence doomed within a century unless learning is revived. Moreover, he estimates that a century from now many more languages will be moribund. This may leave as few as 10 percent of today's languages in genuinely safe condition.

Certainly this loss of diversity is the single most serious problem facing linguists, for it affects their ability to accomplish their two most important tasks: reconstructing linguistic prehistory, and determining the nature, range, and limits of communicative behavior and grammatical competence.

More complicated is its impact on individuals in communities where language shift is under way. Especially as language choice becomes politically and socially polarized, many locate in their ancestral language their social identity, their cultural traditions, their aesthetic and expressive achievements and potential, and the texture of their daily interactions with those around them. Perhaps due to the naturalness of such identifications,

Versions of this chapter were given at the 1995 Dartmouth Conference and at the University of Chicago, Department of Anthropology, in April, 1995. The empirical portions are based on work supported over the years by the National Science Foundation (Grants BNS 82-17785, BNS 86-18271, SBR 95-11856), the Elizabeth and Melville Jacobs Fund of the Whatcom Museum Foundation, and the Phillips Fund of the American Philosophical Society Library. I am grateful for their support. I am also grateful to Lenore Grenoble and Lindsay Whaley for their encouragement, and to the following people for their comments: Bill Darden, Paul Friedrich, Susan Gal, Susan Goldin-Meadows, Eric Hamp, Leo Moses, Jerrold Sadock, Michael Silverstein, Nikolai Vakhtin, Hanni Woodbury, and especially Salikoko Mufwene.

it is usually assumed that the loss of language *entails* a loss of social identity or of culture (e.g. Krauss 1992). Yet there has been relatively little
explicit inquiry into the question, leaving little in the way of either theory
or empirical experience. It still is not known what is entailed when a community loses its language.

Indeed, the standard assumption that language loss entails wider
social consequences appears directly to be challenged by some interesting
and important discoveries made in the last few decades in communities
experiencing what I will call *radical language shift*, that is, shift that
is abrupt, and involves languages from different world areas, different
language families, and associated with different traditions of language
use.

Diana Eades, writing about Aboriginal communities in southeast
Queensland, Australia, finds:

> While many Aboriginal people [namely, in southeast Queensland]
> may speak English as their first language, the context of conversation has
> significant Aboriginal cultural and social aspects which lead to distinctively
> Aboriginal interpretations and meanings. While the chosen language code
> is frequently English, there are important continuities in the ways language
> is used.   (EADES 1988:97)

> The Aboriginal priority on developing, maintaining, and strengthening social
> relationships is both reflected in, and created by, the way people speak to
> each other, whether the language variety is English, Aboriginal English, or
> Lingo [namely, any Aboriginal language].   (EADES 1988:101)

For example, she discusses a preference in Aboriginal English for yes-no
questions without inversion, formally like echo questions but functioning
as a proffering of information for confirmation (Eades 1982). She describes
this as a strategy of indirectness and links it to traditional ideas about the
maintenance of privacy and about the careful regulation of information
exchange in the context of specific personal relationships.

This suggests that in a situation of language shift, a language of
wider communication (such as English) can be adapted ideologically, if not
always structurally, to communicative ends that are continuous with those
earlier fulfilled by an ancestral language.

Patricia Kwachka describes rather similar findings in work on radical language shift in Koyukon communities in Alaska's interior:

> A final and, I believe, a most important factor [in the rapid shift from
> Koyukon to English] is that the Koyukon people have been able to transfer
> and permute a very important cultural pattern at the discourse level – the
> tradition of narrative.   (KWACHKA 1992:70)

> Although [stories from a distant time] are rarely told today, the narrative, as
> a social and rhetorical structure, has not only persisted but flourished. (p. 71)

She then speculates: "Perhaps, while semantic domains underlie and relate
social, political, spiritual and economic organization, discourse structures
may well provide, quite literally, the framework for their reorganization
during language and cultural shift" (p. 72). Again, the ancestral grammar
and lexicon are lost, but "language" in the wider sense – what humans do
with their lexicogrammatical knowledge – is the means for continuity.

Likewise, in a study of English writing by Yup'ik and Iñupiaq under-
graduates at the University of Alaska, Fairbanks, Kwachka and Charlotte
Basham found:

> specific areas of English grammar have been systematically exploited to
> encode Eskimo social values and pragmatic perspectives . . . while some
> features of Eskimo student writing may be classified as developmental or
> transfer errors, a third category, which we have labeled "qualification,"
> is based on an important Eskimo discourse strategy, circumspection of
> assertion, and that, in order to fulfil this obligatory relationship between the
> speaker and the universe of discourse, a process of sociolinguistic extension
> has occurred by which Standard English forms have been adopted to
> express Eskimo functions.   (KWACHKA AND BASHAM 1990:413–414)

Moreover, some of the students in this study were not speakers of their
ancestral language, meaning that "circumspection of assertion" is not simply
an effect of bilingual interference. They go on to argue: "These [Native]
writers [of English], rather than suppressing their identity to conform to
the dictates and constraints of western essayist literature, have successfully
extended their ethnicity to a new domain, shaping their written world to
maintain the pragmatic essence of their cultural perspective" (p. 426). The
issue of identity is thus seen as emergent, ongoing, and not necessarily tied
to the retention of specific traditional practices.

These and related studies are examples of "good science" in a number of important respects. First, they focus on actual language behavior in
contemporary speech communities, including, frequently, records of spoken

or written discourse in context.[1] Second, they put an appropriate emphasis on linguistic creativity and adaptivity, seeing language and communication not so much as things, but as ways and strategies. Third, they emphasize the use of language and speech toward discursively and ideologically framed ends or purposes, especially as this is perceived by involved interpreters (including participants). Finally, they show concern for the maintenance of social identity in situations of language shift, one of the key "extralinguistic" issues likely to be affected.

In turn, their findings of continuity in the face of language shift often send a welcome, even empowering, political message. For example, Eades' work was carried out in a context where claims by many southeast Queenslanders to Aboriginal identity, and with it to Aboriginal political and legal entitlements, were being challenged. She argued that a person could be entirely English-speaking while still being Aboriginal in outlook and identity. More broadly, her work posed a serious critique of wide-spread colonial and romantic tropes that pit the purity and fragility of Native culture (including language) in its "original" or "natural" state (such as to be captured by "natural historical" study), against the supposed degeneracy of contemporary natives victimized and denaturalized through contact.

But for all their emphasis on maintenance and continuity, none of these studies addresses what may be *lost* along with the lexicogrammatical code in language shift. By excluding such a focus so consistently, they permit – and even invite – the following inference: if *some* discursive practices and goals are preserved in the larger communicative system of a community where language shift has taken place, then perhaps *all* are (or can be in principle). This inference entails the conclusion that lexicogrammatical codes are interchangeable, contentless vehicles for social expression that have no necessary or privileged role in the construction or maintenance of social and communicative continuity in communities with which they have been associated.

Moreover, just as cultural perseverance has its ramifications in an indigenous political context, so does loss, and especially the minimization of loss or inattention to it. For one might well see the notion that

---

1 Such studies often criticize standard lexicogram-matical research on ancestral languages for their reliance on elicitation and their lack of attention to contemporary context, see Eades 1982 and Scollon and Scollon 1979.

traditional ways are retained, even in the face of language loss, as a salve to the colonial conscience, or as good news for educators uncomfortable with "exotic" languages, happy instead to support an emergent, newly "nativized" variety of English or Spanish.

In light of this, the central research question can be formulated somewhat more comprehensively, as follows:

(1)   What role, if any, does a lexicogrammatical code play in the construction
       and maintenance of social and communicative continuity, and how can
       such a role be documented?

The studies cited above place certain limitations on the answer, for they show it to be inadequate to assert without qualification that the loss of a lexicogrammatical code entails the immediate loss or shift of social identity. These limitations should not be too surprising, since social identity is a more or less fluid, ideologically oriented interpretation of linguistic and social behavior, rather than something strictly determined by it.

Of greater immediate relevance to (1) are those aspects of language more directly and necessarily linked with social behavior. Recently I have begun searching for specific cases where such a linkage may exist and have relevance in situations of language shift (Woodbury 1993). The following is a theoretical principle that has both emerged from and guided this work. Its purpose is to locate and define an immediately fruitful topic for study which I term *form-dependent expression*:

(2)   In any situation where the arbitrary patterns of a lexicogrammatical code
       are harnessed to constitute, shape, or model communicative purpose or
       content, expression is crucially dependent on form; to the extent that such
       form-dependent expression is (or is part of) a socially significant com-
       municative practice or process – as it can be in verbal art, ritual, and even
       ordinary talk – its continuity is dependent on linguistic form, and hence
       is lost if that form is lost.

Note that this dependence would be indirect, since social practices are constituted not by particular lexical or grammatical systems in themselves, but by the way they are *used*. This chapter is devoted to a single – and, I believe, compelling – example of form-dependent expression in a situation of language shift. I conclude by relating how the notion might be investigated further, taking that opportunity also to amplify the general principle.

2   Use of Cup'ik affective suffixes in a traditional setting

The example comes from my ongoing work in Chevak, Alaska, a village of about 600 people on a small river 11 miles inland from the Bering Seacoast and about midway between the mouths of the Yukon and Kuskokwim rivers. Nearly all Chevak people identify themselves ethnically as Cup'ik [ʧu'pːik] Eskimos and consider their ancestral language to be Cup'ik, a dialect of Central Alaskan Yup'ik Eskimo (CAY) that is spoken only in Chevak and (with very slight variation) nearby Hooper Bay. CAY as a whole is now spoken by about 12,000 people, making it the most widely spoken of any of the Alaska Native languages. But this figure is anything but stable. When I first began work in Chevak in 1978, Cup'ik was spoken by nearly everyone, while knowledge of English was restricted: the oldest fluent speaker was forty-five, while the youngest were generally the five-year-olds who had acquired it on entering kindergarten. As I now write – having just returned from a December, 1995 to January, 1996 visit there – very few high-school students have significant proficiency in Cup'ik as measured by standardized tests,[2] and proficiency is still lower among younger children. In effect, Cup'ik in Chevak has gone from vital to moribund in less than a generation's time.

The outline of my argument is as follows. CAY (like all Eskimo-Aleut languages) has a set of suffixes which predicate different affective colorations of noun stems ("poor/dear N", "darned N," "nice N," "funky N," etc.). Their use patterns, it is shown, reflect and exemplify a tradition of aesthetic, rhetorical, and expressive production and evaluation. These suffixes occur in the formation of some kinship, nickname, and other lexical stems, suggesting their integration in an even larger, structurally salient, system for producing and interpreting affective discourse. They also have certain inherent formal properties – including their form as suffixes rather than full words – that are conducive to both low salience and unobtrusive but intensive use. It is shown that when a myth narrative was told in Cup'ik and retold right afterwards in English, this system was retained only partially and in narrowed contexts. This suggests that the system is likely to be lost if the shift from Cup'ik to English ever becomes complete in the community. Because of its expressive value and its traditional associations, its loss is likely to be experienced as a cultural loss.

---

2 Al Weinberg, superintendent of the Kashunamiut School District, p.c. January, 1996.

I argue that the thinning of the system is at least partly due to the difficulty of rendering its Cup'ik form and use patterns into English – that is, the system is a garden-variety case of form-dependent expression. And I theorize that a fuller remaking of the Cup'ik system in English – if even possible in principle – would, because of its *formal* characteristics, yield a result quite at variance with rhetorical and aesthetic principles of "mainstream" English use and therefore be strongly susceptible to loss.

The use of affective suffixes in relatively traditional contemporary Cup'ik interaction can be demonstrated by examining all their occurrences in a four-hour-long tape recording of the proceedings in Chevak's traditional *qaygiq*, or men's house, on the afternoon of November 26, 1978. The *qaygiq* had been constructed, from driftwood and sod, as part of a cultural restoration effort of the Chevak Traditional Council. The participants were about ten elderly men monolingual in Cup'ik; several younger, bilingual men who joined later; an eight-year-old boy who was present intermittently; and me. Activities included conversation, story telling, a sweatbath, sweatbath preparation, maintenance work on the *qaygiq*, and preparation of a program of dance songs for an upcoming Christmas "Eskimo-dance" gathering.

The suffixes are:

(3)   *-rurlur-*   "poor dear N; poor dear (subject) does V"
      -ksagar-   "darned N; darned (subject) does V"
      -rrlugar-   "funky N; funky (subject) does V"
      -llerar-   "shabby old N; shabby old (subject) does V"

Each suffix has a somewhat colorful English gloss that is very approximate, (usually) following Jacobson's (1984) dictionary (whose representations contain a few morphophonemic diacritics that I have suppressed). Notice that each gloss has two parts, pertaining to the suffix in construction with noun versus verb stems, on which more is said later.

A proper linguistic description of each suffix would represent the morphosyntactic constructions it occurs in, and then argue for a parsimonious account of its sense, rules of use, and conventional interpretations in context. My purpose however is less ambitious. I wish only to make observations that will show that the distribution and interpretations of each suffix in a variety of contexts reflect and exemplify the existence of rhetorical strategies, aesthetic principles, and expressive practices highly specific to Cup'ik/Yup'ik society; that these strategies and practices are linked, in turn, to other affective systems, including nicknaming and the invocation of kin categories; and that certain grammatical characteristics of the suffixes enable or promote these functions. It is therefore reasonable that I simply present and comment on the instances of each suffix in the order of their occurrence on the tape. This will allow the reader to develop a picture of them as an adult language learner might when joining the *qaygimiut* – those in the *qaygiq* – armed only with a fledgling ability to understand Cup'ik. The sheer repetitiveness of certain basic phenomena should then seem impressive, as well as the range and extent of the less basic features. I begin with the suffix that occurs most frequently.

2.1   -rurlur- *"poor dear N; poor dear (subject) does V"*
The first two uses occur at the beginning of the tape as part of some general discussion.[3]

(4)   *Taivqaralria**ruluu**m=am, Nukam qetunraa,*   [7]
       "**Poor/dear** Taivqaralria (said) that Nukaq's son . . ."

(5)   *Paka**urluu**m=am, (U: Eng=ng), uptaqkiikut.*   [28]
       "**Poor/dear** Buck, (U: Uh huh), he has provided us with things."

In (4), -*rurlur*- (its surface reflex is in bold face) modifies *Taivqaralria*, the name of a man from another village who was being discussed. In (5), it modifies *Pak'aq* (= Buck), a man from "outside" (namely, outside Alaska) who had married the daughter of one of the participants and was being extolled for his generosity toward the *qaygiq*.

Soon after this Ap'ang'aq, the eldest man and usually the floor-holder, gives an account of his recent trip to a convention in Anchorage, including a description of his encounters with homeless people:

(6)   *Angkelic'ami=ll'^icivaq naklegyukarr, Kassa**urluu**gneng*   [56–57]
       angutngurtellrii[gneng], pekaqtarareraqagneng; nervigmun
       *neryarturaqagneng, naken ^pi**urlu**raqak?*
       "In Anchorage I recently pitied two **poor/dear** white men, getting on in
       years, when they were hobbling along; when they go to the restaurant to
       eat, where do the **poor/dear ones** come from?"

---

3 The utterance numbers from the *qaygiq* transcript range from [1] to [813] and are given in square brackets at the right of each citation.

(7)   *Al' quya**rulur**luni ^taw' anqataami. Anyuumiilingremi ^taw' anluni,*
       *tungupall' rayaga**qegtaareq.**   [66]
       "Oh, the **poor/dear one** was grateful as he was getting ready to go
       out again. Although he didn't want to go out, he went out, a really **nice**
       black man."

In (6), *-rurlur-* occurs on both the noun *kass'aq* "white man" (from Russian
kazák "cossack") giving "poor dear white man," and on the verb stem *pi-*
"do," which together with *naken* "from where" translates as "come from
where." As always when an affective suffix occurs on a verb stem, *-rurlur-*
does not modify the verb stem itself; that is, it does not work like a manner
adverb (e.g. "to poorly/dearly come"). Rather, it modifies the stem's subject, in this case the two individuals referred to earlier and also referenced
pronominally by the third-person dual ending *-k* in *piurluraqa-k*, which
is thus better translated as: "they (dual), poor dear ones, would come (lit.
do)." In (7) *-rurlur-* occurs again on a verb stem. Both (6) and (7) clearly
establish the affectionate character of *-rurlur-* uses.[4]

       (8) shows *-rurlur-* with a verb stem, *assirrlugar-* "for the funky one to
be very nice," but as this gloss suggests, the stem itself contains an affective
suffix (*-rrlugar-* "funky . . .," see section 2.3) together with a simple stem
assir- "be nice." Thus, the whole expression *assirrlugarulurtuq* means "the
poor/dear funky one is nice," doubly modifying the third-person subject,
which in that context referred to me after I had done a chore.

(8)   *Assi**rrlugarulur**tuq qaugyaq=ll' anlluku, qaugyarugar ^antaa.*   [147]
       "The **poor/dear funky one** is very nice, he took the sand out, all of
       that sand."

One might suspect from (4)–(8) that *-rurlur-* is in some sense associated with the sympathetic portrayal of relatively powerless outsiders. But
the situation proves more complex when Ap'ang'aq begins a series of narrations on the doings of various shamans during his youth.

       In (9) he mentions an early twentieth-century local shaman, Kang-
ciurluq, whose name itself contains the suffix *-rurlur-*. That is, *-rurlur-* is a
fixed or *lexicalized* part of the name, so its mention is not specifically
sympathetic (i.e. "poor/dear Kangciurluq," a sense that would only be captured by adding a second *-rurlur-*: *Kangciurlu'rluq*). *-rurlur-* is lexicalized
as part of quite a few personal names, as well as certain other nouns, as

---

4 In (7) this owes partly to the use of *-kegtaarar-* "nice N," an affective suffix not otherwise occurring in
the transcript.

discussed below. Even so, *-rurlur-* in these formations is still segmentable and recognizable to any speaker of the language. Therefore, when such names happen to occur they at very minimum call attention to both the form and the sense of *-rurlur-*. I call this process *evocation* and will discuss it further below.

(9)   *Kangciurlurmun=ga ^taw' mayurtengnaqsaaqniaqekiit.*   [178]
       "It was Kangci**urluq** (lit. **poor/dear** sodhouse wall) who was said to
       have tried to cause him to ascend."

Examples (10)–(16) are from a longer narrative in which Ap'ang'aq uses *-rurlur-* repeatedly in references to a series of hapless characters. In (10) and (12) he uses it in his reference to two companions, one of whom, Ciutailnguq, is a powerful local shaman who has worked a trick on a Nunivak Island man – in turn referred to with *-rurlur-* in (11) – but is about to get his comeuppance. As Ciutailnguq comes under the control of enemy shamans from the Yukon River, the suffix applies to him in references to his past prowess ((13), on the verb stem *angarvau-* "be a great shaman"), to his struggle with the Yukon shamans (15), and to the discovery of his situation by his painfully surprised cross-cousin (16), who likewise is tagged with *-rurlur-*.

(10)   *Atakutalliniluteng ikani, Ciutailnguunkuk, aipaurluni=llu;*   [190]
       "Also eating, across from them, were Ciutailnguq and his **poor/
       dear** buddy"

(11)   *Tunraruaruluq ^kan'', kumalillernun inangqaluni;*   [204]
       "**Poor/dear** Tunraruaq was lying down on the ashes in the fire pit
       down there"

(12)   *Aipaurluqelriik=g' taukuk piniaqekegket. Aipaurluqelriik taukuk.* [206–207]
       "Those two **poor/dear** buddies were the ones who were said to
       have done it. They were **poor/dear** buddies, those two."

(13)   A: *Angarvaurulungraan, . . .*   [210]
       TM: *Niitellra angarvauguq.*
       A: "Even though the **poor/dear** one was a great shaman . . ."
       TM: "From what is heard, he was a great shaman."

(14)   *. . . maaken qaygimeng camaken, Nunarulurneng; nunaneng.*   [218]
       ". . . from the *qaygiq* down there, from **Poor/Dear** Village
       (= Kashunak); from the village."

(15)   *Aa, taw' ^arulairerrluni piurluryaaqelliniuq; kiatmun eglerquurluni.*   [221]
       "Oh, he stopped, and the **poor/dear** guy tried to do something about it,
       but it was already too late."

(16)   *Aa maaten=gguq uyangt**u'rlu**rtuq, ilurii kan'a, im' angarveg**urluq**.*   [233]
"Well, to his surprise, when the **poor/dear one** peered down, there
was his cousin, that **poor/dear** great shaman."

Nunarulurneng in (14) is an affectionate nickname for Kashunak, Chevak's
ancestral village. It is composed of *nuna-* (pl) "village" plus *-rurlur-*. Since
these elements would normally combine to give a form with the broader
meaning "dear old village," the "Kashunak" sense should be considered
lexicalized. Note that the nickname's affective value is inherited from *-rurlur-*
following normal principles of productive morphosemantic composition.

Together, evocation and inheritance illustrate two different levels at
which lexicalized affective suffixes are relevant to the more concrete systems of affective representation that are encoded in the language lexically
– in these instances, the naming of specific places and people. Moreover,
the process is dialectical – uses of the productive suffixes color speakers'
"readings" of the lexemes, while knowledge of the lexical patterns provides
the productive suffixes with associative resonances. I will term this property the *interwovenness* of the affective suffixes in wider systems for the
production and interpretation of affect in discourse.

After these narrations, Ap'ang'aq uses *-rurlur-* several times in
addressing me:

(17)   *Umyugartuara**urlur**tuten=qaa^tawa? Waten piureluten.*   [252]
"Are you thinking a bit, **poor/dear** one? You're going like this."

(18)   A: *Waq' ca**urlur**qatarcit?*   [280–281]
W: *Qerrutaanga.*
A: *Aa. Nakl**u'rluq**.*
A: "What are you doing, **poor/dear** one?"
W: (Putting on parka) "I'm cold."
A: "Aa. **Poor/dear** one, poor thing."

In both cases the suffix appears on a verb stem (*umyugartuarar-* "to think
a bit"; *ca-* "do what"). In (18) it also occurs with the expletive particle
nakleng "poor thing!," whose sense it amplifies. While *-rurlur-* is often used
when adults address children, there are no instances on the tape where it is
used between peers. It is likely then that Ap'ang'aq's use of it to me reflects
not only affection, but also my age (twenty-five years old) and inexperience.

In the next use, Ap'ang'aq suffixes *-rurlur-* to the name of his son
Elias:

(19)   *Ilayassa**ruluq** taneksagglugaullran, miktellran, nuyarpaungnaqengraan*
        ^taw', nuyarpaurtellran, aa nengaurqelluk' ^taw' aymegtaqluku.   [303]
        "**Poor/dear** Elias, when he was a boy, when he was little, even though
        he tried to have long hair, when his hair got long, oh, I kind of scolded
        him and cut his hair."

Soon after, he applies *-rurlur-* to himself, as subject of the verb stem *caite-*
"to lack anything." Given the patterns so far seen, this usage is probably
self-deprecatory:

(20)   *Qayugga=ll' ^wii cameng muragaaremeng cait**urlu**ama.*   [314]
        "For a change, **poor** me didn't even get any little piece of wood."

The last two uses (21)–(22) apply to the hapless victims in another
shaman story by Ap'ang'aq. They occurred when the taped session was little
more than half over. It is probably significant that the talk thereafter of the
session differed from that of the first half: whereas the first half included
large amounts of narrative and talk about people – just the kinds of passages in which most *-rurlur-* examples occurred – the second half did not.
It was more highly interactive and was generally focused on such topics as
qaygiq maintenance, fishing, and the recollection of dance songs.

(21)   *Apaya**urlur**=am taw' – ^tawken ^un' pillermini keplermini, cingilleni*
        pivkenaki, mayurluni.   [378]
        "When **poor/dear** Apayaq did this when he cut loose (the thong), he
        couldn't free his ankles, as he was climbing up."

(22)   *Apayar=am ^taw' pilliat; cakneq ^taw' icunglluku: "Aa*
        *alinguryugpakarniluni ^taw" naklekqa**urlu**qaasqelluni, mingqun*
        ^taw', tamalleq piluku, [. . .]   [396–397]
        "So they called on Apayaq, kindly imploring him: saying 'Oh,
        he is really scared', asking him to have pity on the **poor/dear one**
        that had lost the needle, [. . .]"

Because the foregoing discussion is based on a chance set of attestations in
a given setting, only a sketchy view of *-rurlur-* emerges. But it still demonstrates the points I have set out to prove in this section. First, it suggests the
presence of principles that must be defined with reference to very specific
aspects of Cup'ik/Yup'ik discourse, social structure, and sensibility. Some
are clear in outline, thus *-rurlur-* is seemingly applied to individuals "on the
outside," individuals of lesser competence, and individuals to be pitied.

Others are certainly present but their details are fuzzy: To whom would it be applied normally and whom only daringly or figuratively? It can be applied in direct address, but where is the line between affection and insult? It can be applied to oneself, but who can or should do so, and when? It is common in narrative, but in many other kinds of discourse it can be absent. None of this can be answered without extensive experience of and insight into traditional rhetorical strategies, aesthetic principles, or affective practice. Moreover, the eventual loss of *-rurlur-* and categories like it would deprive these traditional practices of a major arena of expression.

The second point that is demonstrated here is that *-rurlur-* is lexicalized in the formation of names. (It is also lexicalized in the formation of such kin terms as *tutgararuluq* "grandson" and *anuuruluq* "grandmother.") Depending on the productivity of the formation, the terms then inherit, or else at least evoke, the sense of the suffix, interweaving the suffixal system into a wider lexical system for affective expression.

The third point is that *-rurlur-* has certain formal characteristics – it is a suffix that can occur on both noun stems or verb stems – and these characteristics enable or promote the system of use. As a suffix it is somewhat less salient than an independent word: for example, suffixes are not traditionally uttered or discussed in isolation in Cup'ik/Yup'ik metalinguistic discourse, whereas whole words certainly are. Furthermore, its referentiality is low in that it does not affect the truth conditions for an utterance, expressing instead an evaluation or judgment by the speaker (see Silverstein [1981] for more general discussion about the relationship of both these characteristics to speakers' metalinguistic and metapragmatic awareness). All things being equal, such a system can be used more intensively than a lexical system without becoming overwhelmingly salient in an aesthetic or poetic sense: compare, for example, how English speakers react when the same noun or verb is repeated several times nearby, but still seem to tolerate multiple repetitions of affixes (e.g. possessive *-s* or the prefix *un-*). That is, repeated use of *-rurlur-* may "slip under the radar" more easily than would repetition of a whole word. This ability is enhanced by the possibility for *-rurlur-* to occur on verb stems since it can then apply to subjects that are expressed only pronominally (compare the relatively awkward English translations for this taking the form "the poor one does V" in (6)–(8), etc.).

2.2   -ksagar- *"darned N; darned (subject) does V"*

Whereas *-rurlur-* is used on the tape only in reference to people, *-ksagar-* is used there for things (23), (24), (26) and people (25), (27) both. The contexts suggest it reflects and implies annoyance: a timber in an uneven floor (23), a wash water can that was in the way (24), a man whose blurted suggestion spoiled a shamanic conjuring (25), metal fasteners on an old sled being used for firewood (26), and a visitor (me) who might open the door and run out when the heat and smoke of the firebath reaches maximum intensity (27). None of the examples occurred in narrative except (25), and even here it is an embedded quotation. In these ways *-ksagar-* clearly reveals another side of Cup'ik/Yup'ik discourse, social structure, and sensibility.

(23)   *Kumlanengqe**ksaga**ami ^taun', enkegtenqegcaareyungremi.*   [14]
"Because that **darned** one (floor timber) has permafrost, even though it seems to be well in place."

(24)   *Qurru**ksaga**an ^taun', tegulluuqerrutekevkenaku; qurruten tauna.*   [129]
"Your **darned** wash water can (lit. urine vessel), you should set it aside."

(25)   *Uum=am Culuk' am atiin cagivikengraaku Qailla**ksaga**am, heh,*
"[ɒ:::::::::]! *Teguyaqunaku::!"*   [179]
"And then Culuk'aq's father extended his arms toward him, but that **darned** Qaillaq [uttered]: 'Ooooo! Don't grab him!' "

(26)   *Cavilqu**ksaga**at awkut tumarutai.*   [325]
"He held it (a sled) together with those **darned** strips of metal."

(27)   TM: *Maqicurlagcite**ksagar**ciqaakut=ll'=am.*   [527–528]
A: *Maqicurlagcite**ksagar**ciqaakut=ll'=am.*
TM: "The **darned one** might ruin our bath."
A: "The **darned one** might ruin our bath."

Unlike *-rurlur-* there are no lexicalized examples of *-ksagar-* on the tape (nor do I know of any). This almost surely reveals a conflict between the sense of *-ksagar-*, and the affective and aesthetic principles governing the formation of kin terms, names, and other lexicon.

Like *-rurlur-*, *-ksagar-* is suffixed to noun stems (24), (25), (26) and to verb stems (23), (27), where it implicates the grammatical subject.

2.3   -rrlugar- *"funky N; funky (subject) does V"*

The gloss "funky" is very approximate (Jacobson [1984:551] uses "good old"). The suffix seems to be used for individuals inherently lacking in power, strength, or grandeur: a child (28), (35), me (30), (31), or, self-deprecatorily, the speaker and his companions in their youth (32). For all this, the examples and their context show that its tone is still affectionate and home-spun. It is particular to Chevak and a few other localities, where it takes over functions otherwise assigned to -*rurlur*-, which is more far more widespread in CAY. Therefore, its use must index a speaker's Chevak identity in addition to all else. In these ways, it reveals still more about traditional Cup'ik discourse.

(28)   *Yura**rrlugar**ciquten ^qaa ^taw'? Ai? Aa=gguq.*   [20]
       "You, **funky one**, will Eskimo dance? Huh? He says yes."

(29)   *Eng=ng, Kassauyaaqluni ^taw' Kasqapik; Ayaskam=ggur ^uum*
       *tutga**rrlug** [aa]; tutgaraa.*   [79]
       "Uh huh, he was white OK, a true white man, but he was the (lit. **funky**)
       grandson of Ayaksaq, his grandson."

(30)   *Quyana ^taw' nevuq antaa. Asqi**gglugar**tur ^awna.*   [85]
       "I'm grateful that he took the mud out; the **funky** one is quite
       satisfactory, the one out there."

(31)   *Assi**rrlugar**ulurtuq qaugyaq=ll' anlluku,*   [147]
       "The **funky** one is very nice, he took the sand out, . . ."

(32)   *Nunaniryu**gglugar**naurtukut caciq –, cameng ^taw'*
       enqak'ngarailengremta. Cakner ^nunaniryugluta.   [290]
       "**Funky** us, we used to have such fun, although we had nothing
       [special] to remember about. We had lots of fun."

(33)   *Ilayassaruluq taneksa**gglugа**ullran, miktellran, nuyarpaungnaqengraan*
       ^taw' nuyarpaurr –, nuyarpaurtellran, aa nengaurqelluk' ^taw'
       aymegtaqluku.   [303]
       "When poor Elias was a (lit. **funky**) boy, when he was little, even
       though he tried to have long hair, when his hair got long, oh, I kind
       of scolded him and cut his hair."

(34)   *Pamkut, ukut M**arrluga**nkut eniit, pama=i avirpatuiluni, . . .*   [356]
       "Back there at the house of Marrlugaq (lit. **funky** grandmother) and
       family, (I heard) the door slamming back there,"

(35)   *Ah hah hah! Tang' aya**rrluga**ma! Hehehehe.* <Leslie also laughs>   [707]
       "Ah hah hah! My Tang'ayarrlugaq (= Leslie; lit. '**funky** go-and-see').
       Hehehehe." <Leslie also laughs>

-*rrlugar*- is lexicalized in kin terms (29), (although as revealed here, -*rrlugar*- is omissible with this particular stem); in certain kin-term-based nicknames (34); in an affectionate term for 'boy' (33); and in an *inqun* (affectionate nickname for a child) (35). *-rrlugar-* is by far the most prevalent formative in kin terms in Cup'ik, a role that is fulfilled by *-rurlur-* in most other Yup'ik dialects. (29) is interesting because it shows that the stem for "grandchild" appears both with and without *-rrlugar-*. In general then, *-rrlugar-* shows is a high degree of lexical interwovenness.

It happens that all the productive (i.e. non-lexicalized) examples of *-rrlugar-* are suffixed to verb rather than noun stems.

2.4   *-llerar- "shabby old N; shabby old (subject) does V"*

The last suffix occurs three times with things (an ax in (36), a sled in (38), and a snow machine in (39)). In these uses it functions more or less literally, predicating a shabby, dilapidated condition of the noun stem to which it is added. Its single reference to a person (37) is part of a lexeme where *-llerar-* together with *+pag-* "big N," and *-yagar-* "baby N," are frozen into an idiomatic affective formation. Moreover, the second appearance of the lexeme in (37) is modified by another productive suffix expressing positive affect, *-kegtaarar-* "really nice N" (cf. fn. 4). *-llerar-* is also relatively common in the formation of kin-based nicknames.

(36)   U: *Qalqapaipagg! Qalqap –*   [30]
        A: *Qalqapaipagg!*
        U: *Qalqapagtaitelliniami=ll' kiwna, . . .*
        A: *Qalqapacua**ller**angqerrsaaqua Avrulriim ^im' taitellruyaaqaa*
            qalqapapaarrluk.
        U: "There's no ax! An ax – "
        A: "There's no ax!"
        U: "When it appeared there was no ax there, . . ."
        A: "I had a **shabby** little ax, but Avrulria was going to bring a huge ax."

(37)   *Una=ll' ^tawan, tungupa**ll'ra**yagaq, elatemteñi uitaurallrani,*
        ing'um Qemiim it'rulluku . . . Anyuumiilingremi ^taw' anluni,
        *tungupa**ll'ra**yaga**qegtaareq**.*   [64–66]
        "And this one fellow, a black man (lit: baby **old** big dark one), when
        he was hanging around outside our hotel, Qemiq brought him in . . .
        And although he didn't want to go out, he went out, a **really nice**
        black man."

(38)   *Ikamra**ll'ra**agk' ^ingkuk caak pina – tegunaqsaaqug ^yaa=i.*   [322]
        "My **old** sled over there, who knows what condition the wood is in –
        it is available over there to be used (for wood)."

(39)   *Senuku**ll'ra**qa assiriluk' taqkeka; atakuqanrakun.*   [633]
        "I finished improving my **old** snow machine, just when night was
        falling."

2.5   *Conclusion*

Each of the four affective suffixes discussed (and a few others not used on this tape) reveals the existence – if not the details – of different parts of an extremely nuanced rhetorical, aesthetic, and expressive tradition in Cup'ik. The system is interestingly (but asymmetrically, cf. *-ksagar-*) interwoven, through lexicalization, in such other effectively important areas as personal and place names, nicknames, kin terms, and names for classes of individuals. And the affective suffixes are united as a paradigmatic set by their status as suffixes, as well as their ability to occur with both noun and verb stems. Both these characteristics, it was claimed, lower their inherent saliency and facilitate intensive use.

3   Affective suffix outcomes in two Cup'ik-to-English translation experiments

On November 16, 1978, Leo Moses of Chevak told a *quliraq* (traditional myth), in Cup'ik, at his home. I taped him. He then retold the story in English. Both versions lasted about twenty-five minutes. Much later, in 1983, I played the Cup'ik tape for him in roughly paragraph-sized chunks while he performed a running "United Nations" style translation/interpretation of it for a second tape recorder. In all then, there is one Cup'ik version and two English versions.[5] The translations are experiments in the sense that they test the fate of given features of the Cup'ik under different conditions of interlinguistic performance. In this discussion, the fate of affective suffixes will be considered.

At the time of the telling Leo Moses was forty-five years old, a little more than a generation younger than the oldest men present on the *qaygiq* tape just considered. He was also the oldest person in the village with real fluency in English (although by no means the first ever to have known English well). He was and is widely recognized for his skills as a translator and simultaneous interpreter. Therefore, his renderings must be seen not as some sort of "typical" translation, but rather as instances of performed interlinguistic mediation by a skilled, methodical practitioner making creative choices that draw on mature narrative abilities in both languages.

5   A third English version by Leo Moses was obtained by asking him for word-by-word translations of the Cup'ik text once it was transcribed.

In the myth, a young man is such a proficient hunter that his grandmother whom he lives with blinds him in order not have such a large catch
to process. His sight is restored by loons in a nearby lake, whom he paints
in their present-day colors out of gratitude. He then wins a wife after
undergoing several tests, eventually returning with her to his original home,
where his grandmother has died from inattention. There are just four productive (non-lexicalized) uses of affective suffixes in the Cup'ik telling of
this myth:

(40)   *Anuurulurulua=gguq ^taw' tauna, kivluni ^taw',*   [04]
        "But the **poor/dear** grandmother was depressed"

(41)   *Cuna=gguq cikmi' urlurlun' taun' tutgararulua,*   [16]
        "And so the **poor/dear** one, her grandson, was blinded,"

(42)   *Cuna=gguq nukalpialleraam taum al'kartaa paniminun taumun
        uiknaluku,*   [80]
        "And so that **shabby old** great hunter thought right away to test if he
        would be a suitable husband for his daughter"

(43)   *Unuakuareq=gguq tupagtuq tutgararululleraq.*   [86]
        "So at early dawn he got up that **shabby old** grandson."

(40) contains *-rurlur-*, which modifies the stem *anuurulur-* "grandmother."
Note that *anuurulur-* itself contains a lexicalized instance of *-rurlur* combining with a stem, *anuu(r)-*, which never occurs alone. (41) has *-rurlur-*
with the verb stem *cikmir-* "to become blind," where it modifies the subject,
the grandson. Again, note that *tutgararulua* "her grandson" also contains a
lexicalized instance of *-rurlur-*. In (42) the father of the prospective bride,
and in (43) the grandson, are each modified with *-llerar-* "shabby old N."

Now consider the comparable parts of the English retelling performed the same day (44)–(47). Of them, only (45), depicting the traumatic
climax of the myth, shows any kind of rendering of the affective suffix (via
the lexical adjective *poor*, which modifies the NP "young man" directly).
Elsewhere, there is no reflex of the affective suffixes that appeared in the
Cup'ik.

(44)   (cf. (40)) But the grandmother . . . she was getting tired of handling all the
        things that he brought home

(45)   (cf. (41)) And ever since then that *poor* young man, was blind.

(46)   (cf. (42)) There was a great hunter. That man, he had no need for anything.
        He was the great hunter already. And there was his daughter.

(47)   (cf. (43)) Next morning he went at the early time, the time scheduled to leave, when the day was just about to come.

Although these passages build a prima-facie case for the attrition of affective suffix categories in the English retelling, a careful search reveals two more passages where a literal translation back into Cup'ik would probably involve an affective suffix (48), (49); these, like (45), both use *poor*. In (48) it modifies the loons, whom the grandson had treated with kindness even before his blinding, and in (49) it modifies the grandson after his blinding. It is therefore reasonable to acknowledge that *poor* patterns as a resource in the narrational style Leo Moses has chosen to use in English. (50) summarizes the occurrences.

(48)   He left nature be. Because there were, more, food around in abundance, in greater form than those two *poor* birds.

(49)   She would bring him food, when it's time to eat, but that *poor* man, was isolated in the *qaygiq* (men's house).

(50) | Cup'ik telling | | Count | English telling | Count |
|---|---|---|---|---|
| *-rurlur-* | "poor/dear" | 2 | *poor* | 3 |
| *-llerar-* | "shabby" | 2 | | |

This much suggests rough comparability between the systems in the Cup'ik and English tellings, but the more fundamental question that remains is whether *poor* does the same quantity and kinds of affective work in the English as *-rurlur-* and *-llerar-* do in the Cup'ik . The most obvious strategy for answering it is to evaluate the Cup'ik in terms of each of the characteristics of traditional Cup'ik affective suffix use identified in section 2, and then see to what extent they, and the system(s) behind them, have been transplanted into English.

Let us begin with the characteristic of *interwovenness* through lexicalization, where lexemes formed with affective suffixes inherit, or at least evoke, the value of the suffix. This characteristic is particularly salient in the Cup'ik telling of the myth. As already pointed out in connection with (40) and (41), the lexemes that designate the two main characters in the story – *anuurulur-* "grandmother" and (usually) *tutgararulur-* "grandson" – are kin terms that are formed with *-rurlur-*. Although these are ordinary (non-affectionate) terms for these kin relations, the formal presence of *-rurlur-* must at least evoke the "poor/dear" category (in the sense of section 2.1), establishing an affective background that is poetically enhanced by the sheer number of repetitions of each word throughout the narration (see (51)), some parts of which will be discussed only later). The two productive instances of *-rurlur-* in the text (40, 41) can then be seen not as two affective suffixes in utter isolation, but as resonators and focusers of the affect already evoked in the background. Furthermore, because of the paradigmatic properties of the affective suffix set, the same can be said, albeit more indirectly, for the two occurrences of *-llerar-* "shabby" (42), (43). In striking contrast, the English telling shows no such interwovenness. The three occurrences of *poor* resonate with nothing else in the telling. And the English lexemes designating the two main characters, though occurring in roughly comparable numbers to the Cup'ik terms (cf. (51)), happen not include *poor* or related adjectives in their etymologies.[6]

(51)	Cup'ik telling		Count	English telling	Count
	anuurulur-	"grandmother"	15	*grandmother*	20
	tutgararulur-	"grandson"	38	*grandchild*	2
	tutgarrlugar-	"grandson"	3	*young man*	12
	tutgarar-	"grandson"	1	*tutgararuluq*	1[7]

Consider another, related point about interwovenness in the Cup'ik telling. As (51) shows, three separate Cup'ik lexemes for "grandson" were used: *tutgararulur-*, containing *-rurlur-* "poor/dear," has just been discussed. In Chevak, it is the term most associated with a literary myth-telling style. The second, *tutgarrlugar-*, formed with the *-rrlugar-*, "funky" suffix (local to Chevak), is the colloquial Chevak term; and *tutgarar-*, with no affective suffix, also sometimes appears. The differences between these three terms are partly inherited from the suffixes, and partly simply evoked by them (since the sense of all three is nominally just "grandson"). But it is clear that while *tutgararulur-* is the default or neutral choice, the choice of the other two puts their inherited or evoked characteristics to use. Thus in (52), the unsuffixed "grandson" stem (*tutgarar-*) occurs at just the point where the grandson's one flaw is mentioned and where *-rurlur-* implicates sympathy toward the grandmother (this is from the same passage as (40)). And

---

6 It is also noteworthy that Leo Moses pursued an aesthetic in English where the grandson was designated *young man* rather than kin-relationally in most cases, thus weakening further the overt *tutgararulur-* : *anuurulur-* antonymy present in the original.

7 At one point in the English retelling, the Cup'ik word *tutgararuluq* was used for "grandson."

in (53), the colloquial "grandson" stem (*tutgarrlugar-*) occurs twice at a point where the narrator appears to be groping for his phrasing. Again, because English lacks the suffixal system and the differentiation that it has created among "grandson" terms, these affective nuances are not lexically expressed in the English retelling.

(52)   *Anuurulurulua=gguq ^taw' tauna, kivluni ^taw' tauna, kivluni ^taw',*
        *caliamineng makuneng, taum **tutgarami** pitaineng.*   [4]
        "But the **poor/dear** grandmother was depressed, by all this work she had, **her grandson's** catch."

(53)   *Piqerluni ^taw' anuurulua tauna mernurialliqlermini, taw' umyugangelliuq*
        *qaillun tauna **tutgarrlugar**=mi taum anuuruluan, **tutgarrlugani** tauna*
        qaillun . . .   [10]
        "But then the grandmother, because she got so tired, began to think how that **grandson** the grandmother's, how that **grandson** of hers . . ."

A second characteristic noted in section 2 is that affective suffixes form a small paradigmatic set whose use depends on rhetorical, aesthetic, and expressive dimensions of traditional Cup'ik discourse. Three members of this set are involved (productively or lexically) in the Cup'ik telling; only *poor* occurs in the English telling, making it seem less rich by comparison. Moreover, it is not clear whether *poor* in the English telling can be said to stand in a paradigmatic relationship with a small number of other English adjectives in the context of local English, let alone precisely and rigorously invoke traditional values and practices in the way the affective suffixes in the Cup'ik telling can.

A third characteristic mentioned in section 2 is the affective suffixes' suffixal form itself, and their ability to occur on both noun and verb stems. It was argued that as a result of both these characteristics, the suffixes are less salient (and hence capable of more intensive use). Striking further support for this claim is provided by Leo Moses' running, utterance-by-utterance Cup'ik-to-English interpretation of the original Cup'ik telling (played for him on tape piece by piece). Consider the renderings in (54)–(57) of the four Cup'ik passages that contained productive affective suffixes (40)–(43). Strikingly, none contains *poor* or any other likely adjectival rendering of affective suffix categories. Thus, the direct-translation exercise appears to have been particularly unconducive to the transplant of the Cup'ik affect system into English. Why should the putative "low salience" of affective suffixes be more of a factor in the translation than in the retelling? Part of the answer may lie in the fact that attention to Cup'ik versus English linguistic form is much higher in a translation, leading to the loss of low-salience parts of the original.[8] That claim is supported by the fact that in the word-by-word Cup'ik-to-English translations that Leo Moses also performed at my request (and for that matter in word-by-word translations he did of the *qaygiq* tape), affective suffixes in the Cup'ik word are not accounted for in the English at all. By contrast (as already suggested) *poor* in the retelling appears to pattern as a resource in the narrative style Leo Moses chose to use in English, perhaps under influence from the original Cup'ik practices.

(54)   (cf. (40)) The grandmother was very depressed at the amount of work she had to do, in caring for all the game the grandson had brought home, caught.

(55)   (cf. (41)) So the grandson became blind, and therefore could not hunt.

(56)   (cf. (42)) So that *nukalpiaq* ("great hunter") rather thought right away to see if he would be suitable as his daughter's husband.

(57)   (cf. (43)) So at early dawn, the *tutgararuluq* ("grandson") rose very early.

It was asked in this section whether *poor* in the English versions of the myth does the same quantity and kinds of affective work as *-rurlur-* and *-llerar-* do in the Cup'ik telling. It is now clear that it does not. In the English retelling, *poor* occurs but as part of a much larger poetic interaction with the terms for the main characters; nor does it bear any clear relationship to the whole system and tradition of affective use and practice that *-rurlur-* and *-llerar-* are part of. In the running English translation, *poor* and comparable renderings have been omitted entirely. Without these resources, the English versions are not enactments of traditional Cup'ik values in anything like the same sense as the Cup'ik version is.

Ironically, an astute observer of just the English telling would perhaps notice the uses of *poor* in the English and suspect their connection to the affective suffix system, in much the fashion that similar observations about Native Englishes served as the basis of the work reviewed at the beginning of this article. But when fully bilingual individuals in

---

8 I am grateful to Susan Gal and Susan Goldin-Meadows for pointing out this focus on language and discussing some of its implications. See Woodbury 1986 for discussion of this same phenomenon in Sherpa.

communities where radical language shift is under way reflect on the impending loss of their language, they do not look only at the local use of the new language. Rather, they compare the old and the new and can then see what is missing in the new. It is this wider prespective that I have been trying to develop in this chapter.

4   The future of affective suffixation

The foregoing section is an empirical demonstration of the attrition of affective suffixation in the context of language shift. But in a more theoretical sense, I am arguing that affective suffixation is *form-dependent expression*, hence that the losses pointed to are (practically) predictable on principle. To amplify this point, imagine a local Cup'ik/Yup'ik English that incorporated a much more faithful rendering of affective suffixation than the English of the retelling: let it assign an English adjective (say *poor, shabby, funky*, etc.) to each suffix category and let the use of the adjective follow all the traditional principles governing the original; let it use the adjectives to coin new kin terms (*poor grandma, shabby grandson*, etc. in place of *grandmother* and *grandson*), new nicknames, and so on; and let it permit them to be used as intensively as the Cup'ik suffixes are in some of the *qaygiq* passages cited in section 2. Such an English would almost certainly be judged unusual against the rhetorical and aesthetic principles of "mainstream" English: thus the adjectives would appear to be used too noticeably, too repetitively, and at times incorrectly; the kin and other lexical coinages would add to these impressions, while also appearing ungainly for their bulk; and in general the system would attract such negative characterizations as "too wordy," "too cute," or "too sharply evaluative." It is unlikely, moreover, that such an English could attract the necessary loyalty or achieve a stability of use patterns, sufficient for Cup'ik/Yup'ik communities, with their small populations, to resist the pressure from "mainstream" English norms.

I have so far discussed the problems of transferring and maintaining a system of form-dependent expression from one language to another in the context of radical language shift. But is it not possible that at least some traditional rhetorical and aesthetic values might be reflected and promulgated in forms and strategies that have been newly innovated in the course of radical language shift rather than reconstructed on the pattern of the traditional language?

The answer seems to be yes. Kwachka and Basham (1990) argue for such cases among Yup'ik and Inupiaq speakers of English, and in general, significant innovation in the course of language shift has been linked to the creativity and goals of "imperfect" speakers (Gal 1989). But from the point of view of accounting for feelings of loss in situations of language shift, this is also utterly beside the point, for at least two reasons. First, innovations that reflect or promulgate community values will take place whether or not there is language shift. The issue is whether the continuity of intricate, complex, delicately tuned, deeply interwoven systems like Cup'ik/Yup'ik affective suffixation, and their contributions to aesthetic and rhetorical practice, are to be cut off abruptly as a (nearly) automatic consequence of a sociopolitical situation, radical language shift. Second, it is not at all clear that quickly innovated forms compensate for the loss of forms whose possibilities of use have been explored and learned for many generations. Rather, both innovations and retentions may have a joint and largely complementary role in reflecting and promulgating community values – one that is drastically disturbed by radical language shift.

5   Prospects for future work

I have presented a case where aestheticized and emotionalized traditions of language use are dependent for their stability – if not their very definition – on particular features of a traditional lexicogrammatical code and are therefore not transplanted (or readily transplantable) into a new language. My purpose in doing this has been to document some of the wider effects of radical language shift and thus to locate some concrete sources of the common perception that language loss means cultural loss (see Woodbury [1993] for another case study). It is also to support the wider, more theoretical project of exploring the relationship between linguistic diversity and linguistic meaning (cf. Lucy 1992; Friedrich 1986).

Where might one find other linguistically embedded systems from a traditional language that have become the basis of community-specific rhetorical, aesthetic, and expressive practices? That is, what are some typical independent characteristics of the form in form-dependent expression? In general, one should seek forms or systems of forms whose functionality depends on its relationship to the speech situation or its immediate textual environment, or on a perception of non-arbitrariness in the relationship between its form and its function. (That is, its "semiotic" mode should involve indexicality or iconicity.) Categories of language structure that often meet these criteria include deictic systems; aspectual, modal, mood, and evidential systems; postlexical prosody, including intonation, prosodic phrasing, and rhetorical distortion; formal poetics, including morphological and syntactic parallelism, meter, rhyme, and assonance; and systems of lexical relations such as kinship, biological classification, positional verbs, and sets of affective elements (like the ones described here).

To show that these linguistic systems have become the basis of community-specific practices, it is crucial to make and study careful records of natural speech of different kinds (as has been done here). The kind of material found in grammars, dictionaries, or even (narrowly conceived) text collections is not enough. In particular, it is important to document and compare the use of both the old and the new language in order to gauge processes of transfer (or non-transfer) of the systems under study. It is also highly desirable to make longitudinal records since they may help identify actual patterns of loss and change.

Part IV Mechanisms of language loss

11 Impact of language variation and accommodation theory on language maintenance: an analysis of Shaba Swahili

ANDRÉ KAPANGA
Department of Foreign Languages, Illinois State University

1 Introduction

In recent years, the dialect of Swahili spoken in Shaba, Zaire, has been one of the few African languages that have raised a certain level of curiosity in the field of pidgin and creole studies, in large part because Shaba Swahili (Sh.S.) exhibits many differences when compared to other Swahili subdialects spoken in East Africa (and eastern Zaire). These variations have generally been considered as instances of decay, colloquialism, corruption, and even a threat to the "homogeneous nature" of the Swahili-speaking community.

However, one of the areas for which Sh.S. has not been studied is its usefulness for our understanding of the process of linguistic maintenance or language revitalization. In other words, since Sh.S. has generally been considered as a less prestigious variant, there has been a concerted effort to bolster the more prestigious subdialect, Standard Sh.S. These efforts, which have generally been witnessed in churches, schools, some courts, and in the local and national media, have proven to be unsuccessful. The "ordinary" or less prestigious dialect is still very strong and is thriving in all spheres of the Shabian society.

In this chapter, I will not discuss the policies put in place to bolster the Standard Subdialect. I will rather concentrate on the study of some of the natural, linguistic, political, attitudinal, psychological, and social factors that have contributed to the entrenchment of a subdialect which is naturally more prominent than the more prestigious subdialect, namely Standard Sh.S. This chapter will try to explain the factors that have contributed to the maintenance and expansion of a less prestigious dialect at the expense of a more prestigious one. Put differently, in most cases where one identifies endangered languages, they are less prestigious, and they have been supplanted by languages that have more prestige and that also enjoy some kind of institutional support (Brenzinger, Heine, and Sommer 1991). In Shaba, Standard Sh.S. enjoys more prestige than Sh.S. (see Kapanga 1990); this prestige is recognized by the ordinary people as well as those who are involved in those institutional systems that are trying to strengthen it in the Shabian community. Then why has a subdialect with less prestige consistently been displacing one with known prestige despite the concerted effort by various institutional organizations to reinforce and promote a wide use of the Standard variant?

Using data from Sh.S., this chapter argues that the process of linguistic accommodation as well as the notion of ethnolinguistic vitality in bilingual and multilingual areas can be used to understand the processes of language maintenance, language revitalization, and language obsolescence. It will be shown that linguistic accommodation will generally take place in the direction of a subgroup that is characterized by one or more of the following factors: demographic prominence, social status, and economic power within a community. For each of these factors, however, there exists a set of social variables which are generally ranked in terms of their vitality within the community. Such ranking is for the most part unconscious and is in essence culturally determined. The variables with the highest degree of linguistic vitality are the ones that will determine the direction of linguistic accommodation in a society. The argument in this chapter is that such findings can also be used in the search for means to preserve languages that face the prospect of disappearance within a community. In other words, the task of those working toward the preservation of a language would then be to find ways to attribute one or more of the social factors (social status, demographic prominence, and economic power) to an endangered language. This can be done by identifying the endangered language with social variables associated with the daily lives of a community; these variables must in turn have the highest degree of ethnolinguistic vitality within the linguistic community where the endangered language is spoken. Thus, the best approach to revitalize a language would be to relate it to the social variables that are closely associated with allegiance to the vernacular culture of a linguistic community. In other words, following Fishman (1991), the revitalization of a language can generally take place if it is accomplished at the intimate levels of communal life. For Fishman, the intimate or lower levels which constitute "face-to-face, small scale social life must be pursued in their own right and focused upon directly rather than merely being thought of as obvious and inevitable by-products of higher level" (1991:4) for language revitalization to take place. Taking this view will foster a positive attitude vis-à-vis the endangered language and sustain its viability by encouraging its members to promote it.

2   Historical overview of Sh.S. and its linguistic impact on Sh.S.
The development of Swahili in Shaba took place in three stages:

1   the pre-colonial stage which involved the introduction of a subdialect of Swahili in Shaba which is close to the East African Standard Sh.S., and the expansion of Swahili in the Sanga-speaking areas;
2   the development of the industrial mines and the Christianization of the province. This period also corresponded to the importation of the Luba Kasai labor force. This group greatly influenced the region in all spheres of life (economic, political, social, cultural, educational, judicial).
3   the post-colonial period which corresponds to the spread of the educational system and a drastic expansion of French as the official language of the country (for education, the court system, external commerce).

I have shown elsewhere (Kapanga 1991, 1993) that for each historical period, there corresponds a given social group that had a certain influence on the linguistic form of Swahili produced in Shaba. That is, for each historical period, one social group or another had a high degree of ethnolinguistic vitality in the community and so determined the direction of linguistic change undergone by the Swahili of the region. Thus, at the introduction of Swahili in southern Zaire, Sanga had the greatest influence on Swahili since Bukenya was the economic and political center of Shaba. The creation of the mining company led to the development of Lubumbashi as a political and economic center. Its development corresponded to the large migration of laborers from the Kasai and surrounding African countries. In terms of numbers, the laborers from the Zairian provinces of Kasai far exceeded those of other ethnic groups in most urban centers. In addition, they took advantage of the educational system created by the colonizers and ended up being placed in charge of the educational system by the Belgians. In addition, they proved, according to Heine (1970), to be the most zealous ethnic group with regard to learning Swahili. Their influence in the educational system as well as their willingness to readily learn the language of wider communication, namely, Swahili, allowed them to become one of the groups of people that were given the task of spreading Swahili both by the colonial authority and the Church. These various factors contributed to the great impact that the Luba had on Swahili.

Given that Lubumbashi was created in an area that is predominantly inhabited by the Bemba ethnic group, their numbers were similarly greater and they had what Ryan, Giles, and Sebastian (1982) refer to as demographic status; this explains the presence of some of the Bemba features in the Shabian subdialect of Swahili. Since independence, however, French has had a very big influence since it is the language of social and economic advancement. This explains the greater incidence of French lexical items in the local subdialect of Swahili. However, since the above-mentioned changes have taken place, and given the desire by the political system to invigorate Standard Sh.S., it is fruitful to analyze this situation to see what factors have contributed to the maintenance of Sh.S. and the neglect of Standard Sh.S.

3   Sh.S. versus Standard Sh.S.: linguistic maintenance

In this section, I discuss the issues of linguistic variation in a multilingual context, and analyze the factors that generally cause linguistic variation to see how these forces interact to bring about language maintenance. In collecting data, I used the network approach. In this approach, two kinds of linguistic variants are important in the study of linguistic data. The first variant is that used by a group of speakers who identify themselves as a distinct entity. This variant is seen by Le Page (1978:176), quoted in Milroy (1982:143), as a natural result of a more general cultural process involving the emergence of a distinct sense of group solidarity and identity. The second variant displays linguistic patterns of people who are geographically and socially mobile. Generally it is not considered to belong to any specific accent because it is a concoction of sundry social and regional accents (Milroy 1982).

The subjects for this study were essentially drawn from two kinds of social networks. The two networks exhibit the type of structures that Milroy (1987:20) calls high-density personal network structure and low-density personal network structure, respectively: the high-density network essentially involves an intense interaction within the constituent group members; and the low-density network is characterized by interaction with individuals outside one's constituent group.

In the high-density network, the members are expected to display their allegiance or devotion to the sociocultural norms of the vernacular through their use of certain sets of linguistic features. In the low-density network, because members are in contact with people from diverse backgrounds, there is not the strong polarization found in the high-density network. Consequently, the individuals found in this category generally tend to violate the rules of the communities they belong to. They generally produce a subdialect which, for the most part, reflects the many linguistic subgroups they are in contact with, or they may simply display a somewhat low frequency in the use of the features which are associated with strong allegiance or loyalty to the vernacular culture.

In the first category are generally found Shabians who are not linguistically or geographically mobile. Such individuals include mostly users of the auxiliary vernacular[1] who interact only with people they identity with linguistically, socially, and culturally. The second category includes people who blend with both people in and outside their direct social network (in church, at work outside the area they live in, in schools outside their immediate social environment, etc). The subjects were first observed interacting with individuals belonging to their own social networks. Their interaction with relatives, close friends, and individuals they "intimately" socialize with on a daily basis was recorded by non-participating observers. Then some of the subjects with outside connections were also observed spending time with individuals outside their immediate subgroups. Of particular importance was the fact that these individuals included mostly users of two different kinds of Sh.S. subdialects: the "Educated subdialect" (strongly influenced by French) and the Standard Sh.S. subdialect. The linguistic performance yielded by each set of data collected is discussed in the following sections.

---

1 This name refers to the subdialect of Sh.S. used by individuals with little or no formal education. The other variant used in Shaba is known as the Educated subdialect which is spoken by the segment of the population that is exposed to the European school system where French is the dominant language; the main feature of this variant is its extensive use of French lexical items. The last subdialect is known as Standard Sh.S. which is characterized by the use of many words of Arabic origin as well as structures that are very close to East African Swahili. For further details regarding the various features that typify each one of these subdialects, see Kapanga 1991.

3.1   *Social-network approach and Sh.S.*

Milroy (1987) and Cheshire (1982) have both shown that the frequency in use of non-standard features is correlated with the type of social
networks in which speakers are involved. The use of these features essentially conveys a certain loyalty to the vernacular culture by the speakers.
To investigate this claim in the case of Sh.S., the subjects were divided into
two groups. The members of each group were presented with some linguistic features from each of the three subdialects of Sh.S. found in the
community. Group members were asked to give the differences between
their own speech and that of the other two subdialects. Then their attitudes
toward these features were requested in order to establish the *vernacular
culture index* for the group of speakers associated with each of the three
subdialects. The speakers of Auxiliary Sh.S. describe themselves as true
speakers of Sh.S. for it is not a reflection of any outside group or culture.
Users of Educated Sh.S. associate it with stature, grandeur, and loftiness
conferred on it by the influence of French as the consequences of its high
social status in Zaire. The group that uses Standard Sh.S. thinks of its
subdialect as representative of Swahili in the true sense of the word; that
is, their Swahili is similar to the subdialect of Swahili recognized in the
Swahili community at large as the most prestigious of all the variants of the
language. Thus, linguistic nationalism or regionalism, superstratum association, and native-dialect association were considered the cultural foci in the
cross-subdialect communication. Linguistic nationalism was essentially
reflected in three ways: avoidance of the French pronunciation in borrowed
words, avoidance of words of Arabic origin in their speech and avoidance
of East African Swahili (EAS) features in speech. Superstratum association
is marked by the French pronunciation of words borrowed from French as
well as a heavy dose of code-mixing. EAS dialect association is marked by
a heavy use of structural features of EAS; it includes the use of the noun
classification of EAS,[2] the use of a "light dose" of words of Arabic origin,
and the preferred use of the non-impersonal passive. As can be seen, all
the vernacular-culture indicators are linguistic features. In some communities, daily activities can be used as indicators of the vernacular subculture

---

2 Swahili nouns are traditionally divided into noun classes according to their morphology; each of these
classes is assigned a number.

(see Cheshire 1982). Given that this is not the case in Shaba, only linguistic features are used as indicators or markers. That is, an individual performing manual jobs can use EAS features better than one who is educated and frequently uses Sh.S. In a more concrete way, the use of some of the features of the three main subdialects of Sh.S. were analyzed to ascertain whether they embody a social or cultural function of one kind or another. The features used for each subgroup are given below.

3.2   *Auxiliary Sh.S.*

Auxiliary Sh.S. is characterized by a lack of mixing patterns, i.e. there is no code-mixing or code-switching using French or any other local language during interaction. In addition, this subdialect reveals peculiar characteristics at all grammatical levels. At the phonological level: [ʃ] is used instead of [s] as in *šmama* "stand up", *škiya* "listen"; the sound [l] is realized as [r] as is the case in the words *ripa* "pay" and *rima* "cultivate." Auxiliary Sh.S. is also characterized by an almost total deletion of EAS [h] as in *abari* "news," *apa* "here" in place of *habari* and *hapa*, respectively. At the morphological level, this subdialect is typified by a reclassification of EAS class 10 words into class 6 as in *manyumba* "houses" and *manyota* "stars" instead of *nyumba* and *nyota*, respectively. The suffix *-ko* is always used to express politeness or a polite request as in *unifungiyeko mlango* "please close the door for me" in lieu of the EAS *tafadhali, nifungie mlango*. The lexicon of Auxiliary subdialect is set apart from the other subdialects by its extensive use of words borrowed from local ethnic languages; for example, *(m)bandakwe* "tortoise," *masengo* "horns," *ribaya* "blouse," *kabunji* "fox," *mpombonfuko* "gophers." Words borrowed from French are almost always nativized when adopted in Auxiliary Sh.S. Examples include, among others, the words *fulu* "stove," *futubolo* "football," *jipe* "skirt," *pantalo* "trousers," *mashini* "machine," *lampi* "lamp," *biro/bilo* "desk," *filme* "movie," *shesheti* "sock," *pantufu* "tennis shoes," *alumeti/alumechi* "match", which in French are: *four, football, jupe, pantalon, machine, lampe, bureau, film, chaussette, pantoufles*, and *allumette*, respectively.

At the syntactic level there are impersonal passive constructions such as *barimutuma Safi kuko mama* "Safi was sent by mom" instead of *Safi alitumwa sokoni na mama*; the temporal clause markers *-po-* and *-kapo-* are not used by Auxiliary Sh.S. speakers; for example, *wakati/pale nirimwona* "when I saw him," *wakati/pale nitamwona* "when I will see him" are used instead of the EAS (*wakati*) *nilipomwona* and (*wakati*) *nitakapomwona*.

3.3   Educated Sh.S.

At the phonological, morphological, and syntactic level, this sub-dialect is exactly the same as Auxiliary Sh.S. The difference between the two subdialects stems essentially from the production of borrowed French words which are not nativized in Educated Sh.S. Therefore, the nativized examples found on the lexical level in the description of Auxiliary Sh.S. are always produced in the Educated subdialect as: *four* [fuʀ], *football* [futbal], *jupe* [ʒyp], *pantalon* [pãtalõ], *machine* [maʃin], *lampe* [lãp], *bureau* [byro], *deux* [dø], *film* [film], *chaussettes* [ʃosɛt], *pantoufles* [pãtufl], *allumettes* [alymɛt], etc. The grammatical levels do not exhibit differences with Auxiliary Sh.S. Most of the disparities detected in the data can be attributed to individuals rather than considered idiosyncrasies attributable to a social dialect.

3.4   Standard Sh.S.

The linguistic attributes associated with this subdialect are found at all grammatical levels. At the phonological level, there is frequent use of the sounds [s] before a high front vowel, [j] instead of the glide [y]. Other features include the non-use of [l] in words such as *kidogo, midomo, kidonda, dawa, damu* and *udongo* (Sh.S.: *kiloko* "small," *milomo* "lips," *lawa* "medicine," *kilonda* "wound," *lamu* "blood," and *bulongo* "earth/dirt," respectively); the non-use of the initial nasal in words such as *kuku* "chicken," *kuni* "wood," *kopo* "cup." etc. (These are realized in Sh.S. as *nkuku, nkuni,* and *nkopo,* respectively.) Standard Sh.S. morphology is characterized by infrequent use of the syllabic nasal as a noun class marker, the use of the noun prefix *ji-* instead of the Sh.S. *ri-*, the use of *vi-* instead of *bi-* for class 8, and the use of *amba-* as a relative marker. While quite a few French words have found their way in this subdialect of Sh.S., it still displays quite a few words of Arabic origin such as *fikiri* "think," *šukuru* "thank," *fariki* "die" as well as the Arabic-based time-telling system. At the syntactic level, the most common item is the use of the non-impersonal passive construction, the use of *-op-* with the appropriate tense marker in clauses denoting time.

4   Linguistic markers and the vernacular culture

Following Cheshire (1982), I arranged the features into three classes which indicate the degree to which these traits specify allegiance to the sub-vernacular culture for each of the subgroups of Sh.S. Class A comprises features whose frequency of use is closely related to the vernacular culture of Auxiliary Sh.S. speakers; class B incorporates linguistic features which operate as indexes of vernacular allegiance for speakers of Educated Sh.S., but the kind of loyalty these features represent for the Auxiliary subdialect speakers is less than that denoted by class A traits. The last class, C, includes features which denote loyalty to the culture of Standard Sh.S. users, but disloyalty to the other groups' subcultures. The data-gathering took place in three different contexts: the church, radio broadcasting, and the home environment. The different contexts were used to ascertain to what extent the context affected the frequency of occurrence of some items. The subjects recorded for this analysis exhibited a high frequency of interaction among themselves in daily communication. In the home environment, the recordings involved eleven people. Three of them generally speak Standard Sh.S., four use the Educated subdialect and four use the Auxiliary Sh.S. Auxiliary Sh.S. speakers included three people with very little or no formal education; three were female (17, 18, and 42 years of age) and one male (37 years old). Educated Sh.S. users included two university students (21 and 22 years of age, male), a high-school student (20 years old, female) and an administrator (31 years old, male). Among the Standard Sh.S. users, two are church-goers (23 and 33 years old, males) and one (41 years of age, female) works for the radio station. Every effort was made to allow interaction to take place naturally in all three different contexts of interaction.

The recordings made in the home environment were conducted in a very informal setting. Figure 11.1 gives the frequency of occurrence of the features for each group. This was the only environment where individuals from all the three groups were brought together in the same environment. The features observed were: the use of [f] for [v], the use of [s] for [ʃ] before high front vowels, the use of the relative marker *amba*+suffix, and the use of time marker *-po-*. After the recording had taken place, the observer isolated the first 100 instances where there was the possibility of using either of the above variables. The results are given in Figure 11.1.

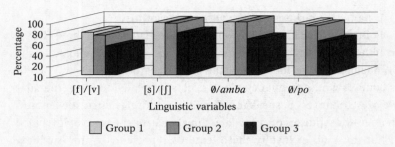

Figure 11.1 Occurrence of subgroup forms: instances of Auxiliary Sh.S. features

In figure 11.1 the users of Auxiliary Sh.S. seem to show a large use of features from their subdialect. That is, for [f]/[v] alternation, 79% of items which would exhibit EAS [v] are realized with [f]; 97% of the features display [ʃ] instead of the EAS [s]; 97% use structures without *amba* in the relative clause while 97% of temporal clauses have no *-po-* unlike in EAS. In other words, Auxiliary Sh.S. speakers used the Sh.S. features found in Figure 11.1 on an average of 92.5%. During the same interaction, Educated Sh.S. speakers had an average of 90%, which makes the difference between them and Auxiliary Sh.S. users insignificant. The speech of the Standard Sh.S. speakers showed a reduction in the use of such features. That is, for these people, who essentially use features of EAS, the average use of traits from Auxiliary Sh.S. is 65.25%. While this percentage is lower than that of group 1 and group 2, it shows, however, that group 3 speakers have reduced the use of features of their own subdialect in a very significant way to conform to the speech of their interlocutors. In essence, this confirms Bossevain and Mitchel's (1973) view developed in the social-network approach which states that a man is "an interacting social being capable of manipulating others as well as being manipulated by them." This notion has been used extensively by, among others, Gumperz (1972), Blom and Gumperz (1972), Labov (1973), and Milroy (1980, 1982). Milroy's (1987) asserts that non-standard speakers, when interacting outside their close-knit communities, suppress all but their most careful linguistic styles. However, it can be seen that it is the Standard speakers who attempt to suppress their own features at the expense of the non-standard speakers. Their linguistic behavior is not based on the assumption that non-standard speakers cannot use Standard Sh.S. as the result of its complexity. Rather, non-standard speakers can

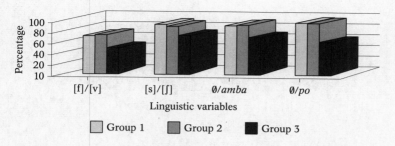

Figure 11.2 Adherence to subculture: use of Auxiliary Sh.S. features

adequately use the features of Standard Sh.S. as shown below. In the environment where the Educated subdialect is mostly used, the results obtained were very close to the those figure 11.1, as can be seen in figure 11.2.

On average, the features of Sh.S. were found in 88%, 87.5%, and 62.73% of all the cases for each group respectively. Thus, there is no significant difference between the results of figure 11.1 and figure 11.2. This is, in essence, due to the fact that the features associated with the Educated Sh.S. are essentially words borrowed from French which generally tend to conserve their French forms or pronunciation. To create an environment for this subdialect, many more users of the Educated Sh.S. were brought in; the context was basically dominated by the educated group. This was done to create the most favorable conditions for production of Educated Sh.S. The only features observed are the same as the four variables shown in figure 11.2; in addition, only the data produced by the original subjects of the study were analyzed. In this respect, the results of the variations presented in figures 11.1 and 11.2 concur with those found in Milroy (1982, 1987; Russell 1982).

In the church and radio broadcasting, where Standard Sh.S. is the norm, there was a drastic decrease in the use of the vernacular norm as suggested by the low number of occurrences in each group. In both environments, only three members of each group were represented giving a total of nine subjects. Although there were interactions with non-participants in the survey who were heavy users of Standard Sh.S., only the features used by survey participants are used in figure 11.3.

Unlike figures 11.1 and 11.2, there is a systematic reduction in the use of traits pertaining to Auxiliary Sh.S. In group 1, [f]/[v] deviation is found

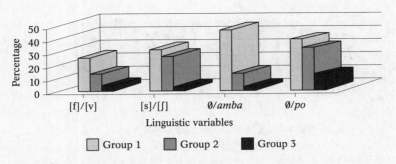

Figure 11.3 Adherence to vernacular subculture: use of Auxiliary Sh.S. features

in only 25% of the uttered words, while [s]/[ʃ], Ø/*amba*, and Ø/*po*- alternations display 31%, 46%, and 39%, respectively. In other words, the average use of the Sh.S. features in the church is about 35.25% for group 1. In group 2, the average use of Auxiliary Sh.s. is also reduced significantly; [f] is used instead of [v] in 13% of the cases, [s] is realized as [ʃ] in 26% of the cases while *amba* and -*po*- are not used in only 13% and 31% of the cases, respectively. In group 3, however, the change is even more dramatic. The features of Auxiliary Sh.S. have all but disappeared. They are used only an average of 5.25%. This group basically expresses through the use of a certain set of features its allegiance to the codified norms. Such norms are diametrically opposed to the norms of the vernacular culture for Educated and Auxiliary Sh.S. These results show that non-standard speakers (i.e. the speakers of Educated Sh.S. and those who speak Auxiliary Sh.S.) are indeed capable of speaking (to a large extent) the Standard subdialect. In addition, they show a drastic reduction in the use of features of their own subdialect through heavy use of EAS features.

The data in figures 11.1, 11.2, and 11.3 show, in principle, that the use of the features associated with the vernacular culture is not determined by the participants. Rather, the variant speakers use is determined by the context, at least in the case of Sh.S. The subjects were basically showing, through the use of the local vernacular, a certain allegiance to the local vernacular culture. The consistent use of Auxiliary Sh.S. features by the Educated and Auxiliary Sh.S. speakers does not demonstrate a lack of knowledge of Standard Sh.S., since, if this were the case, these groups would not have used Standard Sh.S. in such contexts as the church, and radio broadcasting which require more refined language. In this case, the language of the radio and the sanctity of the church take precedence over loyalty to the vernacular culture. This behavior is expected in view of findings by Gumperz (1976, 1982) that code selection is influenced by domain and context. It should be noted, however, that loyalty to the vernacular culture has been so strong in Shaba that more and more programs that used Standard Sh.S. in the late 1970s and early 1980s are switching to the local vernacular. Among such radio programs are found: *Bibi wa Sasa* ("The new wife"), *Baraza la Bib* ("The woman's council"), and parts of local news and communiqués. For the most part, these programs are a mixture of both the Auxiliary, the Educated, and the Standard Shabian subdialects.

5   Shaba Swahili and the accommodation theory

In this section, I analyze the linguistic interaction between speakers of different subdialects of Sh.S. I examine the level of accommodation between speakers of Auxiliary Sh.S., Standard Sh.S. and five speakers of EAS during the summer of 1987. I make use of quantitative methods as used by Coupland (1984) and Trudgill (1986) to analyze the exact quantification of the degree of linguistic accommodation. However, my analysis differs from that of Trudgill and Coupland in that it evaluates both long- and short-term accommodation as opposed to one or the other alone. It also involves data gathered in a multilingual area in both formal and informal interactions among subjects. Given that accommodation is multidimensional, all levels of grammar have been analyzed.

5.1   *Phonological level*

This analysis investigated three linguistic variables:

1.   [g] versus [k] in *mugging* versus *making* "backs"
2.   /h/ versus Ø in *habari* versus *abari* "news"
3.   Ø versus [n] in *kuku* versus *nkuku* "chicken"

The sound [g] of EAS is realized as [k] in Sh.S. when it occurs in syllable-initial position. Finally, there is a strong tendency among Sh.S. speakers to add [n] in initial position to words that begin with consonants other than nasals.

The first analysis involved the interaction between the five EAS speakers and Standard Sh.S. Figure 11.4 shows the occurrence of the

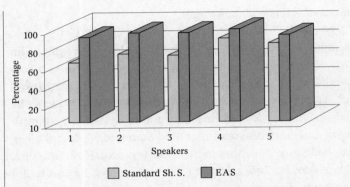

Figure 11.4(a) Use of [g] and [k]: occurrence of [g] in Standard Sh.S. and EAS

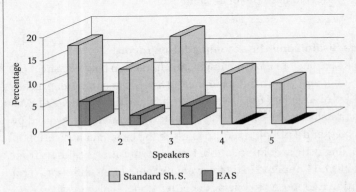

Figure 11.4(b) use of [n] and ∅: occurrence of [n] in Standard Sh.S.

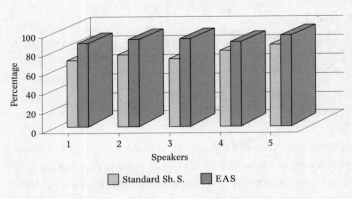

Figure 11.4(c) Use of [h] and ∅: occurrence of [h] in Standard Sh.S. and EAS

different variables in the speech of the subjects whose speech was selected for representation in this figure.

Figure 11.4 shows that in syllable-initial position, the variants of EAS are commonly realized as such by the native EAS speakers who reside in Shaba, when they are interacting with Standard Sh.S. speakers. In syllable-initial position, [g] occurred, on average, in 94.8% of the cases. [h] had 92.6% occurrence, while the epenthetic [n] occurred only in 1.8% of all the cases. The same variants occurred in 76% of the cases for [g], 77.8% for [h], and, 13.6% for the epenthetic nasal. Among the Standard Sh.S. speakers, the occurrence of the Shabian variants is somewhat reduced in comparison with that of EAS. This possibly reflects some influence of their speech community. Such an influence can also be seen in the speech of some of the EAS speakers who have incorporated the feature of Sh.S. here and there. In light of this, nonetheless, it is hard to speak of accommodation in the sense that Standard Sh.S. Shaba displays a great deal of the features of EAS. What is remarkable, however, is the occurrence of some features attributable to the Educated and the Auxiliary Subdialect in the speech of both EAS locutors who live among Shaba and Standard Sh.S. speakers.

The next stage of the analysis was to allow interaction between each of the above subgroups and the speakers of Auxiliary Sh.S. Here the changes in both instances were very dramatic, as shown in figures 11.5 and 11.6.

As indicated in figure 11.5, the Auxiliary Sh.S. speakers essentially stick to their subdialect. They do not use the feature [g] in syllable-initial position when interacting with Standard Sh.S. speakers. That is, the speakers of Auxiliary Sh.S. show 0% in their use of EAS [g] in syllable-initial position; however, their counterparts (i.e. Standard Sh.S. speakers) reveal a drastic change as far as syllable initial [g] is concerned. The percentage of the syllable initial [g] use has decreased to a mere 6.6% (from 76% in figure 11.4). This reduction is also observed in the case of [h], which they almost systematically drop when interacting with Auxiliary Sh.S. speakers. For Standard Sh.S. speakers, when prattling with Auxiliary Sh.S. speakers, [h] occurs in only 13.6% of all cases as opposed to 77.8% when interaction takes place with EAS speakers (cf. figure 11.4). As for the epenthetic [n], its occurrence has significantly increased among the Standard Sh.S. users. They use it in 53% of the cases as opposed to 13.6% in figure 11.4. The Auxiliary Sh.S. speakers display an average of 73.4% in the frequency of [n] addition in their utterances. In essence, the results of figure 11.1 concur with

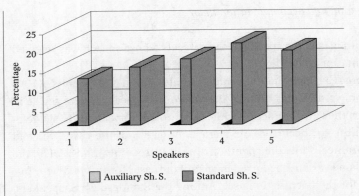

Figure 11.5(a) Use of [g] and [k]: occurrence of [g] as [g] in initial position

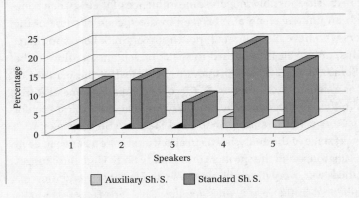

Figure 11.5(b) Use of [h] and ∅: presence of [h] in Auxiliary Sh.S. and Standard Sh.S.

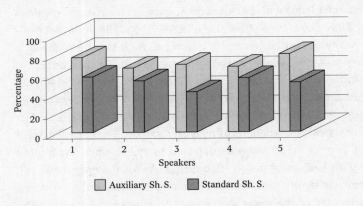

Figure 11.5(c) Use of [n] and ∅: presence of [n] in initial position

Giles and Powesland's (1975) accommodation theory in that they show that the speakers of Standard Sh.S. modulate their linguistic patterns toward that of their interlocutors. They reveal a behavior modification pattern which can be defined as convergence strategy.

In figure 11.6, however, the EAS speakers were placed among the Auxiliary Sh.S. speakers in a very informal situation. The results for the occurrence of the three variables ([g] in syllable initial position, deletion of [h], and addition of [n] in word initial position) are given in figure 11.6.

Once again Auxiliary Sh.S. speakers remain loyal to their own dialect by producing, on average, only 15% of items that contain [g] in syllable-initial position, 3.6% for words that require the production of [h] in EAS, and their use of epenthetic [n] in word-initial position is still very high (i.e. 70.4%). The EAS speakers, on the other hand, reveal the features of Auxiliary Sh.S. to a higher degree. They replace [g] with [k] in syllable ini-tial position in 29.2% of the cases, the production of [h] is reduced to 46.4%, and the word-initial nasal is found in 13.2% of the cases. There is basically an increase of approximately 24% in the production of syllable-initial [g] as [k]. The production of [h] is drastically reduced by 46.2% while the pro-duction of the epenthetic nasal increases by 11.4%. Clearly, accommoda-tion occurs in this particular case.

The linguistic data analyzed in figures 11.4, 11.5, and 11.6 show accommodation of a striking sort at the phonological level. Figure 11.4 shows a tendency, by Standard Sh.S. speakers, to use the feature [g] in syllable-initial position, [h] in all positions, and [n] before consonants when interacting with EAS users. However, there is a dramatic reduction in the EAS variants when the groups of both EAS and Standard Sh.S. speakers are addressing Auxiliary Sh.S. users, as can be seen in figures 11.5 and 11.6. That is, the two groups exhibit a very high degree of accommoda-tion to the speech of the users of the so-called less prestigious subdialect. This reduction is not due to the ignorance of Standard Sh.S. by Auxiliary Sh.S. users. Rather it is due to factors which will be discussed below. In essence, this accommodation seems to defy all the stated rules whereby non-standard speakers generally tend to reduce non-standard features when interacting with Standard subdialect users (Milroy 1982, 1987).

Figure 11.7 provides an example of EAS and Standard Sh.S. speakers interacting with Auxiliary Sh.S. users. The only difference with the situation seen in figures 11.4, 11.5, and 11.6 is that the context of interaction for the

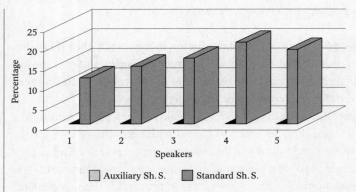

Figure 11.6(a) Use of [g] and [k]: presence of [g] in syllable-initial position

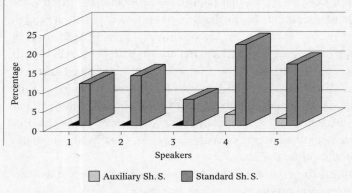

Figure 11.6(b) Use of [h]: presence of [h] in speech Standard Sh.S.

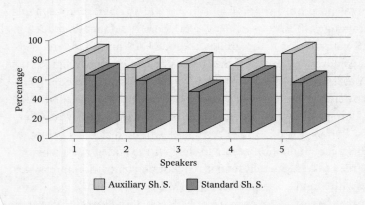

Figure 11.6(c) [n] before consonant: presence of [n] in word-initial position

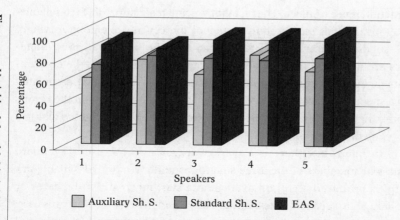

Figure 11.7(a) Use of [g] between vowels: presence of [g] in church/radio-broadcasting environment

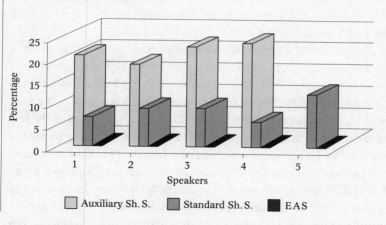

Figure 11.7(b) [n] in syllable-initial position: [n] before words with consonants in initial position

data in figure 11.7 is a church (for three of the Standard Sh.S. users) and a formal radio interview (for the other two subjects). In this specific case the Auxiliary Sh.S. users have a higher incidence of the EAS or Standard Sh.S. features; this can be ascribed to the formality of the context in which interaction is taking place. The fact that voicing realization of [g] in syllable-initial position has increased in frequency of occurrence among Auxiliary Sh.S. subdialect users attests to the fact that the interlocutors by themselves are not likely to bring about accommodation; rather, the environments (a church, a studio) can do that simply because they are associated with a specific dialect. Such a conclusion is essentially based on the results found in figure 11.3 where the Standard variants users reduced the features that typify these variants.

In figure 11.7, there is a marked increase in the use of standard features by members of the three subgroups under study. The syllable initial [g] is produced as [g] on average in a startling 72.2% of the cases by Auxiliary Sh.S. speakers. The Standard Sh.S. and EAS speakers, in this case, prefer to use features of their own "subdialects." The average percentage of occurrence of [g] in syllable initial position is 79.8% for Standard Sh.S. speakers and 95.4% for EAS speakers. As for [n]-epenthesis, it occurs in 23.6% of the cases for Auxiliary Sh.S. speakers, 8.6% of the cases for Standard Sh.S. speakers, and only 0.4% for EAS speakers.

The context in which interaction takes place plays a role as far as accommodation is concerned. This is confirmation of the importance of the context of situation in daily interactions (e.g. Firth 1934). Rather than use the Auxiliary subdialect or the Educated subdialect as was the case in figures 11.4, 11.5, and 11.6, the Standard Sh.S. speakers as well as the few EAS speakers selected for this part of the study find it necessary to use the subdialect with which they generally feel comfortable. That is, in the church or radio environment, the activity in which they are engaged requires the use of a certain register; this register is essentially the language required or expected in church and radio-broadcasting domains. As a consequence, the opposite group, i.e. the users of Auxiliary Sh.S., finds itself in such a position that they have to alter their dialect despite their own belief as to which dialect is appropriate in their part of the country. At the same time, this seems to contradict the claim that Auxiliary Sh.S. speakers (in some contexts) exhibit a certain inability to learn the Standard dialect because of its linguistic complexity.

5.2   *Lexical level*

To investigate the extent to which accommodation occurs throughout the entire accent spectrum of Sh.S., Educated Sh.S. was compared to

Auxiliary Sh.S.; then Educated Sh.S was also compared to Standard Sh.S. These two comparisons centered on the analysis of lexical items. As indicated earlier, the difference between the Auxiliary and the Educated subdialect is more a matter of the lexicon or lexical choice than of phonology, morphology, or syntax. The interaction that occurred involved two kinds of pairing: younger speakers of the Auxiliary subdialect were matched with speakers of the Educated Sh.S.; and older speakers of the Auxiliary dialect were paired with the users of the Educated subdialect. The object of this task was twofold: (1) to study the structural differences, per se; and (2) to examine the impact of age on accommodation. The data uncovered in these instances suggested no striking differences among both groups as far as phonological features are concerned. However, the lexical items used in both instances were very revealing from the perspective of accommodation. The words analyzed in this study fall in the category of words that have been borrowed from French, as they are the features that most characterize Educated Sh.S. In the speech of Educated Sh.S., these words are generally realized with the French pronunciation; but in Auxiliary Sh.S., the same words are used but their pronunciation has been nativized to the phonological patterns of Sh.S. Lexical items of this type included Educated Sh.S. words such as [ʃɛmiz] "shirt," [ʒyp] "skirt," [avjõ] "plane," [ʀadjo] "radio," [maflœʀ] "flowers," [simã] "cement," [aʀbitʀ] "referee" which are realized in Auxiliary Sh.S. as [ʃemize], [ʒipe], [anvjo], [lario/ladjo], [mafulele], [ʃima], and [albitre], respectively. The expectation is that the Educated Sh.S. users will stick to the forms they identify themselves with in both situations. In analyzing the speech of younger Auxiliary Sh.S. users, older Auxiliary Sh.S. users and Educated Sh.S. users, it was found that when young Auxiliary Sh.S. speakers interact with Educated Sh.S. speakers, borrowed French words are pronounced with a French accent in 63% of the cases. However, the educated counterparts show a percentage of 88.2%. Still, the same Educated Sh.S. speakers reveal a severe reduction of the French accent in the production of borrowed French pronunciation when they are talking with old(er) Auxiliary Sh.S. speakers. Their average, as far as French-accent production is concerned, has fallen to a mere 34.2%. The average for the older people basically reflects their lack of French knowledge, and it stands at 24.4%.

In this part of the study, the observers indirectly imposed some topic of conversation to allow the subjects to use the same words during both interactions. Based on the results of figure 11.7, clearly, accommodation has taken place in both instances. However, its direction is different in both cases. There is an approximation of the two lines in both instances; that is, on the one hand the line representing the auxiliary group converges towards the line symbolizing the educated group; on the other, the line representing the educated moves in the direction of the line that symbolizes the older speakers of Auxiliary Sh.S. However, as can be seen, the young(er) Auxiliary Sh.S. speakers try to accommodate to the speech of the Educated Sh.S. users. Whereas in the case of interaction between the older locutors of Auxiliary Sh.S. and Educated Sh.S. speakers, the former adhere to their own non-French pronunciation, the latter, on the contrary, change their French pronunciation in accordance with that of their elders despite the prestige associated with French pronunciation in the community. The accommodation by younger people is simply the corollary of the prestige associated with the French variants. However, the reduction observed in their interaction with older Auxiliary Sh.S. users seems to suggest a certain deference, on their part, vis-à-vis their older interlocutors. To use the French variant in this specific case amounts to mocking or making fun of their older interlocutors, which in itself goes against the cultural values of the community. The other factor that leads to the selection of this particular type of pronunciation is the need to be understood by their interlocutors. The use of French pronunciation generally assumes a certain level of education. And it so happens that most of the speakers of Auxiliary Sh.S. have little or no formal education. Consequently, using French pronunciation is nothing more than being pretentious, or it may impede one from conveying a message effectively.

In the case of Sh.S., vocabulary is one of the grammatical levels that shows greater variability between Sh.S. and its native counterpart. However, Standard Sh.S. locutors have a characteristically high frequency of use of words unique to Sh.S. The frequency of accommodation in speech of the Standard Sh.S. subdialect was analyzed in two situations. The Standard Sh.S. speakers were observed while interacting with the Educated Sh.S. speakers, on the one hand, and Auxiliary Sh.S. ones, on the other. They were also observed talking with EAS users, using the same topic as with the other groups. The frequency of occurrence of Arabic loanwords in the speech of Shabians differed significantly from that of the EAS interlocutors.

In conversations between Standard Sh.S. speakers and those who use EAS, the average frequency of occurrence of Arabic words in the speech of EAS speakers was 83% (for a possible 100% for which Arabic loan could have been used); but for Standard Sh.S. speakers the average was only 49.6%. When interacting with speakers of Auxiliary Sh.S., that average falls to a low 5.6% among Standard Sh.S. speakers; here however, it needs to be noted that the Auxiliary Sh.S. speakers show only an average of 4.6%. The interaction between Standard Sh.S. speakers and their counterparts who use Educated Sh.S. exhibits results that are close to those that involve interaction between speakers of Standard Sh.S. and Auxiliary Sh.S. That is, on average the Educated Sh.S. speakers use Arabic words in 5.4% of the cases while their counterparts use these words in only 14% of the cases.

In essence, the Standard Sh.S. speakers constitute the only group of people that find themselves torn between two worlds: that of the majority which prefers the subdialect with fewer Arabic loans, and their own "world" which requires the use of a very close variant of EAS. The consequence in this case is that the speakers of Standard Sh.S. accommodate their style to that of each group of people with whom they interact. What is remarkable, however, is the unwillingness of both the Auxiliary and the Educated Sh.S. speakers to accommodate to the speech of the users of the Standard Sh.S. subdialect despite the fact that this latter subdialect is viewed by both groups as being very close to the more prestigious EAS. Note, however, a slight increase of words of Arabic origin when the Standard Sh.S. locutors interact with the Educated group. This is due to the fact that there is a tendency by many to assume that education implies some knowledge of EAS. However, this is not true in that the language of education is Swahili only for the first three years of elementary school, and French is used in the last four years of elementary education, in high school, and at the university. The impact of Auxiliary Sh.S. has been so great that it is the predominant variant used in elementary school.

5.3   *Morphological and syntactic levels*

Accommodation was limited to the phonological and lexical levels. The data analyzed consistently showed that accommodation is a multilevel phenomenon which can affect phonology, morphology, and syntax as well as the lexicon. Non-users of Auxiliary Sh.S. consistently accommodated or used the convergence strategy when interacting with Auxiliary Sh.S. users. The only instances where they diverged from this rule was in interactions that involved the sanctity of the church and the radio environment where the social rules require the use of a standard subdialect of Swahili (EAS or Standard Sh.S.).

6   Linguistic accommodation as an explanation

Throughout this chapter, it can be seen that people seem to alter their linguistic behavior in order to be accepted by members of social groups other than their own. Nonetheless, it is remarkable to see that the data analyzed here and elsewhere (Kapanga 1990) suggest that the rate of Standard Sh.S. use is falling drastically. In other words, more and more people prefer to use Auxiliary Sh.S. rather than the Standard one. The usage of Standard Sh.S. is shown to be limited to three environments: radio broadcasting, in the church, and among Standard Sh.S. users. In essence, this subdialect is used only in situations/contexts that require a certain allegiance to the vernacular culture proper to its context of use. Speakers of Standard Sh.S., as shown in Kapanga (1990), use that dialect only in cases where the vernacular-culture indexes (sanctity of church, radio broadcasting requirements or government support, intra-group pride) require it. These vernacular-culture indexes have a vitality which overrides the vitality of other social variables. However, in contexts other than the church, radio broadcasting or among Standard Sh.S. users, these variables (e.g. prestige of Standard, sanctity of the church, governmental support) do not have an overriding power; instead they have a low vitality and consequently do not determine the direction of accommodation. Variables such as age, regionalism, or local pride seem to determine the selection of the linguistic variant to be used. Consequently, it can be claimed that these variables have a high degree of vitality outside the contexts of radio, the church, the court, etc. In a context where older people are involved (outside the church, radio, etc.), it is noticed age seems to act as a variable in determining interlocutors' linguistic behavior; thus it can be claimed that age, which is associated with respect for elders in the African context, has a high degree of vitality in that specific context. Given this shift in the vitality of social variables from one context to another, it can be claimed that in each speech community, there exists a "repertoire of social variables" that may affect people's linguistic behavior. For each context of interaction, some variables are more prominent than others and they can have an impact on linguistic behavior. Put differently, one can claim that in different contexts, different variables have more vitality than others; thus they can govern people's linguistic behavior which can translate into either accommodation or the use of divergence strategy (see Giles and Smith 1976). For each context, members of a community are aware of the social variables that are likely to influence their linguistic behavior. Thus, these variables are assigned a high degree of vitality or a higher indexation marking. In a different context where they may not impact linguistic behavior, these variables will have a low degree of vitality and will in this way be assigned a lower indexation marking. In other words, one can say that for each context of situation, a speaker will give prominence to social variables that govern his or her linguistic behavior. These variables may be connected with the low levels of daily life, or with the high levels which are dependent on society. Therefore, it can be said that speakers have an internal hierarchy as far as social variables are concerned. This hierarchy is unconsciously determined by society as a whole, and it is heavily governed by the social and cultural values of the community. Each member of the community is aware of the hierarchy and will usually rank these variables in harmony with the context of interaction, and according to communal "rules." That is, in each context of situation, social variables are indexed in such a way that some are more pre-eminent than others; the most potent variables are assigned the highest index(es) and accommodation will be constrained by such variables. A change in context will require a re-indexation which, in all likelihood, will sway the "direction" of accommodation. This way of analyzing synchronic data can also be extended to the analysis of diachronic ones (see Kapanga 1991).

7   Implications for endangered languages

It is certainly obvious that societies attribute some value to the linguistic variables that are likely to influence people's linguistic behavior. The variables that reflect one's vernacular culture and that are highly functional in a given community are likely to occasion accommodation or the convergence strategy on the part of the interlocutors. Those that contradict one's vernacular culture will cause the use of what is known as divergence strategy (or lack of accommodation).

To allow communication to take place during any linguistic interaction, individuals generally make use of the convergence strategy (Giles and Smith 1979). This can be seen in their selection of linguistic variants or items that are appropriate for the context in which they find themselves. In the case of endangered languages, we have already stated that these languages are generally associated with low prestige; in addition, the social variables associated with these languages do not in any way denote any type of positive allegiance to a specific culture or vernacular culture; rather they are negatively perceived by members within and outside the context(s) in which they are used. In the case of Shaba, however, we have seen that a subdialect with low prestige (Sh.S.) has supplanted one with high prestige (Standard Sh.S.). The reasons for this state of affairs are the demographic prominence of Sh.S. speakers, its denotation of local pride, its association with an allegiance to the local culture, and its association with a certain regionalism by its speakers. As can be seen, most of these variables are dealing with the lower levels of communal life in the Shabian environment. While this association happens unconsciously in most linguistic communities, it may be applied consciously in cases where linguists and others are dealing with the revitalization of a given language. That is, in order to revitalize a given language, linguists and other language-revitalization experts will need to find ways to associate that language with social variables that are positively perceived and that are associated with allegiance to a local culture. Among these are found cultural pride, linguistic regionalism or nationalism, local pride, educational opportunity, cultural heritage, religion. In other words, the endangered language will need to be consciously associated with any of the variables which essentially have a high degree of ethnolinguistic vitality within their respective communities. For example, languages such as Gaelic and Occitan were at a given period associated with social variables found at the lower end of the spectrum (e.g. languages of the countryside, language of farmers, languages of uneducated people, etc.). However, their relative revitalization occurred only after a campaign was carried out to specifically associate them with variables found at the higher end of the spectrum, namely, education, cultural pride, nationalism, cultural heritage, and the like. These variables, as can be seen, have a high degree of vitality, and they have contributed to the resurgence or the revitalization of these languages. While the indexation process as well as the linguistic behavior are unconscious in Shaba, in an endangered language they will have to be consciously promoted to actively eradicate negative misconceptions in the minds of potential speakers. In other words, the endangered languages have to be associated with variables that are at the high end in terms of ethnolinguistic vitality, and that are likely to positively impact the speakers of the community where an endangered language is spoken.

8   Conclusion

This chapter has essentially shown that in linguistic interaction, paralinguistic variables that relate to the small-scale social lives of a community are the ones that determine the direction of variation (Kloss 1966; Fishman 1991; Kapanga 1990). These variables are generally indexed hierarchically based on their degrees of vitality in different contexts of situation. The variables with the most potent vitality in a given context are likely to determine the type of variation witnessed in that context. Members of each speech community somehow consciously or unconsciously acquire this hierarchical ordering of paralinguistic variables likely to determine variation and change in language. This model is also applicable to linguistic changes that have occurred at various periods over time. The understanding of this hierarchical indexation can be useful in finding ways to reverse the phenomenon of language endangerment. That is, languages that are endangered are generally associated with paralinguistic variables that have a low degree of ethnolinguistic vitality in communities where they are spoken. To revitalize them, there is the need somehow to find a way to consciously assign, at what Fishman (1991) refers to as the "lower levels" of communal life, a high degree of vitality to the paralinguistic variables associated with these languages. It needs be emphasized that these variables should be the ones that members of the endangered language use to generally express their allegiance to their culture. They may include: linguistic pride, cultural heritage, nationalism, sociocultural self-sufficiency, self-help, self-regulation, education, etc. This explains, for example, the sudden interest of Catalan and Basque in Spain, Occitan and Breton in France, and Gaelic in Great Britain; these languages which were all associated with a low degree of vitality in these countries have undergone a drastic change of perception in their respective communities. Instead of simply being considered as languages of "farmers, villagers, uneducated, or neglected minorities," these languages have consciously been assigned attributes that generally have a high degree of vitality in communities; namely nationalism, regional pride, cultural identity, etc. Such a deliberate change has contributed to their relative revival and their possible survival and removal from the endangered list. Thus, the key in preserving endangered languages is to find a way to assign to them attributes associated with a high degree of vitality. This will guarantee that languages with low prestige will be associated with variables that have high vitality and that in turn may contribute to their maintenance or expansion as is the case for the low-prestige subdialect in Shaba, Zaire.

12   A way to dusty death: the Matrix Language turnover hypothesis

CAROL MYERS-SCOTTON

Linguistics Program, University of South Carolina

1   Introduction

This chapter proposes a set of predictions to explain the general morphosyntactic structural outlines found across all types of bilingual speech. Bilingual speech is defined as showing either morphemes or lexical structure, or both, from two or more languages. One encounters bilingual speech most typically in code-switching by proficient bilinguals, but not all language-contact situations are so viable or capable of sustaining themselves. Specifically, the paper accounts for cases of what have been called structural borrowing, especially in relation to language attrition. Languages can sustain structural incursions and remain robust, but the taking in of alien inflections and function words is often a step leading to language attrition and language death. This is not to say, however, that all endangered languages in their late stages show structural borrowing; that is, all the following arguments do not apply to all endangered languages and certainly not to the speech of final fluent speakers.

1.1   *Assumptions and claims of the proposed model*

What makes the model presented here different from previous discussions of structural borrowing in the literature are these claims:

> Heavy cultural contact is a necessary precondition for structural incursions of one language into another (Thomason and Kaufman 1988), but contact itself obviously is not the structural mechanism involved.
>
> The hypothesis developed here is that the actual mechanism which sets the stage for structural change is a turnover (from one language to another) in

This research was supported under NSF grant FBR 9319780. I thank Janice L. Jake for helpful comments on an earlier draft. "The way to dusty death" is from Shakespeare's *Macbeth* and the famous "Tomorrow and tomorrow" soliloquy in act v ("And all our yesterdays have listed fools/The way to dusty death").

the role of the Matrix Language (i.e. morphosyntactic frame builder) in bilingual speech. The Matrix Language (ML) as a theoretical construct is discussed below.

In addition, it will be argued that the key necessary conditions for such structural change are either widespread intra-sentential code-switching in a community or convergence, or both. 'Classic' intra-sentential code-switching is redefined here as the use of morphemes from two or more linguistic varieties in the same CP (projection of Complementizer), formerly S-bar. Convergence is defined as the use of morphemes from a single linguistic variety, but with parts of their lexical structure coming from another source. Thus, code-switching (CS) and convergence are prototypical of the two types of language-contact phenomena which I include under bilingual speech: CS shows morphemes from two or more languages, and convergence shows lexical structure from more than one language.

Note that while either intra-CP switching or convergence is a necessary condition for the turnover to occur, neither is sufficient. A turnover is motivated by socio-political factors, as discussed below, as is the extent of the turnover (i.e. extent can vary from a complete Matrix Language turnover and subsequent language shift to limited structural incursions into a maintained language).

In order to understand the effects of a turnover of the ML, a more complex analysis of lexical structure is necessary. Specifically, an analysis must recognize two points. First, there are two classes of morphemes, content versus system morphemes. Difference in class membership makes a difference in what types of morphemes are borrowed in any type of contact phenomena or affected in language attrition. Second, lexical structure has at least three subsystems or levels which are present simultaneously, but not necessarily activated at the same time. They are: lexical–conceptual structure (semantics and input for pragmatic readings); predicate–argument structure (relations between verbs and prepositions and their arguments, i.e. θ-grid mappings onto hierarchical P-markers); and morphological realization patterns (surface requirements for well-formedness, including word order). In monolingual speech, all aspects of lexical structure normally come from a single language. However, in language-contact situations, resulting structures show parts of lexical structure for lexemes and their relations coming from more than one language.

2   Bilingual speech: a coherent perspective

I will cite data from a number of language-contact situations to argue two propositions:

> The same structural processes figure in all forms of bilingual speech, from code-switching to interlanguage in second-language acquisition, to language attrition, to mixed languages or pidgins and creoles (Myers-Scotton forthcoming).
>
> While the precise ways in which these processes are played out in any single contact situation depend on a number of factors, including the sociolinguistic milieu and how it changes, typological characteristics of the languages in contact, and speakers' proficiency in the languages involved, *not* anything can happen in language contact. Rather, one can make principled, rather specific, predictions about expected effects.

Thus, while cross-speaker comparisons, especially at early stages of pidgin formation or L2 learning or L2 attrition, may show high variability due to different "repertoire histories," the thesis here is that the form which structural variation may take is limited to a finite set of options. Of course the details of these options will be language-specific, but the outlines are universal.[1]

Two universally present principles are hypothesized to be part of speaker competence and to drive and organize bilingual speech.[2]

2.1   *The Matrix Language Recognition Principle*

Ample evidence indicates there is a "dominant language" mechanism at work when two languages are brought together in production. This mechanism assigns one language status as the Matrix Language. The ML is defined as the language supplying the grammatical frame of constituents with morphemes from the two languages.[3] "Frame" means the lexical structure. Most obviously, this means morphological-realization patterns:

1 Of course not all cases of language-contact phenomena involve structural modifications in the participating languages. For example, there can be language shift or language death without attrition. Note the title of this chapter is "a way," not "the way," indicating that there can be other routes to language death than through the Matrix Language turnover and accompanying structural borrowing.

2 For the sake of brevity, I will avoid saying "two or more languages" and assume "two languages"

although what follows applies when more than two languages are involved as well.

3 Note that the Matrix Language versus Embedded Language distinction applies only to constituents within a CP showing morphemes or lexical structure from two or more languages. Thus, the ML designation is not relevant to switching between CPs. And while there may be a dominant language for such inter-CP switching, such "dominance" is a characteristic of the discourse. In contrast, the ML is a structural feature relevant only within a CP.

morpheme order and system morphemes (see below) signaling grammatical relationships; this is how "frame" has been defined in my writings on "classic" CS (e.g. Myers-Scotton 1993a). In "classic" CS, content morphemes from another language (the Embedded Language) may appear in this frame, as well as ML content morphemes.

There is always an ML in bilingual constituents, and there is always only one ML at a time; however, in some types of contact phenomena the ML is a composite of lexical structure from two or more sources. The possibility of a composite ML arises because the grammatical frame, in fact, includes more than just morphological-realization patterns; it includes all aspects of lexical structure. Recall that lexical structure also consists of the lexical–conceptual and predicate–argument levels. Thus, for example, in convergence, part of the "frame" may be aspects of these levels which come from another language outside of the source of the actual morphemes. See (1) in which the Pennsylvania German speaker uses morphemes from German only, but in a pattern which shows the presence of English lexical structure at two levels. She uses a pattern from English so that *habe* "have" (corresponding to English *have*) is used as an auxiliary for the perfect where German would historically require *sei* "be" for verbs of motion or change of state. Second, this surface (morphological-realization) pattern reflects the neutralization at the lexical–conceptual level of semantically based specification in main verbs as requiring either *habe* or *sei*. It is in cases such as this that one can speak of a composite ML as structuring the grammatical frame. The ML of Pennsylvania German "converges" towards English at the abstract levels of lexical–conceptual structure and predicate–argument structure; the new ML is a composite (Fuller 1996).

(1)   a. Pennsylvania German
           Mer hab-e   da   auf-ge-wachsen
           We have-1pl there up-part-grow

       b. Standard German
           Wir sind da   auf-ge-wachsen
           We be.pl there up-part-grow
           "We grew up there."

2.2   *The Morpheme-Sorting Principle*

There is also obvious evidence that not all morphemes have the same freedom of appearance in either monolingual or bilingual production.

For example, data from monolingual speech errors and aphasia show that content and system morphemes are subject to different sentence-building procedures (i.e. the abstract lemmas underlying them are "called" differently).[4] Also, language-acquisition studies, including among adults, indicate that learners are sensitive to the content versus system morpheme distinction and that content morphemes are acquired first (Klein and Perdue 1992).

Morphemes are assigned to the two categories largely based on the lexical feature of plus or minus thematic-role assignment. Content morphemes assign or receive thematic roles while system morphemes do not.[5] I refer to such familiar thematic roles as "agent," "experiencer," "beneficiary," and the like. Prototypical content morphemes are nouns, descriptive adjectives, and most verb stems. Prototypical system morphemes are inflections and determiners, possessive adjectives, and intensifier adverbs. While most verbs achieve content-morpheme status by assigning thematic roles within a CP, discourse particles, such as *but, well, also* are content morphemes because they can be thought of as assigning a different type of role, discourse-level thematic roles. Such discourse-relevant concepts are involved as "contrast" (e.g. signaled by *however, but* in English) and "conclusion" (e.g. consider *therefore* in English).[6]

4 See Levelt 1989 or Garrett 1988 for psycholinguists' views of the differential accessing of different types of morphemes in speech production.

5 See Myers-Scotton 1993a or 1995 for a fuller discussion of the content versus system morpheme distinction. Note that this distinction differs from other categorizations in the literature. First, the demarcation is theoretically independent of the lexical categorization features of the morpheme (i.e. whether a morpheme is a verb or pronoun or preposition). Second, the category content morpheme is similar to, but not the same, as "open class words" since some "closed class words," such as discourse markers and some prepositions, also are content morphemes. In turn, the category "system morpheme" is not the same as "closed class word" or "functional element", since some functional elements, such as some conjunctions and some prepositions are content morphemes. Finally, membership in the category system versus content morpheme may vary cross-linguistically. Jake (1994) argues that pronouns cannot be uniformly characterized as either content or system morphemes; however, she also shows that the principles for assigning a particular pronoun to the class of content morphemes or system morphemes are universal.

6 One consequence of their membership in the category of content morphemes is that in contact situations discourse particles from one language are readily inserted into morphosyntactic frames prepared by another language; this means they are in a position to be easily borrowed. In many languages, complementizers also should be considered as content morphemes since it can be argued that they also assign thematic roles at the discourse level; however, this is a topic which needs more study.

2.3   *Explaining outcomes in language-contact situations*

While one or both of these principles explain outcomes in most language-contact situations, researchers often imply, but just miss, the generalizations following from these principles. For example, the most common outcome in language contact is lexical borrowing from the more sociolinguistically dominant language by the less dominant one. But are all types of lexical items borrowed? All researchers know the answer is "No"; but they do not take the next step and recognize the principled basis for what they find.

Lexical borrowing is almost categorically restricted to content morphemes. As will become clear below, the explanation is that when one language sets a morphosyntactic frame, it accepts only *content* morphemes as (singly-occurring) foreign insertions in that frame. While other researchers do not state the Matrix Language Recognition Principle and the Morpheme-Sorting Principle as such, they make many statements or cite data which are clearly in support of the operation of these principles. For example, in their study of Spanish influence on Nahuatl or Mexicano, Hill and Hill (1986:194) write, "In spite of the breadth of borrowing from Spanish into Mexicano, few Spanish affixes have been incorporated into Mexicano speech except in borrowed fixed phrases . . . we have found only three borrowed Spanish affixes." Of these affixes, two are derivational (diminutive and agentive) and only one is inflectional (= system morpheme), the plural suffix *-s/-es*. Among other content morphemes borrowed are a range of Spanish discourse particles.

And when Drewes (1994) discusses the extensive borrowing into Maltese, his examples make clear that, in fact, what are borrowed are Italian and English content morphemes, not system morphemes. With genetic affiliations as a Western Arabic dialect akin to North African Arabic dialects, Maltese is spoken on the Maltese islands of Malta and Gozo south of Sicily. It has been estimated that more than 50 percent of the lexicon is of Romance origin (largely from Italian). Drewes' most explicit comment is this (p. 87): "While the influence of Italian and English on Maltese is immediately obvious in the lexicon and idiom . . . the morphology of Maltese is predominately Semitic. Verbs of English or Italian origin are conjugated with the Arabic prefixes and suffixes." And later he states that "The morphology of the noun is also basically Semitic" (p. 91). Example (2) shows how many Italian nouns have been incorporated into Maltese, in some cases with their plural suffixes.[7] Italian borrowings are in bold face.

(2)   *il-**bzonn**-ijiet ta' l-**individw-i**   j-rid-u   j-kun-u **akkomodat-i***
       det-need-pl of det-individual-pl 3pl-want 3pl-cop accommodated-pl
       indipendentemente** mil-l-**karattarestic-i**   **fizic-i**   u   **mental-i
       irrespective   of-det-characteristics-pl physical-pl and mental-pl
       "The needs of the individual must be accommodated irrespective of physical
       or mental characteristics."   (DREWES 1994:85)

3   Illustrating the principles in code-switching

Awareness of the patterns encapsulated in the two principles is clear from some comments in the code-switching literature as well. For example, in writing about CS between SeSotho and English in South Africa, Khati (1992: 189) states, "in trans-lexical mixing only the affixes can be in Sesotho, while the roots must always be in English. This rule can apply equally to other mixed speech categories with N being substituted by an appropriate lexical category, for example, V, ADV, etc." That is, while Khati does not explicitly refer to SeSotho as the ML, he recognizes that if there are mixed constituents, the mixing can go only in one direction (i.e. system morphemes must be from SeSotho, the ML, and having the lexical category from English is what makes the construction mixed). He cites such examples as (3a) and (3b). In this and the following examples, the Embedded Language (EL) is in bold face.

(3)   a. *Ba-tho   ba-e-a-ng   **space**-eng ke ba-nna*
          cl 2-person cl 2-go-**indic**-rel space-**loc cop cl** 2-man
          "People who go into space are men."   (KHATI 1992:189)

       b. *Le   li-**comment**-s   li-a-hlok-ahal-a*
          even **cl** 10-**comment**-pl cl 10-t/a-need-**n**-fv
          "Even comments are needed."   (KHATI 1992:195)

I take CS as my starting point to illustrate more fully how these principles work for two reasons. First, this paper argues that the main principles explaining CS apply to other bilingual phenomena, albeit in a modified form. Note that this is not saying that all forms of bilingual speech

---

7 Nouns of the Embedded Language often appear with EL plural affixes in CS data. Explaining their occurrence is beyond the scope of this chapter, but see Myers-Scotton and Jake 1995 for further discussion.

are one and the same as "classic" CS. Second, as noted above, the presence of CS in a community is a necessary condition to explain the development of many other language-contact phenomena.

4   The Matrix Language Frame model of "classic" intra-CP CS

Most generally, CS is the use of morphemes from two or more linguistic varieties in the same discourse. However, the interest here is only in switching between languages within a syntactic unit. Such CS can be viewed most precisely with the CP (projection of Complementizer) as the unit of analysis. Previous work on switching often refers to intra-sentential CS; however, the basis for labeling a sentence as showing intra-sentential CS may be two or more monolingual CPs whose production brings the two grammars in contact only in a limited way. Only studying CS within a CP where the two grammars are in contact allows us to examine fully permissible combinations. A CP, of course, is synonymous with a clause with a Complementizer, although this Complementizer is often null.

The two languages present in a CP showing CS do not participate equally. One of these languages, the ML, frames the CP. The other language(s) are called Embedded Languages (EL). A CP showing CS includes minimally two of the three constituent types allowed under the Matrix Language Frame model (MLF model) of Myers-Scotton (1993a). These constituents are the ML + EL, or mixed constituent; the EL island; and the ML island.

4.1   *The ML + EL constituent or mixed constituent*

These constituents show the morpheme order and morphosyntactic structure (including all syntactically active system morphemes) from the ML. Such constituents are illustrated with African data, in example (4) from Swahili/English from Kenya (*u-na-anza ku-behave* "you begin to behave" and *wa-na-vyo-behave* "as they behave") and (5) from Adamne/English in Ghana (***house red*** o [ə] "the red house").

(4)   Swahili/English
       . . . *U-na-anza*   *ku-**behave***   *kama wa-tu   w-a huko*
       2**sg-non-past**-begin **infin-behave** as   people of   there
       *wa-na-vyo-**behave***
       3**pl-non-past-manner-behave**
       ". . . You will begin to behave as people from there behave."

(MYERS-SCOTTON 1993A:103)

(5)   Adamne/English
    é   *he* **house red** *o[ə]*
    3sg past (tone) buy **house red det**
    "He/she bought the **red house**."   (NARTEY 1982:187)

4.2   *The EL island*

Example (6) illustrates these types of constituents. Under the MLF model, in (6) *la semaine* "the week" is such an EL island, as is *les permis* "the permits."

(6)   Moroccan Arabic/French
    . . . jazni w   kant dak **la semaine** *djal . . . tajzawalu*   **les permis**.
    I mean   and it was that the week   where they take away the permits
    ". . . I mean, and it was (that) the week where they take away the driving
    licenses."   (BENTAHILA AND DAVIES 1992:449)

Such islands must be maximal projections; that is, they show internal dependency relations (e.g. NP, PP). They must be well-formed from the standpoint of the EL grammar; yet they are still under ML control in various ways, some occurring within ML maximal projections which are hierarchically superior to the EL maximal projection. (Note that *la semaine* is also part of the ML maximal projection headed by *dak*, *dak la semaine* "that the week").[8]

4.3   *The ML island*

Finally, in addition to mixed constituents and EL islands, there are many ML islands in most CPs showing CS. ML islands are simply maximal projections with all morphemes coming from the ML.

5   CS versus other language-contact phenomena: some differences

In "classic" CS, it is assumed speakers are proficient enough in the languages involved that they could produce monolingual utterances in

---

8 *La semaine* is what is termed an "internal EL island" (cf. Myers-Scotton and Jake 1995). While such islands are maximal projections from the standpoint of the EL grammar, they are "intermediate constructions" in the sense that they are not well-formed maximal projections from the standpoint of the ML. In Arabic, in order to be well-formed, an NP including *dak* must be followed by a DET + N, not simply an N. In the case of *dak la semaine*, the DET + N comes from French, the EL, and *la semaine* forms an internal EL island. An indication that all EL islands in a CP are under ML control is their placement in the CP; if there is a conflict between the ML and EL regarding EL positioning, ML requirements are followed.

either language, even though they probably are more proficient in one language than the other. The motivations for CS among such speakers are social or sociopsychologically based, as discussed in Myers-Scotton (1993b). There are, of course, instances of CS which occur because speakers cannot continue in the language in which they began (whether because of proficiency or some performance issue), but they are relatively rare, folk views notwithstanding. This is one of the ways in which CS differs from attrition: except in its early stages, speakers showing language attrition are *not* proficient in both the languages which they are using. For this reason, while the two constructs introduced above – recognizing the role of a Matrix Language and content versus system morpheme sorting – will apply to attrition as well as to CS, we can predict the products will differ in detail. This difference is developed later.

Note that central to the MLF model for CS is the ML versus EL opposition. The ML's dominant role is most obvious in mixed constituents where the ML supplies the morpheme order and all syntactically relevant system morphemes. The EL can supply only content morphemes.[9] Further, there are restrictions on these morphemes as well. In order to qualify for insertion in an ML frame, content morphemes must be sufficiently congruent with an ML counterpart (see the Blocking Hypothesis discussed in Myers-Scotton [1993a] as well as a more extended discussion in Myers-Scotton and Jake [1995]).

5.1   *Extending the Matrix Language Recognition Principle*

With the principles structuring CS in place, two riders on the Matrix Language Recognition Principle should now be comprehensible and will prove relevant in discussing other types of bilingual speech.

---

9 Even though there are many researchers today who are interested in CS, there is still some disagreement about what constitutes CS (cf. Sankoff, Poplack, and Vanniarajan 1990). Under the MLF model, CS includes the singly-occurring content morphemes in mixed constituents, as well as full constituents from the EL, that is, EL islands. Some raise the issue that singly-occurring content morphemes are really borrowed forms. Discussing this issue is beyond the scope of this paper, but see chapter 6 in Myers-Scotton (1993a). Suffice it to say here that, synchronically, borrowed forms and CS forms are treated very similarly, if not identically, from the standpoint of their insertion in an ML frame. Therefore, if there is a distinction to be made between content morphemes which are CS forms and established borrowings, it is irrelevant to this discussion.

(a)   Because ML assignment is dynamic, a "turnover" of the ML is possible.
An ML turnover means that the main language which had structured
constituents becomes the minor or Embedded Language (EL); in turn, the
language which had been the minor language regarding structure becomes
the ML. The result is that grammatical structuring in CPs showing CS is
now the task of the new ML.[10]

(b)   A second rider on the ML Recognition Principle has already been introduced: the ML of bilingual production is not always a single language;
in some cases it is a composite ML instead.

We can now turn to the notion of a composite ML. ML assignment
of a single language to the role of setting the morphosyntactic frame only
operates completely when speakers can produce well-formed utterances in
a dialect of that language, whether or not it is the standard dialect. In many
cases of language contact, this is not so. The example for which there is
copious data is adult second-language acquisition. In second-language
acquisition (SLA), the target ML is the language which the speaker is
trying to acquire; however, imperfect knowledge of this language results
in the speaker's producing a composite ML (Jake 1996; Wei 1996). This
composite ML structures the speaker's learner-stage interlanguage; it has
features of the target ML, but also features of the speaker's L1, as well as
some structures which perhaps can be attributed to Universal Grammar
or to universal learning strategies.

Also, when there is a change in progress in a bilingual community
involving a turnover in ML for CS from one language to another, the ML,
in fact, is a composite, based on some structures from each of the participating languages, but obviously moving toward the new ML. The composite
often has a complex nature; for example, certain system morphemes may
still come from the "old" ML; some may have been reanalyzed in terms of
similar system morphemes in the "new" ML.

Thus, a main argument advanced here is that two related abstract
theoretical constructs, the notion of ML turnover and the notion of a composite ML while a turnover is in progress, explain many of the structural

10   In some communities (but not all), turnovers
in the language structuring mixed constituents are
possible within a conversation with a change in
situational factors, such as participant make-up or
topic, or if the speaker wishes to index a different
"attitude" toward the topic. However, such intra-
conversational turnovers are not directly relevant
here since their duration is limited; instead, more
permanent ML turnovers, which may well be
community-wide, are our concern.

configurations found in advanced stages of convergence, structural borrowing, or attrition.

6   Matrix Language turnover

The same external conditions which promote language shift promote an ML turnover. Thus, a turnover is predicted if the "socio-political
balance" for individuals or an entire community changes considerably.
This balance is altered by such major social changes as immigration on the
part of individuals or the takeover of a community by a foreign power.

6.1   *Conditions for a turnover*

While an ML turnover may be a step on the way to language shift, an
ML turnover differs from some shift situations in requiring the ML versus
EL opposition to be relevant. This opposition only holds where there are
morphemes or lexical structure from two or more languages in the same
CP. That is, it applies only to communities where there is CS or convergence within a CP. Therefore, the notion of an ML turnover is not relevant
to all cases of languages in contact. Also, it cannot be demonstrated after
the fact that a turnover occurred earlier in the communities where linguistic varieties today show structural borrowing or attrition.

Consider this hypothesis for future testing: in communities where
there is widespread CS or convergence within a CP and where there is a
dramatic shake-up in the socio-political balance in favor of the "infring-
ing" language, an ML turnover will result. What has been called structural
borrowing (incursions into the "old" ML) is an outcome of the turnover. A
way to falsify this hypothesis would be to show that structural borrowing
occurs where these conditions are not present.

What can be the results of an ML turnover? Based on existing situations, three scenarios seem possible.

(a) The ML turnover is arrested, with the "old" ML maintained as
the community's main medium of communication. However, because its
content morphemes were used with system morphemes from the "new"
ML when speakers engaged in CS, some of these system morphemes are
reproduced in the "old" ML in those collocations where they had been
used in CS. Extensive CS is not necessarily still present. This scenario
would account for most cases of structural borrowing; it seems to be what
happened in regard to Ilwana, to be discussed below.

(b) CS, with its composite ML, can fossilize as the main medium of communication in the community in question. Theoretically, this could happen at any stage of the ML turnover. Most of the various examples of what have been called mixed languages can be explained as fossilizations at some stage in the turnover. Such languages largely show the grammar of one language and the lexicon of another. Individual cases have appeared to be unique because different cases show fossilization in different stages of completion of the turnover. In the case of Ma'a to be discussed below, fossilization happened rather late in the turnover.

(c) The most common outcome is that the turnover does go to completion and, in fact, is so "successful" that language shift follows; that is, CS falls away and any composite ML is replaced by a single, probably standardized variety of what was the "new" ML during CS. Under this scenario, speakers may shift so rapidly that they never even show much attrition in their original language. In many cases, this is what has happened and is happening with endangered languages. Some aspects of abstract lexical structure from the "old" ML (the L1), which were part of the composite ML, may remain after the shift as substrate features in the new community language.

7   **Examples of outcomes: communities**

Two cases of mixed languages will be discussed as examples in support of the ML turnover hypothesis developed here. Ilwana, a Bantu language spoken on Kenya's northern border, is treated as an example of an early arrested turnover to a Cushitic ML. Ilwana has retained a Bantu grammatical base, but shows Cushitic structural influences. Ma'a or Mbugu, a language spoken in northeastern Tanzania which has a fully Bantu structure but also has many Cushitic lexical items, is considered a case of a nearly complete turnover.

7.1   Ilwana/Orma contact

Nurse (1994) provides data on the Ilwana community, situated on the banks of the Tana River in northeastern Kenya just south of Somalia. Historical accounts indicate that the Ilwana were engulfed by a Cushitic speaking people, the Orma, who dominated the area until 1875. At that point, incoming Somalis (also speaking a Cushitic language) changed the balance of power. Nurse states (1994:214), "Although Somalis were the dominant presence after 1875, the superiority of the Orma and their language lived on among the Ilwana for some time. Young people report that their fathers' fathers in the twentieth century were bilingual in Ilwana and Orma." Today all Ilwana are fluent in Swahili and Ilwana and some members of the community speak Somali and/or Orma.

In regard to vocabulary, external influences are clearly evident. Nurse states (1994:215), "Of about 2200 Ilwana verbal stems and non-verbal lexemes currently available, 77.5% appear to be not inherited, that is, only 22.5% have passed into today's Ilwana by direct oral transmission from its Bantu ancestor." Some of the non-inherited lexemes come from Swahili (about 22.5 percent), probably its nearest relative, Nurse states. Of most interest, however, is that Nurse states as well that the percentage from Orma, "while less clear and currently slightly less than 22.5%, will ultimately probably equal or exceed that."

A period of contact, inducing Ilwana speakers to become bilingual, first in Orma and then in Swahili, and to practice extensive CS between Ilwana and Orma and then later between Ilwana and Swahili, could account for lexical borrowing. Even borrowing on this scale could take place with Ilwana still in place as the ML of any CS.

To explain what happened to the morphosyntax of Ilwana, however, the initial stages of a turnover in the ML are posited. This is because Ilwana shows some structural features from Orma. Recall that the argument of this paper is that such structural incursions *only* occur when (a) CS (or convergence) is a common community pattern and then (b) there is a turnover of the ML in that CS, stimulated by a change in socio-political factors. Without the turnover in ML assignment, Orma structural features – that is, Orma system morphemes – could not appear in Ilwana/Orma CS and then find their way into Ilwana. As long as Ilwana is the ML in any CS, Ilwana, and only Ilwana, supplies syntactically relevant system morphemes to CS.

Negative evidence for the argument that an ML turnover is necessary for structural borrowing is found in studies of CS in communities all over the world: even where CS is extensive, there is no structural borrowing unless an ML turnover is in progress. On this view, structural borrowing is a concomitant of an ML turnover and, as such, is not independent evidence that a turnover took place or is taking place. However, demonstrably dramatic changes in the socio-political balance in the community in favor of the "invading" language do offer independent evidence of a turnover in progress.

Because Ilwana today has a mixed morphosyntax, partially attributable to Bantu and partially to Cushitic, the ML turnover was never completed and seems to have been reversed. I will briefly discuss some of the evidence from Nurse (1994).

(a) The Ilwana nominal system shows two clear innovations to the typical Bantu noun class system. Nurse, however, is cautious in attributing them to Orma, pointing out that they are not distinctively characteristic of structures in the Cushitic languages in the area. There are two sets of innovations. Along with the usual pairings and agreements of a Bantu system of nouns classes, Ilwana has two unusual pairings (classes 1–10 and classes 9–2). Both refer to human relationships.[11] Nurse (1994:216) does say, "Certainly 1–10 (ethnonyms) and probably 9–2 (kinship terms) are based on Orma models." Another change in the noun class system is the use of suffixes, a dramatic change since Bantu classes are usually marked by prefixes. Nurse notes that the suffixes appear mainly on the one pair (9–10) which is morphologically unmarked. Example (7) illustrates this.

(7)   *si:ba* "lion": *sib:be:na* "lions"
        (compare Swahili *simba* "lion": *simba* "lions.")

(b) Ilwana does have a new set of possessive pronouns which follow a pattern found in Cushitic (e.g. *a* "of" + *imi* "I" = *emi* "my", mine')

(c) Verb structures: compared to other Bantu languages, Ilwana has a reduced set of tense/aspect markers. Further, the present-day system resembles the Cushitic pattern in certain ways, such as in seemingly being more of an aspect system than a tense/aspect system, which is more characteristic of Bantu languages.

(8)   a. *tw-a-ko: soma* "we will read"
           Note: *ko* is a vowel harmony variant of *ku*
        b. *to-mo-ko-som-e:ni* "we are reading"
           Note: progressive = present; Nurse cites *-mo-* as a variant of *-ko-*

---

11 Bantu nouns are traditionally divided into noun classes according to their morphology; each of these classes is assigned a number.

Nurse comments that a tense marker consisting of a linker clitic (-*a*-) plus infinitive marker "is definitely anomalous and would hardly arise spontaneously" (1994:218). While -*a*- is widespread in Bantu with a range of meanings (often non-past), as Nurse comments (1994:218), "[it] is not and never has been an auxiliary." He goes on to say, "The very close parallel between the Ilwana future and progressive forms and those in Orma would suggest they are calques on the Orma forms, and could presumably only have been introduced at a time when large sections of the Ilwana spoke Ilwana and Orma" (1994:218).

In addition, Nurse points out that, compared to other Bantu languages, Ilwana has a reduced set of verbal derivational extension. Cushitic is characterized by fewer extensions, Bantu by many.

(d) There is no evidence that syntax, specifically word order, was affected by Orma. Nurse's interviews were conducted in Swahili, and he remarks that gross differences between Swahili and Ilwana would have become apparent.

What are the effects of a partial ML turnover? In summary, Ilwana has retained its Bantu structure, but with apparent inroads from Orma. The modifications in the noun class system, the new possessive pronouns, and especially the likely reanalysis of some Ilwana verbal system morphemes in terms of Orma lexicalization patterns are all reasons to claim that the Ilwana situation shows the effects of having had a composite ML at an earlier point in its history when CS would have been more common, I argue.

Nurse concludes his discussion by accepting borrowing of stage 5 from the typology of types of contact-induced language change presented by Thomason and Kaufman (1988:75). That is, Nurse accepts "heavy cultural pressure" as the mechanism to induce structural borrowing. A moment's reflection indicates two problems with this as an explanation: (a) how does one distinguish cultural pressure, which results only in lexical borrowing, from *heavy* cultural pressure? (b) What about the many contact cases of demonstrably "heavy cultural pressure" where only lexical borrowing, but no structural borrowing, occurs?

A better explanation is to consider an ML turnover in CS as the mechanism for structural borrowing. In its role as "new" ML in CS, Orma would gradually take over as the source of the morphosyntactic frame of any CPs showing morphemes from both languages. Nurse himself writes (1994:220), that "if the process had not been halted by external force in the late nineteenth century, Ilwana might have become an Orma dialect or have been given up entirely in favor of Orma."

Any ML turnover from Ilwana to Orma appears to have fossilized in its very early stages. Reasons to argue that the turnover never progressed far are the retention of Bantu word order and the relative paucity of system morphemes clearly from Orma. Recall that the main Orma structural influences which Nurse documents are *reanalyses* of Ilwana material along Orma lines. In an elaborated version of the MLF model, Myers-Scotton and Jake (1995) argue that "congruence" between lexical entries across languages (and therefore affecting possible borrowing) must be considered in terms of the three levels of complex lexical structure outlined above in section 1.5. On this view, reanalyses, such as those of Ilwana tense/aspect inflections or of Ilwana noun class pairings, represent structural borrowing, *not of morphemes as such, but of lexical-conceptual structures*. This argument is an example of why a more abstract analysis of lexical structure, going beyond viewing morphemes holistically, is desirable.

Such a scenario fits the sociohistory which Nurse assembles. In the period of "high bilingualism," Orma was the more prestigious language: Ilwana learned Orma and Orma men married Ilwana women, not vice versa. But Nurse also gives indications that the Orma influence either waned or was reversed. He notes that while there were two sets of low numerals in Ilwana, one inherited and one from Orma, the Orma set is now receding in use. Also, he stated (1994:214), "The two young men with whom I worked in 1992 were quite nationalistic and bridled at suggestions that Ilwana material originated in Orma." Thus, an earlier period of high bilingualism (and presumably use of CS) gives way to a change in sentiments. CS may cease altogether, and the first language of the community, having taken in some structural features of the L2 through the L2's role in CS, fossilizes with those features now part of the language.

The ML turnover hypothesis for Ilwana is a better explanation than "heavy cultural contact" because it is at the same time more specific as to a mechanism and more general because it is related to explanations of outcomes in other contact cases.

7.2 *Ma'a/Mbugu as a mixed language*

The case of Ma'a/Mbugu is often mentioned when the structural results of heavy cultural contact are considered (e.g. Thomason and Kaufman 1988). This language is spoken in northeastern Tanzania and has always been referred to as a language with a Bantu grammar and a lexicon coming largely from Cushitic. Recent fieldwork (1990–1994) by Maarten Mous (1994 and p.c.) provides new information about this often cited example of a mixed language.[12]

Mous' data show that what exists in the community in question are two overlapping varieties, not one, which he refers to as registers. One of the varieties corresponds to what has been called Ma'a; this is the variety with Cushitic lexical items. Mous calls this Inner Mbugu, after local usage. The other variety is more of a typical Bantu language, with very close resemblances to the Bantu languages spoken in the area. This variety Mous refers to as Normal Mbugu; the speakers call it their "usual" language. Mous asserts (forthcoming: 1) that "people who speak Inner Mbugu also speak Normal Mbugu to varying degrees."

Mous's data clearly indicate that the grammar of the two varieties is identical. That is, except for free-form pronouns, possessives, and demonstratives, all system morphemes in the two varieties are the same. If one accepts that free-form pronouns, possessives, and demonstratives are content morphemes, their retention from Cushitic would be no surprise, although Mous notes (1994:191) that "the origin of the actual forms is difficult to establish." However, even these particular closed-class items in Inner Mbugu make the same three-way distinction which is found in Normal Mbugu and which follows the general Bantu pattern and is different from the Cushitic pattern.

An example sentence in (9) shows the lexical differences between the two varieties, but the system morphemes and morpheme orders are identical. Swahili is given for comparative purposes, as a representative Bantu language. Note, however, that Swahili is unusual among Bantu languages in the area in signaling LOCATIVE with a suffix, not a prefix.

---

12 Another case of mixed language (discussed in this volume by Nikolai Vakhtin), Copper Island Aleut, can also be explained in terms of an ML turnover, a turnover from an Aleutian variety to Russian as the ML. This variety, which is almost extinct, was spoken on an island off the Soviet coast in the Bering Sea. It shows Aleut content morphemes and Russian system morphemes.

(9)   a. Swahili
           a-ta-fich-a   vi-tu   vi-chaka-ni
           3s-**fut**-hide-**fv** **cl** 8.**pl**-thing **cl** 8.**pl**-bush-**loc**
       b. Inner Mbugu
           e-ne-matu vi-gi   he-ki-maye
           3s-**fut**-hide **cl** 8.**pl**-thing **cl** 16(**loc**)-**cl** 7-bush
       c. Normal Mbugu
           e-ne-fis-a   vi-nthu   he-ma-zungo
           3s-**fut**-hide-**fv** **cl** 8.**pl**-thing **cl** 16(**loc**)-**cl** 6.**pl**-bush
           "S/he will hide things in the bushes."   (MOUS FORTHCOMING: I)

The lexicons of the two Mbugu varieties overlap, but Inner Mbugu includes distinctive lexemes, many of which can be attributed to Cushitic origins. In a forthcoming article, Mous states categorically that "the difference between Inner Mbugu and Normal Mbugu is lexical." In his 1994 article, he makes some more specific comments, such as this: "If a word is from Pare, it belongs to the Normal Mbugu register. If a word can be shown to be Cushitic (Southern or Eastern Cushitic) or Masai [Eastern Nilotic], it is Inner Mbugu, excluding the Cushitic loanwords in Pare. It should be noted that for many Inner Mbugu forms, the origin is not clear" (1994:197).

Today there is a good deal of CS between the two registers, Mous states. He says, "If one maximizes the Ma'a register, one speaks *Ma'a* [Inner Mbugu]. If one minimizes the Ma'a register, one speaks *Mbugu* [Normal Mbugu]" (p.c.).

In line with the argument of this paper, I suggest that Ma'a or Inner Mbugu is the result of a late arrested ML turnover from Cushitic to the Bantu variety of the neighboring groups, an argument also made in Myers-Scotton (1992, 1993a). Stated in the terms of the main hypothesis argued here, the present structural make-up of Inner Mbugu came about because at an earlier stage the community met two conditions: there was widespread CS between the original Cushitic L1 and a local Bantu language; and sociopolitical conditions accorded more prestige to the Bantu variety. A plausible conclusion is that Ma'a/Mbugu of today represents how a substituted variety has evolved: the CS variety, with the Bantu variety as the ML supplying the morphosyntax, but with Cushitic elements as well, has replaced the original Cushitic L1 of the community.

At this point we can hypothesize the stages in Mbugu development. An outline of five stages of linguistic development shows how the Ma'a/Mbugu (hereafter Mbugu) situation conforms to the main ML turnover hypothesis.

Stage 1 The premise is that the original speakers of "proto-Mbugu" were of Cushitic origin. Mous (1994:199) objects to this historical reconstruction on the grounds that "the first stage cannot be shown." Yet, strong implicational evidence indicates that the population originally spoke a Cushitic language. The extensive Cushitic component in the Inner Mbugu lexicon of today obviously supports such a claim. The argument that the Mbugu simply borrowed some lexical items from Cushitic, as did other (Bantu) groups in the area, is not convincing because of the quantitative evidence: other languages have a few Custhic items; Mbugu has many. Additional support comes from the fact that there are still a few pockets of Cushitic speakers in northern Tanzania, indicating Cushitic expansion southwards could have reached the Mbugu area. In summary, these facts argue for a Cushitic origin for the Mbugu.

Stage 2 The Mbugu find themselves surrounded by Bantu speakers. It is known that some Mbugu speakers assimilate to neighboring Bantu groups, such as the Pare, shifting to the Pare language. The remaining Cushitic speakers become bilingual in one of the neighboring Bantu languages, presumably Pare, for very instrumental reasons: to communicate with their Bantu neighbors, including the assimilated Mbugu with whom it is known they have periodic ethnic ceremonies. Among themselves, the Mbugu gradually engage in CS between their original language and the Bantu variety which they have learned.

Eventually, CS becomes their unmarked mode of daily communication. There is ample evidence in many contemporary African societies, as well as in other communities throughout the world, that CS can become a major medium of daily life, For example, Swigart (1992) argues that what she calls Urban Wolof, but what is Wolof/French CS, is the unmarked code among Senegalese in Dakar today. Similar arguments are made for the Bantu townships in South Africa (Calteaux 1994) and elsewhere (Myers-Scotton 1993b).

Mous (1994: 199) finds the postulated presence of CS implausible. His reasoning is that if CS existed in the early Mbugu community, "it is hard to understand why other cases of code-switching did not lead to a mixed language."[13] As should now be clear, the hypothesis advanced here would *not*

---

13 In addition, Mous (1994:199) argues that "CS involves a positive attitude toward the languages involved ... whereas for Ma'a a *negative* attitude towards Bantu languages/peoples seems to have

predict that a mixed language will result from CS *alone*. Rather, to repeat, the prediction is that extensive CS or convergence within the CP must be coupled with a dramatic shift in the socio-political balance in order for the stage to be set for an ML turnover. This change in the socio-political balance in favor of the "invading" language is not present in those many other cases which show CS, but no turnover resulting in a mixed language. Further, a mixed language such as Ma'a/Mbugu is only one of three possible outcomes when a turnover begins. A mixed language only results *when a shift does not go to completion*. There is a social motivation for its not going to completion – ethnic identity. I address this matter below under stage 4.

Stage 3 In this CS, there is a turnover in the ML, from Mbugu to the Bantu language. Given the realities of the socio-political situation, the Mbugu cannot avoid such Bantuization. This means their Cushitic L1 loses its primacy in CS as the source of the grammatical frame, with the Bantu L2 taking its place.

Stage 4 This CS variety becomes the L1 of the community; as such, it retains some Cushitic content morphemes and a few sounds. The Mbugu avoid shift to a neighboring Bantu language in this way. This variety is what Mous calls Inner Mbugu. At the same time, because of environmental pressures, the Mbugu also speak what Mous calls Normal Mbugu, a Bantu variety which is intelligible to their Bantu-speaking neighbors.

been a force in its origin." True, elsewhere I have argued that "unmarked" CS involves a positive evaluation of the identities associated with both codes (Myers-Scotton 1993b:177ff.). There is no evidence that there were open hostilities between the Mbugu and their Bantu neighbors and there is evidence (from Mous himself) that today there is CS between Inner and Normal Mbugu. Given these facts, any argument against the likely presence of CS in the formation of Inner Mbugu loses force.

Evidence elsewhere shows that for CS to occur, speakers need not embrace the languages involved at all levels. There are many contemporary examples of unmarked CS in communities where both varieties are not positively valued for the same reasons. There is no evidence that the attraction of ingroup ethnic identity prevents CS which juxtaposes the ethnic language with a community language which does not index that

identity, but which is in use because it has a more significant population or power base. For example, in many African settings, the alien official language (e.g. French or English) is valued mainly for status-building functions (instrumental reasons), not for solidarity-building functions. Yet, this language is a typical code found in unmarked CS. Such is the case in South Africa or Zimbabwe with English today.

At the same time, I agree with Mous that a desire to avoid total identification with the Bantu was probably the major force in the origin of Inner Mbugu. That is, the desire to retain ethnic distinctiveness is the reason the language shift did not go to completion; in fact, all cases of mixed languages are not cases of language shift for this same reason, I argue. In this sense, mixed languages are one of the strongest cases which show how social factors can affect the outlines of structural outcomes.

Step 5 Those persons who were left behind when the present speakers of Mbugu moved to the Usambara mountains completely forget Mbugu and speak only a local Bantu variety.[14]

Mous's own argument for the origin of Inner Mbugu is that community members, wishing to retain ethnic distinctiveness, purposefully constructed a variety. They did this by adding Cushitic words to what they were already speaking. The idea of purposeful *addition* has a number of problems. First, it is counterintuitive; retention, reanalysis, and deletion are the unmarked processes in language change, but not addition. Second, where would speakers "find" the words in order to add them? Retention of some Cushitic content morphemes during the ML turnover is simply more likely since it requires no "discovery procedure." Finally, this scenario requires a good deal of conscious activity on the part of speakers.

8   Examples of outcomes: individuals

In the two cases discussed above, Ilwana and Mbugu, an ML turnover can only be hypothesized; that a turnover actually happened cannot be demonstrated because the communities were not studied when the hypothesized turnovers supposedly took place. However, the claim that ML turnovers can happen in a community receives strong support from evidence in the literature today on individual cases of evolving linguistic repertoires which can best be explained as instances of an ML turnover in progress. Consider three cases of children in the process of losing either a first or second language and/or in developing a composite ML.

14 I thank Maarten Mous for suggesting that I add step 5 to the scenario. Mous (p.c.) correctly stresses the need for fieldwork in which discourses are collected, preferably as naturally occurring data. For example, he pointed out that he found on a recent field trip to Tanzania that Swahili words are replacing many indigenous words in the Bantu languages of Tanzania; Swahili, of course, is the official language in Tanzania, giving it more prestige than local languages. However, this ongoing replacement process has not been noted, perhaps because for many researchers, their only source of data is the questionnaire form/word list. When directly questioned, consultants may report archaic words which, in fact, they do not use.

Mous's comment is relevant here because I would add that the true structural situation in a language also can only be studied in samples of naturally occurring conversations. More to the point, hypotheses about language attrition and language death involving CS and the ML turnover require such discourse-level data for testing.

In the first case, Kuhberg (1992) reports on two Turkish girls (seven and nine years old) who previously had acquired German as an L2 while living in Germany. He studied them longitudinally after their families moved back to Turkey. Except for their test conversations with the researcher, both girls received exposure only to Turkish in Turkey. Over the time of the study, their German showed attrition. What is interesting for this paper is that their language-use patterns clearly showed a turnover in the ML from German to Turkish. In the parlance of the model developed here, the girls moved from speaking monolingual German, to CS with German as the ML, and then to a turnover of ML to Turkish in their CS, at the same time as they were losing fluency in German.

The second case, a child's loss of a first language, shows a similar ML turnover pattern when the child studied moved from a Hebrew-speaking environment in Israel to an English-speaking milieu in the United States (Kaufman and Aronoff 1991). Entering the United States at age 2;6, the child is a fluent speaker of Hebrew, on par with her peers. By age 3;1, the child is "a balanced bilingual – at ease with the use of both L1 and L2" (p. 180). She now shows intersentential CS and some intra-sentential CS, the latter consisting of L2 words inserted into an L1 frame. She then begins producing defective Hebrew verb forms, modeled on a canonical triliteral root (third-person masculine singular past). This bilingual period is short, with the child's utterances becoming L2 (English) dominant and with the child expressing an unwillingness to speak the L1. Example (10) illustrates her use of deviant L1 verbs in an L2 morphosyntactic frame at age 3;6:

(10)   *I'm **me-nagev**-ing myself. I want to **i-nagev**   myself.*
        I'm **pres-dry**-ing myself. I want to **imperf-dry** myself.
        "I'm drying myself. I want to dry myself."

                                        (KAUFMAN AND ARONOFF 1991:182)

Example (11) at 4;4 months shows that her ML has turned over to English, with only a single holistic form for all of her Hebrew verbs which then receive English inflections.

(11)   *When it **i-calcel**-z I will turn it off*
                verb formative-ring-3sg.pres
        "When it rings, I will turn it off."   (KAUFMAN AND ARONOFF 1991:187)

Kaufman and Aronhoff stress the child's creativity in their concluding remarks, stating, "the resulting system, which, while perfectly intelligible to

all those in the child's family environment, is entirely her own, is a powerful reminder of the fact that languages are individual creations constrained
only by the social needs to communicate" (1991:187). The argument of this
paper, however, would offer a different set of concluding remarks. That is,
the resulting system is *not* the child's own. While the child may be creative
in her formation of Hebrew verbs, she is otherwise acting out universally
present strategies in very predictable ways: she moves from Hebrew as the
language setting her morphosyntactic frame to English as the ML and the
framer of her utterances. In so doing, she offers dramatic evidence for
the ML turnover hypothesis.

A third case, that of a young Hungarian girl who lives in the
United States with her Hungarian parents and brother, but who goes to an
English-speaking daycare facility, offers extensive data relevant to the ML
turnover hypothesis (Bolonyai 1996). When recordings were first made of
the subject at age 3;7, her main medium is monolingual Hungarian. When
she does engage in limited Hungarian/English CS (only 4.8 percent or 7 of
a total of 143 CPs studied showed CS), Hungarian is typically her ML and
English is the EL. That is, Hungarian is projecting her grammatical frame
and English provides only content morphemes, as example (12) shows:

(12)   *Mi-t*   **cook**-*sz*
        what.sg-acc **cook**-2sg.pres
        "What are you cooking?"   (BOLONYAI 1996:4)

By age 4;2, English is the ML in 38 percent (19 out of 50) of CPs showing CS
and there is a composite ML in 6.8 percent of these CPs. Example (13) illustrates the composite ML taking the form of convergence.

(13)   *Mom, en meg-**find**-t-am   a   ket **quarters**-t*
        Mom, 1sg. perf-**find**-past-1sg det two **quarters**-acc
        "Mom, I found two quarters"   (BOLONYAI 1996:12)

Like other pro-drop languages, Hungarian requires the use of an overt
subject/object pronoun only for emphasis and other such functions. Yet, in
(13) the subject is using an overt subject; thus, this example shows convergence to English. Also, the content morpheme *quarters* includes the plural
affix; yet, Hungarian well-formedness conditions require a noun to be
singular when preceded by a numeral. One can say that the English plural
affix of *quarters* has been reanalyzed as part of the noun stem; this reanalyzed stem received the Hungarian case marker.

9   Conclusion

Based on the model developed here of the role of CS and ML turnover in language attrition, some predictions specifically relevant to language attrition are the following.[15]

9.1   *Unchanged ML:EL socio-political balance*

Keeping in mind that what qualify as system morphemes can vary cross-linguistically, one can expect that only content morphemes will be borrowed when a contact situation includes bilingualism and even extensive CS, but the ML:EL 'sociopolitical balance' remains unchanged.

9.2   *Types of CS constituents: mixed languages*

If CS is present, EL islands may be borrowed from the EL into the ML. This apparently is what happened with Michif, a Cree-based language

---

15 Many of the authors in a volume on mixed languages, edited by Bakker and Mous (1994), argue or at least imply that when languages show structural borrowing, the structural mix must be the result of *conscious* effort on the part of the speakers. Some of them, for example, equate mixed languages with the making up of a secret language. A moment's reflection, however, indicates this need not be so. Indirect counterevidence is that a product synonymous with structural borrowing is produced with no conscious awareness on the part of speakers. I refer to producing mixed constituents in CS – content morphemes from one language and system morphemes from the other. If speakers were consciously organizing their utterances in CS, it would be more than fortuitous for all CS speakers in the world to manipulate them in the same way (i.e. with system morphemes always coming from the ML). Yet, the evidence from naturally occurring CS data shows uniformity across diverse language pairs, with very few counterexamples. Surely this uniformity is evidence of universally present cognitively-based strategies, not the result of conscious manipulation.

Of course the *reason* for engaging in CS or for an ML turnover or for attrition is indeed available for conscious reflection. Also, lexical choices (i.e.

content morphemes) are open to careful choice. For these reasons, speakers are able to make the choice to attempt to retain content morphemes from an L1 because they convey ethnic associations or for whatever reason. But once the production process goes beyond choices at this level, that is, once production moves to associating these lexical choices with predicate–argument structures and morphological realization patterns, the actual *process* of language production is not open to conscious decision-making.

Bakker and Muysken (1995:42) assert that mixed languages arise through an intertwining process: "an intertwined language has lexical morphemes from one language and grammatical morphemes from another." This resembles the argument presented in Myers-Scotton (1992, 1993a) and made more specific here. Their conception differs, however, because they refer to intertwining as "a type of language genesis" (1995:42) but without any specific structural motivations. As such, "language genesis" seems to exclude relations to principled language processes structuring language change. For this and other reasons, "intertwining" may be descriptively adequate but lacks explanatory power.

which shows French NPs today, as in (14). That is, what is called Michif today is a case of fossilized CS between Cree, as the ML, and French, the EL. NPs from French (what would be called EL islands in CS) fossilized in what became Michif.

(14)   Michif text
  un **vieux** *opahike-t* *e-nohcihcike-t,* ekwa **un matin**
  art.m old man trap-he.conj comp-trap-he.conj and art.m morning
  e-waniska-t   *akhosi-w* **but** *keyapit ana* *wi-nitawi-wapaht-am*
  comp-wake up-he be-sick-he but still this one want-go-see.it-he.it
  ses   *pieges*
  3s.poss.pl traps
  An English version of the same story to this point: "That old trapper, way up
  north, he was old, the old bugger. He was trapping up there in a cabin. He
  took sick, you see. And when he got up on the morning . . . he had a little bit
  to eat and then he had to go and see, visit his traps." (BAKKER 1994:29–30)

9.3   *Complete ML turnover*

CS is a necessary condition and a turnover in the ML is a necessary mechanism for system morphemes from the "other" language to appear in bilingual production. Such turnovers have not been documented often, but they do occur, although few seem to be so complete as in the case of Inner Mbugu. Evidence of a turnover, independent of the structural outlines of production, will be changing socio-political dynamics in the community. In many instances, turnovers show modularity; for example, word order may change independently of turnover of system morphemes (cf. Nahuatl/Mexicano in Hill and Hill 1986).

9.4   *Community CS and L1 attrition*

When attrition of an L1 occurs, CS and a turnover of the ML are necessarily involved. While attrition affects all L1 morphemes when the L1 falls into disuse, it affects L1 system morphemes disproportionately. This happens because CS, potentially both a cause and a symptom of L1 attrition, becomes prevalent. For CS to have this effect, of course, it would be CS between the L1 and a more sociolinguistically dominant L2. As the L2 becomes the ML of this CS, the system morphemes of the new ML are employed. While such CS means that L1 content morphemes are still used frequently (since content morphemes from the EL can appear in mixed constituents framed by the ML), L1 system morphemes become forgotten.

9.5   *Individual L1 attrition*

In the initial stages of attrition, ML turnover will show itself first in mixed constituents; constituents with morphemes from both the initial L1 and the other language will be framed by the other language as the new ML, instead of by the L1. That is, they will begin to show the grammatical frame of the new ML (i.e. ML morpheme order and/or some system morphemes). At the same time, speakers will still produce well-formed EL islands in their L1.

In later stages of attrition, L1 material will consist only of content morphemes in mixed constituents (either as bare forms or morphosyntactically integrated into the ML). Finally, while speakers will still produce EL islands, they will consist of bare forms (i.e. no system morphemes) except for formulaic expressions retained from the EL.

9.6   *ML turnover in progress: convergence*

Few cases of attrition *in progress* will show a complete turnover of the ML; rather they will show a turnover in progress. This means that the ML of mixed constituents will include ML system morphemes but a composite of lexicalization patterns from the L1 and the new ML. In some cases, depending on the sociolinguistic profiles of the community (i.e. how crucial the L1 is to group identity), convergence in the L1, not CS itself, will be evidence of the turnover in the ML in progress. This is the case with some varieties of Pennsylvania Dutch (Fuller 1996). Because of their association with the religious life of the community, Pennsylvania Dutch varieties are maintained and classic CS is resisted. In such cases, convergence is the form of bilingual production during the ML turnover, not CS as such.

Convergence is defined here as the use of morphemes from one language only. However, what makes it bilingual is that it involves the introduction of lexicalization patterns (i.e. lexical–conceptual structures, predicate–argument structures, and morphological-realization patterns) from an external source, the ML.

These hypotheses are motivated by the principles encapsulated in the model presented here: a Matrix Language Recognition Principle and a System Morpheme Principle or Morpheme-sorting Principle are at work in structuring any bilingual speech (morphemes or abstract lexical structure from two or more languages). That is, there is always a Matrix Language in such bilingual speech, and it is the source of the morphosyntactic frame of the relevant CPs. Also, while content morphemes in such language may come from either language, syntactically relevant system morphemes – those structuring mixed constituents – must come from the ML only. In these ways, attrition can be related to other forms of bilingual language production.

Given the sociolinguistic and psycholinguistic characteristics of the speech community in question, the possibility of language attrition can be predicted. When there is a shake-up in the values attached to varieties so that the "encroaching" variety is accorded high prestige, attrition in the L1 is likely. What makes its structure predictable, however, depends on the presence of two structural conditions, in combination with the change in valuation of structure-external characteristics of the community. First, there must be extensive CS, including switching within CPs, or there must be convergence. Second, the structural "borrowing" characterizing language attrition only occurs when constituents showing this CS or convergence are structured by a composite ML, indicating an ML turnover is in progress.

13 Copper Island Aleut: a case of language "resurrection"

NIKOLAI VAKHTIN

Institute of Linguistics, Academy of Sciences, St. Petersburg

1 Introduction: language "life" versus "death"

When "endangered languages" are mentioned, normally people have in mind the danger of language death, the danger of a language disappearing from the linguistic map of the world. However, in my opinion the situation here is more complicated than one of just "the language is alive versus the language is dead." Language is a highly viable and an extremely flexible system; it is often not at all easy to eradicate a language.

I would like to present here an example of the outstanding viability of a native language. This particular case exemplifies a Russian–Native contact of extreme intensity and duration (of over 150 years). Current linguistic research in language endangerment suggests that the native language in question should have become extinct long ago, but in reality the situation is very different. This does not mean I am overly optimistic about the fate of endangered native languages; I simply wish to stress that there are other possibilities besides linguistic "life" and "death," especially at times of sharp turns of history, such as the one Russia is living through now. To an external observer, a caterpillar in a cocoon does not show any sign of life. It looks dead, but it is not dead: it has ceased to be a caterpillar, but in due time it will become a butterfly, and the life of the organism will continue, though the form of life will become different. Some languages find such a new form of life in creolization.

2 Copper Island Aleut

The language I am discussing here is the language of the Copper Island Aleuts, which Evgenyi Golovko and I have somewhat ironically dubbed CIA (Golovko and Vakhtin 1990). Copper (or in Russian *Mednyj*) Island is one of the Commander Islands, a small group of islands about 90 km from the eastern coast of Kamchatka and about 150 km from Attu, the

317

westmost island of the Aleutians. In 1982 and 1985 I conducted fieldwork there together with Golovko. In 1988 Golovko returned to work alone collecting field data on CIA. The data are partly published, in Russian and in English, both as joint papers as well as articles written individually by one of us (see Vakhtin 1985; Asinovskij, Golovko and Vakhtin 1983; Golovko, Vakhtin and Asinovsky 1987; Golovko and Vakhtin 1990; Golovko 1988, 1989, 1994).[1]

The first Aleuts were brought to the islands by the Russian American Company in 1812, at first as just one working team, then subsequently more were brought in. By 1815, there were 15 inhabitants on Copper Island, but the settlements were temporary. The first permanent settlement, Preobrazhensky village, was founded on the island in 1828. After the 1840s the Company pensioners began to settle down on the island; the last large influx of newcomers came in 1872 (30 Aleuts from the island of Attu) and in 1888 (26 Aleuts and Eskimos from Kadyak and Kuril Islands). The population of Copper Island grew as follows: 1860–90 people, 1870–153 people, 1880–192 (200) people, 1890–238 (281) people; 1900–253 people; 1910–232 people, 1921–171 people.[2] In the late 1960s the Preobrazhensky village was abandoned, and its population relocated to Bering Island.

There were several ethnic groups in the village: Aleuts who spoke Aleut and Russian; Creoles who spoke Russian and Aleut; Russians who spoke Russian (and probably some Aleut), and others (e.g. Eskimos, Kamchadals) who, in all probability, spoke languages other than Russian or Aleut. The linguistic structures of the populations on Copper Island and on Bering Island were more or less similar. However, on Bering Island the present language situation is very much the same as in other parts of the northeastern part of Russia: the majority of the population has switched to Russian and has almost ceased to use Aleut. The dialect spoken on the Bering Island is more or less identical to Atkan Aleut. Atkan Aleut is the language of Atka, an island in the eastern part of the Aleutians, which is

1 I wish to stress that I long ago lost track of what data and/or ideas are mine and which are Golovko's. Similarly, in the case of the ethnohistorical research on CIA, I can no longer determine which data and interpretations belong to Golovko and myself and which to Igor Krupnik and Michael Chlenov who did fieldwork on the island in 1983:

the four of us shared the data and discussed the problem to too great an extent for me now to be able to distinguish between individual and collaborative contributions.

2 Statistics from Lyapunova 1987: 179–80, 196; alternative figures from other sources are given in parentheses.

still spoken by at least part of the population. But on Copper Island a very unusual mixed language has emerged.

In the following examples, Indo-European elements, i.e. those of Russian origin or, in (1a), of English origin, are in bold face:

(1)   a. Young Atkan Aleut
        fish=*i*=*za*=*xx*
        "he usually fishes"   (BERGSLAND 1979)
    b. Copper Island Aleut
        chali=*y*=**it**
        "he usually fishes"

In the Aleut language of the younger Aleuts on Atka a well-known process of borrowing English stems and adding Aleut derivation and inflection is evident. On the other hand, Copper Island Creole *mirrors* the process: the stem is Aleut, while the derivation and inflection are Russian. This is a paramount characteristic of CIA, cf. examples (2)–(6):

(2)   a. CIA
        axsa=*y*=**it** > *axsa*=*chaa*=*y*=**u**
        DIE-/-3sg > DIE-caus-/-1sg
        "he dies" > "I kill"

In both words, stems are Aleut, and in the second word an Aleut causative suffix is present. The person/number inflection is Russian, cf. Russian *vid-it* "he sees", *vizh-u* "I see", etc.

(2)   b. CIA
        sagyin > *sagyi*=*ggii*=*y*=**ish'**
        GUN > GUN-poss-/-2sg
        "you have a gun"

The derived verbal form consists of an Aleut nominal stem and an Aleut verbalizer =*ggii*= "possess N," where N is expressed by the stem. The person/number inflection (-*ish'*) is Russian, cf. *vid-ish'* "you see."

(2)   c. CIA
        ayuu=**l**=*i*   > **ni**=*ayuu*=**l**=*i*
        LONG-past-pl > neg-LONG-past-pl
        "(they) were long" > "(they) were not long"

In both words in (2c), the stem is the only Aleut element. All other morphemes are Russian: -*l*- past tense, -*i* plural, *ni*-negation, cf. Russian *ne*

xodi-l-i "they (we, you(pl)) did not go." (Since Aleut lacks the vowel [e], it
is consistently changed to [i] in all borrowed words.)

(3)   a. CIA
   vchira   *angalim guzuu qaka=yaa=l,* *tin*
   YESTERDAY DAY FULL DRY=caus=past, 3sg.obj
   ni=*qaka=chaa=l*
   neg=DRY=caus=past
  b. Russian
   Vchera ves' den' soxnul, ne vysoxnul
   "Yesterday it was drying all day, (but) never got dry"

One of six stems (*vchira*) is Russian, while the other five are Aleut. Causative *-yaa-* and *-chaa-* are Aleut, and tense (*-l-*) and negation (*-ni-*) morphemes are Russian.

(4)   a. CIA
   stiiklaxx *sixxa=xxtaa=y=it* **davnu**
   GLASS BREAK=result=/=3sg LONG.AGO
  b. Russian
   steklo razbito davno
   "The glass has been broken for a long time"

Out of three stems in (4), two are Russian (*stiiklaxx,* from Russian *steklo*
"glass", and *davnu*, from Russian *davno* "long ago"), and one stem is Aleut.
The resultative marker *-xxtaa-* is Aleut; personal inflection *-it-* is Russian.

(5)   a. CIA
   ya bud **ivo** *hayaa=t'* **ukushkaxx** *haksii=t'*
   I WILL HIM ASK=inf WINDOW OPEN=inf
  b. Russian
   ya poproshu ego otkryt' okno
   "I will ask him to open the window"

Three of the five stems here are Russian (*bud* from Russian *budu* "I will,"
ivo from Russian *yevo* (written *ego*) "him", and *ukushkaxx* from Russian
okoshko "small window"), while two verbal stems are Aleut. The infinitive
marker *-t'* is Russian, cf. *xodit'* "to walk."

(6)   a. CIA
   ni=*ugunuu=y* **chivnonibut'** *aqaasaa=t'*
   neg=FORGET=imp SOMETHING BRING=inf
  b. Russian
   ne zabud' chto-nibud' prinesti
   "Do not forget to bring something"

One stem is Russian (*chivonibut*,' Russian *chego-nibud'*, pronounced [tʃivonibut']); the two verbal stems are Aleut. The negation *ni-*, infinitive *-t'* and imperative *-y* are Russian (cf. *ne dava-t'* "not to give," *dava-y* "give!").

Clearly, what we have here is a mixed language, with both the lexicon and morphological markers coming from two sources, Russian and Aleut. Roughly speaking, the majority of verbal stems and many noun stems are of Aleut origin, as is the derivational morphology. Most auxiliaries and adverbs are of Russian origin, and all of the verbal morphology is Russian as well. This mixed language resembles Mitchif as described by Bakker (1994).

If one thinks of the possible origins of a language like this, it will become clear that the answer is not easy to find. This is obviously "language mixing," but the term only describes the *result* we witness, it does not *explain how* this language could have appeared.

Note that this could not have been simple "borrowing" of Russian grammatical features into Aleut, or vice versa: it is hardly possible to "borrow" inflectional or derivational morphology because a morpheme is not a linguistic unit which is consciously registered by speakers. In numerous pidgins, creoles and mixed languages throughout the world inflection is always "native," not borrowed. Consider, for example, the jargon of Russian black-market dealers of the 1970s: having borrowed English stems, they attach Russian endings to them, producing as a result phrases like the following:

(7)   *vayt=ovye*   *shuz=y*   *vayt=ovyx*   *shuz=ov*
       WHITE=pl.nom SHOES=pl.nom WHITE=pl.gen. SHOES=pl.gen
       "white shoes"

Consider also the jargon of Russian immigrants in the United States:

(8)   *dva*   *slajs=a*   *turk=i*
       TWO SLICE=gen TURKEY=gen
       "two slices of turkey"

Jargons normally emerge in a situation when a community or a group is surrounded by speakers of a more prestigious and/or socially dominant language. If CIA had developed from a jargon into a mixed language, then *Russian* is the only possible language which could have been the native language of those who developed the original jargon.

This is the principal assumption of the present analysis, namely, that *CIA could have originally emerged only in a Russian-speaking community in the North Pacific*. But *why* would this community need such a language? That is, why should a bilingual community develop another, third language? This situation is in distinction to numerous other areas of the world where a socially dominant group (such as the Portuguese, British, etc.) caused the native population (or quasi-native, as in the case of plantation workers) to develop a jargon, or a pidgin (English, French, or Portuguese). This pidgin, according to Robert Hall (1966), later develops into a creole language. Why on earth in Russian America of the nineteenth century did a pidgin *Aleut* appear which later evolved into CIA? Why was it not a pidgin *Russian*?

The answer that seems to me most probable is this: there must have existed in the area, on Copper Island or elsewhere, a Russian-speaking *and* socially dominated group which needed a means to communicate with an Aleut-speaking *and* socially dominating group.

In Golovko and Vakhtin (1990) we attempted to demonstrate that one of the candidates for such a group was the Creoles, an intermediate social group occupying a position somewhat in between the Russians and the Aleuts. I will not repeat all the arguments for and against this position here, as it is clear to me now that this hypothesis is not a strong one. What is indisputable, however, is that for such a language to emerge, a social situation is required which can be characterized as a situation of *sociolinguistic tension*: a strong necessity for different groups to communicate in a situation where their common language is lacking or insufficient.

In the following section of the paper I will suggest an alternative model of mixed-language formation which, if provable, may be significant for the future of endangered languages of the Far Northeast: *the possibility of mixed languages emerging as a result of sociolinguistic tension not between social or ethnic groups, but rather between generations*.

3   Linguistic change across generations

A common linguistic situation in the Far North today is when elderly people are unable to communicate with their grandchildren because the two age groups are separated by what I have called elsewhere the *turning-point generation* (Vakhtin 1993). This can be schematized as in

<table>
<tr><td>
Junior group, Russian-speaking,
with a very limited knowledge of
the native language
</td></tr>
</table>

<table>
<tr><td>
Middle group: "semi-lingual,"
with insufficient command of
either the native language or Russian
</td></tr>
</table>

<table>
<tr><td>
Senior group, native-speaking,
with a very limited knowledge of Russian
</td></tr>
</table>

Figure 13.1 Typical generational differences in the languages of the Far North

<table>
<tr><td>
Junior group, Russian-speaking,
with a very limited knowledge of
the native language
</td></tr>
</table>

<table>
<tr><td>
Senior group, native-speaking,
with a very limited knowledge of Russian
</td></tr>
</table>

Figure 13.2 Radical generational differences in the languages of the Far North

figure 13.1. In some cases, this linguistic gap between generations can open even within the lifetime of *one* generation (figure 13.2). However, if for some reason the sociolinguistic situation changes, and the native language gains prestige, the younger generation may attempt to talk to their (grand)parents in the native language which they do not know.

Independent data from another community of the Far North can be provided in order to support the viability of the suggested model. This is not conclusive evidence, of course; however, what is important in the following is that the process of a mixed-language formation between generations has been documented and witnessed by the present author *today*.

In 1985 I had the lucky opportunity to witness and record in the Yupik Eskimo village of Sirinek two utterances by a five-year-old girl who was trying to talk to her mother "in mother's language." When asking her mother if she should pour something out, she said:

(9)   ***Mam***,   ***ya èto***   <u>*quuv*</u>*=a=y=u*?   ***ya èto***   <u>*niv*</u>*=a=y=u*?
       MOTHER I THIS POUR-OUT=SV=1sg I THIS POUR-INTO=SV=1sg
       "Mom, shall I pour this out? Shall I pour this (into something)?"

Out of seven morphemes, five are Russian (in bold face): *mam* "Mom," *ya* "I," *èto* "this," SV (stem vowel), and *=y=u* (1sg). But the two verbal stems are Yupik (underlined): *quuv=* "pour out," and *niv=* "pour into something."

Interestingly, her mother reacted to the question quite normally, hardly even noticing that her daughter was speaking a jargon. She replied:

(10)   ***Ladno***,   <u>*quuv*</u>*=a=y*
       ALL RIGHT, POUR=SV=imp
       "All right, pour it out"

If we compare the resulting word *quuv=a=y=u* with CIA *axsa=chaa=y=u* "I kill" (example (2) above), we shall see that the two look very much alike, although, obviously, the word structure is more complicated in CIA: it has an Aleut causative morpheme preceding the inflection. It is quite probable, though, that CIA could have emerged from a jargon of the kind exemplified in (9) and (10), a jargon the 5-year-old Yupik girl invented to talk to her mother. What would be needed for this hypothesis to be substantiated is, of course, an attested historical shift in the social status of the Aleut language at some time in history. If this could be proven, then it would be logical to claim that at a certain point in the island's history the children may have found themselves in a situation where they felt the need for a different language as a means of ensuring their identity. Russian, their native language, could no longer serve this purpose. They did not speak Aleut – but their (grand)parents did. The children could have constructed a jargon using Russian as a grammatical and lexical basis and filling in Aleut stems they knew. The process received support from their (grand)parents and/or other (newcoming?) groups of people who spoke Aleut better than Russian. The number of Aleut stems in the new mixed language increased and after some time a bilingual situation had formed: the inventors of the mixed language, now used as a means of everyday communication, would have restored contact with (Atkan) Aleut proper. The extensive influence of Atkan Aleut brought in derivational morphology and was responsible for the considerable expansion of the Aleut lexicon. After several generations, CIA emerged.

At present there is no solid historical support for this, although there do exist some indications that such a shift of social status and prestige of the Aleut language might have taken place. However, theoretically this hypothesis is not new: it is in accord with the well-known thesis of Le Page and Tabouret-Keller who write: "Since individuals use language to communicate not only their meaning but also their social identity, they can shift their habits to signal a shift in their social allegiance; similarly, an entire speech community can shift language habits to signal a more focused or cohesive identity" (1985:2). A striking example of this kind of shifting is provided by Kapanga (this volume) with Shaba Swahili.

Other parts of Siberia, as well as other parts of the world show numerous cases of such status shift. For example, in the publications of the Select Committee on Race Relations and Immigration in Britain, it is reported that many young black British who show no sign of creole usage in their earlier years and use the language of the neighborhood suddenly start talking BEV around the age of 14–15. This use is interpreted by the authors as a deliberate social and psychological protest, an assertion of identity (quoted in Romaine 1993:188). Individuals "create the patterns for their linguistic behaviour so as to resemble those of the group or groups with which from time to time they wish to be identified" (Le Page and Tabouret-Keller 1985:18).

Boretzky and Igla (1994) report on the situation of Romani mixed dialects (RMD), i.e. dialects that evolved in total independence from one another under the strong influence of different languages spoken in Europe and the Near East. Their article contains the argument and conclusions which are very much along the same lines I am suggesting here. Many of their conclusions about RMD apply to CIA as well. Boretzky and Igla assert that "the evolution of these varieties cannot be the result of normal contact-induced language change" (1994:61); that the necessary condition for the emergence of a language like RMD is "the stage between bilingualism and language shift, when the speakers as an entire group are no longer fully bilingual, but have not accomplished language shift yet" (p. 62); and that "those who took the most active part in creating the new mixed idiom did not have Romani as their mother tongue any longer" (p. 63). They also suggest that there were three groups of speakers within the linguistic community in which RMD formed: (a) those who have a perfect command of Romani; (b) those who speak it imperfectly (semi-speakers); and (c) those who have but a passive knowledge (p. 63); compare figures 13.1 and 13.2. This should be the structure of any community capable of forming a language like RMD. Boretzky and Igla also suggest that a mixed language like RMD (and CIA, I shall add) could have appeared not as a result of language contact but "as a group-internal development" (p. 64), and, just as I do in the present paper, assume that the "changing attitudes of the Roma vis-à-vis their old vernacular play an important role" (p. 65) and may have been the driving force behind RMD formation. That is, a desire to preserve Romani may have been instigated as a counterreaction to their reduced fluency. And finally, Boretzky and Igla argue, just as Golovko does in (Golovko 1994), that speakers must have, to some extent, consciously elaborated and used the new code.

That it is at all possible to create a language intentionally can be supported not only by the RMD data, but also by what Ken Hale writes on Damin as opposed to Lardil (North Queensland). Damin is the language of initiated men whose mother tongue is Lardil; Damin serves as a means of communication between the initiated and those who are involved in their initiation; and, Damin is also "fun" (K. Hale 1992:37; see also Hale, this volume). Damin, according to Hale, was entirely a product of the people's intellectual work. It was *an invention*: its lexicon had no support or source in any of the languages of the area; its phonology included sounds found nowhere else in the world. At present it has almost disappeared (1992:36). Interestingly, the structure of Damin very much resembles that of CIA: as Hale puts it, Damin is a lexicon, not an entire language. The correct way to use Damin is to replace all Lardil lexical items by Damin items; the inflectional morphology and syntax remain intact (p. 37).

In this respect, Damin resembles CIA to some extent. In the case of CIA, the "invented" language must have originally had Russian grammar (native to its inventors), while its lexicon was borrowed by the younger generation from "the language of the elders" – Aleut, which by that time must have been unknown to them. After CIA emerged and began functioning as a means of communication and a support for the ethnic identity of the Copper Island community, it underwent further evolution. It is important to remember that CIA has been in close contact with Russian and, until one generation ago, was in permanent contact with Aleut. This accounts for the fact that it has obviously undergone "decreolization" in the sense of Bickerton (1980:109), as well as for the fact that CIA is today extremely viable: one can almost claim that the greater the Russian influence, the stronger the language stands. One of my informants, when asked to translate a Russian sentence into CIA, said: "It will be just the same." The sentence is identical, although one or two Aleut stems are thrown in, and the resulting sentence is seen by the speakers as "native." Note that CIA is considered by all its speakers to be a 100 per cent native Aleut language: all the informants are unanimous in flatly rejecting any resemblance of CIA to Russian, which, for an outsider, is striking.

4   Conclusion

To conclude, why is the history of CIA important for the issue of endangered languages? The reason is that the situation which a century ago caused the formation of CIA may become the future of some of the native languages of the Far Northeast, one of a number of possible "stable states," to use a term from the catastrophe theory. The prestige of native languages has grown considerably since the collapse of the Soviet Union, the Russian influence is decreasing, and, although the majority of their population are Russian-speaking, many local communities are now looking for support for their identity. It is possible that in a decade or two linguists will suddenly discover new jargons which will later develop into pidgins, which will become native languages for the coming generation and further evolve into creoles, or mixed languages.

This is one of the reasons why it is so difficult to make a prognosis about language death: language development is a non-linear process, with more possibilities than simply "living" or "dying."

Appendix

Nancy C. Dorian
dorian@henry.bowdoin.edu

Nora C. England
nora-england@uiowa.edu

Lenore A. Grenoble
lenore. grenoble@dartmouth.edu

Colette (Craig) Grinevald
cgrineva@docsrvr.mrash.fr

Ken Hale
klhale@mit.edu

Christopher Jocks
christopher.jocks@dartmouth.edu

André Kapanga
akapanga@rs6ooo.cmp.ilstu.edu

Nora Marks and Richard Dauenhauer
jfrld@acadl.alaska.edu

Marianne Mithun
mithun@humanitas.ucsb.edu

Carol Myers-Scotton
carolms@sc.edu

Nikolai Vakhtin
nikolay@vakhtin.spb.su

Lindsay J. Whaley
lindsay.whaley@dartmouth.edu

Anthony C. Woodbury
acw@mail.utexas.edu

References

Abbi, Anvita. 1995. Language contact and language restructuring: a case study of tribal languages in Central India. *International Journal of the Sociology of Language* 116.175–185.

Adelaar, William F. H. 1988. Search for the Culli language. *Continuity and identity: essays in honor of Benedikt Hartmann*, ed. by Marteen Jansen, Peter van der Loo, and Roswitha Manning, 111–131. Leiden: E. J. Brill.

1991. The endangered languages problem: South America. In R. H. Robins and E. M. Uhlenbeck (eds.), 45–91.

Aikhenvald, Alexandra Y. 1994. Classe nominal e género nas línguas Aruák. *Boletim do museu Goeldi* 10.137–259.

1995. Person marking and discourse in North-Arawak languages. *Studia Linguistica* 49.152–195.

1996. Areal diffusion in Northwest Amazonia: the case of Tariana. *Anthropological Linguistics* 38/1.73–116.

Albó, Xavier. 1995. *Bolivia plurilingüe: Guía para planificadores y educadores*. La Paz, Bolivia: UNICEF-CIPCA.

Alfred, Gerald. 1995. *Heeding the voices of our ancestors*. Toronto: Oxford University Press.

Amadio, Massimo and Louis Enrique Lopez. 1993. *Educación bilingüe intercultural en América Latina: guía bibliográfica*. 2nd edn. La Paz: UNICEF-CIPCA.

Appel, René and Pieter Muysken. 1987. *Language contact and bilingualism*. London: Edward Arnold.

Asinovskij, A. S., E. V. Golovko, and N. B. Vakhtin. 1983. Ètnolingvisticheskoe opisanie Komandorskix aleutov. *Voprosy jaykoznanija* 6.108–116.

Bakker, Peter. 1994. Michif, the Cree-French mixed language of the Métis buffalo hunters in Canada. In P. Bakker and M. Mous (eds.), 13–33.

Bakker, Peter and Pieter Muysken. 1995. Mixed languages and language intertwining. *Pidgins and creoles, an introduction*, ed. by Jaques Arends, Pieter Muysken, and Norval Smith, 41–52. Amsterdam: Benjamins.

Bakker, Peter and Maarten Mous, eds. 1994. *Mixed languages: 15 cases in language intertwining*. Amsterdam: IFOTT (University of Amsterdam).

Banks, Arthur S. and Robert B. Textor. 1965. *A cross polity survey*. Cambridge, MA: MIT Press.

Barber, Carroll G. 1973. Trilingualism in an Arizona Yaqui village. *Bilingualism in the Southwest*, ed. by Paul R. Turner, 295–318. Tucson, AZ: University of Arizona Press.

Bauman, James A. 1980. *A guide to issues in Indian language retention*. Washington, DC: Center for Applied Linguistics.

Bender, Gerald J. 1978. *Angola under the Portuguese: the myth and the reality*. Berkeley and Los Angeles: University of California Press.

Bentahila, Abedali and Eirlys E. Davies. 1992. Code-switching and language dominance. *Cognitive processing in bilinguals*, ed. by Richard J. Harris, 443–458. Amsterdam: Elsevier.

Benton, Richard A. 1991. Tomorrow's schools and the revitalization of Maori: Stimulus or tranquilizer? *Bilingual education: Focusschrift in honor of Joshua A. Fishman on the occasion of his 65th birthday*, ed. by Ofelia Garcia, 135–47. Amsterdam: John Benjamins.

Bergsland, Knut. 1979. The Comparison of Eskimo-Aleut and Urali. *Fenno-Ugrica Suecana* 2.7–13.

Bernard, H. Russell. 1992. Preserving language diversity. *Cultural Survival Quarterly* 16.15–18.

Bickerton, Derek. 1980. Decreolization and the creole continuum. *Theoretical orientations in creole studies*, ed. by Albert Valdman and Arnold Highfield, 107–128. New York: Academic Press.

Biggs, Bruce. 1968. The Maori language past and present. *The Maori people in the nineteen sixties*, ed. by Eric Schwimmer, 65–84. Auckland: Blackwood and Janet Paul.

Blake, Barry J. 1979. Pitta-Pitta. *Handbook of Australian languages*, vol. 1, ed. by R. M. W. Dixon and Barry Blake, 182–242. Canberra: The Australian National University Press.

Blom, Jan-Petter and John Gumperz. 1972. Social meaning in linguistic structures: Code-switching in Norway. *Directions in sociolinguistics: the ethnography of communication*, ed. by John Gumperz and Dell Hymes, 407–434. New York: Holt, Rinehart, and Winston.

Bolonyai, Agnes. 1996. Turning it over, L2 dominance in Hungarian/English acquisition. Unpublished MS.

Boretzky, Norbert and Birgit Igla. 1994. Romani mixed dialects. In P. Bakker and M. Mous (eds.), 35–68.

Bossevain, Jeremy and J. Clyde Mitchell, eds. 1973. *Network analysis: studies in human interaction*. The Hague: Mouton.

Bowers, John. 1968. Language problems and literacy. *Language problems of developing nations*, ed. by Joshua A. Fishman, 381–401. New York: John Wiley & Sons, Inc.

Bradley, David. 1989. The disappearance of Ugong in Thailand. In N. Dorian (ed.), 33–40.

Brenzinger, Matthias. 1993. Minority languages, a cultural legacy. *Diogenes* 161.1–18.

Brenzinger, Matthias, ed. 1992. *Language death: factual and theoretical explorations with special reference to East Africa*. Berlin and New York: Mouton de Gruyter.

Brenzinger, Matthias, Bernd Heine, and Gabriele Sommer. 1991. *Language death in Africa*. In R. H. Robins and E. M. Uhlenbeck (eds.), 19–44.

Briggs, Lucy Therina. 1985. Dialectical variation in Aymara. In H. E. M. Klein and
L. R. Stark (eds.), 595–616.

1993. *El Idioma Aymara: Variantes Regionales y Sociales*. La Paz: Ediciones
ILCA.

Broadwell, George Aaron. 1995. 1990 census figures for speakers of American Indian
languages. *International Journal of American Linguistics* 61.145–149.

Brown, Robert McKenna. 1991. Language maintenance and shift in four Kaqchikel
Maya towns. Ph.D. dissertation, Tulane University.

Bruton, John. 1995. Address to the National Press Club, Washington, DC, March 17,
1995. (Federal News Service, Inc., broadcast transcription.)

Bulatova, Nadezhda Ja. 1994. Evenkijskij jazyk. *Kransnaja kniga jazykov narodov
Rossii. Enciklopedicheskij slovar'-spravochnik*, 68–70. Moscow: Academia.

Calteaux, Karen. 1994. A sociolinguistic analysis of a multilingual community. D.Litt.
and D. Phil. thesis, Rand Afrikaans University, Johannesburg.

Cameron, Deborah, Elizabeth Frazer, Penelope Harvey, Ben Rampton, and Kay
Richardson. 1993. Ethics, advocacy and empowerment: issues of method in
researching language. *Language and Communication* 13.81–94.

Campbell, Lyle. 1988. Review of *Language in the Americas* by J. H. Greenberg.
Language 64.591–615.

Campbell, Lyle and Martha C. Muntzel. 1989. The structural consequences of
language death. In N. Dorian (ed.), 181–196.

Carbaugh, Donal. 1989. *Talking American: cultural discourses on DONAHUE*.
Norwood, NJ: Ablex Publishing Corporation.

CEPAR. 1985–1986. *Boletines Sociodemográficos*. Quito: CEPAR.

Cerrón-Palomino, Rodolfo. 1987. *Lingüística Quechua*. Cuzco: GTZ and Centro de
estudios rurales andinos "Bartolomé de las Casas".

1989. Language policy in Peru: a historical overview. *International Journal of the
Sociology of Language* 77.11–33.

Chafe, Wallace. 1962. Estimates regarding the present speakers of North American
Indian languages. *International Journal of American Linguistics* 28.162–171.

1994. *Discourse, consciousness, and time: the flow and displacement of
conscious experience in speaking and writing*. Chicago: University of
Chicago Press.

Cheshire, Jenny. 1982. Linguistic variation and social function. In S. Romaine (ed.),
153–166.

Chiodi, Francesco, ed. 1990. *La educación indígena en América Latina: México,
Guatemala, Ecuador, Perú, Bolivia*. Quito, Ecuador: *EBI, Abya-Yala*.

Chomsky, Noam. 1991. Some notes on economy of derivation and representation.
Principles and parameters in comparative grammar, ed. by Robert Freidin,
417–454. Cambridge, MA: MIT Press.

Cojtí Cuxil, Demetrio. 1991. *Configuración del Pensamiento Político del Pueblo
Maya*. Guatemala: Asociación de Escritores Mayances de Guatemala.

1994. *Políticas para la Reivindicación de los Mayas de Hoy*. Guatemala: Cholsamaj.

Cole, Peter, Gabriella Hermon, and Mario Daniel Martin, eds. 1994. *Language in the Andes*. Newark, NJ: Latin American Studies, University of Deleware.

Collier, Ruth Berins. 1982. *Regimes in tropical Africa*. Berkeley and Los Angeles: University of California Press.

Comrie, Bernard. 1981. *Languages of the USSR*. Cambridge: Cambridge University Press.

CONFEMEN (Conférence des Ministres de l'Education des Etats d'Expression Française). 1986. *Promotion et intégration des langues nationales dans les systèmes éducatifs*. Paris. Champion.

Cornelius, Carol. 1994. Languages as culture: preservation and survival. *Native American expressive culture*, special issue, *Akwe:kon Journal* 11.146–149.

Coulmas, Florian. 1992. *Language and economy*. Oxford: Blackwell.

Coupland, Nikolas. 1984. Accommodation at work. *International Journal of the Sociology of Language* 4–6.49–70.

Craig, Colette. 1992a. A constitutional response to language endangerment: the case of Nicaragua. *Language* 68.11–16.

1992b. Miss Nora, rescuer of the Rama language: a story of power and empowerment. *Locating power. Proceedings of the Second Berkeley Women and Language Conference*, vol. 1, ed. by Kira Hall, Mary Bucholtz, and Birch Moonwoman, 80–89. Berkeley: BLS.

1992c. Language shift and language death: The case of Rama in Nicaragua. *International Journal of the Sociology of Language* 93.11–26.

1993. Fieldwork on endangered languages: a forward look at ethical issues. *Proceedings of the XVth International Congress of Linguists*, vol. 1, ed. by Andre Cochetiere, Jean-Claude Boulanger, and Conrad Ouellon, 33–42. Quebec: Presses de l'Université de Laval.

1995. The Rama language revitalization project: a ten year perspective. Paper presented at the Linguistics Society of America, New Orleans.

1997. Language contact and language degeneration. *Handbook of sociolinguistics*, ed. by Florian Coulmas, 257–270. Oxford: Blackwell.

Craig, Colette and Ken Hale. 1995. Language revitalization projects: what works best is relative. Paper presented at the MIT Workshop on Endangered Languages.

Crawhall, Nigel and Carol Myers-Scotton. Unpublished Shona – English data.

Croese, Robert A. 1985. Mapuche dialect survey. In H. E. M. Klein and L. R. Stark (eds.), 784–801.

Crosby, Alfred W. 1986. *Ecological imperialism: the biological expansion of Europe 900–1900*. Cambridge: Cambridge University Press.

Dauenhauer, Nora Marks. 1995. Tlingit at.óow: tradition and concepts. *The spirit within: Northwest Coast Native art from the John H. Hauberg collection*, ed. by Helen Abbott, Stephen Brown, Lorna Price, and Paula Thurman, 21–29. Seattle: Seattle Art Museum.

Dauenhauer, Nora Marks and Richard Dauenhauer. 1984. *Tlingit spelling book*. 3rd, revised edn. (1st edn., 1974; 2nd edn., 1976.) Juneau, AK: Sealaska Heritage Foundation.

1987. *Haa shuká, our ancestors: Tlingit oral narratives*. Seattle: University of Washington Press.

1990. *Haa tuwunáagu yís, for healing our spirit: Tlingit oratory*. Seattle: University of Washington Press.

1991. *Beginning Tlingit*. 3rd edn., revised. Juneau, AK: Sealaska Heritage Foundation.

1992. Native language survival. *Extinction*, ed. by Linny Stovall. Special issue, *Left Bank* 2.115–122.

1994. *Haa ḵusteeyí, our culture: Tlingit life stories*. Seattle: University of Washington Press.

1995. Oral literature embodied and disembodied. *Aspects of oral communication*, ed. by Uta M. Quasthoff, 91–111. Berlin: De Gruyter.

Dauenhauer, Richard. 1994. Seven hundred million to one: making a difference in Alaska Native language and literature. Keynote address to the Alaska Native Education Council, 8th Annual Statewide Conference, October 10–11, 1994, Anchorage.

Decime, Rita. 1994. Un projet de trilinguisme intégré pour les enfants des écoles maternelles de la Valée d'Ayas. *International Journal of the Sociology of Language* 109.129–137.

Deering, Nora and Helga Harries Delisle. 1995. *Mohawk. A teaching grammar*. Revised edn. Kanien'kéha: Kanien'kéha Cultural Center.

Derbyshire, Desmond 1990. Comparative survey of morphology and syntax in Brazilian Arawakan. In D. Derbyshire and G. Pullum (eds.), 469–566.

Derbyshire, Desmond and Geoffry Pullum, eds. 1986. *Handbook of Amazonian languages*, vol. I. Berlin: Mouton de Gruyter.

1990. *Handbook of Amazonian languages*, vol. II. Berlin: Mouton de Gruyter.

Dimmendaal, Gerrit J. 1983. *The Turkana language*. Dordrecht: Foris.

1989. On language death in Eastern Africa. In N. Dorian (ed.), 13–31.

Dixon, R. M. W. 1991. The endangered languages of Australia, Indonesia and Oceania. In R. H. Robins and E. M. Uhlenbeck (eds.), 229–255.

Djité, Paulin Goupognon. 1985. Language attitudes in Abidjan: implications for language planning in the Ivory Coast. Ph.D. dissertation, Georgetown University.

Dorian, Nancy C. 1986. Abrupt transmission failure in obsolescing languages: how sudden the "tip" to the dominant language communities and families. *Proceedings of the twelfth annual meeting of the Berkeley Linguistics Society*, ed. by Vassiliki Nikiforidu, Mary Van Clay, Mary Niepokuj, and Deborah Feder, 72–83. Berkeley: Berkeley Linguistics Society.

1993a. Discussion note. A response to Ladefoged's other view of endangered languages. *Language* 69.575–579.

1993b. Working with endangered languages: privileges and perils. *Proceedings of the xvth International Congress of Linguists*, ed. by Andre Cochetiere, Jean-Claude Boulanger, and Conrad Ouellon, vol. I, 11–22. Quebec: Presses de l'Université de Laval.

1995. Sharing expertise and experiences in support of small languages. *International Journal of the Sociology of Language* 114.129–137.

Dorian, Nancy C., ed. 1989. *Investigating obsolescence: studies in language contraction and death*. Cambridge: Cambridge University Press.

Drewes, A. J. 1994. Borrowing in Maltese. In P. Bakker and M. Mous (eds.), 83–111.

Eades, Diana. 1982. You gotta know how to talk . . . : Information seeking in South-East Queensland Aboriginal Society. *Australian Journal of Linguistics* 2.61–82.

1988. They don't speak an Aboriginal language, or do they? *Being black: Aboriginal cultures in "settled" Australia*, ed. by Ian Keen, 97–115. Canberra: Aboriginal Studies Press.

Echeverri, J. A. and J. Landaburu. 1994. Los nonuya del Putumayo y su lengua: huellas de su historia y circunstancias de un resurgir. In M. Pabón Triana (ed.), 39–60.

Edwards, John. 1992. Sociopolitical aspects of language maintenance and loss: towards a typology of minority language situations. In W. Fase, K. Jaspaert, and S. Kroon (eds.), 37–54.

England, Nora C. 1995. Linguistics for indigenous American languages: Mayan examples. *Journal of Latin American Anthropology* 1.122–149.

Exploring mathematics. 1991. Agincourt, Ontario: Gage Educational Publishing Company.

Fabian, Johannes. 1982. Scratching the surface: observations in the poetics of lexical borrowing in Shaba Swahili. *Anthropological Linguistics* 24.14–50.

1986. *Language and colonial power: the appropriation of Swahili in the Belgian Congo, 1880–1938*. Cambridge: Cambridge University Press.

1990. *History from below*. Amsterdam: John Benjamins.

Fase, Willem, Koen Jaspaert, and Sjaak Kroon, eds. 1992. *Maintenance and loss of minority languages*. Amsterdam and Philadelphia: John Benjamins.

Fedorov, A. N. 1983. Nacional'no-jazykovye problemy v Sibiri i ix reshenie. *Voprosy jazykoznanija* 4.102–108.

Firth, John R. 1934. Linguistics and the functional point of view. *English Studies* 16.2–8.

Fishman, Joshua A. 1968. Some contrasts between linguistically homogeneous and linguistically heterogeneous polities. *Language problems of developing nations*, ed. by Joshua A. Fishman, 53–68. New York: John Wiley & Sons, Inc.

1985. Mother-tongue claiming in the United States since 1960: trends and correlates. *The rise and fall of ethnic revival*, ed. by Joshua A. Fishman, 107–194. Berlin: Mouton.

1989. *Language and ethnicity in minority sociolinguistic perspective*. Philadelphia: Multilingual Matters.

1991. *Reversing language shift: theoretical and empirical foundations of assistance to threatened languages*. Bristol, PA: Multilingual Matters Ltd.

Fishman, Joshua A., ed. 1966. *Language loyalty in the United States*. The Hague: Mouton.

Flinn, Juliana. 1990. We still have our customs: being Pulapese in Truk. *Cultural identity and ethnicity in the Pacific*, ed. by Jocelyn Linnekin and Lin Poyer, 103–126. Honolulu: University of Hawaii Press.

1992. *Diplomas and thatch houses: asserting tradition in a changing Micronesia*. Ann Arbor: University of Michigan.

Foster, Charles R., ed. 1980. *Nations without a state*. New York: Praeger.

Friedman, Jonathan. 1994. *Cultural identity and global process*. London: Sage Publications.

Friedrich, Paul. 1986. *The language parallax: linguistic relativism and poetic indeterminacy*. Austin, TX: University of Texas Press.

Fuller, Janet. 1996. When cultural maintenance means linguistic convergence: Pennsylvania German evidence for the Matrix Language turnover hypothesis. *Language in Society* 254. 493–513.

Gal, Susan. 1989. Lexical innovation and loss: use and value of restricted Hungarian. In N. Dorian (ed.), 313–331.

Garrett, Merrill. 1988. Process in sentence production. *The Cambridge linguistics survey*, vol. III, ed. by Frederick Newmeyer, 69–96. Cambridge: Cambridge University Press.

Garza Cuaròn, Beatriz and Yolanda Lastra. 1991. Endangered languages in Mexico. In R. H. Robins and E. M. Uhlenbeck (eds.), 93–134.

Garzon, Susan. 1991. Language variation and viability in a bilingual Mayan community. Ph.D. dissertation, University of Iowa.

1992. The process of language death in a Mayan community in Southern Mexico. *International Journal of the Sociology of Language* 93.53–66.

Gellner, Ernest. 1983. *Nations and nationalism*. Ithaca, NY: Cornell University Press.

Gibson, John Arthur. 1912/1993. *Concerning the League: the Iroquois League tradition as dictated in Onondaga by John Arthur Gibson*. Newly elicited, edited and translated by Hanni Woodbury in collaboration with Reg Henry and Harry Webser on the basis of the A. A. Goldenweiser manuscript. Memoir 9, Algonquian and Iroquoian Linguistics. Syracuse, NY: Syracuse University Press, distributed for Algonquian and Iroquoian Linguistics, University of Manitoba.

Giles, Howard and Peter Powesland. 1975. *Speech style and social evaluation*. London and New York: Academic Press.

Giles, Howard and Philip Smith. 1979. Accommodation theory: optimal levels of convergence. *Language and social psychology*, ed. by Howard Giles and Robert St. Clair, 45–65. Oxford: Basil Blackwell.

Giles, Howard, Richard Y. Bourhis, and Donald M. Taylor. 1977. Toward a theory of language in ethnic group relations. *Language, ethnicity and intergroup relations*, ed. by Howard Giles, 307–348. London: Academic Press.

Giles, Howard, Klaus R. Scherer, and Donald M. Taylor. 1979. Speech markers in social interaction. *Social markers in speech*, ed. by Klaus R. Scherer and Howard Giles, 343–381. Cambridge: Cambridge University Press.

Giles, Howard, Donald M. Taylor, and Richard Y. Bourhis. 1973. Towards a theory of interpersonal accommodation through speech: some Canadian data. *Language in Society* 2.177–192.

Girfanova, A. X. 1994. Udègejskij jazyk. *Kransnaja kniga jazykov narodov Rossii. Enciklopedicheskij slovar'-spravochnik*, 57–58. Moscow: Academia.

von Gliech, U. and W. Wölck. 1994. Changes in language use and attitudes of Quechua–Spanish bilinguals in Peru. In P. Cole, G. Herman, and M. D. Martin, 27–50.

Goddard, Ives and Kathleen Bragdon. 1988. *Native writings in Massachusett*. Philadelphia: The American Philosophical Society.

Golovko, E. V. 1988. Materiali dlja izuchenija jazyka mednovskix aleutov I. *Lingvisticheskie issledovanija* 1988. *Problemy vzaimodejstvija jazikovyx urovnej*, 73–78.

1989. Materiali dlja izuchenija jazyka mednovskix aleutov II. *Lingvisticheskie issledovanija* 1989. *Struktura jazyka i ego evoljutsija*, 67–74.

1994. Mednyj Aleut or Copper Island Aleut: an Aleut–Russian mixed language. In P. Bakker and M. Mous (eds.), 113–121.

Golovko. E. V. and N. B. Vakhtin, 1990. Aleut in contact: the CIA engima. *Acta Linguistica Hafniensia*, 22.97–125.

Golovko, E. V., N. B. Vakhtin, and A. S. Asinovskij. 1987. *Ètnolingvisticheskaja situacija na o. Beringa. Raciol'noe prirodopol'zovanie na Komandorskix ostrovax*. Moscow: Moscow State University.

Goody, John R. 1968. *Literacy in traditional societies*. Cambridge: Cambridge University Press.

Greenberg, Joseph H. 1987. *Language in the Americas*. Stanford, CA: Stanford University Press.

Grenand, Pierre and Françoise Grenand. 1993. Amérique Equatoriale: Grande Amazonie. *Situation des populations indigènes des forêts denses et humides*, ed. by Serge Bahuchet, 89–176. Luxemburg: Office des publications officielles des communautés européennes.

Grenoble, Lenore and Lindsay Whaley. 1996. Endangered languages: current issues and future prospects. *International Journal of the Sociology of Language* 118.209–223.

Grillo, Ralph D. 1989. *Dominant languages: language and hierarchy in Britain and France*. Cambridge: Cambridge University Press.

Grimes, Barbara F., ed. 1984. *Ethnologue: languages of the world*. 10th edn. Dallas: Summer Institute of Linguistics.

1992. *Ethnologue: languages of the world*. 12th edn. Dallas: Summer Institute of Linguistics.

Gumperz, John. 1972. The speech community. *Language and social context: selected readings*, ed. by P. P. Giglioli, 219–231. Harmondsworth: Penguin.

1976. *The sociolinguistic significance of conversational code-switching*. Working
Paper 46. Berkeley: Language Behavior Research Laboratory.

1982. *Discourse strategies*. Cambridge: Cambridge University Press.

Gustafson, B. 1995. Linguistic autonomy and standardization in Bolivia: the case of
Guarani. Paper presented at Languages South of the Rio Bravo Conference,
January 1995, Tulane University.

Haarmann, Harald. 1985. The Impact of group bilingualism in the SU. *Sociolinguistic
perspectives on Soviet national languages: their past, present and future*, ed.
by Isabelle T. Kreindler, 313–344. Berlin: Mouton de Gruyter.

1986. *Language in ethnicity: a view of basic ecological relations*. Berlin: Mouton
de Gruyter.

Haboud, M. 1991. *Distribución del uso del quichua y castellano en Ecuador*. Quito:
EBI.

1994. Seleccionar investigadores: Un reto a los estereotipos. Unpublished MS.

1995. Tension, balance and empowerment in Ecuadorian Quichua. Paper
presented at the Conference on Andean Linguistics, July 1995,
Albuquerque, NM.

Hale, Horatio. 1881. Hiawatha and the Iroquois Confederacy: a study in
anthropology. Paper presented at the Cincinnati meeting of the American
Association for the Advancement of Science, August, 1881, under the title
of "A lawgiver of the Stone Age." Salem, MA: The Salem Press. Reprinted,
in *The Iroquois Book of Rites*; and *Hale on the Iroquois*. Ohsweken, Ontario:
Iroqrafts, 1989.

Hale, Kenneth. 1992. Language endangerment and the human value of linguistic
diversity. *Language* 68.4–10.

Hale, Kenneth, Colette Craig, Nora England, LaVerne Jeanne, Michael Krauss,
Lucille Watahomigie, and Akira Yamamoto. 1992. Endangered languages.
Language 68.1–42.

Hall, Robert. 1966. *Pidgin and creole languages*. Ithaca, NY: Cornell University Press.

Haugen, Einar. 1971. The ecology of language. *The Linguistic Reporter* 13,
supplement 25.19–25.

Heath, Shirley Brice. 1972. *Telling tongues: language policy in Mexico, colony to
nation*. New York: Teachers College Press.

Heath, Shirley Brice and Richard Laprade. 1982. Castilian colonization and
indigenous languages: the cases of Quechua and Aymara. *Language spread*,
ed. by Robert L. Cooper, 118–147. Bloomington, IN: Indiana University Press.

Heine, Bernd. 1970. *Status and use of African lingua francas*. Munich: Weltforum.

1982. *Boni dialects. Language and dialect atlas of Kenya*. vol. x. Berlin: Reimer.

Heine, Bernd and Wilhelm J. G. Möhlig. 1980. *Language and dialect atlas of Kenya*.
Berlin: Reimer.

Hewitt, J. N. B. 1892. Legend of the founding of the Iroquois league. *American
Anthropologist* 5.131–148.

Hill, Jane H. 1983. Language death in Uto-Aztecan. *International Journal of
American Linguistics* 49.258–276.

Hill, Jane H. and Kenneth C. Hill. 1986. *Speaking Mexicano: dynamics of syncretic language change in central Mexico*. Tucson, AZ: University of Arizona Press.

Hinton, Leanne. 1994. *Flutes of fire*. Berkeley: Heyday Press.

Hock, Hans H. 1986. *Principles of historical linguistics*. Berlin: Mouton de Gruyer.

Hofling, Charles Andrew. 1991. *Itzá Maya texts*. Salt Lake City: University of Utah Press.

Hohenthal, W. D. and Thomas McCorkle. 1955. The problem of aboriginal persistence. *Southwestern Journal of Anthropology* 11.288–300.

Hohepa, P. 1984. Current issues in promoting Maori language use. *Language planning newsletter* 10/3.1–4.

Hornberger, Nancy H. 1989. *Bilingual education and language maintenance*. Dordrecht: Foris Publications.

    1994. Whither bilingual education in Peru? Quechua literacy and empowerment. In P. Cole, G. Hermon, and M. D. Martin (eds.), 74–89.

Isaev, M. I. 1982. *Socio-lingvisticheskie problemy jazykov narodov SSSR*. Moscow: Vysshaja shkola.

Jacobson, Steven A. 1984. *Yup'ik Eskimo dictionary*. Fairbanks, AK: Alaska Native Language Center.

Jake, Janice. 1994. Intrasentential code switching and pronouns: on the categorical status of functional elements. *Linguistics* 32.271–298.

    1996. Splitting the lexical structure: a composite model of adult second language acquisition. Unpublished MS.

Jake, Janice, Georges Ludi, and Carol Myers-Scotton. 1995. Predicting variation in interlanguage. Paper presented at the annual meeting of the American Association of Applied Linguistics, Long Beach, CA.

Jeanne, La Verne Masayesva. 1992. An institutional response to language endangerment: a proposal for a Native American Language Center. *Language* 68.24–28.

Johnson, Jerald Jay. 1978. Yana. *Handbook of North American Indians*. vol. VIII: *California*, ed. R. F. Heizer, 361–369. California. Washington, DC: Smithsonian Institution.

Joseph, John Earl. 1987. *Eloquence and power: the rise of language standards and standard languages*. Oxford: Blackwell.

Kan, Sergei. 1989. Cohorts, generations, and their culture: the Tlingit potlatch in the 1980s. *Anthropos* 84.405–422.

    1990. The sacred and the secular: Tlingit potlatch songs outside the potlatch. *American Indian Quarterly* 14.355–366.

Kapanga, Andre Mwamba. 1990. Language variation and language attitudes: a case study from Shaba Swahili. *Studies in the Linguistic Sciences* 20.175–188.

    1991. Language change and variation: a case study of Shaba Swahili. Ph.D. dissertation, University of Illinois–Urbana.

    1993. Shaba Swahili and the processes of linguistic contact. *Atlantic meets Pacific: a global view of pidginization and creolization*, ed. by Francis Byrne and John Holm, 441–458. Amsterdam: John Benjamins.

1995. A socio-historical linguistics approach to the study of Shaba Swahili: Recreating the parent language. To appear in *Sprache und Geschichte in Afrika*.

Karetu, Timoti S. 1994. Maori language rights in New Zealand. In T. Skutnabb-Kangas and R. Phillipson (eds.), with M. Rannut, 208–18.

Kaufman, Dorit and Mark Aronoff. 1991. Morphological disintegration and reconstruction in first language attrition. In H. W. Seliger and R. M. Vago (eds.), 175–188.

Kaufman, Terrence. 1990. Language history in South America: what we know and how to know more. In D. L. Payne (ed.), 13–73.

1994. The native languages of Latin America. *Atlas of the world's languages*, ed. by Christopher Moseley and R. E. Asher, 31–76. London and New York: Routledge.

Keesing, Roger M. 1992. *Custom and confrontation: the Kwaio struggle for cultural autonomy*. Chicago: University of Chicago Press.

Khati, Thekiso. 1992. Intra-lexical switching or nonce borrowing? Evidence from SeSotho–English performance. *Language and society in Africa*, ed. by Robert K. Herbert, 181–196. Johannesburg: University of the Witwatersrand Press.

Khleif, Bud B. 1980. *Language, ethnicity, and education in Wales*. The Hague: Mouton.

Kibrik, Aleksandr E. 1991. The problem of endangered languages in the USSR. In R. H. Robins and E. M. Uhlenbeck (eds.), 257–273.

Kinkade, M. Dale. 1991. The decline of native languages in Canada. In R. H. Robins and E. M. Uhlenbeck (eds.), 157–176.

Klein, Harriet E. Manelis and Louisa R. Stark, eds. 1985. *South American Indian languages, retrospect and prospect*. Austin, TX: University of Texas Press.

Klein, Wolfgang and Clive Perdue. 1992. *Utterance structure: developing grammars again*. Amsterdam: Benjamins.

Kloss, Heinz. 1966. German American language maintenance efforts. In J. Fishman (ed.), 206–252.

Krauss, Michael. 1992. The world's languages in crisis. *Language* 68.4–10.

1995a. Status of northern languages. Table presented at Dartmouth Endangered Languages Conference, February 3–5, 1995.

1995b. Language loss in Alaska, the United States, and the world. *Frame of reference* 6/1.3–5.

Kroskrity, Paul V. 1993. *Language, history, and identity: Ethnolinguistic studies of the Arizona Tewa*. Tucson, AZ: University of Arizona Press.

Kuhberg, Heinz. 1992. Longitudinal L2 attrition versus L2-acquisition, in three Turkish children – empirical findings. *Second Language Research* 8.138–154.

Kulich, Don and Christopher Stroud. 1993. Literacy in a Papua New Guinean village. *Cross-cultural approaches to literacy*, ed. by Brian V. Street, 30–61. Cambridge: Cambridge University Press.

Kuter, Lois. 1989. Breton versus French: language and the opposition of political, economic, social, and cultural values. In N. Dorian (ed.), 75–89.

Kwachka, Patricia. 1992. Discourse structures, cultural stability, and language shift. *International Journal of Society and Language* 93.67–73.

Kwachka, Patricia and Charlotte Basham. 1990. Literacy acts and cultural artifacts. *Journal of Pragmatics* 14.413–429.

Labov, William. 1973. The linguistic consequences of being lame. *Language and Society* 2.81–115.

Ladefoged, Peter. 1992. Discussion note. Another view of endangered languages. *Languge* 68.809–811.

Laitin, David D. 1992. *Language repertoires and state construction in Africa.* Cambridge: Cambridge University Press.

Lambert, Wallace E. 1967. A social psychology of bilingualism. *Journal of Social Issues* 23.91–109.

Landaburu, Jon. 1979. *La Langue des Andoke (Amazonie colombienne).* Paris: SELAF.

Langgaard, Per. 1992. Greenlandic is not an ideology, it is a language. *Language and educational policy in the north,* ed. by Nelson H. H. Graburn and Roy Iutzi-Mitchell, 167–178. Berkeley: Working Papers of the Canadian Studies Program, International and Area Studies, University of California at Berkeley.

Le Page, Robert B. 1978. *Projection, focussing and diffusion, or step towards a sociolinguistic theory of language, illustrated from the sociolinguistic survey of multilingual communities, stages ı: Belize and ıı: St Lucia.* York Papers in Linguistics 9. University of York: Department of Language.

Le Page Robert B. and Andrée Tabouret-Keller. 1985. *Acts of identity: creole based approaches to language and ethnicity.* Cambridge: Cambridge University Press.

Levelt, Willem. 1989. *Speaking: from intention to articulation.* Cambridge, MA: MIT Press.

Lewis, E. Glyn. 1972. *Multilingualism in the Soviet Union.* The Hague: Mouton.

Lopez, Luis E. 1997. To guaranize: a verb actively conjugated by the Bolivian Guaranis. *Contribution to the sociology of language: indigenous literacy in the Americas,* ed. by Nancy Hornberger. The Hague: Mouton.

Loukotka, Cestmír. 1934. Classificación de las lenguas sudamericanas. *Lingüistica sudamericana* 1, Prague.

1968. *Classification of South American Indian languages.* Los Angeles: Latin American Center, University of California.

Lucy, John A. 1992. *Language diversity and thought: a reformulation of the linguistic relativity hypothesis.* Studies in the social and cultural foundations of language 12. Cambridge: Cambridge University Press.

Lyapunova, R. G. 1987. *Aleuti. Ocherki ètnicheskoj istorii.* Leningrad: Nauka.

McCloskey, James. 1979. *Transformational syntax and model theoretic semantics: a case study in Modern Irish.* Dordrecht: D. Reidel Publishing Company.

Maguire, Gabrielle. 1991. *Our own language: an Irish initiative.* Clevedon: Multilingual Matters, Ltd.

Mannheim, Bruce. 1984. Una nación acorralada: Southern Peruvian Quechua language planning and politics in historical perspective. *Language and Society* 13.291–309.

1985a. Contact and Quechua-external relationships. In H. E. M. Klein and L. R. Stark (eds.), 644–90.

1985b. Southern Peruvian Quechua. In H. E. M. Klein and L. R. Stark (eds.), 481–515.

Margolin, David. 1996. Native American sociolinguistic identity. Unpublished MS.

Markey, Thomas L. 1988. Ladin and other relic language forms in the eastern Alpine region. *Historical dialectology: regional and social*, ed. by Jacek Fisiak, 357–375. Berlin: Mouton de Gruyter.

Maslova, E. S. 1994. Jukagirskij jazyk. In V. P. Neroznak (ed.), 74–76.

Matisoff, James. 1991. Endangered languages of mainland Southeast Asia. In R. H. Robins and E. M. Uhlenbeck (eds.), 189–228.

Matteson, Esther, ed. 1965. *Gramáticas estructurales de lenguas bolivianas*. 2 vols. Beni: Bolivia, SIL.

Maud, Ralph. 1993. *The porcupine hunter and other stories. the original Tsimshian texts of Henry Tate*. Vancouver: Talonbooks.

Meillet, Antoine. 1928. *Les Langues dans l'Europe nouvelle*. Paris: Payot.

Metge, Alice Joan. 1976. *The Maoris of New Zealand*. London: Routledge and K. Paul.

Milroy, Lesley. 1980. *Language and social networks*. Oxford: Basil Blackwell.

1982. Social network and linguistic focusing. In S. Romaine (ed.), 141–152.

1987. *Language and social networks*. 2nd edn. Oxford: Basil Blackwell.

Mixal'chenko, V. Ju. 1994. Jazykovye problemy novoj Rossijskoj federacii. *Jazyk, Kul'tura, Ètnos*, ed. by G. P. Neshchimenko, 176–183. Moscow: Nauka.

Moore, Denny. 1990. Linguistics and Amazonia. Paper read at the 1990 Annual Meetings of the American Anthropological Association, New Orleans.

Moore, Denny and L. R. Storto. 1994. Lingüística Indigena no Brazil. Unpublished MS.

Moore, Denny, Sidney Facundes, and Nádia Pires. 1991. Nheengatú: Notas sobre sintaxe e desenvolvimento histórico. In *Anais do Quinto Encontro da ANPOLL*. Recife, July 25, 1990.

Morgan, Lewis Henry. 1851/1922. *League of the Ho-de-no-sau-nee or Iroquois*, ed. and annotated by Herbert M. Lloyd. New York: Dodd, Mead.

Mous, Maarten. 1994. Ma'a or Mbugu. In P. Bakker and M. Mous (eds.), 175–200.

forthcoming. Ma'a as an ethno-register of Mbugu. To appear in *Sprache und Geschichte in Afrika*.

Moya, R. 1987. *Cultura, conflicto y utopia*. Quito: CEDIME.

Mülhäusler, Peter. 1990. "Reducing" Pacific languages to writing. *Ideologies of language*, ed. by John E. Joseph and Talbot J. Taylor, 189–205. London: Routledge.

Myers-Scotton, Carol. 1992. Codeswitching as a mechanism of deep borrowing, language shift and language death. In M. Brenzinger (ed.), 31–58.

1993a. *Duelling languages: grammatical structure in codeswitching*. Oxford: Oxford University Press.

1993b. *Social motivations for codeswitching: evidence from Africa*. Oxford: Oxford University Press.

1995. A lexically-based model of codeswitching. *One speaker, two languages: cross-disciplinary perspectives on code-switching*, ed. by Lesley Milroy and Pieter Muysken, 233–256. Cambridge: Cambridge University Press.

forthcoming. "Matrix language recognition" and "morpheme sorting" as possible structural strategies in pidgin/creole formation. To appear in *Pidgins and creoles: structure and status*, ed. by Arthur Spears and Donald Winford. Amsterdam: Benjamins.

Myers-Scotton, Carol and Janice Jake. 1995. Matching lemmas in a bilingual language production model: evidence from intrasentential codeswitching. *Linguistics* 33.981–1024.

Nahir, Moshe. 1983. Sociocultural factors in the revival of Hebrew. *Language Problems and Language Planning* 7/3.263–284.

1991. Language planning goals in contemporary Hebrew. *Linguistic studies presented to John L. Finlay*, ed. by H. Christoph Wolfart, 92–122. Winnipeg: Algonquian and Iroquoian Linguistics.

Nartey, Jonas. 1982. Code-switching, interference or faddism? Language use among educated Ghanaians. *Anthropological Linguistics* 24.183–192.

The national atlas of Canada. 1980. 5th edn. (revised). Canada, Surveys, and mapping Branch, geography Department. Toronto: Macmillan.

Neroznak, V. P., ed. 1994. *Krasnaja kniga jazykov narodov Rossii*. Academia: Moscow.

New York Times. 1975. France refuses to recognize six children because of their Celtic names. January 12.

Nicholson, Rangi and Ron Garland. 1991. New Zealanders' attitudes to the revitilisation of the Maori language. *Journal of Multilingual and Multicultural Development* 12.393–410.

Nurse, Derek. 1994. South meets North: Ilwana = Bantu+Cushitic on Kenya's Tana River. In P. Bakker and M. Mous (eds.), 213–222.

Nyman, Elizabeth, and Jeff Leer. 1993. *Gágiwdul.at: brought forth to reconfirm: the legacy of a Taku River Tlingit clan*. Whitehorse, Yukon, and Fairbanks, AL: Yukon Native Language Centre and Alaska Native Language Center.

Okedara, Joseph T. and Caroline A. Okedara. 1992. Mother-tongue literacy in Nigeria. *The annals of the American Academy of Political and Social Science World literacy in the year* 2000, ed. by Daniel A. Wagner and Laurel D. Puchner, 520.91–102.

Onenko, S. N. 1966. Rol' rodnogo jazyka v uslovijax dvujazychija. *Jazyki i fol'klor narodov sibirskogo severa*, ed. by V. A. Avrorin, 27–40. Moscow and Leningrad: Nauka.

Oxford English Dictionary. 1971. Oxford: Oxford University Press.

Oxlajuuj Kaaj Maya' Ajtz'iib'. 1993. *Maya' Chii': Los Idiomas Mayas de Guatemala.* Guatemala: Cholsamaj.

Pabón Triana, Marta. 1995. La recuperación de lenguas nativas como búsqueda de identidad étnica. In M. Pabón Triana (ed.), 165.

Pabón Triana, Marta, ed. 1994. *Proceedings of La recuperación de lenguas nativas como búsqueda de identidad étnica,* VII Congreso de Antropología, Universidad de Antioquia, Medellín. Bogotá: CCELA-Universidad de los Andes.

Parker, Arthur C. 1916. The constitution of the Five Nations, or, the Iroquois book of the Great Law. *New York State Museum bulletin* 184.

Parker, Gary J. 1963. Clasificación genética de los dialectos quechuas. *Revista del Museo Nacional* (Lima) 32.241–252.

    1969. *Comparative papers in Quechua phonology and grammar II: Proto-Quechua phonology and morphology.* University of Hawaii–Working Papers in Linguistics, vol. 1, no. 2.

Payne, Doris L. 1985. Aspects of the Grammar of Yagua: a typological perspective. Ph.D. dissertation, University of California, Los Angeles.

Payne, Doris L., ed. 1990. *Amazonian linguistics: studies in Lowland South American languages.* Austin, TX: University of Texas Press.

Payne, Doris. L. and Thomas E. Payne. 1990. Yagua. In D. Derbyshire and G. Pullum (eds.), 249–474. The Hague: Mouton.

Payne, Thomas E. 1985. Participant coding in Yagua discourse. Ph.D. dissertation, University of California, Los Angeles.

Pollock, Jean-Yves. 1989. Verb movement, Universal Grammar, and the structure of IP. *Linguistic Inquiry* 20.365–424.

Polomé, Edgard. 1967. *Swahili language handbook.* Washington DC: Center for Applied Linguistics.

    1968. Lubumbashi Swahili. *Journal of African Languages* 7.14–25.

    1971. Multilingualism in an urban center: the Lubumbashi case. *Language use and social change,* ed. by W. H. Whiteley, 364–375. Oxford: Oxford University Press.

    1982. *Language, society, and paleoculture.* Stanford, CA: Stanford University Press.

Pottier, Bernard, ed. 1983. *América Latina en sus lenguas indígenas.* Caracas: Unesco and Monte Avila Editores.

Prunier, Gerard. 1995. *The Rwanda crisis: history of a genocide.* New York: Columbia University Press.

Pye, Clifton. 1992. Language loss among the Chilcotin. *International Journal of the Sociology of Language* 93.75–86.

Queixalós, Francesco. 1995. Grammaire Sikuani. Doctorat d'Etat, Université de Paris IV.

Ramsey, S. Robert. 1989. *The languages of China.* Princeton, NJ: Princeton University Press.

Reder, Stephen and Karen Reed Wikelund. 1993. Literacy development and ethnicity: an Alaskan example. *Cross-cultural approaches to literacy*, ed. by Brian V. Street, 176–197. Cambridge: Cambridge University Press.

Robins, Robert H. and Eugenius M. Uhlenbeck, eds. 1991. *Endangered languages*. Oxford: Berg Publishers Ltd.

Rodrigues, Arion D. 1985a. Evidence for Tupi–Carib relationships. In H. E. M. Klein and L. R. Stark (eds.), 371–404.

1985b. The present state of the study of Brazilian Indian languages. In H. E. M. Klein and L. R. Stark (eds.), 405–439.

1986. *Línguas Brasileiras*. Saõ Paolo: Edicões Loyola.

1993. Endangered languages in Brazil. Paper read at the Symposium on Endangered Languages of South America, Rijks University, Leiden.

Romaine, Suzanne. 1993. *Pidgin and creole languages*. London and New York: Longman.

Romaine, Suzanne, ed. 1982. *Sociolinguistic variation in speech communities*. London: Edward Arnold.

Rottland, Frans. 1982. *Die südnilotishcen Sprachen. Beschriebung, Vergleichung und Rekonstruktion*. Kölner Beiträge zur Afrikanistik 7. Berlin: Dietrich Reimer.

Rubin, Joan. 1968. *National bilingualism in Paraguay*. The Hague: Mouton.

1985. Toward bilingual education for Paraguay. *Perspectives on bilingualism and bilingual education*, ed. by James E. Alatis and John J. Staczek, 423–435. Washington: Georgetown University Press.

Rumsey, Alan. 1990. Wording, meaning and linguistic ideology. *American Anthropologist* 92.346–361.

Russell, Joan. 1982. Sociolinguistic variation in an African urban setting. In S. Romaine (ed.), 141–152.

Ryan, Ellen Bouchard and Howard Giles, eds. 1982. *Attitudes towards language variation: social and applied contexts*. London: Edward Arnold.

Ryan, Ellen Bouchard, Howard Giles, and Richard J. Sebastian, 1982. An integrative perspective for the study of attitudes towards language variation. In E. B. Ryan and H. Giles (eds.), 1–19.

Ryan, Peter M. 1978. *Modern Maori*. Auckland: Heinemann Education.

Sabino, Robin. 1994. Establishing the necessary database for the restoration of the Cherokee language to the Alabama Cherokee population: a proposal. Unpublished M S.

Salisbury, Richard F. 1962. Notes on bilingualism and linguistic change in New Guinea. *Anthropological Linguistics* 4.1–13.

Sankoff, David, Shana Poplack, and Swathi Vanniarajan. 1990. The case of the nonce loan in Tamil. *Language Variation and Change* 2.71–101.

Sasse, Hans-Jürgen. 1992. Language decay and contact-induced change: similarities and differences. In M. Brenzinger (ed.), 59–80.

Saulson, Scott B. 1979. *Institutionalized language planning: documents and analysis of the revival of Hebrew*. The Hague: Mouton.

Saville-Troike, Muriel. 1989. *The ethnography of communication.* 2nd edn. Oxford: Basil Blackwell.

Scollon, Ronald and Suzanne B. K. Scollon. 1979. *Linguistic convergence: an ethnography of speaking at Fort Chipewyan.* New York: Academic Press.

   1981. *Narrative, literacy, and face in interethnic communication.* Norwood, NJ: Ablex Publishing Corporation.

   1994. *Intercultural communication: a discourse approach.* Oxford: Basil Blackwell.

Scribner, Sylvia and Michael Cole. 1978. *Literacy without school: testing for intellectual effects.* Vai Literacy Project Working Paper No. 2. The Rockefeller University, Laboratory of Comparative Human Cognition.

   1981. *The psychology of literacy.* Cambridge, MA: Harvard University Press.

Seliger, Herbert W. and Robert M. Vago, eds. 1991. *First language attrition.* Cambridge: Cambridge University Press.

Silko, Leslie Marmon. 1977. *Ceremony.* New York: Viking.

Silverstein, Michael. 1979. Language structure and linguistic ideology. *The elements: a parasession on linguistic units and levels,* ed. by P. R. Clyne, 193–247. Chicago: Chicago Linguistics Society.

   1981. *The limits of awareness.* Working papers in sociolinguistics 84. Austin, TX: Southwestern Educational Laboratory.

Skutnab-Kangas, Tove and Robert Phillipson, with Mark Rannut eds. 1994. *Linguistic human rights: Overcoming linguistic discrimination.* Berlin: Mouton de Gruyter.

Smalley, William A. 1994. *Linguistic diversity and national unity: language ecology in Thailand.* Chicago and London: University of Chicago Press.

Smith, Carol. 1988. Destruction of the material bases for Indian culture: economic changes in Totonicapán. *Harvest of violence,* ed. by Robert M. Carmack, 206–231. Norman, OK: University of Oklahoma Press.

Sorenson, Arthur P. 1967. Multilingualism in the Northwest Amazon. *American Anthroplogist* 69.670–684.

   1985. An emerging Tukanoan linguistic regionality: policy pressures. In H. E. M. Klein and L. R. Stark (eds.), 140–156.

Spencer, Paul. 1973. *Nomads in alliance: symbiosis and growth among the Rendille and Samburu of Kenya.* London: Oxford University Press.

Stark, Louisa R. 1985. Indigenous languages of Lowland Ecuador: history and current status. In H. E. M. Klein and L. R. Stark (eds.), 157–193.

Stern, Asher. 1990. Educational policy towards the Circassian minority in Israel. *Ethnic minority languages and education,* ed. by Koen Jaspaert and Sjaak Kroon, 175–184. Amsterdam and Lisse: Swets and Zeitlinger.

Story, Gillian and Constance Naish. 1973. *Tlingit verb dictionary.* Fairbanks, AK: Alaska Native Language Center, University of Alaska.

   1976. *Tlingit noun dictionary.* 2nd edn. Revised and expanded by Henry Davis and Jeff Leer. Sitka, AK: Sheldon Jackson College.

Swigart, Leigh. 1992. Practice and perception: Language use and attitudes in Dakar. Ph.D. dissertation, University of Washington.

Szwed, John F. 1981. The ethnography of literacy. *Writing: The nature, development and teaching of written communication*, vol. 1: *Variation in writing*, ed. by Marica Farr Whiteman, 13–23. Hillsdale, NJ: Lawrence Erlbaum Associates.

Taylor, Allan R. 1992. Introduction. *International Journal of the Sociology of Language* 93.5–9.

Thomason, Sarah G. and Terrence Kaufman. 1988. *Language contact, creolization, and genetic linguistics*. Berkeley and Los Angeles: University of California Press.

Timm, Lenora A. 1973. Modernization and language shift: The case of Brittany. *Anthropological Linguistics* 15.281–298.

Tobar Ortiz, Nubia. 1994. En el umbral de una muerte inevitable: los tinigua de la sierra la Macarena. In M. Pabón Triana (ed.), 61–74.

Torero, Alfredo. 1964. Los dialectos Quechuas. *Anales científicos de la Universidad Agraria* (Lima) 2.446–478.

Tosco, Mauro. 1992. Dahalo: an endangered language. In M. Brenzinger (ed.), 137–155.

Traditional Teachings. 1984. Cornwall, Ontario: North American Indian Travelling College.

Traill, Anthony. 1995. The Khoesan languages of South Africa. *Language and social history: studies in South African sociolinguistics*, ed. by Rajend Mesthrie, 1–18. Cape Town: David Philip.

Treffgarne, Carew. 1986. Language policy in franco-phone Africa: scapegoat or panacea? *Language in education in Africa: proceedings of a seminar held in the centre of African Studies, University of Edinburgh, 29 and 20 November 1985*, 141–170. (Centre of African Studies). Edinburgh: Edinburgh University Press.

Trillos Amaya, Maria. 1994. El taara: del ocultamiento a la revitalización lingüística –Los chimila del Ariguaní–. In M. Pabón Triana (ed.), 75–89.

Trudgill, Peter. 1986. *Dialects in contact*. Oxford: Basil Blackwell.

Turcotte, Denis. 1983. *Lois, règlements et textes administratifs sur l'usage des langages en Afrique occidentale française (1826–1959)*. Travaux du Centre International de Recherche sur le Bilinguisme, no. 18. Quebec: Presses de l'Université Laval.

Tzian, Leopoldo. 1994. *Kajlab'alil Maya'iib' Xuq Mu'siib': Ri Ub'antajiik Iximuleew/Mayas y Ladinos en Cifras: El Caso de Guatemala*. Guatemala: Cholsamaj.

Vakhtin, N. B. 1985. Nekotorye osobennosti russko–aleutskogo dvujazichija na Komandorskix ostrovax. *Voprosy Jazykoznanija* 5.35–45.

1993. Towards a typology of language situations in the Far North. *Anthropology and Archaeology of Eurasia* 32: 66–92.

Vanderaa, Larry. 1991. *A survey for Christian Reformed World Missions of mission churches in west Africa*. Grand Rapids: Christian Reformed World Missions.

Watahomigie, Lucille J. and Akira Y. Yamamoto. 1992. Local reactions to perceived language decline. *Language* 68. 10–17.

Watson, Seosamh. 1989. Scottish and Irish Gaelic: the giant's bed-fellows. In N. Dorian (ed.), 41–59.

Wei, Longxing. 1996. Variation in the acquisition of morpheme types in the interlanguage of Chinese and Japanese learners of English as a second language. Ph.D. dissertation, University of South Carolina.

Wise, Mary Ruth 1994. Endangered languages of South America. Paper delivered at the International Congress of Americanists, Stockholm.

Woodbury, Anthony C. 1986. Interactions of tense and evidentiality: a study of Sherpa and English. *Evidentiality: the linguistic coding of epistemology*, ed. by Wallace Chafe and Johanna Nichols, 188–202. Norwood, NJ: Ablex.

    1993. A defense of the proposition, "When a language dies, a culture dies". *Proceedings of the first annual symposium about language and society – Austin (SALSA). Texas Linguistic Foruum* 33.101–129.

Woolard, Kathryn A. 1992. Language ideology: issues and approaches. *Pragmatics* 2.235–249.

Woolard, Kathryn A. and Tae-Joong Gahng. 1990. Changing language policies and attitudes in autonomous Catalonia. *Language in Society* 19.311–330.

Wurm, Stephen A. 1991. Language death and disappearance: causes and circumstances. In R. H. Robins and E. M. Uhlenbeck (eds.), 1–18.

Yava, Albert. 1978. *Big Falling Snow: A Tewa-Hopi Indian's life and times and the history and traditions of his people*, ed. by Harold Courlander. New York: Crown Publishers.

Zepeda, Ofelia and Jane H. Hill. 1991. The conditions of Native American languages in the United States. In R. H. Robins and E. M. Uhlenbeck (eds.), 135–155.

Index of languages

Index of names

General index